RE-READING BECCARIA

Cesare Beccaria's slim 1764 volume *On Crimes and Punishments* influenced policy developments worldwide and over decades, if not centuries, after its publication. For those who turn to Beccaria's work today, the encounter is shaped by that knowledge.

Appreciative of *On Crimes and Punishments*' dual nature as historical document and repository of ideas, the contributions in this collection address different aspects of the criminal justice theory Beccaria offered his readers and face up to methodological questions raised by meeting a historical text of this kind – unsystematic and by modern standards often under-argued – with modern scholarly conventions in mind.

Contributions in the first part of the book engage with Beccaria's political theory of criminal justice through the lenses of political and penal philosophy, considering how Beccaria's blending of social-contractarian foundations and proto-utilitarian policy analysis interlinks with the concrete set of criminal justice practices Beccaria presents as justified.

This leads on to the second part where contributors approach Beccaria's ideas with present-day reforms and developments in mind. Many of his policy proposals and arguments remain significant from our contemporary perspective, their limitations and omissions proving as instructive for the contemporary scholar as their more prescient elements.

The third part offers those looking at Beccaria's work today a glimpse into the practical difficulties facing the firebrand author turned public servant during his long career in the Habsburg-Lombardian administration. It puts his work into the broader context of pathways to criminal justice reform in northern Italy, Habsburgian Lombardy, and the Austro-Hungarian Empire in Beccaria's day.

Studies in Penal Theory and Penal Ethics: Volume 8

Studies in Penal Theory and Penal Ethics

A Series Published for
the Centre for Penal Theory and Penal Ethics
Institute of Criminology, University of Cambridge

Ethical and Social Perspectives on Situational Crime Prevention
edited by Andrew von Hirsch, David Garland and Alison Wakefield

Restorative Justice and Criminal Justice: Competing or Reconcilable Paradigms?
edited by Andrew von Hirsch, Julian Roberts, Anthony E Bottoms, Kent Roach and Mara Schiff

Incivilities: Regulating Offensive Behaviour
edited by A P Simester and Andreas Von Hirsch

Previous Convictions at Sentencing: Theoretical and Applied Perspectives
edited by Julian V Roberts and Andrew von Hirsch

Setting the Watch: Privacy and the Ethics of CCTV Surveillance
Beatrice von Silva-Tarouca Larsen

Criminal Law and the Authority of the State
edited by Antje du Bois-Pedain, Magnus Ulväng and Petter Asp

Penal Censure: Engagements Within and Beyond Desert Theory
edited by Antje du Bois-Pedain and Anthony E Bottoms

Re-Reading Beccaria: On the Contemporary Significance of a Penal Classic
edited by Antje du Bois-Pedain and Shachar Eldar

Re-Reading Beccaria

On the Contemporary Significance of a Penal Classic

Edited by
Antje du Bois-Pedain
and
Shachar Eldar

•HART•
OXFORD • LONDON • NEW YORK • NEW DELHI • SYDNEY

HART PUBLISHING

Bloomsbury Publishing Plc

Kemp House, Chawley Park, Cumnor Hill, Oxford, OX2 9PH, UK

1385 Broadway, New York, NY 10018, USA

29 Earlsfort Terrace, Dublin 2, Ireland

HART PUBLISHING, the Hart/Stag logo, BLOOMSBURY and the Diana logo are trademarks of Bloomsbury Publishing Plc

First published in Great Britain 2022

A catalogue record for this book is available from the British Library.

A catalogue record for this book is available from the Library of Congress.

ISBN: HB: 978-1-50995-913-6
ePDF: 978-1-50995-915-0
ePub: 978-1-50995-914-3

Typeset by Compuscript Ltd, Shannon

Acknowledgements

'Opinion of the Undersigned Members of the Committee Charged with the Reform of the Criminal System in Austrian Lombardy for Matters Pertaining to Capital Punishment (1792)', in C Beccaria, *On Crimes and Punishments and Other Writings* edited by Aaron Thomas and translated by Aaron Thomas and Jeremy Parzen (Toronto, University of Toronto Press 2008) 153–159. This material is reprinted with permission of the publisher.

Contents

PART II
LOCATING BECCARIA IN PRESENT-DAY DISCOURSES ON CRIMINAL JUSTICE

PART III
LOCATING BECCARIA IN EIGHTEENTH-CENTURY CRIMINAL JUSTICE

List of Contributors

Vincent Chiao, Professor of Law and Leadership, University of Richmond, VA.

Antje du Bois-Pedain, Professor of Criminal Law and Philosophy, University of Cambridge and Fellow of Magdalene College, Cambridge.

Antony Duff, Professor (emeritus) in Philosophy, University of Stirling and Honorary Professor, University of Edinburgh.

Shachar Eldar, Professor of Criminal Law, Ono Academic College.

Rachela Er'el, Advocate, Affiliated Lecturer, The Hebrew University of Jerusalem.

Adi Gal, JSD candidate, Yale Law School.

Miriam Gur-Arye, Professor (emerita), Judge Basil Wunsh Chair in Criminal Law, The Hebrew University of Jerusalem.

Mordechai Kremnitzer, Professor (emeritus) of Law, The Hebrew University of Jerusalem and Senior Research Fellow, Israel Democracy Institute.

Shai Lavi, Professor of Law, Tel Aviv University and Director, Van Leer Jerusalem Institute.

Sandra Marshall, Professor (emerita) in Philosophy, University of Stirling.

Matt Matravers, Professor of Law, University of York.

Amit Pundik, Senior Lecturer in Law, Tel Aviv University.

Paul Roberts, Professor of Criminal Jurisprudence, University of Nottingham.

Anat Scolnicov, Professor of Public Law, University of Winchester.

Leslie Sebba, Lawrence D Biele Chair of Law, The Hebrew University of Jerusalem.

JR Spencer, Professor (emeritus) of Criminal Law, University of Cambridge.

Malcolm Thorburn, Professor of Law, Chair in Legal, Ethical and Cultural Implications of Technological Innovations, University of Toronto.

Lorenzo Zucca, Professor of Law and Philosophy, King's College London.

Introduction

ANTJE DU BOIS-PEDAIN AND SHACHAR ELDAR

CESARE BECCARIA IS one of the few authors who could unashamedly claim to have influenced policy developments worldwide, and over decades, if not centuries. In this, his slim 1764 volume *On Crimes and Punishments*[1] stands alone in the history of philosophical writings on criminal justice. For those who turn to Beccaria's work today, the encounter is shaped in part by that knowledge. It is a book that stands for more than it contains: it stands for an historical trajectory of criminal justice reform, often summed up in the key terms humanisation, rationalisation and constitutionalisation of criminal justice. How did it reach that elevated position?

Franco Venturi has observed that from the start there have been two different, and at bottom fundamentally opposed, ways of understanding Beccaria's project.[2] The first has been to see it as reformist: a set of proposals for discrete

[1] Beccaria's *Dei delitti e delle pene* was first published anonymously in July 1764, the published version already bearing the imprint of his then close friend and mentor Pietro Verri's efforts to tidy up the manuscript. Soon pirate editions, further authorised editions under Beccaria's name and numerous translations appeared, the most influential of these last (by the French Abbé André Morellet) deftly reordering the text. Voltaire effectively recruited the book for the pursuit of his own reformist concerns by writing a commentary that was subsequently added to many French and even Italian editions, as well as to translations into other languages. Tracing the extent to which the various versions of Beccaria's book correlate with Beccaria's original manuscript has been the subject of extensive scholarly efforts. Beccaria scholars now accept the fifth Italian edition, the last one Beccaria personally edited and authorised, as the version that presumably most accurately reflects his ideas. Modern English translations are based on this version. Most of the chapters in this book, including this introduction, use C Beccaria, *On Crimes and Punishments and Other Writings* edited by R Bellamy and translated by R Davies (Cambridge, Cambridge University Press, 1995). For the history of Beccaria's text, see ibid, "Note on the texts" at xli–xliv. For additional detail, esp on Verri's influence on the text, see 'Note on the Text', in C Beccaria, *On Crimes and Punishments* edited and translated by GR Newman & P Marongiu (New Brunswick NJ, Transaction Publishers, 2009) at lvii–lxv. For reactions to the book by the Church and the wider public, see A Thomas, 'Preface', in C Beccaria, *On Crimes and Punishments and Other Writings* edited by A Thomas and translated by A Thomas & J Parzen (Toronto, Toronto University Press, 2008) at xxiii–xxviii. On Morellet's translation, see further P Audegean, 'L'ombre de Morellet: les premières traductions françaises de Beccaria (1765–1822)', in M Porret & E Salvi (eds), *Cesare Beccaria. La controverse pénale, XVIIIe–XXIe siècle* (Rennes, Presses universitaires de Rennes, 2015) 119. On Voltaire's commentary and its influence, see E Groffier, 'Voltaire vulgarisateur de Beccaria', in P Audegean & L Delia (eds), *Le moment Beccaria: naissance du droit pénal moderne (1764–1810)* (Liverpool, Liverpool University Press, 2018) 15.

[2] For Venturi's reading of Beccaria's work and its reception, see F Venturi, *Utopia and Reform in the Enlightenment* (Cambridge, Cambridge University Press, 1971) 100 ff, esp at 106.

improvements of the criminal justice system and more generally of practices of government. When read in this way, a broader critique could question the coherence of the proposals, and it would be quite possible to pick and mix between them, supporting some and rejecting others. The rulers inspired by Beccaria's book took what he said in this way: as a list of policy changes to consider and implement, reject or adapt, as it appeared appropriate to them from a good governance perspective.[3] The most influential of these proposals were the two to which Beccaria himself had given particular prominence, the abolition of the death penalty and of torture. Other suggestions made by him would, from this perspective, appear more like tentative ideas, passing observations or speculative hints, and these would be ignored or charged with vagueness and lack of clarity, and frequently be embellished or improved upon by Beccaria's ardent followers.[4]

There is, however, also a second way of understanding Beccaria's project, which Venturi refers to as utopian. In this utopian reading, what agitates Beccaria is the state of a deeply corrupt society, where the nobles enjoy their unfair and undeserved privileges, the poor are poor and obviously suffer, the Catholic Church's teachings drape a cloak of constructed meaning over the naked and unvarnished truth of that suffering, and so-called criminal justice, in all its brutal splendour, keeps the socially harmful actions that arise from such suffering in check. This reading, as Venturi shows, is invited by Beccaria's stressing the problems of inequality and poverty.[5] In so doing, Beccaria tapped into a different strand of philosophical thinking from that of Hobbes and Montesquieu, hearkening rather to the radical proto-socialist critiques of the existing social order.[6] Would but a tinkering with the extremes of the practices underpinning this order (torture and the death penalty) effect any real change at all? Was such tinkering even possible, or would genuine reform always falter on the hurdle of the underlying social forces driving people towards crime, and authorities towards brutalities?

[3] These rulers included Peter Leopold, Grand Duke of Tuscany (1765–1790) and later Holy Roman Emperor, King of Hungary and Bohemia, and Archduke of Austria (1790–1792), and – most famously – Catherine II of Russia, who even unsuccessfully tried to entice Beccaria to advise her in person on law reform. About one-third of Catherine II's extensive instructions on law reform, her *Nakaz*, were copied directly from Beccaria's treatise. See T Cizova, 'Beccaria in Russia' (1962) 40 *The Slavonic and East European Review* 384 at 390–393. For Beccaria's influence on reform projects in Austria and Northern Italy, see ch 14 in this volume.

[4] Emblematic of this reading is Voltaire's approach to Beccaria's text in his commentaries, on which see Venturi, above n 2 at 108–109. See also C Cave, 'Voltaire lecteur de Beccaria, Le commentaire sur le livre "*Des délits et des peines*"', in P Audegean et al (eds), *Le Bonheur du plus grand nombre: Beccaria et les lumières* (Paris, ENS editions, 2017) 257; Groffier, above n 1; and MT Maestro, *Voltaire and Beccaria as Reformers of Criminal Law* (New York, Columbia University Press, 1942). Gianni Francioni's reconstruction of Beccaria's original text for the critical edition of Beccaria's book (C Beccaria, *Edizione Nationale delle Opere*, vol 1 (Milan, Mediobanca, 1984)) also shows that Beccaria's initial draft (which was heavily edited by Pietro Verri before being sent to the publisher) was both more radical in content and less lawyerly in style than the published version.

[5] Venturi, above n 2 at 106.

[6] Ibid at 103. For critical discussion of Venturi's perspective, see P Audegean, *La philosophie de Beccaria: savoir punir, savoir écrire, savoir produire* (Paris, Vrin, 2010) 15–21.

That implementation of Beccaria's practical proposals would, of necessity, fail for these reasons was not an objection raised only by aggressive critics such as Beccaria's arch-opponent, the monk Facchinei (who, slyly observing that hard labour as a mode of punishment looked suspiciously like the free labour engaged in by poor people, queried what message, exactly, hard labour as a punishment 'worse than death' could send to the would-be assassin if there were people aplenty who as supposedly free men lived just such lives of endless drudgery and misery?).[7] And not only does punishing people by hard labour make little sense in a world where many in any event had to live lives like that, but how can their punishment be just in a world that is so unjust? Both challenges were put to Beccaria even by some of his most admiring and excited readers among the French *philosophes*, some of whom were for this very reason inclined to jettison the project of gradual reform as unworkable and to embrace full-scale revolution instead.[8] Moreover, if crime really was (as Beccaria claimed) the result of misery more than of deliberate evil, of being denied the physical and educational resources to better one's lot, was not Beccaria's imaginary culprit's protest against the execution of the law against him – 'What are these laws which I have to obey, which leave such a gulf between me and the rich man [who] denies me the penny I beg of him, brushing me off with the demand that I should work, something he knows nothing about …'[9] – unanswerable? In short: the 'just punishment in an unjust society' problem threatened to collapse the whole reformatory endeavour and made Beccaria's reformist vision appear mired in contradiction.

This is where, for his contemporaries at least, the intellectual attraction of taking Beccaria's vision to be utopian in character came in. If what Beccaria seeks is a world that cannot be reached but through a revolution, doubts as to whether this world could be reached by gradual reform are simply by the way. However, Beccaria's own character and inclinations meant he abhorred violence and was attracted to working within the system, on the path of gradual reform.[10] He offered a reply to those who would deem gradual reform impossible (a reply many of his contemporaries were ready to dismiss outright as wishful thinking but that turned out to be the most prescient of his many predictions): that, as daily life became better and safer and people more educated, serious crimes would become less frequent, and milder punishments would suffice to bring

[7] F Facchinei, 'Notes and Observations on the Book Entitled "On Crimes and Punishments"', in Beccaria (Thomas ed), above n 1 at 89, 96. Facchinei's opposition is also discussed by Venturi, above n 2 at 102–106.

[8] See esp Venturi, above n 2 at 115 ff. See also J Bart, '"*Des délits et des peines*" dans les débats révolutionaires francais', in Porret & Salvi (eds), above n 1, 153; E Salvi, '"Adoucir le sort des hommes accablés par l'oppression légale". La réception de Beccaria dans la Bibliothèque philosophique (1782–1785)', in Audegean et al (eds), above n 4 at 271.

[9] Beccaria (Bellamy ed), above n 1 at 69 (ch 28).

[10] This is stressed by Venturi, above n 2 at 101.

their incidence down to a socially bearable level.[11] (Beccaria, from his economic perspective, views crime as deterrable but not as completely avoidable.[12]) Knowing, with hindsight, that Beccaria's bold speculation about the longer-term impacts of social change was right,[13] we can feel more confident that the reformist reading of his text will take us somewhere. In what is perhaps the ultimate historical irony, what did prove politically unstable, economically unsustainable and culturally unacceptable were the various revolutionary attempts to re-mould collective socio-economic life wholesale in a post-private-property mode. In most places, gradual legal and institutional reforms were eventually able to reshape government and criminal justice in sufficiently legitimate forms.

A major theoretical puzzle for contemporary readers of Beccaria's text arises from the use he makes of the social contract – both as regards his understanding of the notion of the social contract, and as regards the very fact of his perceived need to rely on it. As Matravers points out in his contribution to this collection, from a present-day philosophical perspective, it is unclear why Beccaria would need or want to draw on social contract theory at all, given that he adopts a utilitarian value system. One way of responding to this puzzle is to reflect on the limitations of utilitarianism as a comprehensive political doctrine. It is all very well for a focus on the costs and benefits of the consequences of our collective policies and actions to guide legislative and administrative decision-making and to be prominent in political debate. But Beccaria sees clearly that utilitarianism thus conceived[14] cannot serve as a complete theory of political authority. Any such theory must include limits on what we can do to each other – even in the name of utility. This is so because complete agreement on, and consequently genuinely self-motivated endorsement of and submission to, the policies generated by utilitarian calculation is farfetched. Disagreement in politics is pervasive, and it is by no means limited to disagreement about empirical facts and their processing within the calculus. It is also always disagreement about values and priorities. What follows from this – apart from a need to allow different voices in the debate – on a normative level is that any political decision is one in which other reasonable positions have not prevailed. For those whose positions

[11] Beccaria (Bellamy ed), above n 1 at 113 (ch 47): '[P]unishments ought to be relative to the state of the nation itself. Stronger and more easily felt impressions have to be made on a people only just out of the savage state. … But as souls become softened by society, sensitivity grows. And as it does so, the severity of punishments ought to diminish …'

[12] Ibid at 19 (ch 6). For further discussion, see MD White, 'On Beccaria, the Economics of Crime, and the Philosophy of Punishment' (2014) 2 *Philosophical Inquiries* 121.

[13] A process analysed from a normative-sociological angle by Norbert Elias and empirically by Manuel Eisner. See N Elias, *The Civilizing Process* (Oxford, Oxford University Press, 1969) [first published in German in 1939] and Manuel Eisner, 'Long-term Historical Trends in Violent Crime' (2003) 30 *Crime and Justice* 83.

[14] This is not to claim that modern utilitarian theorists fail to develop better accounts but only to stress that the first proponents of utilitarianism did not develop them. While Matravers in his discussion of Beccaria's approach shows that it would be possible to recast Beccaria's position as a rights-protective version of utilitarianism, Beccaria's explicit reliance on the social contract indicates that he found it easier to derive such limits from a separate theoretical foundation.

have not prevailed, compliance means submission to the will of another. Any legislative and administrative scheme therefore always contains a dimension of coercion. This is so simply because it requires compliance, cuts discussion short (or, to speak with Raz, because it introduces exclusionary reasons).

Utilitarianism as initially conceived by Helvétius, Beccaria and others, therefore falls short as a comprehensive theory of political legitimacy and must be relegated to just one component within such a theory. This is arguably how the matter appears to have been perceived by Beccaria himself. The way Beccaria treats utilitarianism, it cannot give us sufficient reason in itself why we must comply with laws.[15] For this, we need a different theoretical foundation.

This is precisely what social contract theories seek to provide. They seek to offer us reasons why we must subject ourselves to a political authority. One major reason (that also often functions as a limitation) is that it is not just in our collective but also in our personal interest to participate in the political system and submit ourselves to its laws. That such participation remains in our interest can, however, only be assured to us in advance if the system is set up so that it will not become too costly for us as individuals to comply with decisions that do not go our way (think of Rawls' theory of justice as a modern working-out of this basic thought).[16]

Arguably, this is the kind of link between utilitarianism and social contract theory that informs Beccaria's position. Beccaria's attraction to the idea of the social contract is closely connected to his concern with individual freedom and wellbeing. It is his concern with individual freedom that guides Beccaria to his specific articulation of contractarianism. He is not oblivious to the inherent contradiction between assuming contractual obligations of obedience and maintaining individual freedom, or blind to the danger that contractarianism can become a vehicle for justifying a Hobbesian sovereign. But he starts from another contradiction, which is that absolute freedom cannot be safely maintained in conditions of absolute freedom; that is, the state of nature can only guarantee 'a freedom rendered useless by the uncertainty of retaining it'.[17] He is then able to resolve both contradictions by devising his signature brand of minimalist contractarianism (contra Hobbes), under which the social contract

[15] Bellamy might disagree. For him, the utilitarian element is the dominant one, with the social contract's becoming 'both a means for expressing the central utilitarian concern that in minimising pain and maximising pleasure we show equal respect for the interests of each individual and a device for justifying our obligation to uphold this maxim', with the further consequence that 'the only rights that either state or citizen might validly claim flowed from their mutual obligation to preserve those human interests necessary to the reduction of pain and the promoting of happiness' (Bellamy, 'Introduction', in Beccaria (Bellamy ed), above n 1 at ix, xx).

[16] The affinity between Beccaria's contractarianism and Rawls' is often noted, see eg M Ricciardi & F Santoni de Sio, 'Cesare Beccaria: Utilitarianism, Contractualism and Rights' (2014) 2 *Philosophical Inquiries* 79 at 83. Compare also Bellamy 'Introduction', in (Bellamy ed), above n 1 at ix, xxi–xxiii.

[17] Beccaria (Bellamy ed), above n 1 at 9 (ch 1).

can legitimately demand from individuals to surrender to the collective only the smallest portion of their freedom needed to secure the protection by the collective of their remaining freedom.

While Beccaria does not express himself in the language of fundamental political rights, his main conclusions and commitments are certainly capable of being restated in terms of such rights. Proportionality enters Beccaria's thought first and foremost as a notion that is determinative of specifying which portion of his freedom a citizen has ceded to the polity.[18] Deterrence similarly does not supply lawmakers with a freestanding justification[19] – which, if it were available, could potentially justify any punishment that could be shown to operate as a stronger deterrent than its alternatives.[20] Punishments must be proportionate also from the perspective of the individual who is being punished on a particular occasion. This is the Copernican revolution brought about by Beccaria's political theory of punishment that Zucca rightly stresses in his contribution to this volume. From this perspective it makes perfect sense to ask, as Beccaria famously does in his discussion of the death penalty, whether any individual could plausibly be expected to consent to a political system that might impose *this punishment* on him.

Beccaria draws on his contractarianism to specify the basic principles of collective political life. As such, his contractarianism lends itself to being translated into constitutionalism.[21] For Beccaria, unlike for Hobbes, the fact that humans possess no viable alternatives to living in political associations does not preclude constraints on the exercise of public authority. Quite the opposite: the inevitability of contracting obliges the polity to adhere to principles that make this communal existence valuable for each of its members.[22] This requires certain protections to ensure that politics serve the interests of all individuals within that polity.

From this perspective, the use that was made of Beccaria's treatise by some of the American founding fathers, who took from his work elements of a blueprint for a written constitution,[23] involved no bastardisation or cheapening of Beccaria's thought. To the contrary: this use of Beccaria's ideas was not

[18] L Picotti, 'Der Grundsatz der Verhältnismässigkeit von Verbrechen und Strafen als Quelle und Beschränkung für die Legitimation der Strafgewalt bei Beccaria', in L Picotti (ed), *An den Wurzeln des modernen Strafrechts. Die juristische Aufklärung Cesare Beccarias und die Strafgewalt* translated by T Vormbaum (Wien, LIT Verlag, 2017) 71.

[19] Beccaria (Bellamy ed), above n 1 at 13 (ch 3).

[20] For some discussion, see MD White, 'The Neglected Nuance of Beccaria's Theory' (2018) 46 *European Journal of Law & Economics* 315.

[21] Eberhard Weis considers Beccaria 'an early proponent of bourgeois rule-of-law and, albeit more veiled, constitutional thinking': E Weis, *Cesare Beccaria (1738–1794), Mailänder Aufklärer und Anreger der Strafrechtsreformen in Europa* (Munich, Verlag der Bayerischen Akademie der Wissenschaften, 1992) 16–17.

[22] Beccaria (Bellamy ed), above n 1 at 10–11 (ch 2).

[23] Beccaria's influence in, and on, early American law and politics is extensively traced in JD Bessler, *The Birth of American Law: An Italian Philosopher and the American Revolution* (Durham NC, Carolina Academic Press, 2014).

only consistent with the practical-political aim of enlightened criminal justice reform that underpinned his treatise but it arguably constituted the decisive step that brought Beccaria's ideas into their natural habitat. It is in constitutions that we expect, and find, guarantees and principles of political organisation that will ensure to all members of the polity equal protection of their rights and equal concern for their interests. Translated into a constitutional framework, Beccaria's particular blend of contractualist and utilitarian thinking makes perfect sense.

Beccaria is sometimes portrayed as someone too shy, withdrawn and lethargic to be able to take his rightful place among the public intellectuals of his time, and it is suggested that he had little to offer the world after the publication of his bold, youthful treatise that so wonderfully expressed, condensed and encapsulated the political beliefs and reformist ambitions of the intellectual avantgarde of his age. This is a perception much encouraged by stories his former friends and intellectual mentors, the Verri brothers, put about after Beccaria's return from an extended trip to Paris that he had, at the invitation of some leading French intellectuals, undertaken in the company of one of the Verri brothers.[24] One can, of course, only ever speculate about such matters, but considering how he chose to spend the rest of his life – as a faithful servant to the Habsburg administration – one might hazard the guess that the truth of the matter might have been somewhat different. It is at least conceivable that Beccaria did not want to occupy this role – that, if he discovered anything in Paris, he discovered that life as a public intellectual was not for him. Not for him the constant proffering of opinions to no immediate end other than the response and reaction of similarly placed others. Not for him the veiled competition for the most interesting remark, the most striking turn of phrase, the most devoted attention of admirers. Looking at his life as a whole, one might even begin to wonder whether his very participation in the Accademia dei Pugni – the political discussion circle of like-minded friends created by the Verri brothers – was in part a holding operation, a youthful pursuit for someone with a lot of time on his hands and a vague, unformed hope to one day be able to influence for the better how things are done. What we do know is that this hope fastened itself on contact with those whose actions could make a difference: to wit, the Habsburg-installed administrators of Lombardy, who just might be persuaded to turn their minds to modernisation and reform.[25] It would be unsurprising, then, that Beccaria jumped at the opportunity to take on a newly-created chair of economics in which this

[24] The best biographical account of Beccaria's life and work is still MT Maestro, *Cesare Beccaria and the Origins of Penal Reform* (Philadelphia PA, Temple University Press, 1973). Other biographical sketches include J Hostettler, *Cesare Beccaria. The Genius of 'On Crimes and Punishments'* (Hook, Waterside Press, 2010), the well-known C Phillipson, *Three Criminal Law Reformers: Beccaria, Bentham, Romilly* (London, JM Dent & Sons, 1923), and recently M Pisani, *Cesare Beccaria* (Milan, Giuffrè, 2015).

[25] On the Accademia dei Pugni, see esp SA Reinert, *The Academy of Fisticuffs: Political Economy and Commercial Society in Enlightenment Italy* (Cambridge MA, Harvard University Press, 2018).

administration gave him his first role; and that after two years of lecturing and educating (when the tedious regularity of having to repeat himself all over again for a new group of students might have set in) he was keen to switch across to the administration itself, commissioned over subsequent years to look into a great variety of issues that impeded effective rule and caused trouble to governors and governed alike. Beccaria liked to get his head round a problem and solve it. His reports and proposals for the Habsburg administration were not hesitant but bold. With the repeated experience of being listened to by his superiors, and seeing his proposals implemented, there is little reason to doubt that, in working for the Habsburg administration on various projects of practical reform, he had found what suited him as an occupation in life.[26]

Given this history one can, on the one hand, see the point of looking at Beccaria's book separately from the man who wrote it: he separated himself from it rather quickly, in that the kind of project the book was – a contribution to political-philosophical debates – was not Beccaria's life project. On the other hand, however, this history invites us to take a closer look at Beccaria's later brushes with criminal justice reform – and particularly, to trace the fascinating and still underappreciated connections between Beccaria's work and Habsburgian criminal law reform. Practical political uptake of Beccaria's ideas by the self-styled enlightened rulers of his day was not a foregone conclusion, successful reform even less so. This collection does not offer a thoroughgoing historical appreciation of Beccaria's influence, which would require historians' methods and extensive, often archival, research. But it aims to provide those looking at Beccaria's work with contemporary concerns in mind a glimpse into the practical difficulties facing the firebrand author turned public servant during his long career in the Habsburg-Lombardian administration. Other aims of this collection are to take a fresh look at *On Crimes and Punishments*' lasting contribution to political and penal theory, and to discover what contemporary criminal law thinkers, who have the benefit of two and a half centuries of post-Beccaria scholarship, can derive from this canonical text.

I. THE INDIVIDUAL CHAPTERS

Lorenzo Zucca's magisterial opening chapter on 'Beccaria's Political Theory of Criminal Justice'[27] offers a precise, contextualised and nuanced appreciation of the central lines of thought in Beccaria's book. No reader of Zucca's chapter

[26] On Beccaria's career in the Habsburg administration, see esp C Capra, 'Beccaria fonctionnaire et l'évolution de ses idées', in Audegean et al (eds), above n 4 at 177; and A Ortolja-Baird, 'Cesare Beccaria: Functionary, Lecturer, Cameralist?: Interpreting Cameralism in Habsburg Lombardy', in E Nokkala & NB Miller (eds), *Cameralism and the Enlightenment: Happiness, Governance, and Reform in Transnational Perspective* (Abingdon, Routledge, 2019) ch 8.

[27] Ch 1 in this volume.

can fail to grasp why Beccaria was so exciting to his contemporary readers, and ultimately why his thinking – not only his conclusions, but also his exposition, outlook and specific arguments – proved so influential. As Zucca highlights, 'Beccaria's *On Crimes and Punishments* was the first attempt to apply the principles of political economy to the practice of punishment with the intent of humanising and rationalising the use of coercion on the part of the state', having previously explained that:

> Political economy for Beccaria was not just a tool with which to administer the state more efficiently; it was a Copernican revolution in how to understand the place of man in the society, and the importance of reconceiving politics to serve the interests of the society. Political economy aimed to be the science of happiness and was intended to replace religion, which was perceived as the source of misery.

Zucca stresses that 'Beccaria's project of rationalising law extended also to politics, and in particular to the understanding of political justice and political order.'

> Beccaria resisted traditionalists by denying their eschatology: human freedom and human goals can only be evaluated within the realm of immanent civil societies. Divine justice addressed intentional wrongdoing, commonly defined in religious language as sin. Sin had to do with intentions and a man's heart. It was within God's jurisdiction to punish this kind of wrongdoing. Civil societies, insisted Beccaria, had jurisdiction on crimes, which must be separated from sins. A crime is what damages society, and the crime's cost to the society can be measured.

Beccaria's originality, Zucca argues, lies in the unique way in which Beccaria combines utility, political freedom and the social contract to 'arrive at a compromise between freedom and utility in the name of justice'.

The relevance of the social contract to Beccaria's thinking is explored further in Matt Matravers' chapter, 'Reconstructing Beccaria's Social Contract'.[28] Matravers' discussion highlights how, and why, Beccaria's use of this concept confounds contemporary contractarian thinking. This is so in part because Beccaria deploys two arguments – one from natural equality and one utilitarian – that could each be used without any recourse to the social contract. Beccaria's account thus strongly resembles the rule utilitarianism of Mill and, with respect to punishment, Rawls. Why, then, rely on the notion of a social contract as well? Matravers suggests that Beccaria's use of the social contract may be not so much as a theoretical device than as a rhetorical one: contractarian language enables Beccaria to give particular strength and power to the question 'Why should we accept this as an authoritative principle?', and to make his argument a more vivid one.

[28] Ch 2 in this volume.

Matravers' reconstruction of Beccaria's arguments allows us to appreciate the coherence of Beccaria's approach. With emphasis on some very different aspects of Beccaria's proposals, the coherence of Beccaria's position is also at issue in Antony Duff and Sandra Marshall's chapter on 'Beccaria's Contractarian Criminal Law: Jurisdiction, Punishments and Rewards'.[29] Duff and Marshall explore the implications that Beccaria's views of the state's socially reformatory, citizen-improving and welfare-oriented functions have on the reach of criminal law. They connect this to another distinctive element in Beccaria's thought, one that follows inexorably from stepping away, as Beccaria did, from perceiving crime in its pre-political aspect, whether as sin or as serious interpersonal wrong. This element is that crime becomes – conceptually – restricted to a breach of the criminal law of *this* polity, an understanding that generates an equally restrictive approach to criminal jurisdiction, confining prosecution to conduct criminalised within a particular polity. In Duff and Marshall's view, such a 'hands-off' approach to the crimes committed elsewhere at first blush sits uneasily with various suggestions Beccaria makes about how the state might prevent crimes by engaging in various character-building strategies through education and through publicly rewarding good behaviour. They argue that we can, however, make sense of both these suggestions by reading Beccaria as concerned with the duties of citizenship of a free subject – a reading that dissolves the apparent tension between the restriction of crime to the polity, on the one hand, and an extension of the subject matter of crime-control policies to matters well beyond crime, on the other hand. In their view, Beccaria successfully develops a '(proto-) version of a "public law" conception of criminal law' similar to that developed by modern writers such as Thorburn and Chiao – despite their doubts as to whether Beccaria's account of the criminal law can be sufficiently grounded in the contractarian framework in which Beccaria sets it.

Beccaria's contractarian framework for criminal law is further explored in Antje du Bois-Pedain's chapter on 'Crime, Punishment and the Social Contract: Towards the Constitutionalisation of Criminal Law'.[30] While the contract model has obvious theoretical strengths when laying the foundations for state authority, in the criminal law context, contractarian approaches have struggled to generate plausible accounts of state punishment. The conception of crime as a breach of the contract, which Beccaria shares, has proved a troublesome starting point – indeed, Hobbes, by catapulting the lawbreaker outside the communal realm constituted by the contract, notoriously succeeded only in rendering punishment an extra-legal act of war against an ex-citizen. That Beccaria resolves this problem (or perhaps more accurately: reveals it to be a non-problem) is owed to his public law conception of criminal law, which is in turn linked to his utilitarian conception of government. Beccaria's unique

[29] Ch 3 in this volume.
[30] Ch 4 in this volume.

combination of contractarian and utilitarian lines of thought allows him to treat the law-breaking subject as a continuing member of the polity, subject to and protected by the contract's terms during the process of criminal-law enforcement. This breakthrough in punishment theory is made possible by Beccaria's treatment of the 'social contract' less as a hypothetical device than as a set of shared assumptions about good and appropriate government: in other words, as an existing political constitution.

A challenge to the coherence of Beccaria's foundation of state punishment comes from a different direction. Treason has often been taken to be a pivotal offence by those writing in the social contract tradition, and Beccaria is no exception in this regard. In historical terms, this is in part explained by the cultural memory of feudalist political practices such as oaths of allegiance and even actual contracts of government, which naturally placed treason at the apex of possible violations of the contract's terms. It is much more difficult to explain the elevated status of treason when the contractarian basis of political obligation is not taken literally but metaphorically, and when the ultimate justification of political authority resides in its capacity to secure 'the greatest happiness for the greater number'. Against this background, Anat Scolnicov, in her chapter on 'Beccaria, Treason and the Social Contract',[31] asks whether Beccaria's views on treason and on extradition follow coherently from his account of the foundation of political authority. Scolnicov argues that Beccaria's positions on treason and on extradition expose tensions in his bold attempt to reconcile utilitarianism with social contract theory, in that the most important offence according to Beccaria himself – treason – is not sufficiently justified by his theory of the criminal law (which includes utilitarian components), whereas extradition for this offence undercuts his conception of the social contract.

In his chapter on 'Beccaria's Secular Metaphysics: Pain, Time and State Authority',[32] Shai Lavi picks up on another of Beccaria's key influences on punishment theory: his decisive break with metaphysical or religiously oriented justifications of punishment (and of sovereign authority). In Lavi's analysis, the 'demystification' of punishment (which fits well with Beccaria's, and legal positivism's, larger commitment to the demystification of law also discussed by Zucca) has deeper destructive effects on the theoretical foundations of punishment than is often appreciated by philosophers of punishment (although these effects were, as Lavi also perceptively explores, immediately noted by Beccaria's contemporaneous religious opponents). The point of state punishment is no longer to respond to an act that, *qua* sin, also puts the offender's eternal salvation at risk; it is simply to contribute through enforcement of the law to an overall scheme of good governance of the polity.

Beccaria's fully secularised perspective on criminal justice entails a pivotal lowering of what is at stake in public punishment practice: not – ultimately – the

[31] Ch 5 in this volume.
[32] Ch 6 in this volume.

eternal salvation of criminals, the expiation of crimes (entailing, if one were to judge wrongly, the possible damnation of the judge into the bargain), but merely the managerial organisation of public life by responding to socially injurious activities. This is not just a decisive lowering of the stakes for punishment practice, it is – far more fundamentally – a reorientation in which the distinctive moral valence of the act of state punishment disappears. Punishment is just one among many possible ways of dealing with socially injurious behaviours, and at that – as Beccaria also says – not necessarily the best or most effective one. Responding to socially injurious behaviours by criminalising these behaviours and then sanctioning their breach is very much second best to preventing such behaviours by means of general social policy and cultural improvements involving the inculcation of styles of living and working that lead to less violence and less crime. In such a perspective, punishment is not the central part of the system but the ancillary support that is needed to prop up what matters: the prohibition itself, which is in turn rationally embedded in a wider scheme of legal and political behavioural guidance.

Lavi concludes:

> Beccaria's reversals of the Catholic teachings on the temporality of punishment and the morality of pain mark the importance of his contribution to the history of penology. His nascent utilitarianism and his reliance on social contract theory are important but secondary. While the latter are broad conceptual frameworks to which Beccaria may have contributed, his revision of penal theory is far-reaching and original.

Malcolm Thorburn's chapter on 'Public Institutions Without Public Offices: Beccaria's Use of Political Theory in the Reform of Criminal Justice'[33] draws attention to another feature of Beccaria's contractarian argument: that, as Thorburn puts it, 'Beccaria uses the idea on a retail level, measuring a wide variety of criminal justice policies by considering whether free persons would consent to be governed by such rules'. Thorburn views this tendency as problematic as, in his view, 'some extra-legal yardstick such as hypothetical consent' is ill suited to the purpose of 'evaluat[ing] specific criminal justice policies'. Thorburn also draws attention to another problematic aspect of Beccaria's thought: his conceptualisation of judicial determinations involving interpretation of unclear law as exposing the law's subjects to 'the petty tyrannies of the many individuals enforcing the law'.[34] Having identified the problem, the 'theoretical flimsiness' of Beccaria's account of public authority leaves him unable 'to follow up his powerful critique of unbridled judicial discretion with a plausible alternative'. In Thorburn's estimation, it is the absence of 'a conception of public office' that leads Beccaria to insist 'that all officials must be reduced to mechanical tools for giving effect to the law, without the need for the exercise of judgment' – a

[33] Ch 7 in this volume.
[34] Beccaria (Bellamy ed), above n 1 at 15 (ch 4).

position that Thorburn castigates as 'an implausible account not only of judicial decision-making, but of the rule of law more generally'.

Given these limitations in Beccaria's approach, it is particularly interesting that Vincent Chiao, in his chapter on 'Realism and the Rational Administration of the Law in Beccaria',[35] reads Beccaria not only 'as a precursor to a particular strand of American legal realism' but also 'as a prophet of the administrative state'. What he means by the former is Beccaria's deflationist account of judicial decision-making, his critical, rational and scientific approach to law, and his scepticism that law could be treated as a closed system of interlinked concepts. What he means by the latter is that Beccaria's attitude towards law more broadly is

> instrumental and bureaucratic, largely sceptical of case-by-case discretion and optimistic about the power of scientific administration. ... For Beccaria, ... [t]he criminal law should, in Weber's terms, be taken out of the domain of charismatic leadership and be subjected to norms of instrumental and bureaucratic rationality – what we today might call 'evidence-based policy'.

Chiao also points out that Beccaria himself may not have been aware of the extent to which 'this vision renders law an essentially bureaucratic institution: impersonal, instrumentally rational, and rule bound' – a conclusion reinforced by Thorburn's analysis of Beccaria's inability to provide a constructive solution to the problem of judicial discretion, which Thorburn links to Beccaria's failure to conceive of the judge's role in terms of public office. It is therefore all the more fascinating that, as Chiao maintains, '[i]t is by reading Beccaria as a precursor to Weber's account of bureaucratic rationality ... that the groundbreaking character of *On Crimes and Punishments* is best appreciated'. One reason why Chiao may well be right about this is that, while Beccaria's understanding of the judicial function may, as Thorburn argues, have been antiquated and confused, Beccaria did have a clear sense of the potential for effective reform residing in new modes of governance through modern administrations – the main reason why he and many others in the self-styled 'Academy of Fisticuffs' had set their hopes on becoming engines of change themselves on joining the Habsburg administration.

While the essays in Part I of the book engage, in different ways, with Beccaria's ongoing contribution to political and penal theory, the essays in Part II take up the editors' invitation to contemporary criminal justice scholars to reflect on how Beccaria's work and ideas could influence their current scholarship – to contemplate a conversation with Beccaria, to imagine him as the enigmatic retired professor who wanders into their office and asks the eternal question 'What are you working on?'

[35] Ch 8 in this volume.

This part of the collection begins with a chapter by Paul Roberts on 'Beccaria Now: (Re)reading *On Crimes and Punishments*'.[36] Roberts reads Beccaria as 'through and through the modern rationalist penal reformer, arguably the first and the one who led the way'. Roberts also stresses the significance of Beccaria's '[holistic] approach to penalty'. Because he 'conceived crime and punishment as part of the more general problem of enlightened liberal government', he was able to anticipate 'the central tenets of what became, during the nineteenth-century reforms and ever after, orthodox civilian criminal process'.

Roberts acknowledges that Beccaria, writing as he did before modern differentiations developed between different academic specialisms, and when many of those regarding themselves as public philosophers drew no clear line between theoretical philosophy, on the one hand, and policy advice and advocacy, on the other, 'could not reasonably be expected to match the technical finesse of twenty-first century analytical philosophy or the methodological rigour of modern empirical social science'. But he still notes as a source of frustration for the modern reader that '[h]is commentaries on the more specifically evidentiary aspects of criminal adjudication are patchy, underdeveloped and antiquated in ways that Beccaria the arch-modernist would have been mortified to realise'.

So why bother with Beccaria's book today? For Roberts, the main reasons are that Beccaria's 'liberal instincts generally save him from any corresponding dogmatism at the substantive level of practical ethics and policy choice', and that his innovative 'commitment to treating criminal justice reform as a problem of public administration susceptible of rational analysis and (a more capacious adjective in Romance languages than in modern-day English) *scientific* solutions' itself is of lasting value. His conception of good legislation is 'more nuanced, pluralistic and humane' than Bentham's later efforts, with Beccaria stressing that 'it is a false idea of utility to sacrifice the thing to the name and to separate the public good from the good of each individual'.[37] For Beccaria, thus, legitimate political authority is, at least, side-constrained by a conception of the person mandating respect for individual rights. It comes as no surprise that Beccaria can also be read as anticipating twentieth-century ideas of human dignity as the basis for universal human rights.

In a chapter entitled 'Should Murder Be More Difficult to Prove than Theft? Beccaria and Differential Standards of Proof',[38] Amit Pundik picks up on one of Beccaria's ideas that is illustrative of Beccaria's tendency, noted by Roberts, to advance rationalistic arguments that appear peculiarly unscientific to the modern reader. This is Beccaria's suggestion that the graver the nature of a crime, the less frequent that crime is and hence the more likely the accused is to be innocent of it, from which he takes it to follow that a grave crime should

[36] Ch 9 in this volume.
[37] Beccaria (Bellamy ed), above n 1 at 102 (Ch 40).
[38] Ch 10 in this volume.

require more proof of guilt than pettier crime. Pundik first tightens and reconstructs Beccaria's argument. He then explores two possible interpretations of it – one that would support the introduction of what in modern parlance is termed naked statistical evidence in all criminal proceedings, and another that permits the introduction of such evidence only in respect of low-frequency crimes (when it tends to favour the accused). Pundik's reading of Beccaria's empiricist claims gives rise to an argument for requiring stronger proof for certain crimes that differs from contemporary arguments in both its theoretical foundations and practical implications, showing that a re-reading of Beccaria's work can offer important contributions to the theory of evidence and proof.

As stressed by Zucca and Lavi in their appreciations of Beccaria's contributions to political and penal theory, Beccaria instantiates prevention as the only legitimate function of the criminal law, and reconceptualises punishment as a deterrent of law-breaking behaviour. In their chapter on 'Cesare Beccaria's Integrative Deterrence Approach',[39] Mordechai Kremnitzer and Adi Gal revisit Beccaria's concept of deterrence. While, as they stress, there are good theoretical and empirical reasons to doubt that deterrence can stand by itself as punishment's justification and criterion for measurement, they argue that a more careful reading of Beccaria's approach to punishment can offer ways of balancing different punitive approaches, producing what is best termed an 'integrative deterrence approach'. They suggest that

> the principle of deterrence is an important and valuable tool that should not be marginalised. Instead – and provided that it is better implemented and integrated, based on guilt and limited by justice considerations – it should be combined with retribution, and given an important place in punishing particular types of crimes and certain types of perpetrators.

The two final chapters in this part of the book address, from different directions and with different emphases, the connection between Beccaria and human rights discourses with a bearing on criminal justice. In her chapter on 'Human Rights and Criminal Law: From Beccaria's *On Crimes and Punishments* to Modern Criminal Law',[40] Miriam Gur-Arye approaches the question from a constitutional criminal law angle – a perspective that is in line with Zucca's interpretation of Beccaria's work, in the opening chapter to the collection, as developing 'principles for the constitutionalisation of criminal law' by 'creating a number of substantive and procedural guarantees against the abuse of power and in favour of limitation of power'. Gur-Arye shows that such constitutionalisation should go further than suggested by Beccaria's text. As she argues,

> over-criminalisation is one of the main concerns of modern criminal law and it cannot be remedied solely by reforming social institutions, as suggested by Beccaria.

[39] Ch 11 in this volume.
[40] Ch 12 in this volume.

> Over-criminalisation unduly infringes upon offenders' freedom and other basic rights. Therefore, modern criminal law should move towards subjecting the issue of criminalisation itself to constitutional control.

In their chapter entitled 'Beccaria on the Human Rights Committee? An Excursus on the Parameters of Human Rights and Penology',[41] Leslie Sebba and Rachela Er'el trace the common roots of Beccaria's treatise and of modern human rights law in Lockean notions of the social contract, as well as the convergences of outcomes and similarities of reasoning and approach between Beccaria's text, on the one hand, and historical and modern texts enshrining human rights commitments concerning specific human rights issues, on the other. Sebba and Er'el's attention is focused on Beccaria's contribution to the culture of international human rights – a contribution that does not run through the creation of new institutional structures and authorities but through inserting ideas into debates and giving such ideas political and cultural traction. Indeed, as they point out, in Beccaria's time, human rights and penology did not yet exist as distinct fields and practical discourses outside the boundaries of moral and political philosophy. The discussions stimulated by *On Crimes and Punishments* did much to remedy this.

Part III of the book places Beccaria's influence on criminal justice policy in an historical context, specifically in the context of reform efforts in Northern Italy and Habsburg Lombardy. The chapter by Antje du Bois-Pedain on 'Criminal Justice Reform in the Austro-Hungarian Empire, Habsburgian Lombardy and Tuscany: Beccaria's Policy Memoranda in Context'[42] describes these developments. It traces the landmark steps of criminal justice reform in the Habsburg crownlands from their abortive beginnings during Maria Theresa's rule to the ambitious but problematic reforms pursued by her immediate successor Joseph II, and their modifications during the brief reign of Leopold II, and considers their repercussions on Habsburg-ruled Lombardy,[43] as well as the trajectory of reforms pursued by Leopold during his long reign as grand duke of the constitutionally separate Tuscany prior to his accession to the Habsburg throne.[44] Both Joseph and Leopold aspired to enlightened rule and sought to make their mark on criminal justice reform, and their successes and failures help us appreciate the potential as well as the difficulties of implementation faced by Beccaria-inspired reforms, and the truly innovative dimensions of his work.

[41] Ch 13 in this volume.

[42] Ch 14 in this volume.

[43] Lombardy was ruled directly through Habsburgian officials sent by Vienna to administer the Italian provinces of the Empire, who were consequently Beccaria's employers for most of his life.

[44] Tuscany was constitutionally separate from the Habsburg Empire. The title of grand duke of Tuscany had passed to Maria Theresa's husband, Francis Stephen of Lorraine, and from him was passed to his second son, Peter Leopold, in 1765. Leopold had to relinquish governance of Tuscany when he became Emperor, in 1790, in succession to his brother Joseph II.

This chapter is followed by translations of two policy memoranda Beccaria was instructed to produce towards the end of his years of service. The first concerns the possible legislative introduction in Lombardy of the (deeply problematic) penal code promulgated in Austria by Joseph II on 13 January 1787; the second concerns the question of the abolition or retention of the death penalty in Lombardy, where Beccaria found himself – much to his chagrin and disappointment, one must suppose – unable to convince the Committee at whose helm he had been placed to favour abolition, being reduced to setting out the case for abolition in a minority report. Both reports are of interest not just because they are some of the last things Beccaria wrote, thus allowing us to appreciate the trajectory of his views from his youthful treatise to the end of his career, but also because in these reports he had to approach the subject from the vantage point of a public servant advising on concrete policy options and not as a political commentator and interested public-spirited citizen taking a bird's-eye perspective on politico-legal change.

II. ACKNOWLEDGEMENTS

We are most grateful to all who attended our workshops in April 2018 and in July 2019. The first workshop was hosted by Ono Academic College in Tel Aviv, the second by the Centre for Penal Theory and Penal Ethics at the Institute of Criminology, University of Cambridge. We are greatly indebted to all our contributors for their intellectual generosity, spirited discussion and patience. Lorenzo Zucca and Paul Roberts deserve special mention, in addition, for their willingness to prepare full chapter drafts in good time before the second workshop, such that their drafts could serve to ground and focus our thinking. In respect of the dating difficulty that exists for Beccaria's internal memorandum on Joseph II's Criminal Code, we sought the advice, which was generously given, of Professor Paolo Rondini of the Università degli Studi di Milano-Bicocca, the author of a leading study on the draft criminal code for Lombardy prepared by Luigi Villa[45] for which Joseph II's penal code served as the starting point. Lastly, we want to record our gratefulness to François du Bois for discussion of ideas and drafts, as well as for his ever-patient and skilled help in preparing the manuscript for publication.

[45] P Rondini, *Il progetto di Codice Penale per la Lombardia Austriaca di Luigi Villa (1787): Pietra scartata o testata d'angolo?* (Padova, CEDAM, 2006).

Part I

Locating Beccaria's Contribution to Penal and Political Philosophy

1

Beccaria's Political Theory of Criminal Justice

LORENZO ZUCCA

On 12 April 1764, the citizens of Milan witnessed the brutal killing of Bartolomeo Luisetti. Bartolomeo had been condemned to death after being accused of sodomy. He was killed by asphyxiation and then burnt at the stake in front of the crowd. Throughout Europe, ruling elites believed that criminal justice had to be done and to be seen to be done; and criminal punishment had to be cruel so as to instil the fear of God in the people watching the gruesome spectacle. Beccaria observed the scene with horror. It was hard to believe that such cruelty could be regarded as a rational response to crime. At the time of the event, Beccaria was only in his mid-twenties, but already had strong political and philosophical views. In the same year, Beccaria's *On Crimes and Punishments* was published.

His manifesto against cruel punishment and abuse of power spread through Europe like a wildfire, and inspired radical reforms of repressive and coercive institutions throughout the Continent. But what made Beccaria's tract so popular with Enlightenment rulers and thinkers? My hypothesis is that Beccaria managed to offer a vision of radical reforms that would follow a rational, and moderate, path. It pleased *Les Philosophes* and the administrators in equal measure. His novelty resided in the criticism of criminal law from the viewpoint of those who were immediately affected, rather than from the viewpoint of the lawyers. It was a Copernican revolution in perspective and one that stood with the many against the privileged few.

There are two key insights in Beccaria's political theory of criminal justice. First, the law should not be an instrument of oppression but rather a tool to foster life in common. Second, to constrain the abuse of political power, every political system needs constitutional guarantees that minimise the interference of criminal law in people's lives and promote social welfare policies so as to prevent crime.

I. BECCARIA'S LEGAL AND POLITICAL PHILOSOPHY

A. The Context: Inequality

> For the most part, men leave the care of the most important regulations either to common sense or to the discretion of individuals whose interests are opposed to those most foresighted laws which distribute benefits to all and resist the pressures to concentrate those benefits in the hands of a few, raising those few to the heights of power and happiness, and sinking everyone else in feebleness and poverty.[1]

Beccaria wrote *On Crimes and Punishments* in 1764, 25 years before the French Revolution. Europe was then a profoundly hierarchical society, where a few privileged people ruled over the entire population with an arbitrary and unaccountable authority. Enlightenment philosophers condemned inequality as the germ of social injustice, and Beccaria was passionate about it even though he belonged to an aristocratic milieu. He was a member of the academy of fisticuffs, a group of young Milanese aristocrats who rebelled against the stifling oppression of the local élite, which included their families.

The interests of the few systematically trumped the interests of the many, and the laws were designed to increase the power of the few while keeping the many under the thumb. That situation afflicted Milan, Italy and Europe. Beccaria and his fellow young pugilists had the ambition to radically reform their society, its institutions and laws. It was an ambition shared by all enlightenment thinkers in Europe, although the means to achieve that reform were the object of disagreement. We know that France took a revolutionary path, while Milan engaged in steady reforms from within; indeed, Beccaria and other pugilists were to play an important part in the local administration.

European enlightenment thinkers agreed that the Church was one of the strongest forces of inequality and subjection, and religion was the instrument of mass control. Italian publicists – scholars of political philosophy and public law – never ceased to be inspired by Machiavelli's central idea; namely, that Christian morality is incompatible with the morality of Civic Republicanism.[2] The former is passive and requires obedience to the established authority, while the latter is active and demands participation in the political affairs of the city. Everyone must strive to take an active part in the running of the city. In this way, institutions and laws will reflect the interests of the whole society, and not just the vested interests of the privileged ones.

[1] C Beccaria, *On Crimes and Punishments and Other Writings* edited by R Bellamy and translated by R Davies (Cambridge, Cambridge University Press, 1995) 7 ('Introduction').

[2] N Machiavelli, *Discorsi sopra la prima deca di Tito Livio* [c. 1517] available in English as N Machiavelli, *Discourses on Livy* translated by HC Mansfield & N Tarcov (Chicago IL, University of Chicago Press, 2009); see also I Berlin, 'The Question of Machiavelli' *New York Review of Books* (4 November 1971) Special Supplement.

It is with the interest of the many in mind that Beccaria formulated his famous motto: *la massima felicità divisa nel maggior numero* (the greatest happiness shared among the greater number), which was subsequently adopted by Bentham. Beccaria sees this maxim as the centrepiece of a new science, whose object is human society and whose name is 'the science of man'. His ultimate intellectual ambition was very close to Hume's project. Beccaria's keen interest in mathematics and the sciences is poured into the development of political economy; indeed, Beccaria's first public appointment was to the chair of political economy, the second oldest chair of its kind in the world. Political economy in the eyes of the pugilists aimed to replace religion as the guiding light of human behaviour:

> 'Now everyone speaks of public economy as if it were religion,' the Vallumbrosan monk Ferdinando Facchinei lamented in a 1764 manuscript held in the Venetian state archives. His fear was that while the lives of individuals and the ideals of societies alike traditionally had been understood and evaluated in theological terms, what we might call an 'economic turn' was in the process of dramatically recasting how Europeans conceived of themselves and of their polities.[3]

Political economy for Beccaria was not just a tool with which to administer the state more efficiently; it was a Copernican revolution in how to understand the place of man in the society, and a reconceiving of politics to serve the interests of the society. Political economy aimed to be the science of happiness and was intended to replace religion, which was perceived as the source of misery.

Beccaria was aware that much progress had been achieved in public matters through political economic reforms. Trade replaced wars, the press spread new ideas, and the relation between sovereign and subjects had been reconceived. But he also noted that little had been said and done about the cruelty and arbitrariness of criminal laws, the most immediate and visible display of brute force which had not yet been rationalised. It was not uncommon in those years to see people condemned to death and brutally ravaged in the public square.

Beccaria's *On Crimes and Punishments* was the first attempt to apply the principles of political economy to the practice of punishment with the intent of humanising and rationalising the use of coercion on the part of the state. After all, arbitrary and cruel punishment was the most immediate and visual instrument the state had to terrorise the people into submission, so as to avoid rebellion against the hierarchical structure of the society.

The problem that Beccaria faced then was the simple fact that the élite had complete control of the law, which was a highly esoteric language that only the initiated could master. The path leading to the rational reform of penal law required first and foremost a fundamental philosophical rethinking of the role and place of the law in the society.

[3] SA Reinert, *The Academy of Fisticuffs: Political Economy and Commercial Society in Enlightenment Italy* (Cambridge MA, Harvard University Press, 2018) 1.

B. Methodology: De-Mystifying Law

> A few odd remnants of the laws of an ancient conquering race codified twelve hundred years ago by a prince ruling at Constantinople, and since jumbled together with the customs of the Lombards and bundled up in the rambling volumes of obscure academic interpreters – this is what makes up the tradition of opinions that passes for law across a large portion of Europe.[4]

Beccaria's project was to dismantle the edifice of Roman law, which he mockingly refers to as 'a few odd remnants of the laws of an ancient conquering race codified twelve hundred years ago by a prince ruling at Constantinople'. The law, as Beccaria had studied it in Pavia, was an arcane language of power controlled by a very narrow élite; its shape and content were hardly clear as it was made of the odd admixture of Roman law with local customs, and was 'bundled up in the rambling volumes of obscure academic interpreters'. The opacity and abstrusity of the law were deliberate and instrumental to the control of the people.

Beccaria was a trained lawyer as well as a published mathematician; but it was philosophy that was central to his mission of reform. *On Crimes and Punishments* was the first glaring model of an excoriating work of censorial jurisprudence. As HLA Hart reminded us:

> Bentham admired Beccaria not only because he agreed with his ideas and was stimulated by them but also because of Beccaria's clear-headed conception of the kind of task on which he was engaged. According to Bentham, Beccaria was the first to embark on the criticism of law and the advocacy of reform without confusing this task with the description of the law that actually existed.[5]

Beccaria's work is entirely censorial; he is the first legal philosopher to keep the distinction between exposition and criticism of the law very clear in his mind.

Philosophy was the critical tool with which Beccaria wanted to revolutionise the way in which European societies thought about law. He was not even remotely interested in what the law said, as the whole system was designed to minimise the interests and the voice of the people. The rule of law was at the time of his writing a chimera, since law obeyed the rule of lawyers and catered for the interests of the ruling élite.

There is a name for this critical endeavour: *the demystification of the law*. Beccaria was the founder of this approach that would become a great tradition in the philosophy of law. Bentham, HLA Hart and Raz understand that the law is a mere instrument and cannot be venerated or mystified:

> The words 'mystification' and 'demystification' have appeared fairly recently among us in the literature of the radical New Left. The central idea that these words are used

[4] Beccaria, above n 1 at 3 ('To the Reader').

[5] HLA Hart, 'Bentham and Beccaria', in his *Essays on Bentham: Jurisprudence and Political Philosophy* (Oxford, Oxford University Press, 1982) 41.

> to express is that unjust, anachronistic, inefficient or otherwise harmful social institutions, including laws, are frequently protected from criticism by a veil of mystery thrown over them.[6]

Beccaria was a pioneer of the philosophical criticism of the law. He was among the first to apply rational scrutiny to that social institution that had always been presented as unassailable. He was certainly the first who applied that rational critical spirit of observation to the institutions of criminal justice. Beccaria's contribution to the philosophical methodology was monumental. But we should not forget that that philosophical turn had the great ambition of social, political and institutional reform.

First, the law as practised until then should be discarded: it was impossible to navigate the innumerable sources of Roman law, customs and academic opinions. The law had to be democratised and that meant one simple thing: the source of the law must be one and only one, that is to say, legislation. Of course, the idea had already been expounded by Rousseau, who argued for the law to be the expression of the general will. Beccaria reasserted this and clarified its importance by putting his finger on the problem of law as it was practised. The obvious consequence for criminal laws was to demand legislative codification of the crimes and their punishment. Beccaria embraced the movement for a penal code and helped to spread that idea in many parts of Europe, including Russia, where he was invited by the Empress Catherine the Great to advise her on penal reforms.

Beccaria was a proto-legal positivist, and the first to defend a very robust sources thesis, not with the intent to explain the law as it was, but instead with the intent to shape the law around the sole source of legislation. Demystification went hand-in-hand with an obsession for clarity and a revulsion against the obscurity of the laws, which was an evil in itself and also called for a second evil – the discretionary interpretation of the laws:

> And it is the greatest of evils if the laws be written in language which is not understood by the people and which makes them dependent upon a few individuals because they cannot judge for themselves what will become of their freedom or their life and limbs, hindered by a language which turns a solemn and public book into what is almost a private and family affair.[7]

Beccaria was very sceptical of the social and political function of lawyers and judges, and for this reason was also very sceptical of judicial interpretation and judicial law-making. That view was fairly well-established on the Continent, less so in the English-speaking world; but even so, Bentham and Austin adopted Beccaria's 'constant insistence … that the law should consist of general enactments of the legislature and that these should be both as comprehensive and

[6] HLA Hart, 'Bentham and the Demystification of the Law', ibid at 21.
[7] Beccaria, above n 1 at 17 (ch 5).

as clear as possible and that judicial law-making and discretion even under the name of interpretation should be reduced to the minimum'.[8]

Beccaria insisted:

> The judge should construct a perfect syllogism about every criminal case: the major premise should be the general law; the minor, the conformity or otherwise of the action with the law; and the conclusion, freedom or punishment. Whenever the judge is forced, or takes it upon himself, to construct even as few as two syllogisms, then the door is opened to uncertainty.[9]

Beccaria was opposing the abuse of power by judges and lawyers; on this point he is very much in disagreement with Montesquieu, who believed that the courts were well placed to protect the general interest. Of course, the role Beccaria gave the judiciary was too rigidly constrained and could not be a realistic idea of the judiciary's task. As we saw, Beccaria was not describing anything; rather he was criticising the excessive power of the legal professions. What was remarkable was that Bentham and Austin followed Beccaria in shaping the division of labour between legislature and judiciary, and for this reason 'Bentham and his illustrious pupil Austin have often seemed to English lawyers un-English'.[10] If we put these views in context, they make more sense. Beccaria and Bentham disapproved of *ex post facto* legislation by the judiciary: they believed that legal certainty about crimes, and a strictly quantifiable cost of disobedience, was fundamental for their reformist projects.

C. Beccaria's Conception of Political Justice

> Divine justice and natural justice are both essentially unchanging and constant, since the relation between two objects which remain the same is always the same. But human or political justice, being nothing but a relation between an action and the varying state of society, can vary according to how necessary or useful the action is to society. Nor can human justice be well understood except by one who has analysed the complex and ever-changing relations of civil association. As soon as these essentially distinct principles are confused, all hope of thinking clearly about public affairs is lost.[11]

Beccaria's project of rationalising law extended also to politics, and in particular to the understanding of political justice and political order. To begin with, he drew a tripartite distinction between divine, natural and political justice. He also explained that there were three sources of normativity: revelation, natural

[8] Hart, above n 5 at 47–48.
[9] Beccaria, above n 1 at 14 (ch 4).
[10] Hart, above n 5 at 47.
[11] Beccaria, above n 1 at 5 ('To the Reader').

law and the conventions arrived at by society. By singling out the conception of human laws as conventions, Beccaria opened a door for the 'great tradition in the philosophy of law which is realist and unromantic in outlook. It regards the existence and content of the law as a matter of social fact whose connection with moral or any other values is contingent and precarious.'[12] With this move, Beccaria wanted to free society from the grip of traditionalists driven by theology as well as moralists like Grotius and Pufendorf who attempted to shape natural justice in the image of divine justice, but without the theistic assumption: '*etiamsi deus non daretur* [even if God did not exist]', as Grotius put it.

Traditionalists and moralists conceived of justice as a system of unchangeable norms, the truth of which does not depend on local circumstances or contingencies. Beccaria's conception of political justice is independent from divine and natural justice. Political associations are like living creatures: they are born, live and perish; in other words, they change and evolve and respond to local factors and local challenges. Political justice cannot be conceived as 'the relation between two objects which remain the same'.[13]

Beccaria resisted traditionalists by denying their eschatology: human freedom and human goals can only be evaluated within the realm of immanent civil societies. Divine justice addressed intentional wrongdoing, commonly defined in religious language as sin. Sin had to do with intentions and a man's heart. It was within God's jurisdiction to punish this kind of wrongdoing. Civil societies, insisted Beccaria, had jurisdiction over crimes, which must be separated from sins. A crime is what damages society, and the crime's cost to the society can be measured.

Traditionalists and Beccaria nevertheless had some points of agreement: both believed that men seek their own interest and are inclined to follow their passions; that means that they can hardly be guided by reason. As a result, Beccaria distanced himself from moralists who were described as living in a world of fiction far removed from reality: reason is not capable of guiding us to negotiate a contract that is in everyone's interest.[14]

Beccaria not only resisted assimilation with traditionalists and moralists, but also with Hobbes. We certainly want to escape human chaos, but that does not mean that we ought to transfer all our rights in exchange of our security. Beccaria insisted that we only give up a portion of our rights, and we do so grudgingly because our human passions are opposed to the full abandonment of our power.

[12] As Joseph Raz has remarked about HLA Hart in the opening sentence of his essay, 'Authority, Law, Morality' (reprinted in J Raz, *Ethics in the Public Domain* (Oxford, Clarendon Press, 1994) 194).

[13] On this point, Beccaria echoed the great Republican tradition and more precisely the views of Montesquieu.

[14] On this point, Beccaria echoed the influence of Machiavelli and Spinoza, in particular Spinoza's criticism of Hobbes' contractualism.

Beccaria's idea of the political order is very modern. The political order is purely immanent and law within it is a matter of social fact. The connection between social facts and morality is contingent. It is possible to subject social facts to a rational inquiry in order to assess their contribution to the welfare of the society. At this point, we can distinguish two opposite schools of political economy. One school proposes a sharp distinction between the natural order of the economy and the artificial order of law and punishment. It is the school of free-marketeers that counts Physiocrats like Quesnay among its greatest proponents. The idea is that commerce must be left as unregulated as possible. The other school believed instead that the rationalisation of the economic domain should be extended to penal practices, and in return penal discipline should be used to regulate and prevent the distortions in the economic domain.

Some have argued that Beccaria and his fellow pugilists were prototypical socialists: 'In fact, Facchinei's censure of the rise of political economy as an organizing discipline of worldly existence went hand in hand with his equally intriguing charge that Beccaria was a "socialist," in what marked the term's earliest known vernacular appearance.'[15] The charge came from two opposite directions; Facchinei was a traditionalist who dreaded the rise of political economy as an immanent replacement of religion. But Beccaria was also criticised by the Physiocrats and other free-marketeers because his understanding of the role of the state in the economy paved the way for a demanding degree of re-distribution and social justice. Beccaria's political order was defined in terms of social facts that were under the control of human action; he believed that not only was it possible to rationalise the control of human action, but that the point of political institutions was to do so with the aim of maximising happiness for the greatest number.

D. Beccaria's Political Philosophy

Beccaria's political theory is dominated by three different ideas that many philosophers would regard as incompatible: utility, political freedom and the social contract. In his account, utility and political freedom are in conflict with each other, and the social contract is the fruit of the compromise between the two. Let us have a look at each idea separately before we look at how they can hang together.

Some call Beccaria utilitarian, but that is a mistake: they are assuming too quickly that Beccaria is a predecessor of Bentham in ethical matters. The mistake is understandable since Bentham himself acknowledged his debt to Beccaria with regard to the formulation of the principle of utility and the focus on criminal punishment. However, the similarities end there, and the differences are much

[15] Reinert, above n 3 at 2.

more important. Bentham himself voiced criticism of Beccaria whose 'terminology and certain specific forms of argument ... seemed laden with confusion and bad metaphysics'.[16] Beccaria used the language of the social contract, natural rights and even that of dignity. The idea that natural rights could limit sovereignty was deemed by Bentham an absurdity. HLA Hart concluded that

> if Beccaria was a utilitarian his utilitarianism was qualified in ways which Bentham thought absurd. Quite apart from the doctrine of social contract and of the rights created by it there is in Beccaria a respect for the dignity and value of the individual person which is absent in Bentham. This absence indeed at times gives to some of Bentham's speculations an almost inhuman flavour; as if he was concerned with manipulable and predictable animals or machines – pleasure and pain machines – rather than men. Indeed one can find contrasting texts on this very point, though too much importance should not be attached to them as they relate to very different matters. Beccaria says 'there is no liberty when the laws permit that in some circumstances a man can cease to be a person and become a thing'.[17]

Beccaria's idea of utility was not to the exclusion of the idea of human dignity. Indeed, you can even read in the last sentence cited above an early formulation of Kant's categorical imperative.[18]

For Bentham, utility is central to his philosophical doctrine, to his meta-ethics, his moral theory and his normative politics. Not so for Beccaria. Beccaria sharply distinguished between moral theory and political science. He does not have an interest in meta-ethics, and his political philosophy uses the metaphor of the social contract which is explicitly rejected by Bentham. For Beccaria, the principle of utility is just because it is willed by the people, it is not willed by the people because it is just; indeed, a society can decide to overrule an outcome that is supported by utility, since utility for a society is determined by the will of the society itself.

From this viewpoint, Beccaria's conception of utility is much closer to the European tradition of political thought that harks back to Machiavelli and that focuses on the ideas of interest and utility interchangeably. Since Machiavelli, several political theories have put utility at the centre of their attention and have regarded it as an anthropological truth about human nature. Hobbes, Spinoza, Mandeville and Helvétius all put utility or common interest at the centre of their political stances: they share a clear pessimism about human rationality, and they want to take human desires, passions and interests seriously. Beccaria is following them rather than preceding Bentham: utility is an element of his theory of the state in so far as utility can trump morality, and it is also an element of his criminal theory in so far as criminal law can perform the useful functions of deterrence and prevention of crime.

[16] Hart, above n 5 at 49.

[17] Hart, above n 5 at 50–51.

[18] Even though Kant was critical of Beccaria, it cannot be excluded that Beccaria's formulation shaped Kant's.

At first, justice seems to pull in the opposite direction of utility. However, we have to remember that Beccaria focuses on human or political justice as opposed to divine and moral justice. Political justice only exists because of the creation of a political society that is a free association of men through the social contract. People agree to come together on the basis of the social contract because of necessity: the contract is a necessary condition for enjoying political freedom. The people agree to trade natural (unregulated) freedom for political (regulated) freedom because they prefer to have a guarantee of a certain freedom rather than the uncertainty that comes with limitless freedom for all. The contract transfers a minimum amount of natural freedom to the state that becomes the ultimate guarantor of political freedom.

The authority of the state is legitimate if and when it protects the common reservoir of freedom pooled by the people. But at the same time, the sovereign authority is limited by utility: the sovereign has the right to do what is useful to protect political freedom. But what if the sovereign wants to limit equality on the basis of utility? Beccaria has an economic answer: the industriousness and productivity of a society is increased if the greatest number of people are in a position to contribute to the general welfare: it is always useful to the society to protect equality, and always injurious to the general welfare to allow a few people to enrich themselves at the expense of the rest. This example shows that common interest or utility is the basis of political justice and is not incompatible with it.

Common interest has motivated people to come together in order to lessen the uncertainty of the state of nature and to start enjoying political freedom, that is to say, that limited freedom whose domain and protection are made certain by the existence of a legitimate authority. As mentioned above, political freedom is the opinion of one's own security in the society. Feeling secure means to dispel the feeling of uncertainty, and that is the ultimate goal of political society. Political freedom for Beccaria is capable of trumping utility, since people are motivated to come together and pool their common interest for the sake of creating political freedom; but if that result was not forthcoming, then their very interest in maintaining the pact would be debased.

Political freedom is a psychological, qualitative state and not something that can be measured. It is realised when I know that I can do *x*, other people know that I can do *x* and I know that other people know that I can do *x*. This feeling is immaterial, the law cannot quantify or define the areas of freedom. However, the law can certainly help by giving clear and predictable guidance with regard to permissions and prohibitions, which will in turn result in the feeling of security. Indeed, as Montesquieu put it, criminal law's aim is to guarantee political freedom.

Utility and political freedom are in perpetual, apparent conflict, and it is the social contract that balances and reconciles the two concerns. The social contract is not a moment of ideal celebration for Beccaria. People grudgingly accept to sign a pact with each other, and they are always tempted to break the pact to foster their own advantage. What moves them to sign the pact is the feeling of uncertainty, which makes it impossible to enjoy their natural freedom to act according to their immediate passions. That only leads them into conflict, and conflict leads to less natural freedom rather than more. The uncertainty as to how to exercise natural freedom leads everyone to accept a basic necessity: something has to be given away in order for everyone to enjoy political freedom.

A portion of natural freedom must be sacrificed in order to establish political freedom. The latter is the only actual freedom, since the former cannot be exercised without leading to conflict. The sacrifice is grudgingly accepted only because it is strictly necessary. However, it is clear that people can only be moved by necessity to accept the *minimum possible sacrifice* of natural freedom for the sake of achieving political freedom in a more just civil order. The transferral of the minimum portion of natural freedom results in the transformation of natural freedom into political freedom.

Everyone's *minimum* portion of natural freedom constitutes the public deposit of sovereignty that is the basis for the right to punish those actions that are injurious to human society. The right to punish is described as a necessary evil that is exercised by the sovereign in order to respond to the radical uncertainty created by the unfettered exercise of natural freedom.

Beccaria's originality does not lie in developing innovative interpretations of utility, political freedom or the social contract. His originality lies in the way he combines them to arrive at a compromise between freedom and utility in the name of justice. As far as criminal justice is concerned, the right to punish must be as narrow as possible to be considered legitimate. The conclusion of *On Crimes and Punishments* could not be clearer:

> *In order that punishment should not be an act of violence perpetrated by one or many upon a private citizen, it is essential that it should be public, speedy, necessary, the minimum possible in the given circumstances, proportionate to the crime, and determined by the law.*[19]

This conclusion set in motion a cultural revolution. Beccaria's little tract is the symbol of a philosophical movement that was bent on replacing entrenched forms of knowledge that were used by the élites to preserve their privileges. The traditional understanding of law was arcane and inaccessible. Beccaria wanted to replace it with a clear and demystified conception of the law as the product of social fact, the sole source of which would be legislation. Beccaria also knew that religion was still a potent source of normativity that was used to keep the masses in their place. That is why he embraced enthusiastically the turn to political economy as a source of knowledge that government could use to rationalise its policies in terms of measurable properties. It is important to stress, however, that it was Beccaria's philosophical method of censorial – today we would say

[19] Beccaria, above n 1 at 113 (ch 47) (emphasis in original).

normative or evaluative – jurisprudence that shaped his understanding of law and political economy. He used philosophy to undermine the grounds of ancient law and to carve out an immanent domain of politics, free from traditionalist and moralist understandings of justice.

II. BECCARIA'S POLITICAL THEORY OF CRIMINAL JUSTICE

A. Secularising Crime

> My topic is solely those crimes which arise from human nature and the social compact, and not those sins whose punishments, even in this life, ought to be regulated by principles other than those of a limited philosophy.[20]

The birth of modern criminal law is closely tied to the secularisation of criminal justice. Beccaria, through his tract, contributed more than anyone else to separating the domain of crime from the domain of sin. Only God can be the judge of sin; divine justice will be ruthless and implacable, and the sin will be repaid with full retribution. And if the Church insists on temporal punishment of sins, it will still have to be based on different grounds than punishment for crimes. Sin is a wrong against the order created by God, whereas crime is an action that violates 'human nature and the social compact'.

Beccaria carves out a special role for philosophy, which he is quick to call human as opposed to divine philosophy, otherwise known as theology. Sin and its punishment, be it eternal or temporal, have nothing to do with crime and punishment in the immanent world. The two have to be kept separate; not only that: the way in which crime is defined and punished has a different logic from the way in which sin is defined and punished. Divine justice works in a vertical, top down, fashion. It has its own structure and its own principles. But modern European society aims to remove its vertical structure and introduce the organising principle of equality by abolishing social rank. Whatever brings back or entrenches pre-existing privileges is a crime against the political association.

Retributivism resists this suggestion and insists implicitly or explicitly that the logic of crime is the same as the logic of sin: there exists a pre-legal realm of wrongdoing, whether it is defined in theological or philosophical terms matters little, and criminal law must respond to that wrongdoing. Criminal law would thus be driven by legal moralism. Beccaria rejects this logic of crime. In his view, every society is formed with a political aim that is independent from other moral values; broadly defined, the aim of political association is political freedom; crime is defined in relation to the violation of this political aim.

[20] Ibid at 100 (ch 39). Beccaria's book was blacklisted by the Church, but that did not prevent it from becoming a work of reference.

But how do we make political freedom more precise? The answer is in Beccaria's chapter 7: '[T]he one true measure of criminality is the damage done to the nation.' This formula is enshrined in the French Declaration of the Rights of Man and of the Citizen in its Article 5: 'The law has the right to forbid only those actions that are injurious to society.' Article 5 needs to be read in conjunction with Article 4, which states:

> Liberty consists in the freedom to do everything which injures no one else; hence the exercise of the natural rights of each man has no limits except those which assure to the other members of the society the enjoyment of the same rights. These limits can only be determined by law.

The French Declaration asserts the principle of freedom of action within the free political association, unless an action wrongs society in which case the criminal law can set the appropriate prohibitions.

Beccaria inspired the drafters of the French Declaration, which entrenched a substantive limitation of crime. As William Stuntz put it, 'The French Declaration seems almost ideally suited to limiting the power of too-powerful law enforcement agencies, and the Declaration severely limits legislatures.'[21] In chapter 8, Beccaria furthers the point by ranking, according to their harm to society, three different types of crimes:

> Some crimes directly destroy society or its representatives. Some undermine the personal security of a citizen by attacking his life, goods or honour. Others still are actions contrary to what each citizen, in view of the public good, is obliged by law to do or not do.[22]

Injury to society is the only accepted measure of crime. Here we have a criterion of criminalisation that allows for substantive evaluations. Beccaria achieves that by appealing to his notion of common utility. Any action that damages common utility constitutes a public injury and for that reason it is criminalisable. The legislative body has the power to determine what is injurious to common utility in order to draft the penal code. It may be argued that Beccaria's formulation of the utility principle is maximalist and can therefore increase the number of crimes. But there are guarantees against that, which I discuss below.

B. Rationalising Punishment

> Every punishment which is not derived from absolute necessity is tyrannous, says the great Montesquieu. A proposition which may be generalised as follows: every act of authority between one man and another which is not derived from absolute necessity

[21] WJ Stuntz, *The Collapse of American Criminal Justice* (Cambridge MA, Harvard University Press, 2011) 84.

[22] Beccaria, above n 1 at 24–25 (ch 8).

> is tyrannous. Here, then, is the foundation of the sovereign's right to punish crimes: the necessity of defending the repository of the public well-being from usurpations of individuals. The juster the punishments, the more sacred and inviolable is the security and the greater the freedom which the sovereign preserves for his subjects.[23]

Punishment is legitimate only when it guarantees the protection of common utility. It does so when it changes the way in which we feel about our own security. If the existence of a limited right to punish makes us feel more *certain* about our own political freedom, then punishment is legitimate. Its function is chiefly psychological: it aims to deter people from committing crimes, and by doing so it also seeks to prevent the repetition of the crime by instilling the *certainty* that an action will be met with sure consequences. In order to achieve this, political institutions have to work according to a precise framework and follow strict constitutional (political) rules.

Common utility determines the level of punishment for each crime through the principle of proportionality. There must be a clear scale of crimes that correspond to a proportional scale of punishment – proportional, that is, to the level of injury to the common utility. The ranking must be clear to buttress the feeling of certainty in political justice. If a punishment were perceived to be disproportionate from the viewpoint of public morality, it would do more harm than good. Finally, Beccaria's criminal theory prohibits useless punishment: if there is no utility to be gained by the society, then the punishment cannot be justified.

Rationalising punishment means to minimise the quantity and quality of violence within the society. Not only the violence attached to crimes, but also the violence entailed by the reaction to crimes by private parties and by public authorities. The goal of modern secular criminal law in the eyes of Beccaria was to regulate the right to punish and eradicate from its practice all forms of vengeance and religious creed. The idea of rationalising punishment has its advocates and its detractors. Advocates understand that cruel and arbitrary punishment does not build a robust sense of trust in the public authority; they also believe that punishment might be a necessary deterrent against the use of private and public violence, so they accept punishment as expressing the society's commitment against violence. On the other hand, detractors believe that rationalising punishment amounts to giving the state a more efficient instrument with which it could control and discipline us. But for Beccaria the project of rationalising punishment had a deep reformist meaning. It meant moving from a society that wielded punishment as a weapon of mass control to a society in which punishment would only be the last resort.

According to Beccaria, penal law is the law of the weakest or most vulnerable. It replaces the law of the privileged and aims to protect those who are at the mercy of power and violence. But the idea of violence depends on the

[23] Ibid at 10 (ch 2).

relative power relation between two individuals or parties, and it changes with the context. Criminal law is organised in different stages, and at every stage the weakest party is different: At the moment of the commission of the crime, the weakest party is the victim; during trial the weakest party is the accused; and finally, at the stage of the execution the weakest is the party who has been found guilty. Penal law protects the weakest against abuse of power and violence at every stage.

C. Constitutionalising Criminal Law

The principle of legality is at the centre of Beccaria's constitutional understanding of crimes. Laws must be clear, simple and easy to uphold. To promote crime prevention, the state does not have to multiply the number of prohibitions; that only turns more citizens into criminals and disperses public resources. Prevention can be achieved by having fewer and clearer laws that are implemented strictly. The rule of law creates a healthy fear of state institutions, whereas the rule of men (magistrates with discretion) turns men into slaves; devoid of freedom, men tend to be less virtuous and more vicious.

William Stuntz discusses this idea in *The Collapse of American Criminal Justice*. The 'collapse' is an outcome of the unfettered exercise of power by the police in defining crime: 'Law enforcers – state troopers and local cops – define the laws they enforce.'[24] It is also the consequence of overcriminalisation: 'Too much law amounts to no law at all: when legal doctrine makes everyone an offender, the relevant offenses have no meaning independent of law enforcers' will. The formal rule of law yields the functional rule of official discretion.'[25]

Constitutionalising criminal law means creating a number of substantive and procedural guarantees against the abuse of power and in favour of limitation of power. There are several layers to (and guarantees of) the constitutionalisation of criminal law. The first has already been sketched: legality contributes to clarifying, systematising and minimising criminal laws. On the Continent, that resulted in the movement for penal codification. Beccaria hoped to meet the challenge of uncertainty by instituting the principle of legality for crimes and punishments. Beccaria's insistence on certainty through the principle of legality also had surprising consequences: Beccaria argued that when laws are certain, then we should also abolish the practice of mercy. For any act of mercy would simply lessen the certainty of punishment as enhanced by carefully crafted penal codes.

The second layer has to do with the enshrinement of constitutional values that would be legal guarantees against the abuse of power of political institutions.

[24] Stuntz, above n 21 at 3.
[25] Ibid.

One guarantee is the separation of powers, recited in the Declaration of the Rights of Man and of the Citizen, the first example of constitutional codification. Montesquieu and Beccaria are the minds behind this formulation. When it comes to criminal law, it means that only the legislative branch has the power to promote the values of a society. It does so by appeal to the principle of utility and has an eye to the outcome of its policy. The limitation of the legislative power is therefore consequentialist, and criminal law must be the result of utilitarian calculations that should be laid out in a penal code accessible to all. The rules in the penal code are formulated in clear language and their application must be strictly followed. It follows that the limitation on the judicial power is deontological because judges should not have any power of interpretation. Beccaria creates the myth of the judge as a mechanical applicator of the law through the legal syllogism. The distrust of the judges comes from the experience of Beccaria in Italy and France, where magistrates enjoyed hereditary offices that were transmitted from father to son within a very small ruling class. Of course, the idea that judicial discretion can truly be limited by strict laws has been proved to be fanciful. However, the suggestion that the functions of creation, interpretation and application of criminal laws should be separated is still very relevant.

Importantly, in the Continental tradition represented by Beccaria and entrenched in the French Declaration, the power of the legislature is fettered by several substantive clauses. Not so in the case of the American Bill of Rights. Stuntz compares the two bills of rights and concludes:

> The French Declaration seems almost ideally suited to limiting the power of too-powerful law enforcement agencies, and the Declaration severely limits legislatures' ability to define crimes and specify punishments as they wish. Within the realm of criminal justice, the American Bill of Rights establishes limits that police officers and prosecutors find it easy to evade, and places nearly no restrictions at all on legislative power.[26]

A third guarantee has to do with prevention and is formulated by Beccaria thus: 'One cannot say that a punishment for a crime is exactly just (meaning necessary) until the law has instituted the best possible means in a given nation's circumstances for preventing such a crime.'[27] Beccaria introduced the idea that the state needs to put in place all suitable substantive policies that lead to the prevention of crime. By that he means all policies that help the many to meet all the conditions of a decent life, from education to habitation. In short, the third guarantee is about the obligation of the state to ensure social welfare.

The fourth layer of Beccaria's constitutional project is implied rather than explicated, but it is very much part of its ethos. The constitutional limitation of public powers should be followed by a constitutional limitation of private

[26] Stuntz, above n 21.

[27] Beccaria, above n 1 at 82 (ch 31).

powers. The latter are to be more easily found in the economic and financial conglomerates that wield enormous influence on society without being part of the public institutions. A society that gives a blank cheque to private powers is a society that lets gross inequalities blossom amongst the people. When the many are left in a state of poverty and need, the state will have failed its mission and will have lost the justification for its right to punish.

D. 'Diritto Penale Minimo'

'Minimal Criminal Law' is an apt formula to describe Beccaria's modern impact on the philosophy of criminal law.[28] It refers to the specific nature of Beccaria's social contract, which only stipulates a minimum transfer of natural freedom. As a corollary, the contract will only justify a minimum restriction on natural freedom. The principle of minimum restraint is deduced from the sacrificial nature of the contract: the minimum transfer of natural freedom for the maximum gain of political freedom. That is where the principle of utility can also contribute by arguing for decriminalisation and a focus on prevention rather than retribution.

Because the intervention of criminal law is limited through the qualifier of necessity, the state can only use criminal law as the *ultima ratio*. If there are other means to prevent crimes, they should be used. This part of Beccaria's thought is often ignored by those who consider him the forefather of utilitarianism in England or the ancestor of law and economics in the United States.[29] This is so because Beccaria asks for the least penal intervention, and for the maximum provision of social services as part of the same package. It is criminal law that must be minimal, not the state. There is no doubt that Beccaria follows Rousseau in demanding robust intervention by the state to redress the situation of inequality and to prevent crimes by educating and assisting people, not by repressing them.

III. CONCLUSION

Beccaria's slim book *On Crimes and Punishments* is being rediscovered today. The natural question to ask is 'Why?' I suspect that his radical reformist spirit strikes a deep chord with many people. Inequality is again on the rise. In most countries, criminalisation is also on the rise: criminal law attempts to micromanage the behaviour of the many, while giving a blank check to wealthy

[28] This expression was coined by L Ferrajoli, *Diritto e Ragione: Teoria del garantismo penale* (Bari-Roma, Laterza, 1990).

[29] See the seminal essay by G Becker, 'Crime and Punishment: An Economic Approach' (1968) 76 *Journal of Political Economy* 169.

billionaires whose tax-dodging and exploitative behaviour go unpunished. This points to a fifth constitutional guarantee against abuse of power at the supranational level that is implicit in Beccaria's work. The rule of the few super-rich must be kept in check by international law. Beccaria would stand for international legal reform to reduce global inequality and to protect international human rights law against the abuse of private and public powers. His political theory is democratic, socialist and (implicitly) internationalist.

But even at the national level, we have reached a point where we again have to re-think the whole system of criminal justice. It is not about tinkering with what we have; it is about radically reforming criminal law to make it a law for the many and not for the few. Should we invest endless amounts of resources to criminalise all sorts of behaviour and track all minor infringements, or should criminal justice focus its attention on grand-scale criminality that undermines the welfare of the state? Beccaria's answer would be in favour of less criminalisation and the targeting of actions that undermine the public interest, in particular the interest of equality among citizens.

Beccaria denounced inequality between the ruling class and the masses: he insisted that inequality is bound to increase the crime rate because of the criminogenic force of poverty and indignation over injustice. In turn, the increase in crime is likely to entail more social conflict and less certainty about one's own security in the society. As a result, criminal law becomes again the law of the strong against the most vulnerable. In our societies, which are deeply polarised by inequality, Beccaria's perceptions still ring true: we need more social justice and less criminal punishment.

2

Reconstructing Beccaria's Social Contract

MATT MATRAVERS*

According to Newman and Marongiu in their introduction to Beccaria's *On Crimes and Punishments*, the social contract is

> the lynchpin to the entire *Treatise*. It provides the theoretical basis and justification for the rule of law as we know it today. Without it, the right to punish dissolves. Without it, the law cannot exist.[1]

Yet, as they also note, the social contract is expounded only 'briefly and superficially' in the *Treatise*.[2] Indeed, there is no chapter heading that references the social contract and no sustained discussion of the nature of the contract as Beccaria conceives of it. Inevitably, then, any attempt to describe the contract as deployed in the *Treatise* is in large part reconstructive.

This chapter begins by asking how Beccaria addresses the pertinent elements of any social contract theory, to wit: the nature of the contract, the depictions of the choosing situation and of the choosing parties, and the contract's terms. Having thus identified the central features of Beccaria's contractarian approach and the degree to which his contractarian and his utilitarian arguments converge, section II of the chapter examines to what extent the contract occupies a foundational role in this account of the foundations of the polity, and of legitimate authority. The argument is that it does not have such a role – the philosophical 'work' in Beccaria's exposition is done in the main by his commitments to equality and utilitarianism – but that it is nevertheless important in emphasising and amplifying the propositions that emerge from those commitments. In addition,

* In addition to the project workshops, an earlier version of this chapter was also presented to the Cambridge Criminal Jurisprudence and Philosophy Group. I am grateful to participants on all these occasions for their comments. I also want to thank Anthony Bottoms for his extensive comments on the arguments.

[1] GR Newman & P Marongiu, 'Introduction to the *Treatise*', in C Beccaria, *On Crimes and Punishments* 5th edition edited and translated by GR Newman and P Marongiu (New Brunswick NJ, Transaction Publishers, 2009) ix.

[2] Ibid.

the language of contract brings in Beccaria an immediacy and 'person specificity' to the most important aspect of this work, which is the coruscating criticism of the criminal justice practices that surrounded him. Of course, given the indeterminate nature of Beccaria's use of the contract, others may disagree with the reading offered here. If so, then at least the framework should be useful for those others to clarify their own readings of Beccaria's work.

I. MAPPING BECCARIA'S USE OF THE SOCIAL CONTRACT ONTO MODERN SOCIAL CONTRACT THEORY

Social contract theories exist in a variety of forms and for many purposes. As Albert Weale writes:

> As a normative enterprise, modern social contract theory is sometimes directed to questions of personal morality, sometimes to questions of political morality, and sometimes to both. As a normative theory, it offers an intellectual construct the purpose of which is to answer the question of what actions or policies it is right for agents to choose or what principles for the design for social and political practices and institutions are justifiable.[3]

What unites these theories is the 'claim … that the test of rightness or justification is given by determining what principles or practices could be agreed by parties to a hypothetical social contract in which the parties are rational'.[4] Beccaria uses the language of social contract in the main in a negative form of the above: to capture the wrongness or lack of justification of principles and practices and to indicate what arrangements and practices are beyond consent for the members of society.

That said, there are several peculiarities in Beccaria's use of the social contract – at least when considered in relation to current theoretical sensibilities – and teasing these out helps in pinning down Beccaria's main concerns. To identify these, let us consider a number of standard characteristics of contract theories that are often used to distinguish one writer (or even contract tradition) from another. These are: the historical or hypothetical nature of the contract; the depiction of the choosing situation and of the parties therein; the rationality and motivation of the parties; and the terms of the contract.

A. An Actual Historical Event or a Rational Reconstruction?

There are those for whom the contract is a real event or is, at least, modelled on such an event. Locke falls into this category and there is some textual support

[3] A Weale, *Modern Social Contract Theory* (Oxford, Oxford University Press, 2020) 3.
[4] Ibid.

that Beccaria does as well. Early in *On Crimes and Punishments*, Beccaria refers to an increase in the human population that caused scarcity that in turn caused persons ('savages') to form rival groups competing for resources. It is to escape this conflict, he argues, that, out of 'necessity', the contracting parties gave up 'part of their personal liberty' to establish a political authority with the power to punish.[5]

This sounds like a genuine history, and some commentators focusing on this passage seem to think that it is, and that Beccaria is arguing that conflicts over scarcity gave rise to some moment of contracting. For example, Philippe Audegean writes in terms of a 'pact' to escape, 'a pact which arose from the violence of an all-out war which, if it did not necessarily endanger the survival of humanity itself, certainly weakened its resolve to the point of renouncing its inherent liberties'.[6]

Others, such as Richard Bellamy, argue that 'Beccaria employed the idea of a social contract more as a theoretical device for setting limits to the legitimacy of law than as an actual historical act to explain its origins'.[7] Beccaria (as so often) says little more, but the more plausible interpretation is surely Bellamy's. If so, the story of scarcity might be taken either as an account of the evolution of norms[8] or as an explanation of the conditions that make human cooperation under rules both possible and necessary.

In this latter sense, Beccaria's account would resemble David Hume's and John Rawls' 'circumstances of justice'. For Rawls, society is 'a cooperative venture for mutual advantage', but it is also 'marked by a conflict as well as an identity of interests'. The identity of interests arises because 'social cooperation makes possible a better life for all than any would have if each were to try to live solely by his own efforts'. However, 'there is a conflict of interests since men are not indifferent as to how the greater benefits produced by their collaboration are distributed, for in order to pursue their ends they each prefer a larger to a lesser share'.[9] The circumstances that create this include both 'objective' facts about the world – such as the scarcity mentioned by Beccaria – as well as 'subjective'

[5] Beccaria, above n 1 at 11 (ch 2).

[6] P Audegean, 'Cesare Beccaria's On Crimes and Punishments: the meaning and genesis of a jurispolitical pamphlet' (2017) 43 *History of European Ideas* 884 at 886.

[7] R Bellamy, 'Introduction', in C Beccaria, *On Crimes and Punishments and Other Writings* edited by R Bellamy and translated by R Davies (Cambridge, Cambridge University Press, 1995) i at xviii.

[8] Beccaria suggests something like an iterative process of 'momentary pacts' in the chapter 'On the Sciences'. Beccaria, above n 1 at 109 (ch 42).

[9] J Rawls, *A Theory of Justice* (Cambridge MA, Harvard University Press, 1971) sec 22. See also D Hume, *A Treatise of Human Nature* edited by LA Selby-Bigge 2nd edition revised by PH Nidditch (Oxford, Clarendon Press, 1975) bk III, pt II, sec ii, and *An Enquiry Concerning the Principles of Morals* edited by LA Selby-Bigge 3rd edition revised by PH Nidditch (Oxford, Clarendon Press, 1975) sec III, pt I. For an analysis of Hume's and Rawls' accounts of the circumstances of justice, see B Barry, *Theories of Justice: A Treatise on Social Justice* vol 1 (New York, Harvester Wheatsheaf, 1989) 152.

circumstances such as that, as Samuel Freeman puts it, 'we are (naturally) more concerned with our own interests, including the interests of those nearer and dearer to us, than we are with the interests of strangers with whom we have no connections'.[10]

These circumstances explain the possibility and necessity for cooperation under rules. For Rawls, they provide the grounds for reasoning about these rules in terms of abstract principles of justice. For Beccaria, they account for the way in which the rules (the laws) bind members of society to that society and to one another: 'each and every individual is bound to society which in turn is bound to each of its members'.[11]

B. The Nature of the Choosing Situation and of the Parties

In contemporary social contract theory, one of the standard ways of classifying social contract theories is in relation to the knowledge hypothetically possessed by the contracting parties. Some theorists – most famously, Rawls – impose a 'veil of ignorance' on the parties so that they cannot appeal to certain crucial features of their circumstances or condition. Others, such as David Gauthier, impose no such restrictions.[12] No such distinction applies to early modern theories, and Beccaria clearly does not assume that somehow his social contract is between abstract entities unaware of their identities. Indeed, as I shall argue later, some of the appeal for Beccaria of the language of contract depends on the immediacy of the question 'Why should I accept that?', envisaged as asked by actual people in the here and now.

However, it is worth noting two things. First, part of the reason for Rawls' constructing the choosing situation is so that it models freedom and equality. Each person comes to the choosing situation as a free being, and one reason for imposing the veil of ignorance on the people in the original position is that it ensures equality. The contracting parties do not know their relative bargaining strengths, for example, so they cannot exploit these in determining the outcome. Second, this allows Rawls to posit that the contractors deploy standard rational self-interest when choosing between principles (although the exact nature of this is disputed).[13]

Such technical discussions might seem of little interest in a study of Beccaria, but that is not the case. The important point is that parties to a contractual situation can be thought of as reasoning in different ways. Again, the complexities

[10] S Freeman, *Rawls* (Abingdon, Routledge, 2007) 161. Cf Beccaria, above n 1 at 11 (ch 2): 'Every man acts as if he were the center of the world's affairs.'

[11] Beccaria, above n 1 at 13 (ch 3).

[12] Rawls, above n 9; D Gauthier, *Morals by Agreement* (Oxford, Clarendon Press, 1986).

[13] For the best accounts of these issues, see Barry, above n 9 and Weale, above n 3.

need not detain us, but the contrast is important. Weale summarises the range of possibilities with reference to contemporary thinkers as follows:

> In contract theories in which it is assumed that the parties are concerned with protecting and advancing their own interests or conception of the good, the rationality that is ascribed to their reasoning requires only the weak sense of normative. The parties in the original position must be presumed to advance their own interests according to sound principles of reasoning, but the principles of justice to which they agree need not be a motivating consideration of their choice. … At the other end of the spectrum is any theory in which the parties are presented as exchanging sound moral reasons, and in which their rationality is normative in the strong sense. … In between are theories in which the deliberative rationality of parties is primarily of the normatively weak sort, with the contracting parties concerned to advance their own conception of the good, whilst also holding to some procedural values, like the desire to live with others on fair terms, that also shape their reasoning. In this last type of theory, the parties to the original position may be fair-minded and prudent persons, but they are not to be thought of as independent moral reasoners.[14]

So, how does this help in analysing Beccaria? First, Beccaria is clearly inspired by, and belongs to, the Enlightenment with its commitment to the natural freedom, and natural rights, of all persons. His social contract captures that. It is 'independent and isolated individuals' who contract in order to restore a liberty 'made useless by the uncertainty of having constantly to defend it',[15] and who do so 'by necessity' but also 'freely'.[16]

Such a conception of free persons maps on to that deployed by modern social contract theorists. But, what about equality? Here, Beccaria – like his Enlightenment forebears – appeals to something more limited than the expansive conception found, for example, in Rawls. Leon Radzinowicz captured the point well in 1966:

> The doctrine of equality, though given great weight, was more cautiously defined … It was not prepared to go to the length of attacking inequalities in property or rank. Though men had been equal in a state of nature they could not be so in society: authority and subordination must remain though they must cease to be abused. Nevertheless the fact that equality could not be expected in wealth and power made it the more vital to recognize it where it did exist – in the very fact of humanity itself.[17]

I will come back to the implications of all of this when considering the content of Beccaria's 'contract', but before I can do so, we first need to take a closer look at the rationality and motivation of the parties in Beccaria's thought.

[14] Weale, above n 3 at 99. Weale ascribes the first position to GR Grice, *The Grounds of Moral Judgement* (Cambridge, Cambridge University Press, 1967) and Gauthier, above n 12; the second to TM Scanlon, *What We Owe to Each Other* (Cambridge MA, Harvard University Press, 1998); the third to B Barry, *Justice as Impartiality* (Oxford, Clarendon Press, 1995) and Rawls, above n 9.

[15] Beccaria, above n 1 at 9 (ch 1).

[16] Ibid at 11 (ch 2).

[17] L Radzinowicz, *Ideology and Crime: A Study of Crime in its Social and Historical Context* (London, Heinemann, 1966) 5.

C. The Rationality and Motivation of the Parties

For contractarians such as Hobbes and Gauthier, the motivation of each party is self-interest, and they are presumed to reason as rational, self-interested beings to maximise their welfare.[18] Beccaria's position is not entirely clear. In 'To the Reader', he explicitly rejects the Hobbesian account of the state of nature, stating that 'it would be wrong, when speaking of the state of war that existed before society came into being, to assume that it was the Hobbesian state of nature bereft of any overriding human duty or obligation'.[19]

Yet later – in the chapters on 'Honor' and 'On the Sciences' – he refers to the necessity of laws, given the 'intrinsic physical despotism of every man' and 'the inevitable evil of men' respectively. Perhaps most tellingly, when it comes to the right to punish, and the most important invocation of the social contract, he is completely clear that 'Every man acts as though he were the center of the world's [and so, presumably, his own] affairs.'[20]

It seems as if Beccaria's position is this: if the relevant alternative is unregulated conflict for scarce resources, then each person, acting rationally, would agree to cooperate with others as each benefits from that cooperation. Every person enters the contract for what he or she can get out of it, and the outcome is a set of rules 'no more than the constraint that is necessary to hold individual interests together, without which they would fall back into a primitive antisocial state'.[21]

However, there are both exegetical and theoretical problems with this account. Exegetically, when Beccaria is analysing the outcomes of the contract in the remainder of the book, what he says is not consistent with this position. Theoretically, the worry is that any such contract would be unstable. As Brian Barry has pointed out, if one's motivation for agreeing to a contract is only what one can get out of it, then as and when one can free-ride (gain the benefits of the contract without contributing one's share), and/or when one's bargaining power increases so one can negotiate a better 'deal', then it is rational to do so.[22] In short, the answer to the question, 'what reasons do rational agents have to make their behaviour conform to whatever principles of right conduct and just institutions the theory … prescribes?'[23] cannot be solely in terms of unfettered self-interest.

The way out of this conundrum is to appeal to one of the 'in between' accounts of rationality described in the quotation from Weale. That is, to think

[18] Gauthier's main work is above n 12. For discussion, see D Gauthier & R Sugden, *Rationality, Justice and the Social Contract: Themes from Morals by Agreement* (New York, Harvester Wheatsheaf, 1993).

[19] Beccaria, above n 1 at 4 ('To the Reader').

[20] Ibid at 27 (ch 9), 109 (ch 42), 11 (ch 2).

[21] Ibid at 12 (ch 2).

[22] Barry, above n 14 ch 2.

[23] Weale, above n 3 at 10.

of the parties to the contract as prudent and concerned with their own good, but as bound by certain constraints such as the recognition of others as 'free and equal' (in the sense attributed to Beccaria above), and as motivated not simply by the desire to live together with others in peace – which could be achieved, for example, by the strong dominating the weak – but to live together with others on terms that reflect the status of those others as parts of what Radzinowicz calls 'humanity'.

How plausible is it to ascribe such a position to Beccaria? In truth, there is not much textual evidence, but then, given that actual text with respect to the social contract is so rare in the book, there is equally little textual evidence of the opposite. Of course, Beccaria would not have thought in the terms in which I have described the contract. That said, this account of the contract – whilst it will not underwrite the mathematical neatness of Beccaria's suggestions in relation to what each party gives up constituting the right to punish – does capture a great deal of what Beccaria writes in relation to equality and what game theorists would now call the assurance problem. We do not 'give up … [our] personal liberty for the public good' but rather in accordance with the demands of justice, which are no more (or less) than 'the constraint that is necessary to hold individual interests together'.[24] For that reason, I think it is plausible that Beccaria's position is as described, and in the absence of text, the best way to argue for that proposition is to see *how* he argues for the substantive positions he adopts.

To do that, we need to look at content – in other words, at the terms of the postulated contract – and this will bring us to the utilitarian dimension of Beccaria's thought.

D. The Question of Content

If Beccaria were a social contract theorist in the sense in which Locke, Rousseau and Rawls are contract theorists, then one would expect *On Crimes and Punishments* to work through the agreement to determine 'the content of a justifiable set of principles that prescribe the institutions of a just order together with the duties that members of that order owe to one another'.[25] But, strikingly, Beccaria does nothing of the sort. Moreover, what he does do is to introduce a seemingly independent and contradictory theory: utilitarianism. In order to examine Beccaria's contractualism properly, then, we need to examine his utilitarianism, and consider how these fit together (if indeed they do).

In the Introduction, Beccaria states unequivocally that were laws constructed according to 'the scientific study of human nature', then 'one clear proposition

[24] Beccaria, above n 1 at 11–12 (ch 2).
[25] Weale, above n 3 at 10.

would follow: *the greatest happiness for the greatest [or: greater] number*'.[26] This formula – subsequently taken up by Bentham[27] – seems sufficient for a theory of justice (including a theory of punishment). If we wish to know what we ought to do, we ought to do that which will realise the (expected) greatest happiness for the greatest number. This suggests, first of all, that we may not need any reference to contract or to rights (as is clear from Bentham's dismissal of them).[28] In that sense the issue is whether the contract argument is redundant given Beccaria's endorsement of the principle of utility. If it is not redundant then a second issue arises, which is whether reliance on both generates propositions that are in tension with one another. Are either or both of these points applicable to Beccaria's treatment of contractarian and utilitarian arguments?

With respect to the second issue, it is important to clarify the utilitarian principle as such. We can think of the greatest happiness principle in two ways: (i) as the demand that we bring about maximally valuable states of affairs (plus an assumption about human happiness being the correct measure of value), or (ii) as the outcome of treating people as equals (the correct aggregation standard). As Will Kymlicka puts it, 'there is something bizarre' about the first way of understanding utilitarianism because 'it is entirely unclear why maximizing utility, as our direct goal, should be considered a *moral* duty'.[29] The second is the more plausible account. Individual persons matter equally; each person's interests should be given equal weight; so morally right acts will maximise the satisfaction of those interests.[30] The second reading fits better with Beccaria's *critical* approach to contemporary inequalities; each person's interests are to count equally irrespective of, for example, aristocratic status.

[26] Beccaria, above n 1 at 7 ('Introduction'). The translation of the Italian here is contested. Bellamy (Beccaria, above n 7 at xix) insists it should be 'the greatest happiness shared among the greater number'. Newman & Marongiu (Beccaria, above n 1 at 128 note 5) agree that it might be 'greater' but do not think the difference significant.

[27] For discussion of Bentham's use of the phrase, see JH Burns, 'Happiness and Utility: Jeremy Bentham's Equation' (2005) 17 *Utilitas* 46.

[28] Famously, Bentham described natural rights as 'simple nonsense', and 'natural and imprescriptible rights, rhetorical nonsense, – nonsense upon stilts'. J Bentham, 'Anarchical Fallacies', in J Waldron (ed), *Nonsense upon Stilts: Bentham, Burke and Marx on the Rights of Man* (London, Methuen, 1987) 46 at 46. As for the social contract, he thought 'that this chimaera had been effectively demolished by Mr Hume': J Bentham, *The Collected Works of Jeremy Bentham: A Comment on the Commentaries and A Fragment on Government* edited by JH Burns & HLA Hart (London, Athlone Press, 1977) 393 at 439.

[29] W Kymlicka, *Contemporary Political Philosophy: An Introduction* 2nd edition (Oxford, Oxford University Press, 2002) 35.

[30] Ibid. As Hare puts it, when arguing that 'equal concern by giving equal weight to the equal interests of everybody … leads straight to Bentham's formula and to utilitarianism itself': 'To have concern for someone is to seek his good …; and to have equal concern for all people is to seek equally their good … , which is exactly what utilitarianism requires': RM Hare, 'Rights, Utility, and Universalization: Reply to J. L. Mackie', in R Frey (ed), *Utility and Rights* (Minneapolis MN, University of Minnesota Press, 1984) 106 at 107.

With respect to the first issue, one can, of course, endorse the second reading of utilitarianism without needing a social contract (as, for example, does RM Hare[31]). But this reading clearly brings utilitarian and contractarian arguments closer together, and thereby allows a space for 'social contract thinking'. Indeed, some utilitarians have argued that their account would be the preferred one to emerge from Rawls' 'original position'.[32] That said, we are still left with a puzzle. On the account given above, *both* the arguments deployed by Beccaria (the one from natural equality and the one from utility) could be used directly – without the social contract – to derive answers to substantive questions of law and punishment. That is, the first appeals to the freedom and intrinsic equality of persons; the second to an understanding of utilitarianism as requiring each person to be treated with respect, unpacked as the giving of equal weight to each person's interests. These are both substantive principles from which moral conclusions can follow. So, why the social contract?

One possibility is that Beccaria simply used 'all the cards at his disposal', as Pietro Costa puts it in a review of Beccaria and the social contract tradition.[33] That is, seized with reformist zeal and in the face of appalling arbitrariness and cruelty in criminal justice, Beccaria used whatever arguments he could in whatever way he could, irrespective of how they fitted together. There may be some truth in that, and it is true that, to borrow again from Costa, Beccaria moves 'with youthful audacity' through, and adopting from, the arguments of Grotius, Hobbes, Locke and Rousseau.[34] However, there is a second possibility, which is that Beccaria conceived of – or perhaps simply used – the language of contract in two (rather different) ways. On the one hand, and as assumed in the analysis above, the point of the contract is to establish general rules for the governance of society. On the other, the contract – in fact, contract*s* – is a device for examining specific laws in relation to specific people. Each law is conceived of as a contract, hence it would seem that each person has a 'contract' with each law and can ask 'Could I possibly be taken to have consented to this?'[35] Such a move might be understood (as noted above) as primarily negative; to capture what the state cannot justifiably do. So, we need to be careful not to sell Beccaria short. Perhaps his various thoughts can be brought together in one (semi-)coherent frame, and from that we can finally turn to the question of content.

[31] RM Hare, *The Language of Morals* (Oxford, Oxford University Press, 1982); RM Hare, *Moral Thinking: Its Levels, Method, and Point* (Oxford, Clarendon, 1981).

[32] See, for example, JC Harsanyi, 'Can the Maximin Principle Serve as a Basis for Morality? A Critique of John Rawls's Theory' (1975) 69 *The American Political Science Review* 594.

[33] P Costa, 'Lo *ius vitae ac necis* alla prova: Cesare Beccaria e la tradizione contrattualstica' (2015) 44 *Quaderni Fiorentini* 817 at 819.

[34] Ibid.

[35] I am very grateful to Antje du Bois-Pedain for pressing me on this.

II. BECCARIA'S SOCIAL CONTRACT: FOUNDATIONAL, DISTRACTING OR SUPERFLUOUS?

I noted in section I that Beccaria deployed two arguments – one from natural equality and one utilitarian – that could each be used without any recourse to the social contract. That is true, but it need not be seen as a criticism of their deployment in combination with social-contractarian arguments. It depends on what work the contract argument is meant to do. As Brian Barry said of his own contractualist theory, 'the contractual device is helpful but not essential' and can be thought of as 'an attractive way of setting out a conception of justice of a broadly egalitarian nature'.[36] So, how might we set out the basic building blocks of Beccaria's argument?

First, as we have seen, free and equal people face coordination and assurance problems when attempting to gain from cooperation. In the absence of an agreed authority, there will be chaos. Thus, second, it is rational for people to agree to such an authority. Third, in agreeing to that, they do not – as in Hobbes – subsume themselves entirely to the sovereign. Rather, they 'give up' only such liberty as they need to achieve their goals.[37] Those goals, fourth, should be understood as the advancing of each person's interests separately – the greatest happiness *shared* among the greater number – not as advancing total aggregate utility.[38] Finally, fifth, advancing each person's interests separately is to be understood in light of each person's natural status as free and equal.

If this is right, Beccaria's account resembles the rule utilitarianism of Mill and, with respect to punishment, Rawls.[39] That is, the rules enabling and regulating social cooperation are justified in so far as they advance persons' (separately considered) interests; but in their implementation, they are constrained by the demands of justice (or, in Beccaria's case, by the limits of what the state may justifiably do). Such a position is not stable in theory, or as we shall see shortly, in Beccaria's treatise,[40] and of course it is not laid out in any such terms in *On Crimes and Punishments*, but it is recognisably what underpins Beccaria's assault on the practices of his day. This final point is important: Beccaria does

[36] B Barry, 'Something in the Disputation not Unpleasant', in PJ Kelly (ed), *Impartiality, Neutrality and Justice: Re-Reading Brian Barry's Justice as Impartiality* (Edinburgh, Edinburgh University Press, 2000) 186 at 187.

[37] Beccaria suggests some mathematical precision in this: that the sum of the minimal quantities of liberty ceded translates into the sum of the right to punish. This is nonsense, but is in keeping with the times in which he was writing, and so should best be understood as some sort of rhetorical flourish. The key points are that persons only give up a part of their liberty in return for a restrained minimalistic justice system that does no more than it needs.

[38] See n 26.

[39] JS Mill, *On Liberty and other Essays* (Oxford, Oxford University Press, 1991); JS Mill, *Utilitarianism* (Oxford University Press 1998); J Rawls, 'Two Concepts of Rules', in J Rawls & S Freeman (eds), *Collected Papers* (Cambridge MA, Harvard University Press, 1955) 20.

[40] For criticism of the rule utilitarian account of punishment, see M Matravers, *Justice and Punishment: The Rationale of Coercion* (Oxford, Oxford University Press, 2000) 17.

not (even attempt) to use the social contract argument to build, *ab initio*, a theory of criminal law and punishment, still less a general theory of justice. Rather, he starts with current practices and his project is fundamentally critical; to identify and to challenge arbitrariness and abuse. As Radzinowicz puts it, 'reason and common sense [are used] as weapons against the old order … against the unquestioning acceptance of tradition and authority … [and] the inefficiency, corruption and sheer chaos of existing institutions'.[41]

This critical project gains force from the rhetorical power of argument from contract. Consider Beccaria's observations in the face of arbitrary distinctions in punishment between places and those attached to persons' different social status. *Why*, it seems natural to ask, should I accept *this*? Such arbitrariness is inexplicable against the background of natural equality and, as a deviation from equality, cannot be justified by appeal to advancing the interests of each person.

Beccaria's famous argument against the death penalty has a similar tone: 'Who,' he asks, 'has ever wanted to give the right to other men to decide to kill another?'[42] Beccaria argues that no such right can be derived directly from the contract. No one could rationally offer their own life in order to further their own advantage.[43] But, we need to tread carefully, as here – as elsewhere – it matters how we (and Beccaria) conceive(d) of the social contract.

On the one hand, if we think of the contract as establishing general principles, then it is not obvious that the parties could not agree to a *system* of punishment that included the death penalty. To other philosophers, in contrast to Beccaria, it has seemed that it is possible rationally to agree to a general scheme of rules that includes the death penalty – if such a scheme advances one's interests overall – even if, as Hobbes argued, one then has no reason to continue to obey the scheme should one be subject to the particular threat of death.[44] On the other, if we think of the 'contract' between the particular condemned individual and the power of the state to put him to death, then it seems as if no rational contractor could agree to *that*. The latter is clearly what Beccaria had in mind, but also why his argument was immediately picked upon as unstable, for what would stop this reasoning from generalising to lesser punishments?[45]

[41] Radzinowicz, above n 17 at 4.

[42] Beccaria, above n 1 at 71 (ch 28).

[43] Beccaria again turns to his mathematical formula and asks '[H]ow can the smallest sacrifice of liberty of each person ever amount to the greatest of all good, a life?' Ibid at 71 (ch 28).

[44] In pt I, ch XIV, Hobbes is clear that 'a covenant not to defend myself by force from force is always void. … For although a man may covenant thus *unless I do so, or so, kill me*, he cannot covenant thus *unless I do so, or so, I will not resist you, when you come to kill me*'. Thus, for Hobbes, criminals condemned to death may resist, but he is clear that they do so 'notwithstanding that [they] have consented to the law by which they are condemned'. T Hobbes, *Leviathan: With Selected Variants from the Latin Edition of 1668* (Indianapolis IN, Hackett, 1994) 87 (original emphasis). For an instructive discussion, see D Heyd, 'Hobbes on Capital Punishment' (1991) 8 *History of Philosophy Quarterly* 119.

[45] F Facchinei, *Note ed osservazioni sul libro intitolato 'Dei delitti e delle pene'* (Venice, 1765), translated in C Beccaria, *On Crimes and Punishments and Other Writings* edited by A Thomas and

Beccaria may have been in some way aware of this tension, since having asserted that there is no possible right, he immediately goes on to ask if the death penalty can be 'useful'. Beccaria holds that it *would* be a reason – perhaps not a decisive reason, but nevertheless *a* reason – to accept the institution of capital punishment *if* such punishment achieved greater happiness shared among a greater number. Thus, the main part of chapter 28 concerns why, in Beccaria's view, it does not. In short, capital punishment removes a potentially useful member of society; it fails to deter; in its disproportion, it can actually promote criminality.[46]

The fact that Beccaria believes there is no utilitarian case for the death penalty should not blind us to the way in which Beccaria's asking the question reveals the instability in his overall approach noted above. Beccaria's argument here is not consistent with a rule utilitarian approach as described above in section I.D. On that approach, the pursuit of welfare is constrained by justice (i.e., the pursuit of welfare *can only* be done within the demands of justice). It would not be acceptable, then, to say that the death penalty is categorically unjust but could be implemented if it realised enough welfare, which is what Beccaria seems to be saying here. Thus, we have to concede that it is possible that Beccaria had a looser view of the relationship between the two arguments (for example, that they should be 'balanced' rather than that one should have priority over the other), or that he did not really believe that capital punishment was invariably unjust (contrary to right).

Beccaria's model of subjecting existing practices to the question of 'Why should *this* be accepted?', and then examining whether the practice is consistent with the freedom and equality of persons and conducive to general welfare, is replicated in his chapters on the criminal justice practices of his day, and invariably result in his finding those practices wanting. As others have noted, Beccaria's positive policy prescriptions are often ambiguous and equivocal, but that makes sense once one understands punishment as serving certain empirical goals (security, stability, assurance) within the constraints of a set of rules that can be the subject of rational endorsement. For example, what punishments are needed depends not on interpreting the will of God or some celestial mechanics in which each wrong deserves an equal and opposite riposte, but on the circumstances in which we have to live together (including, as Beccaria says, those circumstances we can alter, such as the degree of 'education' of the parties).[47]

In short, Beccaria's argument is more suited to criticism of existing practices than it is to offering detailed policy prescriptions. Some of those practices

translated by A Thomas & J Parzen (Toronto, Toronto University Press, 2008) 89 at 94: '[I]f our author's reasoning were valid, society would no longer have the right to punish anyone, because everyone could say, "What man would leave it up to the will of other men to deny him pleasure, like that, for example, of going to the country … if he so wishes?".'

[46] Beccaria, above n 1 (ch 28).

[47] Ibid at 117 (ch 45).

clearly do not work – although even there, of course, it is an empirical question – just as some arbitrary distinctions cannot be justified by reference to an agreement between naturally free and equal persons, but what does work and what inequalities in status can be justified are more difficult issues to resolve. As a result, *On Crimes and Punishments* is more successful in arguing against 'the existing irregular, particularist and custom-bound legal system, based on hereditary rights and the personal rule of the monarch and nobility', than it is in articulating the details of 'a regular, centralised and rational system of justice that was equal for all and grounded in the rule of law'.[48] However, in this it is both not unusual – it remains easier to say that 'slavery is wrong' than it is to articulate a justified system of labour – and it laid the ground for others to develop reasoned accounts of justice.

III. CONCLUSION: THE ROLE OF THE CONTRACT

I have argued for a reconstruction of Beccaria's underlying argument that appeals to two distinct values: the natural freedom and equality of persons, and the idea that the purpose of authority is to allow people to escape chaos and then to advance the general welfare of the community. As such, it appears that the argument could go through without reference to a social contract. And, indeed, when I was approached about this chapter and first re-visited *On Crimes and Punishments* with a view to writing about Beccaria's social contract argument, I was dismayed to find how little Beccaria had written about the contract. However, it is a mistake to dismiss the contract argument. It does not, I think, ground the rights of the state in the way that Beccaria sometimes suggests. Its role is rather to demonstrate the limits of state power. I do not think that it is essential for Beccaria's argument to work, but I do think that without it the rhetorical and imaginative power of *On Crimes and Punishments* would be significantly weakened. There is a particular power – one well recognised by both parents and children – to the question 'Why should I submit to this demand?', and in political philosophy to its correlate, 'Why should we accept this as an authoritative principle?' Beccaria deploys both in *On Crimes and Punishments*, and for that reason the contract element of the book seems to me best read not as an 'attractive way of setting out an argument', to recall the quote from Brian Barry in section II, but as a way to capture the fury of being confronted by irrational, arbitrary and cruel rules. In the face of such rules, we should ask 'Why should I, and why should we, accept them?' And the answer should be: 'We shouldn't.'

[48] Bellamy, above n 7 at xii.

3

Beccaria's Contractarian Criminal Law: Jurisdiction, Punishments and Rewards

RA DUFF AND SE MARSHALL*

> Some believe ... that one who offends against mankind deserves universal condemnation and to have all mankind as his enemy, that an evil act committed at Constantinople, for instance, can be punished in Paris. As if judges were the upholders of human sensibilities, rather than of the contracts which bind men together.[1]

I. BECCARIA'S CONTRACTARIAN CRIMINAL LAW: CRIMINAL LAW AS PUBLIC LAW

IN *ON CRIMES and Punishments*, Beccaria sketches a familiar contractarian account of criminal law and punishment.[2] We contract with each other in order to avoid the miseries of a Hobbesian 'unending state of war', and to enjoy 'in security and calm' at least some substantial proportion of the freedom that is otherwise 'rendered useless by the uncertainty of retaining it': we thereby 'sacrifice a part' of our freedom, transferring it to a sovereign who is 'the legitimate repository and administrator of these freedoms'. Criminal law functions to protect that 'repository', that sovereignty, 'from the private usurpations of each individual', who would otherwise attempt 'to extract from the repository not only his own due but also the portions which are owing to others'. But if the criminal law simply declared that we must respect the sovereign's authority, it

* The first two sections of this chapter draw on RA Duff, 'Criminal Law and the Constitution of Civil Order' (2020) 70 *University of Toronto Law Journal, Supplement 1* 4. Our thanks go to the journal's editor and publishers for permission to re-use this material.

[1] C Beccaria, *On Crimes and Punishments and Other Writings* edited by R Bellamy and translated by R Davies (Cambridge, Cambridge University Press, 1995) 74 (ch 29).

[2] Ibid at 9 (ch 1).

would be quite ineffective, since 'experience shows that the common run of men do not accept stable principles of conduct': criminal punishment (its threat, its imposition to sustain the credibility of that threat) is therefore central to the functioning of criminal law, since it provides the 'tangible motives' that might 'hold back' our 'self-interested passions'.

Beccaria allied this contractarianism with a pre-Benthamite utilitarianism: all laws must be 'evaluated from the point of view of whether or not they conduce to *the greatest happiness shared among the greater number*'.[3] This leads to a minimalist account of criminal law: 'every act of authority between one man and another which is not derived from absolute necessity [that of 'defending the repository of the public well-being'] is tyrannous'.[4] Punishment is just only insofar as it provides 'the restraint necessary to hold particular interests together, without which they would collapse into the old state of unsociability'.[5]

Consistently with this utilitarian conception of criminal law and punishment as justified only insofar as they efficiently serve the greatest happiness, Beccaria is suitably sceptical of 'broken windows' strategies in criminal policy: '[t]o forbid a large number of trivial acts is not to prevent the crimes they may occasion'.[6] He also recognises the limited role that criminal law and punishment can play in preventing the kinds of contract-threatening conduct that we criminalise: for instance, 'the surest but hardest way to prevent crime is to improve education';[7] we return to this point in section III.

Beccaria can be seen as a precursor of contemporary theorists who argue that we should see criminal law as a species of 'public law', in contrast to the unduly 'moralised' accounts that they find in other theorists – accounts that ground criminal law in non- or pre-political conceptions of moral wrongdoing. Malcolm Thorburn and Vincent Chiao, for instance, have been developing distinctive 'public law' accounts of criminal law, in opposition to the kind of moralist account of which Michael Moore is the most prominent contemporary proponent. For Moore, criminal law is a 'functional kind', whose primary function is 'to attain retributive justice' by punishing 'all and only those who are morally culpable in the doing of some morally wrongful action':[8] to which Thorburn and Chiao reply that criminal law should be understood not as an instrument of the moral law or a mechanism for punishing moral wrongdoers,

[3] Ibid at 7 ('Introduction').

[4] Ibid at 10 (ch 2).

[5] Ibid at 11 (ch 2).

[6] Ibid at 103 (ch 41). For the classic 'broken windows' argument, see JQ Wilson & GL Kelling, 'Broken Windows: The Police and Neighborhood Safety' (1982) 249(3) *Atlantic Monthly* 29.

[7] Beccaria, above n 1 at 110 (ch 45). Compare V Chiao, *Criminal Law in the Age of the Administrative State* (Oxford, Oxford University Press, 2019) 99–101, 226–228, on why we should choose to invest in '*schools, now*' rather than in '*prison, later*'.

[8] MS Moore, *Placing Blame: A Theory of the Criminal Law* (Oxford, Oxford University Press, 1997) 33–35.

but as part of the institutional apparatus of the state, to be justified in terms of its role in serving the public aims of the state – aims that do not plausibly include the infliction of deserved suffering on moral wrongdoers.

The proper purpose of the state, on Thorburn's account, is to 'put in place a rightful context for our actions', so that we can 'interact with others in a way that is respectful of everyone's freedom'; a context 'within which we can be free and independent persons … as we live together with others'.[9] That context is constituted by a range of state institutions, and it is sustained by criminal law as a coercive practice that serves to 'resist any attempt to supplant the law's rules with private preferences'.[10] What the state thus provides, and the criminal law enforces, is a set of jurisdictional provisions, defining what falls within each person's private jurisdiction (as a free and equal moral agent), and what rather falls within the jurisdiction of the state acting in our name and on our behalf: the criminal law is concerned 'with the protection of jurisdiction, both public and private, rather than with the identification of moral wrongs';[11] what the state should therefore criminalise are 'efforts to undermine the whole system of equal freedom itself',[12] by exceeding one's own jurisdiction and invading that of the state. Chiao focuses on the possibility of social life under the rule of law. Criminal law is a 'coercive rule-enforcing institution' whose prime function is to 'promote social cooperation under stable public institutions … by stabilizing shared attitudes of reciprocity'; it 'provid[es] assurance that cooperation with legal rules will not leave one open to victimization or exploitation', thus 'stabilizing the rule of law'.[13]

There are important differences between Thorburn's and Chiao's views – about the nature of the order that criminal law serves to secure, about the way in which criminal law helps to secure that order, about the most significant features of the criminal law itself. What their views share, however, is an insistence on setting criminal law in the context of the state, and of the distinctive ends that the state should serve; a rejection of Moore's suggestion that the state should make the punishment of moral wrongdoing a primary aim – not just because they reject Moore's brand of retributivism, but because they deny that criminal law has any such primary concern with moral wrongdoing; and an argument that criminal law's distinctive function is to make an essentially coercive contribution to the maintenance of a distinctive kind of political order (to a system of equal freedom in which people can live together as free and equal moral agents; to collective life under stable institutions). What is striking is the similarity

[9] M Thorburn, 'Constitutionalism and the Limits of the Criminal Law', in RA Duff et al (eds), *The Structures of Criminal Law* (Oxford, Oxford University Press, 2011) 85 at 88, 97.

[10] Ibid at 88.

[11] M Thorburn, 'Criminal Law as Public Law', in RA Duff & SP Green (eds), *Philosophical Foundations of Criminal Law* (Oxford, Oxford University Press, 2011) 21 at 31.

[12] Thorburn, above n 9 at 100.

[13] Chiao, above n 7 at 36–37 (and see ch 2 generally), 171.

between such accounts and Beccaria's (much sketchier and under-developed) account of criminal law.

For Beccaria, criminal law protects the sovereign's 'repository' of freedom 'from the private usurpations of each individual'; it serves this function by providing 'tangible motives' (the threat and imposition of criminal punishment) that should deter us from trying to usurp the sovereign's prerogatives.[14] Similarly, for Thorburn the criminal law is a coercive practice through which the state can 'resist any attempt to supplant the law's rules with private preferences', and protect its jurisdiction; for Chiao it is a coercive practice that 'stabili[ses] the rule of law'. We do not suggest that Thorburn and Chiao are Beccarians; for one thing, they share neither his sketchy contractarianism nor his crude utilitarianism. But they are alike in portraying criminal law as an essentially coercive institution, whose function is to protect, to sustain, the political arrangements that make a properly functioning society – civil society – possible.

We can also identify a familiar, historical, 'moralist' opponent for Beccaria: a century after *On Crimes and Punishments*, James Fitzjames Stephen famously argued that

> [t]hese acts have … been forbidden and subjected to punishment not only because they are dangerous to society, and so ought to be prevented, but also for the sake of gratifying the feeling of hatred – call it revenge, resentment, or what you will – which the contemplation of such conduct excites in healthily constituted minds.[15]

To which Beccaria had already offered the pre-emptive response quoted at the beginning of this chapter: that we should not see judges as the upholders of human sensibilities (as 'gratifying' those sensibilities), or as 'the instrument of rage';[16] that their role, the role of the criminal law that they administer, is rather to uphold 'the contracts which bind men together',[17] by 'prevent[ing] the offender from doing fresh harm to his fellows and … deter[ring] others from doing likewise'.[18] Analogously, when Moore argues that the proper role of criminal law is to subject moral wrongdoers to the retribution that they deserve,[19]

[14] Beccaria, above n 1 at 9 (ch 1).

[15] JF Stephen, *Liberty, Equality, Fraternity* 2nd edition (London, H Elder & Co, 1874) 162.

[16] Beccaria, above n 1 at 31 (ch 12).

[17] Ibid at 74 (ch 29).

[18] Ibid at 31 (ch 12). Note that Beccaria describes what is to be prevented or deterred here as the doing of harm to others, rather than the usurpation of the sovereign's repository of freedoms (ibid at 9 (ch 2)). We need not pause here to discuss the relationship between these two descriptions: but see S Eldar, 'Criminal Law, Parental Authority and the State' (2018) 12 *Criminal Law and Philosophy* 695, 702.

[19] And indeed, although Moore is not in the business of 'gratifying the feeling of hatred' that is 'excite[d] in healthily constituted minds' by culpable moral wrongdoing, he does argue that the emotions that crime arouses (in particular in our minds as we imagine ourselves committing such wrongs) help to reveal the central truth of retributivism: if I imagine myself having committed a terrible crime, Moore thinks (or hopes) I will feel a guilt that engenders the judgement that I ought to undergo 'the suffering that is punishment' (Moore, above n 9 at 148; the previous few pages provide the background argument).

Thorburn and Chiao respond that its role is rather to uphold those political arrangements that make collective social life possible.

In the remainder of this chapter, we will discuss one line of argument in favour of the public law conception of criminal law that can be found in the quotation from Beccaria at the beginning of this chapter – an argument concerning the ambit and jurisdiction of domestic criminal law (section II); we then turn to a suggestion towards the end of *On Crimes and Punishments* that 'another means of preventing crimes is to reward virtue', to ask what sense we can make of this either within Beccaria's contractarian framework, or within the broader framework of a public law conception of criminal law (section III).[20]

II. QUESTIONS OF AMBIT AND JURISDICTION

The question of the ambit of a system of domestic criminal law is, roughly, the question whether a type of conduct falls under, is defined as criminal by, the law of that particular polity: is a theft committed on the streets of Krakow defined as criminal by, ie does it fall within the scope of, Scots criminal law? Jurisdiction is the question of whether the courts of the particular polity have the standing to try someone for an alleged crime: could someone alleged to have committed theft in Krakow be tried in a Scottish court?[21] It might look as if ambit and jurisdiction must go together. Surely it would be pointless for a national legislature to define a type of conduct as criminal, but not then to give that nation's courts jurisdiction to try those accused of committing that crime; and surely a court can claim jurisdiction over an alleged crime only if it constitutes a crime under the law of the polity whose court it is – which is why 'universal jurisdiction' can be claimed only over extraterritorial conduct that has first been brought within the ambit of the domestic criminal law.[22] However, ambit and jurisdiction could in principle be separated: we could believe that a type of conduct should fall within the ambit of a system of domestic criminal law even if it is committed abroad by and against citizens of other countries, without also holding that it should fall within the jurisdiction of that system's courts.

[20] Beccaria, above n 1 at 109 (ch 44). A further issue, which we do not pursue in this chapter, is whether contemporary public law theorists are right to argue, as Thorburn and Chiao argue, that given the political character of criminal law, it is not essentially concerned with moral wrongdoing: for a defence of a 'public law' version of legal moralism that makes the idea of crimes as public wrongs central, see RA Duff, *The Realm of Criminal Law* (Oxford, Oxford University Press, 2018); RA Duff & SE Marshall, 'Crimes, Public Wrongs, and Civil Order' (2019) 13 *Criminal Law and Philosophy* 27.

[21] On 'ambit' and 'jurisdiction', see M Hirst, *Jurisdiction and the Ambit of the Criminal Law* (Oxford, Oxford University Press, 2003) ch 1; L Farmer, 'Territorial Jurisdiction and Criminalization' (2013) 63 *University of Toronto Law Journal* 225.

[22] See eg Criminal Justice Act 1988, s 134; German *Strafgesetzbuch*, §§ 6–7; L Reydams, *Universal Jurisdiction: International and Municipal Legal Perspectives* (Oxford, Oxford University Press, 2004); and at n 41 below.

To see how such a possibility bears on Beccaria's conception of criminal law, we should turn to another contemporary version of legal moralism, according to which 'an evil act committed at Constantinople' might indeed properly be brought within the ambit of French criminal law, even if it is not made triable in a court in Paris. This is what Nils Jareborg calls the 'radical conception of crime': 'what is wrong with a crime is solely what makes it worthy of criminalization, i.e., an invasion of or a threat to a value or interest worthy of protection by criminal law'.[23] This implies, Jareborg thinks, that domestic systems of criminal law should have an in principle unlimited, universal jurisdiction (by which he seems to mean both jurisdiction and ambit):

> Under the radical conception there is, in principle, reason to take jurisdiction over all acts that invade or threaten interests or values that are protected by criminal law. For example, a murder should be the concern of any country, irrespective of the place of commission or the citizenship of the offender and the victim.[24]

Petter Asp develops this suggestion by clearly distinguishing ambit from jurisdiction.[25] As for ambit, 'the default position must be that offences should be applicable worldwide': for

> [i]f it is seriously wrong to kill, does it really matter whether the perpetrator is Swedish or British, whether the victim is Swedish or British, or whether the offence is committed in Sweden or in the UK?[26]

As for jurisdiction, however, there are principled and practical reasons to limit the jurisdiction of a polity's courts, generally, to crimes committed within its own territory.[27] The practical reasons are obvious: the Scottish police are ill-placed to investigate a theft in Krakow, Scottish courts are ill-placed to try the alleged thief; it usually makes more practical sense to leave jurisdiction to the courts of the polity in whose territory the crime occurred. The principled reason concerns respect for national sovereignty: states should, normally, have the power to make and apply their own criminal laws, as with other internal matters, free from interference by other states.[28]

We might have doubts about aspects of Asp's argument. For instance, if the considerations he cites give us reason to limit the jurisdiction of a nation's criminal courts, do they not give us the same kind of reason to limit the ambit of

[23] N Jareborg, *Scraps of Penal Theory* (Uppsala, Iustus Förlag, 2002) 79.

[24] Ibid at 85–86.

[25] P Asp, 'Extraterritorial Ambit and Extraterritorial Jurisdiction', in A du Bois-Pedain, M Ulväng & P Asp (eds), *Criminal Law and the Authority of the State* (Oxford, Hart Publishing, 2017) 33.

[26] Ibid at 40.

[27] But only 'generally': this 'Territoriality Principle' is subject to exceptions or qualifications. See generally Hirst, above n 21. Note especially the principles of 'nationality' and 'passive personality', according to which crimes committed anywhere in the world by, or against, a polity's citizens fall within the ambit of its criminal law and its courts' jurisdiction: eg German *Strafgesetzbuch*, § 7(1) and (2); French *Code Pénal*, art 113.6–113.7; USC 18 § 2.332.

[28] Asp, above n 25 at 42–45.

its criminal law? The practical reasons are clearly powerful, but there could be cases in which a Polish theft could more practicably be tried in a Scottish court (victim and thief both turn up in Glasgow, the thief is ready to admit his guilt): so they might favour a general doctrine of '*aut dedere aut judicare*',[29] rather than a strict limit on jurisdiction; this would allow that in most cases '*dedere*' will be the appropriate course – the alleged offender is returned to the state in whose territory the crime was allegedly committed; but in some cases '*judicare*' might be appropriate – the alleged offender can be efficiently tried in another state's courts. As for the principled reason, it would clearly be a violation of national sovereignty for the Scottish police to enter Poland in order (without permission from the Polish authorities) to arrest the alleged Polish thief to take him to Scotland for trial; but would it be such a violation to arrest and try him if he happened to come to Scotland, if his guilt could be proved in a Scottish court – perhaps especially if the Polish authorities had neither sought to put him on trial in Poland nor sought his extradition from Scotland?[30] However, our concern here is not with the details of his argument but with the conception of criminal law that it reflects – a conception that gives criminal law, domestic as well as international, an ambit that is in principle unlimited; a conception on which a polity therefore has good reason to extend the ambit of its criminal law and the jurisdiction of its criminal courts across the entire world, even if it must then recognise good countervailing reasons to limit that jurisdiction, and perhaps that ambit, to a more modest, primarily territorial, scope.

Central to that conception, for Asp, is the thought that criminal law must be concerned with wrongfulness as such – with the very fact that a type of conduct is morally wrong: 'the act of criminalising something is an act that expresses a normative statement about an abstract class of behaviour'.[31] What justifies the criminalisation of murder or rape is the wrongfulness of such conduct; thus it would be outrageous for the English legislature to declare that murder or rape committed in England is a wrong, but is not a wrong, or is a 'criminal law-nothing',[32] when committed in another country.

If we now ask why the criminal law should be thus focused on wrongful conduct, or (more appositely) why a polity should maintain an institution with such a focus, one obvious answer is Moore's: those who culpably commit moral wrongs deserve to suffer punishment, and criminal law's function is to ensure the infliction of that punishment.[33] It is a familiar point that Moore's

[29] On '*aut dedere aut judicare*' (either extradite or prosecute), a principle that figures in a number of international conventions, see MC Bassiouni & EM Wise, *Aut Dedere Aut Judicare: The Duty to Extradite or Prosecute in International Law* (Dordrecht, Martinus Nijhoff, 1995).

[30] Compare § 7(2) of the German *Strafgesetzbuch*.

[31] Asp, above n 25 at 41.

[32] Ibid at 40. His argument is illustrated by examples of very serious crimes, but it would also apply to less serious wrongs such as theft.

[33] See Moore, above n 8 ch 1; MS Moore, 'A Tale of Two Theories' (2009) 28 *Criminal Justice Ethics* 27.

legal moralism gives the criminal law an (in principle) vastly expansive scope in relation to the types of conduct that we have reason to criminalise: we ought to criminalise every kind of moral wrongdoing, however 'private' it might be, although we also have better countervailing reasons, flowing from such values as privacy and liberty, not to criminalise many kinds of wrong.[34] What is less often noted is a point that Asp makes clear: a Moorean legal moralism also gives domestic criminal law an in principle vastly expansive, universal, scope as to the location of the wrongs that legislatures have reason to criminalise. If wrongdoing deserves punishment, then it deserves punishment wherever, by whomever, against whomever it is committed. We therefore all have reason to promote the imposition of such penal suffering on wrongdoers anywhere in the world, and reason as legislators to bring all wrongdoers within the reach of our domestic criminal law.[35] Those reasons are not restricted by geography. The French legislature has reason to bring within the ambit and jurisdiction of French criminal law wrongs committed not only within France but anywhere in the world – to count as a crime under French law, triable in French courts, the theft committed by a Turkish citizen on the streets of Istanbul; and the Turkish legislature has reason to count as criminal under Turkish law theft committed by French citizens on the streets of Paris. Moore can argue, as Asp does, that there are persuasive reasons against giving domestic criminal law such global scope, to do with the feasibility of enforcing such a globally ambitious criminal law, and the need to respect other states' sovereignty. But we must appeal to such reasons to show why the French legislature should not give French criminal law such a universal scope.

(A conception of the kind that Asp favours need not rely on Moorean retributivism. It could, for instance, portray the criminal law's concern with wrongdoing as a matter of deterrence rather than of retribution. States should criminalise wrongs in order to deter their commission, but the value of deterring a wrong does not depend on its location: thus the French legislature has reason to seek to deter via criminalisation the commission of wrongs anywhere in the world – though it has better countervailing reasons to focus mainly on wrongs committed within French territory.)

There is something counter-intuitive about this conception of the scope of domestic criminal law: does the German legislature really have reason to criminalise wrongful acts committed not just in Germany, or by or against German citizens, but by anyone against anyone, anywhere in the world? Surely a theft committed between Nigerian citizens on a street in Abuja is not simply a wrong that, all things considered, should not be brought within the jurisdiction of the

[34] See eg Moore, above n 8 ch 18.

[35] '[T]he world is better if it is morally better, and to the extent legislators can achieve that moral betterment through law, they should do so' (MS Moore, 'Four Reflections on Law and Morality' (2007) 48 *William & Mary Law Review* 1523 at 1540).

German courts; it is *ab initio* not the business of Germany's criminal law. Now to call a view 'counter-intuitive' is not yet to provide an argument against it; but we find in Beccaria a different, more plausible conception of the proper role of domestic criminal law.

On Asp's or Moore's view, 'an evil act committed at Constantinople' could, in principle, be 'punished in Paris' – be brought within the ambit of French criminal law and the jurisdiction of French criminal courts: judges, speaking in the name of the law, are in principle the 'upholders' not just of French but of 'human sensibilities' – of the values that speak to those sensibilities.[36] To which Beccaria replies that that is not the business of the criminal law, or of its judges: their role is, more modestly and with less moralistic fervour, to uphold 'the contracts which bind men together'. One *could* take this to imply an equally universal (in principle) scope for the criminal law: if 'the contracts which bind men together' should be upheld, they should surely be upheld wherever and between whomever they are made. A contract made in Constantinople is as worthy of enforcement as one made in Paris; even if it should not in practice be enforceable in a French court, that marks a pragmatic limitation on the in principle universal scope of French law. The same might seem to follow if we read Beccaria (more plausibly) as being concerned not with all contracts but with those social contracts that 'bind men together' in political communities:[37] the contract that binds Turkish citizens together is surely as valuable, as worthy of being upheld, as that which binds French citizens together; it would be odd, indeed outrageous, for a legislature to declare that a breach of the French social contract is a criminalisable wrong, but that a violation in Istanbul of the Turkish social contract is not a wrong, or is a 'criminal law-nothing'.[38]

However, there is another, more plausible way to read Beccaria's contractarian account: that French criminal law is a creation of the particular social contract by which the people of France bind themselves together as the French polity; and that its proper concern is therefore with – and only with – upholding the terms of that specific contract. Criminal law cannot, on a contractarian view, be something apart from the social contract by which a polity or state is created:[39] rather, it is created, with the polity's other institutions, as part of the process of contracting. The contract specifies the terms on which these contractors are to live together, as citizens of this polity: but since the contractors will

[36] Beccaria, above n 1 at 74 (ch 29). Or, as Stephen would say, they uphold the feelings (of hatred, revenge, resentment) that 'the grosser forms of vice' arouse 'in healthily constituted minds': above n 15 at 162.

[37] See Beccaria, above n 1 at 4–5 ('To the Reader'), and ch 3.

[38] Asp, above n 25 at 40.

[39] We can leave aside here the question of whether the social contract should be understood as one through which a polity is created, or one through which the members of a polity create the institutional apparatus of the state.

also require some mutual assurance that those contractual terms will be upheld or enforced (given the certainty that some will be tempted to violate them), their contract will include provisions for dealing with breaches of it; that will be the role of their criminal law. But if that is how we should understand domestic criminal law, we can see why French criminal law should not be concerned with thefts in Turkey: not because such thefts are not, in the French legislature's judgement, wrongs, as violations of the Turkish contract; nor because they are, in the abstract, 'criminal law-nothings'; but because they do not impinge on or violate the French social contract, and are thus not the business of the French legislature. If I contract with you to provide certain services in return for certain payment, we might include in the contract provisions to deal with a breach of its terms: but we have no reason to include provisions to deal with breaches of other contracts between other people, and just the same is true of the parties to a social contract. They need not judge other contracts to be any less worthy of being upheld, or judge breaches of those contracts to be any less wrong: *qua* parties to this contract, they should not be making such judgements – they are not their business.

This is not to say that domestic courts can or should take no interest at all in (alleged) crimes committed by and against foreign nationals in other countries: for nation states might well have extradition treaties with each other under which, if someone is accused of a crime that falls within the ambit and jurisdiction of state *A*'s criminal law, and is found in state *B*, state *A* can request (or even demand) that state *B* extradite her to face trial in state *A*; courts in state *B* may thus have to deal with people accused of offences that do not – in Beccarian terms – constitute violations of the contract that binds the members of state *B* together.[40] But in extraditing the suspected offender, the court in state *B* is not trying (let alone punishing) her for her alleged offence – a Parisian court that orders the extradition of an alleged offender to Turkey is not taking it on itself to punish his (alleged) 'evil act'; it is not treating the alleged offence as its direct business, as something it has an interest in pursuing for the sake of retributive justice or of effective deterrence. It is, rather, assisting state *A* in pursuing *its* proper interest in the prosecution of violations of *its* criminal law (which is why extradition depends on a request from state *A*): in this as in other matters, polities can assist each other in the pursuit of their respective interests. That assistance is not (it should not be) unconditional: a suspect must not be extradited from England, for instance, if the alleged conduct would not 'constitute

[40] See, eg, UN Model Treaty on Extradition (available at www.un.org/documents/ga/res/45/a45r116.htm); Extradition Act 2003; MC Bassiouni, *International Extradition: United States Law and Practice* 4th edition (New York, Oceana Publications, 2002). See also the provisions for European Arrest Warrants (EU Council Framework Decision on the European Arrest Warrant and the Surrender Procedures Between Member States 2012/584/JHA); and the ways in which American States help each other retrieve fugitive suspects, often through the federal offence of 'unlawful flight to avoid prosecution' (Fugitive Felon Act 18 USC § 1073).

an offence' under English law,[41] or if she would then face capital punishment.[42] But that is because, in general, if we are asked either individually or collectively to assist another in some enterprise, our assistance must not be given blindly: we should be ready to cooperate in this way only if we can see the end that the other is pursuing as at least a reasonable one (which is not to say that it must be one that we share as our own).

(Of course, to maintain such an account in the contemporary world we would also need to explain various provisions that seem inconsistent with it – provisions that extend the ambit of domestic criminal law and the jurisdiction of domestic courts to conduct that occurs outside, and has no material impact on, the polity or its citizens:[43] these include conventions and treaties that contain an '*aut dedere aut judicare*' clause, requiring the state in which an alleged offender is found to prosecute him if it does not extradite him,[44] as well as claims to 'universal jurisdiction' for domestic systems of law;[45] not to mention international criminal law itself, whose authority, whose ambit and jurisdiction, cannot be explained in terms of a domestic social contract. That is not, however, a task that we can undertake here.[46])

On a Beccarian account, the proper concern of a system of domestic criminal law is thus not with 'an abstract class of [wrongful] behaviour' as such,[47] not even if its wrongfulness consists in the violation of a social contract; it is with violations of that polity's social contract. To set this kind of account in the larger context of 'public law' conceptions of criminal law, we can say that for Beccaria the proper aim of domestic criminal law is to help to sustain a polity's 'civil order', or 'civil peace'. Adam Ferguson, for instance, writing less than 30 years after Beccaria, gave an account of law very similar in spirit to his:

> We are not to expect that the laws of any country are to be framed as so many lessons of morality, to instruct the citizen how he may act the part of the virtuous man. Laws, whether civil or political, are expedients of policy to adjust the pretentions of parties, and to secure the peace of society.[48]

[41] Extradition Act 2003, s 137(3)(b): this is the 'dual criminality' requirement, which requires not that the alleged conduct *be* criminal under English law (that it fall within the ambit of English law) but that it *would* be criminal if committed in England.

[42] See, eg, art 7 of the Extradition Treaty between the UK and the USA, 2003.

[43] We need to add 'or its citizens' to leave room for the principles of 'nationality' and of 'passive personality' (see above n 27): in Beccarian terms these social contracts bind their signatories wherever they are.

[44] See, eg, Hague Convention for the Suppression of Unlawful Seizure of Aircraft, art 7; Bassiouni & Wise, above n 29.

[45] See, eg, Criminal Justice Act 1988, s 134(1) (following the UN Convention against Torture and other Cruel, Inhuman or Degrading Treatment or Punishment (1984)); and see Reydams, above n 22; A Chehtman, *The Philosophical Foundations of Extraterritorial Punishment* (Oxford, Oxford University Press, 2010).

[46] But see Duff, above n 20 ch 3 sections 1–2.

[47] Asp, above n 25 at 41.

[48] A Ferguson, *Principles of Moral and Political Science* vol II (Edinburgh, W Creech, 1792) 145, quoted by L Farmer, *Making the Modern Criminal Law: Criminalization and Civil Order* (Oxford, Oxford University Press, 2016) 37.

Ferguson's reference to 'the peace of society' belongs to a tradition of thought that portrays law in general, and criminal law in particular, as functioning to secure and preserve 'civil peace',[49] or 'civil order';[50] not civil peace or order in general or in the abstract, but the peace or order of the polity whose law it is. We can indeed say that the criminal law helps not only to sustain, but also to constitute, that civil order: for it defines the kinds of conduct that the polity will not tolerate, thus partly defining its conception of 'civil' conduct; and it prescribes the way in which breaches of such requirements will be dealt with – which is an important aspect of a polity's civil order.[51]

To connect criminal law to civil peace or civil order in this way is not to provide a determinate account either of what kind of peace or order that is, or of just how criminal law can function to sustain it: different political theories will generate different conceptions both of civil order and of the role of criminal law within that order; to talk of 'public law' conceptions of criminal law, or of criminal law as sustaining 'civil order', is to point to a family of conceptions rather than to a single determinate conception, some of which will be very different from Beccaria's. Our aim in this section has simply been to locate Beccaria's admittedly very sketchy account of criminal law within this tradition – a tradition according to which criminal law must be understood in political terms (of its role within the institutional apparatus of the state) and, if we focus on domestic law, as essentially local in its scope: it is concerned not with wrongdoing in the abstract, but with local violations of the norms or institutions that structure the polity whose law it is.

We now turn to examine whether Beccaria's contractarian conception of criminal law as 'public' law is consistent with other aspects of his discussion in *On Crimes and Punishments* – in particular with what he says about 'reward[ing] virtue'.

III. REWARDING VIRTUE?

The final chapters of *On Crimes and Punishments* develop the idea that '[i]t is better to prevent crimes than to punish them'[52] – an idea that flows from Beccaria's utilitarian frugality.[53] A brief, almost throwaway, suggestion is that

[49] See N MacCormick, *Institutions of Law: An Essay in Legal Theory* (Oxford, Oxford University Press, 2007) esp ch 12.

[50] See esp Farmer, above n 48; Duff, above n 20.

[51] Compare Winston Churchill: '[t]he mood and temper of the public in regard to the treatment of crime and criminals is one of the most unfailing tests of the civilization of any country' (HC Deb 20 July 1910, vol 19, col 1354).

[52] Beccaria, above n 1 at 103 (ch 41).

[53] See text at n 4 above. On utilitarian penal frugality, see J Bentham, *Introduction to the Principles of Morals and Legislation* edited by JH Burns and HLA Hart (Oxford, Oxford University Press, 1996) ch XV, sections 11–12.

'[a]nother means of preventing crimes is to reward virtue': we can surely expect that 'prizes distributed by the beneficent hand of the sovereign … [will] increase the number of virtuous actions', since '[i]n the hands of the wise distributor, the coin of honour will prove a lasting investment'.[54] To see what sense we can make of this suggestion, and whether it can be rendered consistent with what else Beccaria says about crime and punishment, we must ask what kind of 'reward' he might have in mind, and what kind of 'virtue' is to be rewarded.

A simple answer to these questions is that what is to be rewarded (in order to prevent crime) is refraining from crime; and that the reward should consist in some kind of material benefit – most obviously, money – that would appeal to our 'self-interested passions': just as punishment can provide a negative 'tangible motive[]' to 'hold back' those passions,[55] a stick with which to beat them back, so material rewards for non-criminality can provide a positive tangible motive to redirect those passions – a carrot to lure them into law-abidance. This suggestion might seem strange, and we will show why it is wholly implausible; but it has received contemporary support. Murat Mungan argues that it could be cost-effective to reallocate part of the criminal justice budget towards providing 'positive sanctions' – 'benefits conferred to individuals who refrain from committing crime' (these might 'be monetary transfers or programs designed to increase potential offenders' benefits from pursuing legal options').[56] It would, Mungan recognises, be expensive to confer such benefits on *all* who refrain from crime; but we could achieve more cost-effective prevention by offering them only to 'marginal potential offenders' who would or might have engaged in crime had they not been offered the benefits.

There are obvious questions to be asked about the operation of such a system. For instance, although the benefits are intended for those who do not commit crimes, Mungan clearly assumes that they would be granted to those who are not convicted of crime, rather than only to those who can offer stronger evidence that they have not offended: but he does not attend to the gap (a large one, given current rates of detection and conviction) between 'has not been convicted of a crime' and 'has not committed a crime',[57] though the size of the gap is likely significantly to reduce the efficacy of the offered benefits. More significantly, if the benefits are to be targeted on 'marginal potential offenders', they would presumably be targeted on members of already disadvantaged groups that are already socially, economically and politically marginalised, given the strong correlation between such disadvantage and crime: but, unless we have in place

[54] Beccaria, above n 1 at 109 (ch 44).

[55] Ibid at 9 (ch 1).

[56] MC Mungan, 'Positive Sanctions versus Imprisonment' *George Mason Law & Economics Research Paper No 19-03* available at papers.ssrn.com/sol3/papers.cfm?abstract_id=3317552.

[57] Thus, he talks about 'provid[ing] positive sanctions to each individual who is not convicted' (ibid at 3), but also says that positive sanctions will be 'receivable only if a person does not commit crime' (at 18).

an adequately secure system of welfare and social security benefits that does not discriminate between those with and those without criminal records, there is an obvious danger that such benefits would become part of a welfare system that in effect further punished those convicted of crimes by depriving them of benefits (such as income, housing, education) to which they would otherwise be entitled. Indeed, it could be argued that we already have just such a system in countries that attach serious welfare-related 'collateral consequences' to criminal convictions:[58] for when those with criminal convictions are denied access to a range of welfare provisions that are available to those without convictions, they are in effect being told that such provisions are 'rewards' (or 'privileges') for those who refrain from crime – for, that is, the 'deserving poor'.

However, the deeper worry about such a suggestion for rewarding non-criminality (or, more precisely, non-conviction) is that it implies that crime would, in the absence of such reward, be a reasonably attractive prospect – one that might motivate reasonable citizens. To offer someone a 'positive sanction', or a reward, or a 'benefit' in return for not behaving in a certain way implies that behaving in that way is (normatively or empirically) 'normal': it is what might reasonably be expected in the absence of such a 'sanction'.[59] But as citizens of what purports or aspires to be a decent polity, we surely should not address each other, or expect the state to address us, as if criminal conduct is normal: instead of seeing refraining from crime as something abnormal that merits recognition by a reward, we should see it as simply what we expect of each other. To put the point in Beccarian terms, contracts (whether social or otherwise) do of course offer benefits to the contractors: the Beccarian contract offers us the benefit of enjoying substantial freedom 'in security and calm', if we 'sacrifice a part of our freedom' by transferring it to a sovereign.[60] But 'positive sanctions' involve the offer of additional benefits beyond those that are part of the basic contract; and whilst contracts can offer bonuses for such things as early completion, they do not offer rewards for mere compliance (beyond the 'reward' of enjoying the security that the contract brings). A reward is offered for something that goes beyond what could normally or reasonably be expected; but refraining from crime is surely what we should be able generally to expect of each other.

If positive sanctions are focused on 'marginal potential offenders', we might suggest that these will be members of disadvantaged groups for whom crime would be a reasonable, normal, possibility – that we need to offer them a positive sanction as a counterbalance to the incentives to crime that their

[58] Most obviously the US: see MC Love, J Roberts & CM Klingele, *Collateral Consequences of Criminal Convictions: Law, Policy and Practice* (St Paul MN, Thomson West, 2016); Z Hoskins, *Beyond Punishment? A Normative Account of the Collateral Legal Consequences of Conviction* (Oxford, Oxford University Press, 2019).

[59] The debates about how to distinguish threats (to make someone worse off than she would otherwise have been) from offers (to make someone better off than she would otherwise have been) are clearly relevant here.

[60] Beccaria, above n 1 at 9 (ch 1).

disadvantaged situation generates: but if that is their situation, in which crime is a reasonable or normal possibility, our aim should be to remedy that situation by removing their disadvantage – not to preserve the disadvantage as the normal or acceptable situation, and offer selective rewards to those who manage to rise above it and resist the temptations of crime. We may reward someone for doing something that was their duty, or that they would normally be expected to do without further reward, if they acted as they should despite being in a situation that made it hard to do so: we reward those who do their duty in the face of serious obstacles or temptations by which they might reasonably have been defeated. But when we have ourselves created, or failed to remove, those obstacles or temptations (as with the obstacles or temptations faced by the seriously disadvantaged), our aim should be to remove them – not merely to reward those who manage to overcome them.

The suggestion that rewarding virtue, in order to prevent crime, might be a matter of offering material rewards to those who refrain from crime is thus not plausible; but Beccaria need not be taken to have had that in mind. For, first, the 'rewards' he has in mind could be symbolic rather than material – they could be awarded in 'the coin of honour' rather than in that of material or financial benefit.[61] Second, the 'virtue' that is to be rewarded need not be understood to consist simply in refraining from crime (as if all those who avoid conviction for a certain period should receive some kind of basic 'civic service' medal). To say that 'the surest but hardest way to prevent crime is to improve education'[62] is not to say that education ought to be focused directly on crime prevention – as if classes in 'How to avoid committing crimes' should be central to the curriculum; nor indeed is it to say that preventing crime should be the primary aim of education.[63] Rather, the plausible claim is that education, which a polity anyway ought to ensure for all its members, will help to develop capacities, to foster dispositions, that will, among other benefits, make people less likely to engage in crime. So too, to say that 'reward[ing] virtue' is a 'means of preventing crime' need not be to say that we should reward merely refraining from crime, as if 'virtue' should be understood simply as a matter of refraining from crime (that would be a strikingly implausible conception of virtue): it could instead, more plausibly, be to say that rewarding virtue is a means of encouraging the development of virtue; and that virtue involves a set of attitudes and dispositions given which people will (among other things) be less likely, less disposed, to commit crimes.

An obvious objection to this suggestion is that what is induced by the offer of rewards is not virtue: for virtue involves not merely appropriate behaviour, but appropriate motivations for that behaviour, and the desire to gain an offered

[61] Ibid at 109 (ch 44).

[62] Ibid at 110 (ch 45).

[63] Thus, Chiao's slogan that we should invest in '*schools, now*' rather than in '*prison, later*' (see above n 7) does not imply that our school curricula should be focused directly on crime prevention.

reward is not such an appropriate motivation. Such an objection is not undermined by noting that the rewards offered will be in 'the coin of honour', since the desire to be honoured is hardly more appropriate as a motive for virtuous conduct than a desire for material reward: but it is rebutted by two other obvious points. First, virtue involves appropriate habits of thought, motivation and conduct; and, as every parent knows, rewards (as well as punishments) can play an important role in the cultivation of such habits.[64] Second, the giving of rewards need not be intended, and need not function, to provide a direct incentive (or a 'positive sanction') for virtuous conduct: it can instead function to identify and recommend role models for citizens to admire, and therefore to seek to emulate.

However, the suggestion that the state (the 'sovereign') should aim to foster 'virtue', in part by rewarding it, will provoke further familiar objections from liberal theorists. To put the point simply, virtue involves not just patterns of appropriate conduct but appropriate motivations that flow from an appropriate conception of the good: a virtuous person is someone who behaves as she should because her practical reason is structured by her understanding of the good.[65] But it is a central slogan of a familiar kind of liberalism that the state must be neutral as between different conceptions of the good – which seems to preclude any attempt to foster virtue, and in particular to do so by means of the law. The objection is not simply that we should not use the *criminal law* as a means of fostering virtue,[66] since Beccaria does not portray rewarding virtue as a task for the criminal law: it is that this is not an enterprise in which the state should be involved at all: neither the criminal law, nor the other institutions of the state, should be in the business of 'making men moral'.[67] In Beccarian terms, freedom-loving signatories of the social contract will have a proper interest in being able to rely on their co-signatories to observe the terms of the contract: but they should not be concerned about what motivates such reliable observance – whether it flows from a recognition of the benefits that the contract brings, or a prudent desire to avoid punishment, or a virtuous commitment to the civil order that the contract makes possible.

One response to this objection would be to espouse some version of liberal 'perfectionism',[68] according to which a liberal state should not (cannot) remain

[64] See Aristotle, *Nicomachean Ethics* Book II.

[65] We rely here on a roughly Aristotelian conception of virtue; but very similar points could be drawn from other conceptions.

[66] Contrast, eg, K Huigens, 'Virtue and Inculpation' (1995) 108 *Harvard Law Review* 1423 at 1424–1425: the purpose of criminal law is 'to promote the greater good of humanity' by 'promoting virtue'.

[67] Compare RP George, *Making Men Moral: Civil Liberties and Public Morality* (Oxford, Clarendon Press, 1993); and see Ferguson's already quoted remark that we 'are not to expect that the laws of any country are to be framed as so many lessons of morality, to instruct the citizen how he may act the part of the virtuous man' (above n 48).

[68] See S Wall, 'Perfectionism in Moral and Political Philosophy' in EN Zalta (ed), *Stanford Encyclopedia of Philosophy* (Summer 2019 Edition) available at plato.stanford.edu/archives/sum2019/entries/perfectionism-moral/.

thus neutral: but a simpler way to defuse the objection is to make clearer what Beccaria means, or should mean, by 'virtue' in this context. The Beccarian contract specifies 'the terms under which independent and isolated men come together in society' so that they may 'enjoy what remains [of their freedom] in security and calm':[69] it thus specifies the conditions of civil order, as an order within which people can safely pursue their own conceptions of the good. Insofar as the contractors, and the state that their contract creates, are concerned with 'virtue' at all, they are concerned only with *civic* virtue, virtue that has to do with the citizens' relationship to the contract and to their fellows *qua* fellow signatories; they are not concerned with the whole range of moral virtues. The state should not aim to 'make men moral'; but it can and should aim to foster good citizenship, or civic virtue.[70] Furthermore, while moral virtue involves not just reliable patterns of conduct but the deeper structure of the person's motivations and habits of thought and feeling (the state of her soul), civic virtue can be understood in much shallower, more behavioural terms: it is, essentially, a matter of how we reliably conduct ourselves towards our fellow citizens, and towards the law.

Civic virtue, we might say (in Dworkinian tones), involves displaying 'equal concern and respect' for all our fellow citizens,[71] as well as respect for the laws under which we live together. Now concern and respect certainly involve attitudes and motivations: but what is central to civic virtue is the *enactment* of the appropriate attitudes, and of the kinds of conduct that flow from the appropriate motivations; and we can enact what we do not feel. If as a public official I am called upon to attend a state funeral, I must display, I must enact, an appropriately solemn attitude of mourning – something that I can do in the way I dress, in my demeanour at the funeral, as well as in what I say in my funeral oration: but I can do this, *and do it appropriately*, even though (in my heart) I despise the person whose funeral it is, loathe this kind of ceremony and would rather be somewhere else.[72] Similarly, I can enact appropriate attitudes of respect and concern towards my fellow citizens, and of respect for the law, even if my feelings towards them are wholly at odds with those attitudes; and in doing so I enact civic virtue of the kind that Beccaria thought (that he should have thought) the state ought to promote. Thus even if the state should be in the business of promoting (civic) virtue, this does not require it to take an (intrusive)

[69] Beccaria, above n 1 at 9 (ch 1).

[70] Compare R Dagger, *Civic Virtues: Rights, Citizenship, and Republican Liberalism* (Oxford, Oxford University Press, 1997).

[71] See RM Dworkin, *A Matter of Principle* (Cambridge MA, Harvard University Press, 1986) 190 (and elsewhere; though Dworkin's concern is with what a state owes its citizens, rather than with what citizens owe each other).

[72] On enactment and its significance, see A Kauppinen, 'Hate and Punishment' (2014) 30 *Journal of Interpersonal Violence* 1719; RA Duff & SE Marshall, 'Criminalizing Hate', in T Brudholm & BS Johansen (eds), *Hate, Politics, Law: Critical Perspectives on Combating Hate* (Oxford, Oxford University Press, 2018) 115.

interest in its citizens' souls: it is still concerned with how they (reliably) behave towards each other, and thus with the attitudes they enact, whether or not they actually feel them.

A radical version of this suggestion is that the state should be concerned *only* with reliable enactments of appropriate civic attitudes in appropriate patterns of conduct: that it has *no* proper interest in what motivates those enactments, in their sincerity, in the 'real', 'private' emotions of those who enact them. Whether I am motivated by self-interested prudence to enact a respect and concern for fellow citizens whom I secretly despise, and respect for a law that in my heart I see as an alien imposition; or by a sincere regard for my fellows as indeed fellows, and for a law that I can see as embodying the values I share with them: I exhibit the civic virtue that the state can properly reward (so long, of course, as my motivation is reliable). That radical thesis is perhaps implausible. If we think about what it is to be a good citizen, what civic virtue (or 'true' civic virtue) involves, we must surely attend not merely to enactments but to their sincerity: someone whose enactments, reliable though they may be, are motivated by prudent self-interest, and who secretly despises his fellows, is a less good, less admirable citizen than one whose enactments express her sincerely felt respect and concern for her fellows and the law. But a more modest version of the suggestion is more plausible, and sufficient to meet the liberal objection: even if we should hope that our fellow citizens come to be truly virtuous, and even if the state should encourage this (for instance through its educational provisions), all it should *demand* of us (all we should *demand* of each other as citizens), and all that it should formally reward, is the reliable enactment of appropriate civic attitudes; it should not inquire into our deeper motivations.

We can make a similar point by attending again to the idea that the rewards Beccaria favours are to be awarded in 'the coin of honour':[73] for it is plausible to interpret 'honour', in this context, in the (primarily) external or conduct-focused terms that we suggested above for civic virtue. Rewards that are paid in 'the coin of honour' bestow honours (medals, titles and the like) of an essentially public, social kind: their (intended) value lies in the status that they give their recipients in the eyes of their fellow citizens, and thus in the respect that their fellows are to enact towards them. We can also say that honour is what is rewarded: I am rewarded for being, or more accurately for showing myself to be, a 'honourable' citizen – a person of honour. Such honour, however, as something that should be recognised in the civic context of a liberal polity, should also be understood in the way in which, we suggested, civic virtue should be understood: as consisting essentially (at least as far as its formal, public recognition or reward are concerned) in the enactment of appropriate kinds of civic attitude.

[73] Beccaria, above n 1 at 109 (ch 44).

Finally, however, such an appeal to rewarding virtue, and to 'the coin of honour', serves to highlight a familiar problem for contractarian theories. The paradigmatic civic virtue, on such a view, must be respect for the contract itself, and for one's fellow contractors – a respect that is enacted in the conscientiousness with which one observes the contract's terms (and takes part in revisions to those terms). But that respect, whether for a contract or for one's fellow contractors, cannot be required or generated by the contract itself: rather, the very possibility of making the contract – a making that must involve an expectation that it will not be futile – depends upon the availability of such respect, which presupposes the existence of a precontractual community. If the 'independent and isolated men' who are weary of 'living in an unending state of war', and seek to protect themselves against 'the uncertainty of retaining' their freedom by 'com[ing] together in society', still realise that in the absence of effective punitive deterrents 'the despotic spirit of every man' will quickly 'resubmerg[e] society's laws into the ancient chaos',[74] it is hard to see how they could make the kind of contract that would rescue them from such chaos: for we can contract only with those with whom we already share a normative understanding of contracts, as agreements that *ought* to be kept – only if, that is, we already exist not merely as an aggregate of 'independent and isolated men', but as a normative community. We cannot pursue this familiar objection, or possible contractarian responses to it, here; but nor does the interest of *On Crimes and Punishments* depend on being able to meet it, since – we have suggested – we can find in (or extract from) Beccaria's often sketchy and dubiously consistent set of remarks an interesting (proto-)version of a 'public law' conception of criminal law that can be detached from the contractarian framework in which Beccaria sets it.

[74] Ibid at 9 (ch 1).

4

Crime, Punishment and the Social Contract: Towards the Constitutionalisation of Criminal Law

ANTJE DU BOIS-PEDAIN

THE METAPHOR OF the social contract has long been used by philosophers to clarify the nature, basis and extent of political obligation.[1] As regards the criminal law, however, contractarian thinking appears to lead into philosophical thickets from which few plausible positions emerge.[2] The perspective that the commission of a crime constitutes a breach of the contract that binds members of the polity together, in particular, has been peculiarly inept at generating a plausible justification for the power to punish.

This chapter explores how contractarian thinking can inform reflection on state punishment, by taking a closer look at Beccaria's use of the concept. Beccaria aspired for his book to provide the theoretical foundations for the exercise of penal authority.[3] He sought to present penal practices as constrained by their consent(-ability) on the part of those governed. Starting from the premise that people would, in the social contract, assign only the minimum amount of their freedom necessary for their protection by the ruler – that necessity being determined by utilitarian calculations of the wellbeing of individuals considered

[1] For a useful introduction, see L Siep, 'Vertragstheorie – Ermächtigung und Kritik von Herrschaft?' in U Bermbach & K-M Kodalle (eds), *Furcht und Freiheit: LEVIATHAN – Diskussion 300 Jahre nach Thomas Hobbes* (Opladen, Westdeutscher Verlag, 1982) 129. See also Matravers, ch 2 in this volume.

[2] For a critical appraisal, see K Seelmann, 'Vertragsmetaphern zur Legitimation des Strafens im 18. Jahrhundert', in M Stolleis et al (eds), *Die Bedeutung der Wörter. Studien zur europäischen Rechtsgeschichte. Festschrift für Sten Gagnér zum 70. Geburtstag* (Munich, Beck, 1991) 443.

[3] L Reuter, 'Die Ansichten des Marchese von Beccaria zu den Strafgesetzen, Verbrechen und Strafen – Strafgesetze, Strafjustiz und strafrechtliches Denken im 18. Jahrhundert', in G Deimling (ed), *Cesare Beccaria: Die Anfänge moderner Strafrechtspflege in Europa* (Heidelberg, Kriminalistik Verlag, 1989) 55 at 59.

qua public good – punishment emerges as justifiable only to the extent that it does not go beyond what is necessary to discourage crimes[4] (which are, in turn, conceptualised as acts of 'unjust despotism against the social contract').[5] Beccaria clearly expected the two grounds of the authority to punish he identified – the social contract, and punishment's utility – to work in tandem towards a minimalist criminal law. To him, it was obvious that utilitarian necessity would legitimate only punishments much milder than those employed in his time, as would reflection on the extent to which subjects can be considered to have given up their liberty under the terms of the social contract. He thus perceived no tension between the utilitarian and the contractarian or rights-based strands in his thinking.[6] Both, for him, inexorably pushed in the direction of penal moderation.

In what follows, I unpack the contractarian element in Beccaria's theory of punishment, starting with his case against the death penalty (section I). The claim that the contracting parties cannot have invested the sovereign with the right to punish by death is the lynchpin of this argument. Engagement with the rebuttals attempted by Kant demonstrates the strength of Beccaria's contractarian model. Against the challenges made by Kant, Beccaria's argument emerges unscathed precisely because he envisions the contractors as full-fledged fallible human beings seeking to protect their interests. Primoratz's suggestion that this very assumption could, however, make Beccaria's position vulnerable to being undermined by demands for capital punishment that could be ascribed to some potential contractors leads across to the broader question of how the Beccarian social contract should be conceptualised so as to deliver on its promise of providing every member of the polity – including those who have committed crimes – with effective protections against arbitrary, cruel or unnecessary punishments.

This question is addressed in section II. This reconstructs Beccaria's understanding of state authority by drawing on historical accounts of contractarian thinking in which the notion of an original contract of polity-formation is distinguished from the notion of a contract of government. It shows that Beccaria approaches the social contract as constituted by a set of practices, understandings and (implicit) commitments that underpin government by enlightened rulers; conventions whose 'perfecting reconstruction' is the enlightened philosopher's task. As such, Beccaria's contractarian approach to punishment's justification

[4] C Beccaria, *On Crimes and Punishments and Other Writings* edited by R Bellamy and translated by R Davies (Cambridge, Cambridge University Press, 1995) 13 (ch 3).

[5] This is Beccaria's somewhat elliptical definition of crime in his brief chapter on theft (ibid at 53 (ch 22)).

[6] See eg P Garnsey, *Against the Death Penalty: Writings From the First Abolitionists – Guiseppe Pelli and Cesare Beccaria* (Princeton NJ, Princeton University Press, 2020) 138; P Audegean, *La philosophie de Beccaria: savoir punir, savoir écrire, savoir produire* (Paris, Vrin, 2010) 167; BE Harcourt, 'Beccaria's On Crimes and Punishments: A Mirror on the History of the Foundations of Modern Criminal Law', in MD Dubber (ed), *Foundational Texts in Modern Criminal Law* (Oxford, Oxford University Press, 2014) 39 at 46.

finds political expression in the constitutionalisation of criminal justice, which in itself constitutes a major advance in punishment's political justification.[7] It is, additionally, Beccaria's de-essentialisation of criminality and crime that makes these advances possible. Crimes, for him, are not committed by persons who are in some essential way different from law-abiding members of the polity; their perpetrators are people who – like everyone – try to make the best of their lot in life, and who have failed or miscalculated in this particular way.[8] This thoroughly psychologised and 'normalising' understanding of criminal behaviour entails the wholesale replacement not only of state punishment's conceptual but also of its ethical foundation, from some notion of annulment of the crime ('expunging sin'), to 'giving effect to sound social policy'. It also makes it plausible that there should be a continuum of membership in the polity and of its protections for the perpetrator, as their grounds remain unaffected by the commission of a crime.

In approaching state punishment from this direction, Beccaria can continue to conceive of laws as 'the contracts that bind men together'[9] but avoid the impasse that arises when crime is understood to sever these contractual ties.[10] This generates a coherent position that can not only be defended successfully against critics such as Kant but also provide a conceptual foundation for criminal justice practice in modern polities.

I. THE DEATH PENALTY AND THE SOCIAL CONTRACT: PLACING PUNISHMENT-BY-DEATH BEYOND THE REACH OF PUBLIC AUTHORITY

Beccaria begins his famous discussion of the death penalty by asking the question 'By what right can men presume to slaughter their fellows?' No such right, he says, can be deduced from the terms on which they have come together for their mutual protection in one polity. This is so because:

> How on earth can the minimum sacrifice of each individual's freedom involve handing over the greatest of all goods, life itself? And even if that were so, how can it be reconciled with the other principle which denies that a man is free to commit

[7] Ferrajoli particularly emphasises Beccaria's contribution to constitutional criminal law guarantees, see L Ferrajoli, 'Two Hundred and Fifty Years since the Publication of *On Crimes and Punishments*: The Currency of Cesare Beccaria's Thought' (2014) 16 *Punishment & Society* 501. See also Zucca, ch 1 in this volume.

[8] Beccaria assumes that 'each individual … is always seeking to extract from the repository not only his own due but also the portions which are owing to others', requiring '*tangible motives* … as a counterbalance to the strong impressions of those self-interested passions which are ranged against the universal good' (above n 4 at 9 (ch 1), emphasis original).

[9] Ibid at 74 (ch 29).

[10] This is a particularly conspicuous problem in the contractarian penal philosophies of Hobbes and Rousseau, which were known to Beccaria and to which he explicitly and implicitly responds. A different solution offered by Beccaria's near contemporary, the German philosopher JG Fichte – involving complex constructions of ever more contracts to allow offenders' re-entry into the polity – is not addressed in this chapter.

> suicide, which he must be, if he is able to transfer that right to others or to society as a whole?[11]

As Adam Sitze points out, the second point made in this quotation – an objection to the death penalty based on the impermissibility of suicide – had previously troubled Rousseau, a contractarian who sought to defend capital punishment.[12] Rousseau had proceeded to deflect this objection based on an absolutist conception of the *volonté générale* (general will) against which his contractors retain no pre-political rights, and which can coherently generate laws that make crimes punishable by death in order to better secure the protection of the contractors' political rights within that order.[13] In the above quotation Beccaria signals that he is unconvinced by this argument – which is unsurprising, since he thinks the public interest cannot be divorced from the interest of each individual member of the public.[14] But – as Sitze also notes[15] – for Beccaria the argument from suicide is merely a supplementary consideration; it points to a self-contradiction in which he sees his opponents embroiled. Beccaria's central objection is *not* that the contractors have *no right they could grant* to another to kill them but that – having proper regard to their interest in self-protection – they just *cannot have granted* public authority any such right.

According to Larrère, what is truly striking is not that Beccaria makes this point but that *he stops there* – that, for him, this argument is dispositive of the matter.[16] Whereas other contractarian theorists who started from the same premise quickly went on to construe the death penalty as a punishment applied to 'un individu disqualifié'[17] – to someone who, by virtue of his criminal act, had placed himself beyond the protection afforded by the social contract and re-entered a state of war with the sovereign – Beccaria was having none of this.

Entwined with the objection from lack of right, but logically separable from it, is Beccaria's denunciation of punishment-by-death as public murder: 'It seems absurd to me,' he writes, 'that the laws, which are the expression of the public will and which hate and punish murder, should themselves commit one, and that to deter citizens from murder, they should decree a public murder.'[18] This provocative equation of the execution of the death penalty with murder

[11] Beccaria, above n 4 at 66 (ch 28).

[12] A Sitze, 'Capital Punishment as a Problem for the Philosophy of Law' (2009) 9 *The New Centennial Review* 221 at 230.

[13] On Rousseau's absolutist conception of the general will, see further the discussion in section II. Compare also G Radbruch, 'Isaak Iselin über Cesare Beccaria', in his *Elegantiae Juris Criminalis* 2nd edition (Basel, Verlag für Recht und Gesellschaft, 1950) 181 at 185 (pointing out that Rousseau's defence of the death penalty depends on what Radbruch calls Rousseau's 'total' conception of the social contract).

[14] Beccaria, above n 4 at 102 (ch 41).

[15] Sitze, above n 12 at 230.

[16] C Larrère, 'Droit de punir et qualification des crimes de Montesquieu à Beccaria', in M Porret (ed), *Beccaria et la culture juridique des Lumières* (Geneva, Librairie Droz, 1997) 89 at 92.

[17] Ibid.

[18] Beccaria, above n 4 at 70 (ch 28).

challenges his opponents to put their cards on the table and provide a positive argument why punishment-by-death is not murder.

Kant's well-known vituperative response takes the argument from the impermissibility of suicide – its lack of centrality to Beccaria's argument notwithstanding – as its main target. Wrapped into this response is Kant's own positive argument in support of the death penalty, which Sitze summarises as follows:

> Kant argues that Beccaria could confuse capital punishment with suicide[19] writ large only because Beccaria did not observe any distinction between the *homo noumenon* (the 'moral personality' who is the locus of 'pure reason within me') and the *homo phaenomenon* (the 'sensuous being' who is the locus of my desire to preserve myself in my 'animal being'). When I consent to suffer the penalty of death at the hands of the sovereign … the *person* within me ([the *homo noumenon* which is] … the nameless force of pure reason, which 'desires' nothing other than universality and necessity itself) dictates a perfectly consistent set of penal laws to which I then subject my own *living being*.[20]

From these considerations Kant seeks to conclude that 'what justice, as the idea of judicial authority, wills in accordance with universal laws that are grounded a priori' is that '[a]nyone who commits murder, orders it, or is an accomplice in it – must suffer death'.[21]

Now, if this is the positive case for the death penalty that Kant offers, then it rests entirely on questionable metaphysics, moreover on metaphysics that are unlikely to attract any serious followers today.[22] For on what grounds should we be prepared to accept that the human being we treat as the locus of value and rights, the reference point for our conception of human dignity, can be divided into a 'noumenal' and an 'empirical' self, into a seat of human reason separable from the seat of human experience, or that (if for some reason such an imagined split may seem attractive in advancing our understanding of the human condition) any normative deductions about what may be done to an embodied human being should be drawn on the basis of what a 'noumenal' self is allegedly committed to?[23]

[19] Or, one might add, with public murder.

[20] Sitze, above n 12 at 233 (emphases original), quoting Kant's definitions of the *homo noumenon* and *homo phaenomenon* in I Kant, *The Metaphysics of Morals* [1797] in *The Cambridge Edition of the Works of Immanuel Kant: Practical Philosophy*, edited by A Wood and translated by M Gregor (Cambridge, Cambridge University Press, 1996) 476 and 546.

[21] Kant, above n 20 at 475.

[22] For pertinent philosophical critiques of Kantian metaphysics, see eg LT Hobhouse, *The Metaphysical Theory of the State: A Criticism* (London, Allen & Unwin, 1960).

[23] This point is forcefully made by P Noll, *Die ethische Begründung der Strafe* (Tübingen, Mohr/Siebeck, 1962) 6. Incidentally, one may also doubt that 'noumenal selves' would have to be committed to the principle of retribution; this principle certainly does not follow from the avoidance of self-contradiction on which Kant's formulation of the moral law insists. I will not pursue this point further here.

The self that 'wills' its own punishment is a chimera that haunts Kant's philosophy[24] but not Beccaria's.[25] It is, in the context of the discussion of the death penalty, part and parcel of Kant's 'desperate proof' (Radbruch) that the parties to the social contract can agree to the death penalty.[26] By construing penal laws as willed by 'noumenal selves', Kant – through an 'artificial move characteristic of his thinking' (replacing the imagined agreement of the contractors as a temporal 'moment' with an imagined transcentendal relation) – seeks to displace the relevance of the question whether anyone could be taken to consent to being punished by death at the point when they are being punished with the 'timeless judgement of reason of [the] necessity [of punishment by death]'.[27] Whether that 'timeless judgement of reason' would, in fact, support the death penalty is (as Radbruch also sees) a separate question. In Radbruch's estimation, Kant's argument falls at that hurdle as well.[28]

What is more – and this is the point Fichte makes in defence of Beccaria – Kant's metaphysical deduction of punishment as a 'categorical imperative' is insufficiently connected to any justification of the content of penal law. To bring out this point, Fichte starts with a concession that Beccaria would not make: that 'in a moral world-order … there is absolutely no dispute about whether a *murderer* has been treated unjustly, if he, too, should lose his own life in a violent manner'.[29] But even if we concede this, Fichte insists, it is 'an entirely different question' (which Fichte thinks was the only question Beccaria sought to answer) 'from where does a mortal get the right of this moral world-order, the right to render the criminal his just deserts?'[30] To this question, however, Kant failed to give a convincing answer, since:

> Whoever ascribes this right to a worldly sovereign will … be required (as Kant's system was) to say that the sovereign's rightful title to it is [grounded on a categorical imperative that is itself not further examinable][31] … [C]laims of this kind are completely out of place in a system of right where legislative authority is ascribed to the people …[32]

[24] On the questionable foundations of Kant's theory, see further MM Falls, 'Retribution, Reciprocity, and Respect for Persons' (1987) 6 *Law & Philosophy* 25.

[25] See further Mario Cattaneo's discussion of the Italian scholar Rodolfo Mondolfo's interpretation of Beccaria on this point, in MA Cattaneo, 'Beccaria und Kant. Der Wert des Menschen im Strafrecht', in his *Aufklärung und Strafrecht. Beiträge zur deutschen Strafrechtsphilosophie des 18. Jahrhunderts* translated by T Vormbaum (Baden-Baden, Nomos, 1998) 7 at 17.

[26] G Radbruch, *Rechtsphilosophie* 5th edition edited by E Wolf (Stuttgart, KF Koehler Verlag, 1956) 272.

[27] Ibid (my translation).

[28] Ibid at 273.

[29] JG Fichte, *Foundations of Natural Right According to the Principles of the Wissenschaftslehre* edited by F Neuhouser and translated by M Baur (Cambridge, Cambridge University Press, 2000) 246. Beccaria, by contrast, not only believes that the death penalty is unnecessary and therefore unjust (even on the assumption that the convict is guilty); he also does not hesitate to speak of those subjected to barbarous penal practices as their 'victims' (again, irrespective of the question of guilt).

[30] Ibid.

[31] Ibid (with the wording in square brackets, at 425, inserted here for clarity).

[32] Ibid at 247.

Fichte's reply stresses that even if there were norms of a moral world-order willed by 'noumenal selves', such norms are one thing and the laws enacted in a polity are another. As regards the latter, we need to identify principles that ought to shape these laws. As a principle of penal legislation, Kant supports the talionic principle, but on the much weaker ground that it is the only principle that can preclude arbitrary exercises of penal power.[33] If we take this to be what the *legal* authority to punish by death rests on, it becomes apparent that – even on Kant's own terms – the claim to its justification as a mode of legal punishment can be defeated by showing that arbitrary exercises of power can be avoided just as effectively, or even more effectively, when penal sanctions are chosen with reference to other principles.[34] It is precisely such a set of competing principles that Beccaria develops when he says that punishment should be apportioned to reflect the harm to society caused by a crime,[35] designed so that the frequency of the commission of more serious crimes is reduced with particular efficiency compared to less serious crimes,[36] and be calculated to 'make the most efficacious and lasting impression on the minds of men with the least torment to the body of the condemned'.[37] While these principles have their difficulties in generating determinate conclusions,[38] they are not obviously less promising in this regard than the talionic principle Kant supports,[39] and which even in Kant's hands immediately begins to crumble as he suggests various modifications to the types of sanctions the principle appears to imply so as not to embroil the state in absurdity or re-enactment of atrocity.[40]

Before leaving this discussion, it is important to highlight just how different Kant's case for the death penalty is from its religiously based justification in Beccaria's time. As Lavi observes, religious doctrine gave a positive valence to the criminal's pain and suffering due to its alleged redemptive capacities.[41] Combined with a world-view where death marked not the end of everything but the transition to another life, the sacralised conception of the death penalty turned it into a corridor to salvation.[42] In this sense it could appear to serve not

[33] Kant, above n 20 at 473: 'only … *ius talionis* … can specify definitely the quality and the quantity of punishment; all other principles are fluctuating and unsuited for a sentence of pure and strict justice because extraneous considerations are mixed into them'.

[34] For pertinent discussion, see also MA Cattaneo, 'Menschenwürde und Strafrechtsphilosophie der Aufklärung', in R Brandt (ed), *Rechtsphilosophie der Aufklärung, Symposium Wolfenbüttel 1981* (Berlin, De Gruyter, 1982) 321 at 329–330.

[35] Beccaria, above n 4 at 22 (ch 7).

[36] Ibid at 19 (ch 6).

[37] Ibid at 31 (ch 12).

[38] This is amply demonstrated by Bentham's unceasing but only partially convincing efforts, on which see HLA Hart, 'Bentham and Beccaria', in his *Essays on Bentham: Jurisprudence and Political Philosophy* (Oxford, Oxford University Press, 1982) 40 at 46–49.

[39] For an illustrative failed attempt to construct defensible (sentencing) propositions out of talion, see J Waldron, 'Lex Talionis' (1992) 34 *Arizona Law Review* 25.

[40] See Kant, above n 20 at 474–475.

[41] See Lavi, ch 6 in this volume.

[42] See H von Thiessen, 'Das Sterbebett als normative Schwelle: Der Mensch in der Frühen Neuzeit zwischen irdischer Normenkonkurrenz und göttlichem Gericht' (2012) 295 *Historische Zeitschrift* 625, esp at 627–629.

only the communal interest but also the interest of the condemned.[43] Stripped of its alleged redeeming power it becomes highly questionable whether religion could support it[44] (and this is why Beccaria's observation, that 'men can run counter to the Almighty' not just 'by blaspheming against him' but 'also by punishing on His behalf', stings.[45]) The religious defence of capital punishment does not rest on anything like a Kantian categorical imperative; that it could do so is excluded by the believer's acceptance of the possibility of God's grace, which also means an ever-present risk that humans may punish when God would not.

Unlike the believer, Kant cannot treat the suffering of death as in some sense positive. He has to treat it as an evil – albeit one justice demands. And, as we have seen above, that latter claim rests on the naked assertion that the penal law is a 'categorical imperative' that mandates punishment of murder by death – an argument which is not only implausible when read against Kant's broader theory of law[46] but also appears to preclude sensible discussion. As the German criminal law scholar Karl Grolman remarked in 1799, 'this alleging of a categorical imperative makes it very easy to avoid proving one's claims; one only has to inform anyone who emboldens himself to ask for such proof, that any attempt to prove a categorical imperative contains a contradiction'[47] – which should, by rights, entitle the unpersuaded to allow 'the unproven theory to rest on its unprovability' and set it aside until it is reasoned for in a manner that allows intellectual engagement with it.[48] Fichte was clearly not alone in his readiness to dismiss Kant's entire argument as what must surely be 'fragments of a very early version … that have found their way to us out of sheer chance'.[49]

Kant's criticism of Beccaria also misses its target when he asserts that Beccaria's argument hangs on a confusion between a legal subject's consent to

[43] J Martschukat, 'Der "Maasstab für die geistige Bildungsstufe eines Volkes und die Moralität eines Zeitalters": Die Todesstrafe in Diskurs und Praxis im 18. und 19. Jahrhundert' (2001) 9 *Historische Anthropologie: Kultur, Gesellschaft, Alltag* 1 at 5–6 (explaining that, according to the religious conception of punishment, serious crime had to be punished in order to avoid bringing down God's wrath onto the community, and that public executions were a way for the authorities to demonstrate that they were fulfilling that duty). Different forms of capital punishment were credited with different effects in the afterlife: executions by sword or axe were believed to cleanse guilt and achieve redemption, whereas executions by hanging were believed not to have this effect. See G Radbruch, 'Ars moriendi: Scharfrichter, Seelsorger, Armesünder, Volk' in Radbruch, above n 13, 141 at 164–165 and 172.

[44] In one of the parliamentary debates conducted in the German Reich in the 1870s, a Catholic priest rejected the death penalty with the argument that 'We, who cannot bestow eternal life, have no right to end anyone's temporal life.' Quoted by C Helfer, 'Todesstrafe', in A Elster et al (eds), *Handwörterbuch der Kriminologie* vol 3 2nd edition (Berlin, De Gruyter, 1975) 326 at 336.

[45] Beccaria, above n 4 at 23 (ch 7).

[46] See Fichte's point discussed in the text.

[47] K Grolman, *Ueber die Begründung des Strafrechts und der Strafgesetzgebung* (Gießen, Heyer, 1799) 219–220. That such a demand would 'contain a contradiction' means that demands for any further grounding of what Kant grounds 'a priori' would be contradictory within Kant's system.

[48] Ibid at 220.

[49] Fichte, above n 29 at 247.

be subject to law, and an embodied legal subject's preparedness to voluntarily undergo the punishment imposed by law. Kant assumes that he has parried Beccaria's point by insisting that it is unnecessary for citizens to consent to the punishment being imposed on them on any particular occasion; what each member of society consents to is to 'subject [themselves] together with everyone else to the laws, which will naturally also be penal laws'.[50] But this very point is based on a misreading of Beccaria.[51] Beccaria never claims (contrary to what Kant apparently assumes) that 'the authorization to punish [has] to be based on the offender's *promise*, on his *willing* to let himself be punished'.[52] For Beccaria, '[l]aws are the terms under which independent and isolated men come together in society'.[53] Beccaria's contractors commit themselves to being governed by the laws of their polity; the judges, who apply these laws, thereby uphold 'the contracts that bind men together'.[54] And

> [t]he judges have not received the laws from our forefathers as if they were a family tradition … Rather, they receive them from the living society or from the sovereign which represents it as the legitimate repository of the current sum of the will of the whole of society … the result of a tacit or express oath which the united wills of the subjects have made to the sovereign.[55]

The commitment to live under the polity's laws is as central to Beccaria's contractualism[56] as it is to Kant's own. The difference between Beccaria and Kant in this regard concerns the determination of the content of the penal law. Kant, as we have seen, construes that content as given through our 'noumenal' selves' legislation (and this is what Kant's construction of the social contract commits the contractors to); Beccaria, by contrast, allows the legislator to determine the content of the penal law according to utilitarian-tinged principles of justice by wielding '[t]he sum of these smallest possible portions [of liberty that] constitutes the right to punish'.[57]

For Beccaria as for Kant, determining the content of the contract involves a critical reconstruction of what political arrangements rational contractors would commit themselves to. The deep differences between the two thinkers

[50] Kant, above n 20 at 476.

[51] This has been pointed out by numerous defenders of Beccaria, see eg Cattaneo, above n 25 at 17.

[52] The quotation is taken from Kant's counterargument against Beccaria (Kant, above n 20 at 476). For a detailed demonstration that Kant misconstrues Beccaria's argument here, see I Primoratz, 'Kant und Beccaria' (1978) 69 *Kant-Studien* 403 at 413–414.

[53] Beccaria, above n 4 at 9 (ch 1).

[54] Ibid at 74 (ch 29).

[55] Ibid at 14 (ch 4).

[56] W Küper, 'Cesare Beccaria und die kriminalpolitische Aufklärung des 18. Jahrhunderts', in his *Strafrechtliche Beiträge zu Rechtsgeschichte und Rechtsphilosophie* edited by M Hettinger & J Zopfs (Tübingen, Mohr Siebeck, 2017) 3 at 7.

[57] Beccaria, above n 4 at 11 (ch 2). Küper rightly stresses that, for Beccaria, laws are not 'just any authoritative command whatsoever' but 'expressions of the reasonable conditions under which contractors agreed to form a polity' (Küper, above n 56 at 9 (my translation)). The proximity to Kant's approach is obvious notwithstanding that Beccaria unpacks 'reason' in a different direction.

as regards the substance of these commitments arise from their fundamentally different conceptions of the human individual (and human rationality).[58] For Kant, rational commitments can only be made by that (imagined) part of the human being unaffected by sensuous experiences of pleasure or pain. Beccaria, by contrast, imagines his contractors as fully-fledged humans, whose interests, on which normative propositions can be built, most certainly include the full range of physical, sensory and emotional experiences. It is this difference that (for the most part) explains their vastly different accounts of what the contracting parties' rational self-commitments entail. Other differences arise due to Beccaria's not purely idealistic conception of the social contract, which is addressed further in section II. These differences are important for Kant's and Beccaria's differing constructions of political authority, but they have no bearing on Kant's critique of Beccaria's argument against the death penalty, which fails on its own terms.

For Primoratz, however, this very construction of the contractors as embodied human beings that makes the Kantian counterargument misfire, is the Achilles heel of Beccaria's argument against the death penalty.[59] Primoratz suggests that it is possible to out-construe Beccaria by assuming that a contractor might face a negotiating situation where some of the other potential contractors insist – as a condition of their entering the contract – on giving the polity the right to punish by death. Primoratz maintains that, on such assumptions, Beccaria would be forced to concede that it would then be rational for the contractors to agree to an arrangement that includes the death penalty, as this would still reduce their personal risk of being killed compared to the risks present in the state of nature.[60] This argument, however, begs the question whether it is indeed compatible with Beccaria's contractual construction to invest some of the contractors with irrational demands[61] (such as demanding the institution of the death penalty even though it is not in their own interest to do so) as their condition for entering the state. We cannot decide this point without a better understanding of Beccaria's contractual argument.

[58] This point is also made by P Costa, '"Un sentiment d'humanité affecté": Kant critique de Beccaria', in P Audegean & L Delia (eds), *Le moment Beccaria: naissance du droit pénal moderne, 1764–1810* (Liverpool, Liverpool University Press, 2018) 65 at 82. To that extent, I would resist the sharp contrast drawn by Scolnicov, ch 5 in this volume, between Beccaria's Hobbesian and Kant's rationalistic constructions of the social contract. In the context of my discussion here, the similarities are more important.

[59] See Primoratz, above n 52.

[60] Ibid at 419–420.

[61] One reason to doubt this is Beccaria's observation in his chapter 'Of debtors', that 'Men's most superficial feelings lead them to prefer cruel laws. Nevertheless, when they are subjected to them themselves, it is in each man's interest that they be moderate, because the fear of being injured is greater than the desire to injure': Beccaria, above n 4 at 89 (ch 34).

Ultimately, then, this discussion brings us to the larger question of the success or otherwise of Beccaria's deduction of limits to punishment based on his construction of the social contract. It is therefore time to move from the discussion of the death penalty to the broader issue of Beccaria's use of the social contract.

II. DEMARCATING THE SOCIAL CONTRACT

As Rother observes when he contrasts Beccaria's and Rousseau's contractarian deductions in respect of the death penalty, Rousseau's construction of political authority leaves no room for natural rights that could, as fundamental rights, set limits to the powers of the polity. For Rousseau, there are no pre-political but only political rights – all of which are extended, shaped and withdrawn, as the general will determines.[62] Moreover, similar to Hobbes, Rousseau views any violation of the criminal law as a violation of the social contract by which the violator catapults himself into a state of war with the polity.[63] As such, he loses all his rights and can, if necessary, be destroyed:

> Every criminal by attacking social rights becomes a rebel and a traitor to his country: by violating its laws he stops being a member of it – he even *makes war* on it. … He has broken the social treaty … so he is no longer a member of the state. … Such an enemy isn't a moral person … and in such a case the right of war is to kill the vanquished.[64]

It is against this extreme construction that Beccaria develops his version of a contractarian foundation of state authority. For Beccaria, the violation of the law does constitute a breach of the social contract – but, regardless of this, the contractor remains a juridical subject (a holder of rights) and a member of the polity. Beccaria's rejection of Rousseau's conception of crime as destroying the contractual bonds between the citizen and the polity entails that he is prepared to protect the 'guilty' citizen as much as the innocent citizen – the legal subject who is guilty of a crime as much as the legal subject who has not

[62] W Rother, *Von Casanova bis Vertrauen. Aspekte der italienischen Aufklärung* (Zürich, Conexus, 2019) 135–136.

[63] Hobbes' and Rousseau's deductions of the right to punish nevertheless differ quite substantially. For Hobbes, the right to punish is the original right to use force that, by the sovereign alone, is retained from the state of nature. For a recent discussion of Hobbes' theory that brings out the strangeness of this construction of the right to punish, see A Ristroph, 'The Imperfect Legitimacy of Punishment', in SA Lloyd (ed), *Hobbes Today* (Cambridge, Cambridge University Press, 2012) 190.

[64] J-J Rousseau, *The Social Contract* [1762] translated by J Bennett, revised 2017 edition (ebook, early modern texts online) 17, available at www.earlymoderntexts.com/assets/pdfs/rousseau1762.pdf.

committed a crime. The commission of a crime makes *a* difference – it makes the citizen liable to punishment – but it does not make *that* difference, the difference between being a citizen and a non-citizen. Crime does not place its perpetrator beyond the protection of the sovereign or outside the contract.[65]

This conclusion is linked to the de-essentialisation of crime that is one of the most modern and important features of Beccaria's thought. By de-essentialisation of crime, I mean three important facets of Beccaria's understanding of criminality. The first is that criminal behaviour is not deeply different from non-criminal behaviour. Quite the opposite: it is ordinary human behaviour that flows from ordinary human motivations and responds, with the same degree of rationality and emotionality as lawful behaviour does, to the circumstances in which the perpetrator finds himself and his perception of his own interests in that situation. As Beccaria puts it, crime flows from the 'despotic spirit of every man' by which he seeks his own advantage.[66] This also means, second, that the commission of a crime is just one act among countless other actions performed by the same person. While this act is problematic since it amounts to an 'usurpation' of the common repository of freedom by one 'seeking to extract from the repository … portions owing to others',[67] it is not a revelation of any deep-seated flaw within the perpetrator's character that sets his nature apart from that of others.[68] For this reason, third, to treat criminality as something approaching a permanent mark or status – a mode of thinking that lingers on, for instance, in Kant's phrasing of our rational commitment to live under laws that will 'naturally also be penal laws *if there are any criminals among the people*'[69] – makes no sense. For Beccaria, Kant's phrasing has no meaning because we are all potential criminals. Nothing new or additional is discovered or revealed 'about the person' when someone commits a crime.

It follows from this reconceptualisation of crime and criminality that criminal law is just one instrument (among others) of social policy and embedded in it. Punishment is an element of that policy instrument.[70] Crime itself – the

[65] Larrère, above n 16 at 97, traces this conception of crime to Montesquieu's depiction of the older, 'pagan' Germanic conception of crime, which was indistinguishable from the concept of a tort and concerned to react to the external dimension of injurious conduct.

[66] Beccaria, above n 4 at 9 (ch 1). In a different context (the differing frequency with which serious and minor crimes are committed) Beccaria remarks that 'The number of motives which impel men to overstep the natural feelings of pity is far fewer than the number of motives which impel them by their natural desire to be happy to violate a right which they do not find in their hearts but in social conventions.' Ibid at 77 (ch 30).

[67] Ibid.

[68] Beccaria's perspective on criminal motivation and behaviour, which spawned the so-called 'classical school' in criminology, is still robustly defended. See AN Carpenter, 'Beccaria, Cesare: Classical School' in FT Cullen & P Wilcox, *Encyclopedia of Criminological Theory* (Thousand Oaks CA, Sage, 2010) 74.

[69] Kant, above n 20 at 476 (emphasis added).

[70] Some of the implications of this shift are explored by Thorburn and by Chiao, in chs 7 and 8 of this volume respectively.

breach of a criminal law – loses its particular high moral valence as a wrong that sets its perpetrator apart from the community of the law-abiding, as an act by which he places himself outside the flock. Most crime, in this new perspective, is truly venial, based either on a false notion of the perpetrator of his own self-interest, or (more worryingly) is a response to external circumstances that could well have made him conclude that crime was in his interest.[71] This is what makes Beccaria's thinking so progressive. Having (as Roberts describes it) thought 'clearly and seriously about the rationality of motivation from the perspective of those most likely to be tempted into a life of crime',[72] he arrives at a conception of criminal behaviour that leaves no room for 'criminal man' set apart from the law-abiding members of the polity.[73] There is no basis, therefore, for excluding him from the polity, from the social contract into which we all enter as (occasionally mis-)calculating advantage-seekers with a tendency, as normal[74] as it is potentially dangerous, to engage in acts of 'unjust despotism against the social contract' (which is Beccaria's conception of crime).[75]

On this basis, Beccaria can turn Rousseau's argument from the state of war between delinquent and state on its head: it is not the delinquent who, by committing a crime, enters into a state of war with the polity, but the polity that declares a state of war with the delinquent when it seeks to punish him by death[76] (a sanction which, as we have seen, the polity cannot impose by right as the right to take a delinquent's life is not part of the 'public repository' of liberty vested in the sovereign).[77]

A successful defence of the limits Beccaria sets to penal authority ultimately depends on his conception of the social contract. But this conception has long puzzled his interpreters. His exposition of the social contract oscillates between the metaphorical and the concrete. Beccaria – unlike Kant – certainly does not appear to be taking the social contract merely as an 'idea of reason' but to treat it in some sense as a fact. But equally clearly its origins are presented in allegorical rather than historical-evidential fashion, and propositions of the arrangements it contains are arrived at through a process of reasoned argument rather than by

[71] Compare eg Beccaria's discussion of theft ('generally the crime of poverty and desperation, the crime of that unhappy section of men to whom the … right to property has allowed nothing but a bare existence' (Beccaria, above n 4 at 53 (ch 22)) and the defiant reasoning of the would-be 'thief or murderer' in the chapter on the death penalty (ibid at 69 (ch 28)).

[72] Roberts, ch 9 in this volume.

[73] For Beccaria, 'each individual … is always seeking to extract from the repository not only his own due but also the portions which are owing to others': Beccaria, above n 4 at 9 (ch 1).

[74] As Beccaria asks (ibid at 10 (ch 2)), if that option existed, would not 'each one of us … wish that the contracts which bind others did not bind us[?]'.

[75] Ibid at 53 (ch 22).

[76] Ibid at 66 (ch 28). For an incisive analysis of Beccaria's complete inversion of Rousseau's position, see D Ippolito, 'Contrat social et peine capitale: Beccaria contre Rousseau', in P Audegean, M Campanini & B Carnevali (eds), *Rousseau et L'Italie* (Paris, Hermann, 2017) 147 at 174.

[77] See Rother, above n 62 at 135–136; and Ippolito, above n 76 at 152–153.

consulting historical sources. And just as clearly, in Beccaria's theory the social contract functions as a source of normative commitments. What, then, 'is' the social contract for Beccaria, and whence does it acquire normative force? These are the questions we must answer in order to successfully defend his view.

To understand Beccaria's use of the social contract properly, it helps to take a step back and look at the philosophical social contract tradition more broadly.

In philosophical texts the term 'social contract' can be used to refer to two rather different notions (one of which is more easily associated with an actual historical moment or phenomenon than the other). That is to say, the notion of the social contract can be used to refer to a society-constituting or polity-forming moment or event – and, in that usage, the notion is clearly allegorical rather than historical, and put to work even by present-day social contract theorists to derive, and make plausible, some basic human commitments that living in organised society necessarily implies. (In the German literature, this is called the *Gesellschaftsvertrag*, the contract that founds the polity.) But the notion of a social contract may also be used to refer to the political arrangements under which a society is ruled or rules itself, its terms of governance. (In this meaning, the older German literature speaks of a *Herrschaftsvertrag* or contract of governance.)[78] It is clear, to the modern mind at least, that the latter notion is capable of application to actual historical events whereas the former is not. These two different meanings or applications of the concept were not, however, clearly distinguished by philosophers of the late Middle Ages who wrote in the Christian tradition – not least because (like early medieval polities before them) these philosophers derived their contractualism in large part from the Old Testament, in which they encountered what they took to be reports of God entering into various covenants with his chosen people, and while we would today tend to approach these biblical stories as allegories or myths, earlier generations took them to refer to actual events.[79]

[78] This terminology was developed by Otto von Gierke in his interpretation of earlier writers; see O von Gierke, *Johannes Althusius und die Entwicklung der naturrechtlichen Staatstheorien* (Aalen, Scientia, 1958) (reprint of the 5th edition 1929, first published 1880). Its usefulness for the interpretation of the philosophical writings of contractarian theorists is, however, sometimes doubted (eg by T Schölderle, 'Fehlperzeptionen der staatsphilosophischen Vertragstheorie' (2011) 58 *Zeitschrift für Politik* 51) and it has been suggested that it would be preferable to reorient historical scholarship around 'the concept of the languages of contractualism' (H Höpfl & MP Thompson, 'The History of Contract as a Motif in Political Thought' (1979) 84 *The American Historical Review* 919 at 944). I consider reliance on these concepts unproblematic so long as one bears in mind that not every writer's position will be illuminated by drawing on the distinction between the two 'ideal types' of contract Gierke identified.

[79] See JW Gough, *The Social Contract. A Critical Study of its Development* 2nd edition (Oxford, Clarendon Press, 1957) at 27–28 and 34. Gough relies here on Gierke's interpretation of the historical sources, which (as Höpfl & Thompson, above n 78, detail) is not uncontested. For a similar reconstruction of social-contractarian thinking that approaches the social contract as 'a living practice, an actual, morally-binding agreement among members of a political society', drawing on and reinterpreting some of Gough's sources, see M Davis, *Actual Social Contract and Political Obligation: A Philosopher's History Through Locke* (New York, Edwin Mellen Press, 2002) at v (emphasis omitted).

By the time Beccaria wrote, philosophers had mainly settled on a non-literal notion of the social contract – certainly for the purpose of explaining the terms on which political society was first founded or created. But when these philosophers moved into the territory of spelling out in greater detail the terms of political rule in their society, the older understanding of those terms as being subject to concrete, historical arrangements could easily creep back in. This was even less surprising because their reflections on the terms of governance in their political order were (at least to some extent) informed by the cultural memory of early medieval political practices of contracts of government – practices that, even after succession to the throne had become fully hereditary, still had an echo in the ceremonies surrounding the taking of office of new kings.[80]

This is the background against which Rousseau's and Beccaria's accounts of the social contract should be read. The distinction between the *Gesellschaftsvertrag* – the self-constitution of a political community – and the *Herrschaftsvertrag* – the assignment of the right to rule – can help us make sense of their theories. As Schottky explains (drawing on Gierke), Rousseau collapses this distinction through his absolutist democracy. Conceptually, if the people are the sovereign, a separate contract of government between the ruler and the ruled becomes an impossibility.[81] Moreover, the 'general will' is conceived of as being logically incapable of violating the true freedom of a citizen. This is so because the citizen's true freedom expresses itself in the general will, and 'when such a will is sovereign, the individual needs no rights *against* the state because his rights are fully contained *within* the sovereign's will'.[82]

Beccaria rejects this construction. His theory brings the notions of a *Gesellschaftsvertrag* and a *Herrschaftsvertrag* together as well, but in a different way. The two contracts become one because the sovereign ruler (the prince) is conceived of as the repository of the ceded freedoms; the sovereign is the 'legitimate repository and administrator of [the part of their] freedoms' sacrificed by the members of society 'in order to enjoy what remains in security and calm'.[83] In this inverse move from Rousseau, Beccaria arrives at a bounded polity precisely because he postulates a sovereign separate from the people. On this basis, Beccaria also resists the reification of law that follows from Rousseau's

[80] Moreover, that past was always readily to hand to be taken up in political agitation against what was perceived to be an unjust government, with rulers being accused of violating their terms of rule, releasing the rebels from any contractual ties and justifying them in disposing of the ruler if they could.

[81] In this paragraph I follow the explanation for Rousseau's position given by R Schottky, *Untersuchungen zur Geschichte der staatsphilosophischen Vertragstheorie im 17. und 18. Jahrhundert (Hobbes – Locke – Rousseau – Fichte)* (Amsterdam/Atlanta GA, Rodopi, 1995) 92–99.

[82] Ibid at 96 (my translation; emphasis original). As Gough, above n 79 at 173, remarks, '[Rousseau's] social contract is no guarantee of the individual's natural rights; it leads instead to the sovereignty of the general will' and 'the general will, while it springs from the people, is not necessarily a democratic idea at all'.

[83] Beccaria, above n 4 at 9 (ch 1).

position. In a few sparse words he brushes aside Rousseau's conception of the general will by insisting that this will is simply 'the aggregate of the individual wills'.[84] In this conception, the possibility that individuals retain rights *against* the state, and that the state's laws could violate these rights, is preserved.[85]

Attention to the historical social contract tradition helps us to resolve another difficulty with Beccaria's use of the social contract: how exactly the social contract can, in a text like Beccaria's, function as a source of normative commitments. As Gough has argued, the social contract tradition arises in part out of a political practice of elected kingship on negotiated terms of rule – a practice that, while not ubiquitous, was not infrequently followed in medieval Europe.[86] It was linked to political systems of fealty,[87] which in any event conceived of the relation between ruler and ruled as a bond created by mutual agreement, and on certain defined terms. Actual contracts of government were not unknown,[88] and while election of the ruler and negotiation of his terms of office were often matters for the few rather than the many, those few were in turn taken to represent larger political units.[89] Of course, as Gough points out,

> [t]he contractual principle, in terms of which these ninth-century Frankish kings occupied their thrones, was not … a social contract, explaining the formation of society; that was something more theoretical, which only appeared with the growth of philosophy. Nor was it an 'original' contract that took place once and for all in the past; it was, rather, a perfectly practical statement of actually existing conditions.[90]

He nevertheless concludes that '[a] contractual principle … was implicit in the political system of Carolingian times',[91] ready to be picked up by writers to be cast into a more theoretical form and to be used to build their theories of government upon it.

As pointed out above, the high level of abstraction and allegorical presentation of the constitution of sovereign power in the opening sentences of chapter 1 of his treatise notwithstanding, Beccaria at other points treats the contract more as – or at least as much as – fact than as fiction. Indeed, at one point in our project workshop the question was raised whether Beccaria might even be thinking of the social contract as an historical, datable event. If we recall the

[84] Ibid at 66 (ch 28).

[85] See Ippolito, above n 76 at 154–157 for Beccaria's position, and Schottky, above n 81 at 108–128 for the unresolved tensions in Rousseau's view.

[86] Gough, above n 79 at 25–28. See also Davis, above n 79 at 47–77.

[87] Gough, above n 79 at 33: feudalism as a form of government was essentially contractual.

[88] Gough mentions numerous examples dating from the 5th to the 9th centuries of documents putting the terms of a king's rule in writing; some of these even used the expression 'pactum' (ibid at 25–26 and 34).

[89] Ibid at 24–26.

[90] Ibid at 27.

[91] Ibid at 28. See further W Schlesinger, 'Karolingische Königswahlen', in W Berges & C Hinrichs (eds), *Zur Geschichte und Problematik der Demokratie. Festgabe für Hans Herzfeld anläßlich seines 65. Geburtstages* (Berlin, Duncker & Humblot, 1958) 207.

examples of actual contracts of government in early medieval times – examples with which Beccaria must have been familiar – this suggestion is not as implausible as it may seem. While clearly incompatible with Beccaria's *method*, it picks up something important about the *ethos* of his approach. He takes it to be the case that the relations of right and authority that constitute the sovereign powers he analyses already *are* in place, not merely that they *should be put* in place. In light of Beccaria's very clear distinction between what is the case and what should be the case, in respect of the content of the polity's laws,[92] this is significant. It shows us that Beccaria thinks of the business of government as underpinned by shared assumptions about good and appropriate government; assumptions that few people consciously bring to their minds or reflect upon, but that are nevertheless the real basis of the sovereign's authority. This is why, if the practices in question are such that, once brought to mind, the laws of the polity are found wanting – because they only advantage the powerful and fail to treat people as equals, and to respect their rights – further voluntary self-subjugation under these laws may be withheld.[93]

If I am right that the set of practices that underpin government by enlightened rulers is what Beccaria means by the social contract, then the social contract Beccaria refers to is not so much a purely theoretical device from which certain conclusions are drawn, but rather reflects what he understands to be an existing political convention. Such a convention can be 'excavated' and interpreted in the manner Beccaria employs in his treatise – by making explicit what is implicit in existing practice. Beccaria's repeated bows to the wisdom of the enlightened rulers of his age can detract us from the critical potential of this reconstruction of sovereign authority. As Sitze has highlighted:

> For Beccaria, the sovereign power is a repository that *minimizes* its own rights in order to *maximize* its ability to represent the personal right to self-preservation that authorizes it. For Beccaria, the sovereign therefore has a duty ... to diminish, as much as possible, its own sovereign rights ...[94]

In Beccaria's minimised and depersonalised[95] construction of the sovereign, the notion of public authority as something more abstract – and at the same time more limited – than a 'flesh and blood' ruler in whom certain powers are vested, emerges. Moreover, this public authority is bounded. It is bounded by principles that follow from the recognition of all men as equal – from according them

[92] This earned him Bentham's admiration and followership. See Hart, above n 38 and Zucca, ch 1 in this volume.

[93] Indeed, Beccaria makes his imaginary assassin consider a 'return to [his] natural state of independence' in which he may just form his own fiefdom and become 'King of a small band of men' who 'put[s] to rights the iniquities of fortune, and [sees] these tyrants blanch and cower at one whom they considered ... lower than their horses and dogs.' Beccaria, above n 4 at 69 (ch 28).

[94] Sitze, above n 12 at 231 (emphasis original).

[95] Ibid at 236. See also ibid at 235 (remarking that sovereign power is for Beccaria 'a warehouse for storing the deposit of public safety and security').

(as Ronald Dworkin would later put it[96]) equal concern and respect – and from the function of all government of ordering men's affairs, with the least encroachment upon their liberty, towards the greatest happiness of the greatest number. This is why Matravers (in chapter 2 in this volume) is right to stress that the substantive bases from which Beccaria generates the principles of legitimate government are his twin commitments to equality and utility. But, as I hope to have shown, this nevertheless leaves room for a particular understanding of the 'social contract' to do substantive work. The social contract is the framing within which Beccaria achieves the distinctive 'conjunction of penal policy and broader theory of government' on which Roberts (in chapter 9 in this volume) remarks. Through the notion of the 'social contract' Beccaria articulates, in the language of his time, a constitutionalised conception of the relations between the governing and the governed.

This analysis opens up another line of response to Primoratz's challenge against Beccaria's contractarian case against the death penalty.[97] If Beccaria's contractarian reasoning is best understood as leading us towards the discovery of constitutional commitments implicit in our understanding of the terms of our association, if – in other words – what it provides is an interpretation of the 'broader theory of government' underpinning that practice, then the situation in which some people cling to the wish that there should be the death penalty is just one of those occasions on which a sensible government should ignore such demands. This is so because they reflect nothing more than '[m]en's most superficial feelings [that] lead them to prefer cruel laws', when what is in fact 'in each man's interest [is] that they be moderate' given that they may find themselves 'subjected to [these laws]' and 'the fear of being injured is greater than the desire to injure'. It is rational to prefer security from cruelty over the satisfaction of one's superficial feelings that can generate a desire to punish others harshly.[98] Since this is what calm reflection shows, the government's duty is clear.

Beccaria's attempt to limit the state's penal power based on an argument about the non-consentability of certain forms of punishment is thus less vulnerable to philosophical objection than Kant's assertion to the contrary would lead one to suspect. This limit is channelled through a constitutional understanding of the constraints on governmental power. In practical-political terms, if a government is prepared to rip off my arm, tie me into a sack and throw me into a river, burn me with hot irons, strangle me, or whip me until I scream and bleed – always, of course, in the name of justice – then this is not a government whose protection is worth having. It is Beccaria's great achievement to have made this clear. Moreover, he has made clear not just that such outrages should

[96] See R Dworkin, *Taking Rights Seriously* (Cambridge MA, Harvard University Press, 1977) 180 (and elsewhere). I do not mean to endorse Dworkin's theory of rights here, merely to claim that the notion of treating people as equals as a principle of government can be unpacked in this way.

[97] See text at nn 59–61 above.

[98] Beccaria, above n 4 at 89 (ch 34).

not be suffered by anyone subject to law, but that anyone could, indeed, be made to suffer the violence of the law, including you or me.

III. CONCLUSION

Beccaria was able to reconcile inalienable human rights with a contractualist foundation of political authority by construing 'the part of their freedom [that men] sacrifice in order to enjoy what remains in security and calm'[99] as minimal: no one is assumed to have 'surrender[ed] to the public repository more than the smallest possible portion consistent with persuading others to defend him', and it is '[t]he sum of these smallest possible portions [that] constitutes the right to punish'.[100] One of the consequences Beccaria explicitly derives from this is that 'the extreme severity of some punishments, even if not directly contrary to the public good and the aim of discouraging crimes [but] merely useless … [is] contrary to … the very nature of the social contract'.[101]

Beccaria's contractualism should be interpreted as a form of constitutionalism. It helps to specify the basic principles of collective political life. Membership in a polity is unavoidable; yet that unavoidability does not mean (as it did for Hobbes) that no effective limits to the exercise of political authority can be set. To the contrary: the inescapability, for humans, of living in a political condition, does not only not prevent but positively calls for the working out of principles that make such an order a valuable and sustainable one. This is what Beccaria does, and why it comes naturally to him to see the potential and the actual lawbreaker as still included in this order, and subject to law and law-enforcement only within the framework of fundamental rights that alone ensures that politics serves the interest of every citizen, of all those subject to (and subjects of) a particular political unit. The contractual model is, for him, not a theory of criminal law enforcement. His contractualism serves to formulate limitations that apply at the level of legislative policy (such as limitations on the kinds of punishments that potential and actual lawbreakers may be faced with). Against the absolutism of Rousseau, it is important to assert that one cannot have defensible government without (to use another one of Dworkin's memorable phrases) 'rights as trumps'.[102] What in the introduction to this book is referred to as Beccaria's 'minimalist social contract' is the only position in the philosophy of punishment that can generate rights-based limitations that protect the delinquent citizen.

[99] Ibid at 9 (ch 1).

[100] Ibid at 11 (ch 2).

[101] Ibid at 13 (ch 3).

[102] Dworkin, above n 96 at ix. Again, I do not mean to endorse Dworkin's particular conception of constitutional rights but use the expression to capture Beccaria's aspiration for government to, as Sitze (cited at n 94 above) put it, 'maximize its ability to represent the personal right to self-preservation that authorizes it' by 'diminish[ing] … its … sovereign rights'.

5

Beccaria, Treason and the Social Contract

ANAT SCOLNICOV*

WHAT IS THE constitutional relationship between the citizen and the state envisaged by the criminal law? For Cesare Beccaria, the social contract was the basic justification for the criminal law. As the ultimate breach of the social contract, treason was therefore the crime of the highest order. This chapter asks whether a social contract theory of the state is indeed capable of justifying this offence and, as a consequence of this enquiry, whether this theory is capable of justifying the imposition of the criminal law by the state.

Section I of this chapter shows that social contract theory forms the basis of Beccaria's account of the criminal law. Section II questions whether this theory can, in fact, justify the imposition of the criminal law by the state. In section III the offence of treason is then utilised to test the conclusion reached, by examining (i) the consequences of the government's breaching the social contract, and (ii) the law and practice of extradition for this offence. Finally, section IV examines the relationship between a social contract theory of criminal law and a community principle of criminalisation in the context of treason, and considers whether the offence can be justified by this principle.

I. BECCARIA'S BASIS FOR CRIMINALISATION – UTILITARIANISM OR SOCIAL CONTRACT?

Beccaria has exerted immense influence on the development of penal theory since the eighteenth century, by virtue of one concise treatise.[1] His thought has

* This chapter was completed during the author's fellowship at the Israel Institute of Advanced Studies. My thanks to Antony Duff and Francois du Bois for reading and commenting on this chapter.

[1] C Beccaria, *On Crimes and Punishments and Other Writings* edited by R Bellamy and translated by R Davies (Cambridge, Cambridge University Press, 1995).

left its mark not only on European reformers of his day and the American founding fathers, but also on those engaged today in the development and application of the criminal law. A testament to this continuing influence is his recent citation by the Supreme Court of Israel in deciding a current question of criminal law doctrine.[2] This continued relevance to contemporary criminal law makes it particularly worthwhile to examine the underpinning theory of criminalisation that he offers.[3]

In *On Crimes and Punishments*, Beccaria relies on two theoretical justifications for the criminal law: social contract and utility. In different parts of this short monograph he seems to switch back and forth between the two. On the social contract, he states that 'the laws, for all that they are or should be contracts amongst free men, have rarely been anything but the tools of the passions of a few men'.[4] And that

> [l]aws are the terms under which independent and isolated men come together in society. Wearied by living in an unending state of war and by a freedom rendered useless by the uncertainty of retaining it, they sacrifice a part of that freedom in order to enjoy what remains in security and calm.[5]

The utilitarian strand in his thinking is evident from the following:

> Here, then, is the foundation of the sovereign's right to punish crimes: the necessity of defending the repository of the public well-being from the usurpations of individuals.[6]

So, what is, for Beccaria, the relation between these justifications? Is the basis for the imposition of criminal prohibitions the social contract, with considerations of utility serving to limit these prohibitions? Or conversely, is he offering a utilitarian theory qualified by the social contract, as he is read by HLA Hart?[7] Or do the two perhaps stand in some other relationship with each other?

As I read him, it is the social contract that for Beccaria is the basis for justifying the state's imposition of the criminal law, while the content of this social contract is discovered by way of a utilitarian test. Any criminal punishment meted out by the state in excess of the utilitarian measure must necessarily

[2] *Tubul v State of Israel* CrA 6201/18, explaining the need to differentiate in the assignment of criminal responsibility between bankrupt debtors who have committed fraud and those who have not.

[3] For a recent exploration of Beccaria's historical significance, see P Audegean & L Delia (eds), *Le moment Beccaria: naissance du droit pénal modern (1764–1810)* (Liverpool, Liverpool University Press, 2018).

[4] Beccaria, above n 1 at 7 ('Introduction').

[5] Ibid at 9 (ch 1).

[6] Ibid at 10 (ch 2).

[7] HLA Hart, 'Bentham and Beccaria', in his *Essays on Bentham: Jurisprudence and Political Philosophy* (Oxford, Oxford University Press, 1982) 40.

exceed what would have been agreed to in the social contract and would for that reason lack justification. As he posits:

> [I]t is therefore certain that none wished to surrender to the public repository more than the smallest possible portion consistent with persuading others to defend him. The sum of these smallest possible portions constitutes the right to punish; everything more than that is no longer justice, but an abuse …[8]

The formulation of the principle of utility by Beccaria is crucially different from Bentham's. Rather than 'the greatest happiness of the greatest number',[9] it is 'the greatest happiness shared by the greater number'.[10] The term 'shared' should be unpacked. Shared how? The 'greatest happiness' and 'by the greater number' are just that, numbers. But 'shared' must necessarily imply some judgement as to the relation between the two. It could be construed as the maximal aggregate sum of happiness, shared by as many as possible without diminishing the total. Or utility could be determined by the formula given by Beccaria's fellow pugilist, Pietro Verri: 'the greatest possible happiness distributed with the greatest equality possible'.[11] In making this determination about the calculation of utility, a non-utilitarian, deontological consideration must necessarily be taken into account.

So, Beccaria's formula cannot be reduced to mere utility. But he does not quite elucidate what that additional deontological criterion is, only going so far as to explain that 'the word "right" is not opposed to the word "power", but the former is rather a modification of the latter, that is to say, the species which is of the greatest utility to the greatest number'.[12]

Utility is constitutive of his social contract, and therefore of Beccaria's justification for the imposition of criminal law by the state. This raises a host of problems. One problem with utility as a basis for the criminal law is that utility is determined through an empirical calculation. One day the calculation of utility might point in the direction of criminalisation or heavier punishment of a particular type of act, and the next day it might not. For instance, in a certain year, home burglaries might be prevalent and a serious cause of public insecurity. The next month the economy might be stronger and burglaries much less frequent. Should the punishment for the same act be different in these two periods?[13]

[8] Beccaria, above n 1 at 11 (ch 2).

[9] J Bentham, *The Collected Works of Jeremy Bentham: A Comment on the Commentaries and a Fragment on Government* edited by JH Burns & HLA Hart (Athlone Press, London, 1977) 393.

[10] Beccaria, above n 1 at 7 ('Introduction'). On the mistranslation of Beccaria's phrase, as 'greatest happiness of the greatest number', and its later development and elaboration by Bentham, see R Bellamy, 'Introduction', ibid ix at xviii–xix.

[11] P Verri, *Reflections on Happiness* [1763], quoted in Bellamy, ibid at xiv.

[12] Beccaria, above n 1 at 11 (ch 2).

[13] See also BE Harcourt, 'Beccaria's On Crimes and Punishments: A Mirror on the History of the Foundations of Modern Criminal Law', in MD Dubber (ed), *Foundational Texts in Modern Criminal Law* (Oxford, Oxford University Press, 2014) 39.

Equally, burglaries might be a widespread problem in one area but not another area in the same jurisdiction. A utilitarian analysis would lead us to conclude that a higher penalty should be given for burglary in the first area. But that would be unjust. A criminal law system that demands individual responsibility cannot mete out punishment based on factors beyond the individual's control. This is a second problem with utilitarianism, specifically with its employment as a basis for the criminal law. It does not account for individual culpability, nor does it consider individual rights, which are necessarily encroached upon by punishment. Utilitarianism was Beccaria's tool for offering an alternative to the criminal law of his day, which was rooted in religious morality. His theory achieves this goal, but at the cost of these conceptual weaknesses.

II. CAN THE SOCIAL CONTRACT JUSTIFY THE CRIMINAL LAW?

A social contract theory of the state does not in itself establish that it should be criminal law that enforces the social contract.[14] A social contract could be upheld by a variety of legal and political methods, either of a civil law type (employing contractual or quasi-contractual remedies) or public law regulation. We might ask why a mechanism for the enforcement of a social contract should not be of a contractual nature, rather than take the form of criminal law? Although the 'social contract' is clearly intended as a metaphor and should not be taken literally as a contract, nothing in the idea of a social contract mandates that it be upheld by penal sanctions, or even by the central government rather than by peers.[15] A social contract theory of the criminal law has found proponents in modern times, but it is still woefully under-theorised.[16]

To try to elicit a justification for state imposition of criminal law from the social contract, we must look first to its original statement by Thomas Hobbes. Hobbes finds the 'Originall of Justice' in his third law, that 'men performe their Covenants made'.[17] But this, *pacta sunt servanda*, is a rationale that can justify a system of contract law, not criminal law. It is not the just or unjust content of the agreement but rather the agreement itself that here provides the moral basis of the system of justice. That seems a poor justification for a system of criminal law.[18] The infliction of pain and physical constraints requires a justification that goes beyond the upholding of the contract.

[14] Further, M Matravers, 'Political Theory and the Criminal Law', in RA Duff & S Green, *Philosophical Foundations of the Criminal Law* (Oxford, Oxford University Press, 2011) 67.

[15] An actual system of social enforcement of (a precursor to) criminal law can be found in the Saxon frankpledge system, in which members of each tithing were responsible for enforcing the law on each other or bearing responsibility for the breach themselves. See LR Poos, 'The Rural Population of Essex in the Later Middle Ages' (1985) 38 *Economic History Review* 515 at 518.

[16] See Matravers, above n 14.

[17] T Hobbes, *Leviathan* edited by Richard Tuck (Cambridge, Cambridge University Press, 1996) ch 15.

[18] D Gauthier, *Moral Dealing: Contract, Ethics and Reason* (Ithaca NY, Cornell University Press, 1990) 135–136.

Gauthier, in critiquing Hobbes' logic of the third law, might have inadvertently given a better rationale for criminal enforcement of the social contract. Hobbes, explains Gauthier, points out a prisoner's dilemma.[19] It is advantageous for each person to enlarge his liberty at the expense of others. But, at the same time, it is in everyone's interest to have peace. If each enlarges his liberty with disregard to others' liberty, we shall have war. Therefore, it is in each person's interest to have a social agreement, and rational for each to perform it so it is mutually upheld.

But, says Gauthier, Hobbes *does not* explain why it would not be rational for a self-interested individual to breach the contract while everyone else obeys it. It is enough that others expect him to obey it; so long as they do so, he may disobey while benefiting from others' observance of the contract. This flaw in the contractarian enforcement of the social contract provides a good reason for adding a different, external type of enforcement, one that is not susceptible to the prisoner's dilemma. It could therefore justify centralised enforcement through the criminal law.[20] But while this thought provides a basis for a centralised enforcement system, such as a criminal justice system, it still offers no justification for such enforcement beyond the bare fact that the agreement was broken. As I have pointed out above, this in itself is too thin a foundation on which to build the sanctioning regime of criminal law.

The Kantian conception of the social contract offers a better basis for a social contract justification of the criminal law than the Hobbesian one, but I get to that later.

III. WHY THE OFFENCE OF TREASON IS A TEST CASE FOR THE SOCIAL CONTRACT JUSTIFICATION

Whilst a justifying theory of the criminal law need not explain every aspect of every offence, if a major offence stands in stark contrast to the explanatory rationale offered by the theory, the inevitable conclusion is that the theory is not sufficient to justify the criminal law.

The difficulties with a social contract justification for the criminal law come into sharp relief when examining the offence of treason.[21]

Beccaria regards treason as a crime of the highest order, indeed the only crime of this category: '[T]he greatest crimes, because the most damaging, are those which are called lèse-majesté or sedition.'[22] This is because '[e]very crime,

[19] Ibid at 17.

[20] Gauthier himself argues that self-interested individuals would rationally come to agree on a moral code (D Gauthier, *Morals by Agreement* (Oxford, Clarendon Press, 1986)).

[21] For my analysis of flaws of other criminal law theories in justifying the treason offence in the liberal state, see A Scolnicov, 'Against the State', in A du Bois-Pedain, M Ulväng & P Asp (eds), *Criminal Law and the Authority of the State* (Oxford, Hart Publishing, 2017) 133.

[22] Beccaria, above n 1 at 25 (ch 8).

even a private one, offends against society, but not all aim at its immediate destruction'.[23] This accords with Beccaria's perhaps pragmatic political stance[24] that harm to monarchs, as representatives of society, is equivalent to harm to society as a whole. Of course, this is not an accurate equivalency, as was evident even to some of Beccaria's predecessors and contemporaries,[25] and as certainly is obvious to any liberal and democratic thinker today.

Beccaria's position on the elevated position of *lèse-majesté* within the criminal law should be viewed in the context of the breadth of the offence in his time, which included such slights as defamation of the king.[26] In somewhat opaque remarks, Beccaria observes that the offence should not include these trivial actions:

> Only tyranny and ignorance, which can confuse even the clearest of words and ideas, could apply this term – and a correspondingly severe punishment – to crimes of a different nature, thus making men the victims of a word, as on countless other occasions.[27]

This qualification only serves to underscore the centrality of the core offence of treason to Beccaria's perception of the criminal law.

Two questions should be examined in an attempt to decipher the social contract justification of the treason offence: (i) breach by government, and (ii) extradition to other states.

A. Rights and Duties when the Government Breaches the Social Contract

A challenge for the social contract justification of the criminal law is that it gives no answer to the question: What should happen if the government breaches the contract, oversteps its powers and abuses citizens' rights?[28]

[23] Ibid.

[24] After all, he was widely read in the courts of European rulers such as Catherine II of Russia, who unsuccessfully tried to invite him to Russia. He himself was an official in the administration of Lombardy, and his work provided inspiration for the drafting of European criminal codes, including the first French Penal Code of 1791. See further, T Cizova, 'Beccaria in Russia' (1962) 40 *The Slavonic and East European Review* 384.

[25] Such as Locke, as will be discussed in section III.A.

[26] See further, A Kelly, 'From Lèse-Majesté to Lèse-Nation: Treason in Eighteenth-Century France' (1981) 42
Journal of the History of Ideas 269. That is still the law on the books, though not enforced, in some European states, and is vigorously enforced law elsewhere (such as in Thailand, see S Baber, 'Shout for Freedom to Curse at the Kingdom: Contrasting Thai Lèse Majesté Law with United States First Amendment Freedoms' (2014) 24 *Indiana International and Comparative Law Review* 693).

[27] Beccaria above n 1 at 25 (ch 8).

[28] Assuming the government is a party to the social contract, as it is in some versions of the social contract, such as John Locke's (in his *The Second Treatise of Civil Government* [1689] edited by CB Macpherson (Indianapolis IN, Hackett Publishing, 1980) sec 122 (ch VIII) and ch XIII), but the analysis applies equally to versions of the social contract such as Hobbes', in which the government is an arbiter and enforcer of the contract between citizens and causes the breach of the contract (see further the text accompanying n 38).

Although this question has general applicability and does not necessarily relate to a specific offence, it is brought into sharp relief when a citizen is charged with treason. The question whether the government should be able to rely on the social contract when it has itself breached the very same contract becomes of urgent relevance when the government levels an accusation of treason against a citizen who claims that he or she was acting against despotic actions by the government.[29]

The existence of an obligation under the social contract does not mean that this contractual obligation should not be balanced against other moral obligations that might outweigh it, such as an obligation towards one's fellow citizens whose rights are being infringed by government. According to John Locke, citizens indeed have the right to resist despotic government (even a constitutionally elected one).[30]

There are some antecedents in Western thought to Locke's right to resist.[31] Locke has also had a clear practical influence. The right to resist an unconstitutional government was a major concern of the American founding fathers, and found its place in the text of the Declaration of Independence.[32] In this respect they departed from Beccaria's teachings, which influenced them in other ways.[33]

The question remains: How can the government be justified in prosecuting a citizen for breaching the social contract when it is the citizen's contention that the government is the one who has breached the social contract? And, if we were to accept that the government cannot be permitted to determine the validity of its own actions, the question is flipped: May the citizen who makes this contention, the defendant in a treason trial, decide his own case against the government?

Immanuel Kant's answer to this conundrum was that citizens cannot be the final arbiters who determine which is the overriding obligation, and therefore should not be able to challenge the government on this point.[34] Although

[29] For example, in the 2016 failed coup d'état in Turkey.

[30] Locke, above n 28 ch XVIII. M Seliger, *The Liberal Politics of John Locke* (Abingdon, Routledge, 2019) points out that Locke did not uphold a distinction between the right to resist external conquest and the right to resist internal subjugation of liberty.

[31] Harking back, amongst others, to Thomas Aquinas, *Summa Theologiae* [1485]: see TA Fay, 'Thomas Aquinas on the Justification of Revolution' (1993) 16 *History of European Ideas* 501. Locke's view had more immediate predecessors, such as George Lawson in his *Politica Sacra et Civilis* [1660]. The right to revolt against an unjust ruler is not only a product of Western thought. The Chinese philosopher Mencius advocated such a right some 2,000 years before Locke. See further T Ginsburg, D Lansberg-Rodriguez & M Versteeg, 'When to Overthrow your Government: The Right to Resist in the World's Constitutions' (2013) 60 *UCLA Law Review* 1184. In Mencius' thought this was connected to the ruler's duty to govern through benevolence: see S Kim, 'Mencius on International Relations and the Morality of War: From the Perspective of Confucian Moralpolitik' (2010) 31 *History of Political Thought* 33.

[32] United States Declaration of Independence (1776), Preamble.

[33] See J Bessler, 'The Marquis Beccaria: An Italian Penal Reformer's Meteoric Rise in the British Isles in the Transatlantic Republic of Letters' (2019) 4 *Diciottesimo Secolo* 107.

[34] I Kant, 'On the Relationship of Theory to Practice in Political Right', in *Kant: Political Writings* 2nd edition edited by HS Reiss and translated by HB Nisbett (Cambridge, Cambridge University

famously a supporter of the French Revolution, Kant in his writings did not support the right of sedition or rebellion.[35] Such was his commitment to the absolute right of government to be the final arbiter of the legitimacy of its own actions that, once a revolution had taken place, no one, including the previous legitimate government, had a right to disobey the new government or to rebel against it.[36]

Hobbes too was opposed to a right to revolt.[37] His conception of the social contract was of one that all rational self-interested actors would accept, in contrast with Kant's conception of the social contract as a moral code (a contrast I explore further in section III.B.ii). If one adopts a rational self-interest view of the social contract then, even if the government breaches the social contract, and certainly if a citizen merely *claims* the government has done so, the interest of other citizens requires that the contract remains intact.[38] Simply put, rational self-interested actors would prefer a final ruler-arbiter, even an unjust one, to the 'mutually assured destruction' in the absence of a final arbiter.

But, as Hampton has shown,[39] Hobbes' own argument leads to a contradictory conclusion. Self-interested actors would want a ruler who is a final decider, including of his own powers. But they would only rationally want this for as long as they collectively see the ruler's decision as still being in their self-interest. So the right to disobey a government (and for Hobbes a right is always the result of what is rational) would exist even under Hobbes' assumptions.

But could there be not just a Lockean right to revolt against the government in certain situations, but even a duty to do so? The American revolutionaries, who owed much to Beccaria in other respects,[40] departed from him on this point as well and sought justification elsewhere for their actions. For instance, they found support in the theoretical writings of Jonathan Mayhew, who believed resisting tyranny was a Christian duty and that the people were the proper judges of civil

Press, 1991) 82. See further LW Beck, 'Kant and the Right of Revolution' (1971) 32 *Journal of the History of Ideas* 411.

[35] I Kant, *The Metaphysics of Morals*, Part I: *The Metaphysical Elements of Justice* translated by J Ladd (Indianapolis IN, Bobbs-Merrill, 1965) 86. For an argument that there is no inconsistency in Kant's thought between his stance on revolt and both his commitment to pre-civil individual rights and his support for the French revolution, see K Flikschuh, 'Reason, Right, and Revolution: Kant and Locke' (2008) 36 *Philosophy and Public Affairs* 375.

[36] Kant, above n 35 at 89. See further S Axinn, 'Kant, Authority, and the French Revolution' (1971) 32 *Journal of the History of Ideas* 423.

[37] As can be seen in his discussion of the English Civil War in *Behemoth* [1668], in T Hobbes, *The English Works of Thomas Hobbes* edited by W Molesworth (London, John Bohn, 1840) vol VI.

[38] Hobbes himself saw the social contract as a covenant between citizens, with the government as enforcer and not a party (*Leviathan* [1651], ibid vol III ch XVIII).

[39] J Hampton, *Hobbes and the Social Contract Tradition* (Cambridge, Cambridge University Press, 1986).

[40] Regarding punishment and the death penalty but also freedom of speech, see J Bessler, *The Birth of American Law: An Italian Philosopher and the American Revolution* (Durham NC, Carolina Academic Press, 2014).

authority.[41] The role Christianity plays in this revolutionary political thought is interesting. Beccaria sought a normative system *not* founded on a divine source, in order to secure greater autonomy for the individual. But when it came to the right to revolt, the American revolutionaries conversely found their source for the protection of autonomy against a despotic leader in a religious text. So, although liberals such as Locke showed that there existed justification for a right to revolt in liberal thought, in the case of the American revolution, religious texts, perhaps ironically, proved a sturdier source of this right than the writings of a liberal reformer such as Beccaria.

The legal outcome of the Kantian approach (that government is the final arbiter of its own actions) is one that both Voltaire[42] and Blackstone[43] highlighted as creating an absurd legal situation. It is impossible for a citizen to know whether his or her actions are treasonous until *ex post facto*. Loyalty to a winning usurper is not a crime. Loyalty to a losing pretender is.[44]

Beccaria does not acknowledge either the existence of the problem or the solution, but Voltaire does so in his commentary on Beccaria's *On Crimes and Punishments*. Interestingly, although Voltaire in this commentary strongly champions Beccaria's views, he differs from him on this point. Voltaire differentiates natural laws from political laws.[45] Natural laws, he explains, include offences like murder, theft and offences of violence. The examples he gives of political laws are descriptions of historical uses of treason in which someone's guilt was ultimately determined by whether he supported the victorious of two contending rulers.[46] This point, that treason can only be determined *ex post*

[41] J Mayhew, 'Discourse concerning Unlimited Submission and Non-Resistance to the Higher Powers' [1750] available at digitalcommons.unl.edu/cgi/viewcontent.cgi?article=1044&context=etas. See further, F Valenzuela, 'Liberalism's Illiberal Obligation: The American Revolutionaries and the Duty to Revolt' APSA 2009 Toronto Meeting Paper (2009) available at ssrn.com/abstract=1451974.

[42] F Voltaire, 'A Commentary on the Book of "Crimes and Punishments" ch XIV', in C Beccaria, *An Essay on Crimes and Punishments with a Commentary by M. de Voltaire* A New Edition Corrected (Albany NY, WC Little & Co, 1872) 204.

[43] W Blackstone, *Commentaries on the Laws of England*, bk IV: *Public Wrongs* (Oxford, Clarendon Press, 1765–1769) ch 6 ('On High Treason'). See further discussion in Scolnicov, above n 21.

[44] Treason is always in the eye of the *de facto* sovereign: Charles I was convicted of treason after the English Civil War, as he was deemed to have acted to further his personal interests rather than those of England.

[45] Voltaire, above n 42.

[46] Ibid at 204:

> 'Or, two ambitious princes contend for a crown: the strongest gains the prize, and punishes with death the partizans of the weaker. The judges become the instruments of vengeance of the new sovereign, and the supports of his authority.
>
> When Richard the Third, the murderer of his two nephews, was acknowledged king of England, the jury found Sir William Collinburn guilty of having written to a friend of the Duke of Richmond, who was at that time raising an army, and who afterwards reigned by the name of Henry VII. They found two ridiculous lines of Sir William's writing, which were sufficient to condemn him to a horrible death. History abounds with such examples of justice.'

facto, is also made by William Blackstone[47] in his discussion of treason, the first statutory offence in England.[48]

For Blackstone, the relative rather than absolute nature of the legality of the actions of the monarch can also be gleaned from his interpretation of the maxim 'the King can do no wrong'. Blackstone regards this as meaning that the King's actions must always be interpreted, by those who want to act upon them, in a way that will not be in breach of the law and that is not injurious to his subjects. This is the meaning of the maxim, rather than its often assumed meaning that anything the King does cannot be deemed unlawful.[49]

That Voltaire in his commentary differentiates between the terms 'natural law' and 'political law'[50] is significant because it signals a shift in the theoretical basis of the criminal law, from Beccaria's contractualism to moralism. (Although Beccaria's use of the term 'natural laws' to describe laws that have a normative non-political basis also hints at a moralist aspect in *his* theory of criminal law.) One of Beccaria's important steps was to divorce the criminal law from moralism and place it on a utilitarian/social contract basis. Voltaire, even prior to commenting on Beccaria, argued for divorcing the criminal law from religious dictates. In endorsing Beccaria, Voltaire also grounded this in a broader utilitarian theory of punishment.[51] But when discussing treason,[52] Voltaire indicates that in his view legitimate criminal laws have a natural law/moral basis,[53] as distinct from illegitimate political laws based on the vagaries of political power.

B. Extradition and the Social Contract

A second difficulty with a social contract account of the criminal law is that it does not provide an adequate theoretical explanation of the normative basis

[47] Blackstone, above n 43.

[48] The Treason Act 1351. See further, Scolnicov, above n 21. Blackstone was familiar with Beccaria's writings (J Innis, 'Book Review: *Le moment Beccaria: Naissance du droit penal moderne (1764–1810), ed Philippe Audegean and Luigi Delia (Liverpool: Liverpool UP, 2018)*' (2020) 135 *The English Historical Review* 495). For the manipulation of treason by successive rulers, see M Cornwall, 'Treason in an Era of Regime Change: The Case of the Habsburg Monarchy' (2019) 50 *Austrian History Yearbook* 124.

[49] Blackstone, above n 43 bk 1 ch 7.

[50] Voltaire, above n 42 at 203–204.

[51] Voltaire, above n 42 ch XII. See E Groffier, 'Voltaire vulgarisateur de Beccaria' in Audegean & Delia (eds), above n 3, 15 at 17.

[52] Voltaire, above n 42 chs XIV and XV.

[53] See further on Voltaire's idea of natural law, the entry 'natural law' in his *Philosophical Dictionary* [1764] translated by T Besterman revised edition (London, Penguin Classics, 1979). Voltaire, too, divorces natural law from the teachings of any specific religion, finding it common even to the 'wretched Jews'. For him every man has it within himself, if he cares not to forget it, harking back to both Plato (in the *Gorgias*, 484 and the *Laws*, 793B) and Aristotle (*Nichomachean Ethics* V.17): see JD Wild, *Plato's Modern Enemies and the Theory of Natural Law* (Chicago IL, University of Chicago Press, 1953) 136.

for extradition, most notably in relation to the offence of treason (and similar offences that fall under the 'political offence' exception, such as sedition and rebellion, as discussed in section III.B.i). Extradition is a vital component of the criminal law. It is common to all modern criminal law systems, although regulated in somewhat different ways.[54] A theory of the criminal law should therefore be able to explain those aspects of the law of extradition common to states, and accepted in international criminal law, even if it does not have to account for the specific characteristics of each state's extradition laws.

Beccaria himself mentions extradition only very briefly in his discussion of asylum,[55] appearing to support universal extradition, though only in a world with no tyranny, not in the current state of the world in his time.

i. Political Offence Exception to Extradition for Treason

Historically, states extradited persons suspected of treason. Indeed, initially extraditions were requested precisely for such crimes, which were of primary concern to rulers, rather than for more common criminal offences.[56] However, since the nineteenth century state practice in international law has included a 'political offence exception',[57] meaning that states can lawfully exempt themselves from extraditing suspects for political offences. States commonly make such exceptions to extradition in their domestic law, and generally do not extradite for such offences. This political offence exception certainly covers the offences of treason, rebellion and sedition.[58]

But what, if any, is the normative basis for this behaviour by states, sanctioned by their respective domestic criminal laws and by international law? Can this state practice be explained and justified by social contract theory? This, too, is a pivotal question for any social contract explanation of the criminal law. If social contract theory cannot explain the state practice of extradition for treason, then either the social contract is an inadequate theoretical justification of the criminal law or the treason offence lies outside the spectrum of offences that can be justified by the criminal law.[59]

[54] For a general discussion of current extradition law, see G Gilbert, *Transnational Fugitive Offenders in International Law: Extradition and Other Mechanisms* (London, Routledge, 1998).

[55] Beccaria, above n 1 ch 35.

[56] See W Magnuson, 'The Domestic Politics of International Extradition' (2012) 52 *Virginia. Journal of International Law* 839.

[57] V DeFabo, 'Terrorist or Revolutionary: The Development of the Political Offender Exception and its Effects on Defining Terrorism in International Law' (2012) 2 *National Security Law Brief* 69 at 70. On the political offence exception since the 1830s, see J Jansson, *Terrorism, Criminal Law and Politics: The Decline of the Political Offence Exception to Extradition* (Abingdon, Routledge, 2020) ch 3.

[58] M Littenberg, 'The Political Offence Exception: An Historical Analysis and Model for the Future' (1990) 64 *Tulane Law Review* 1196.

[59] Cherif Bassiouni, the major international law scholar writing on extradition in the last century, attempted to offer a conceptual framework that both encompassed an international rule of law and

ii. Two Conceptions of the Social Contract

Here we must consider two different accounts of the social contract. In this analysis I rely on the classification offered by Matravers.[60]

One is the conception of Beccaria and Hobbes,[61] that the social contract is a mutual agreement of self-interested individuals. Beccaria, for example, explains:

> No man has made a gift of part of his freedom with the common good in mind; that kind of fantasy exists only in novels. If it were possible, each one of us would wish that the contracts which bind others did not bind us.[62]

This emphasis on the covenant as the one thing preventing humanity from descending into chaos also explains why Hobbes (and implicitly Beccaria) is opposed to a right to depart from this contract, even when it was the government that first diverged from the terms of the covenant. Under this conception it is simply too dangerous to allow individuals to determine whether the contract has been breached, as the uncertainty created thereby would see society descend into anarchy, which is seen as far more perilous than a (possible) breach by the government.

In this conception of the social contract, every sovereign state is constituted by a separate local contract. If this is the conception of the social contract, then any state requesting extradition has just as much justification to enforce *its* contract through use of the criminal law as the potential extraditing state has. Every state should accordingly extradite to every other state (according to the existing extradition treaties), regardless of the requesting state's regime and constitutional values. This conception of the social contract therefore cannot explain a political offence exception. If a state claims justification for its criminal law in the maintenance of its own social contract, it has no reason to deny another state assistance in enforcing *its* social contract.

The second account of the social contract is that of Kant (and subsequently Rawls).[63] Here the contract is a mutual agreement to comply with a moral code of fundamental constitutional principles. It is the moral code that rational people would have arrived at through the use of reason.[64] Since this moral code contains some fundamental constitutional principles, the Kantian concept of the social contract provides a reason for states to refuse extradition when it is not clear that it is the accused, rather than the requesting state, who is in breach of these fundamental principles.

took account of national interest. See MC Bassiouni, 'Ideologically Motivated Offenses and the Political Offenses Exception in Extradition – A Proposed Juridical Standard for an Unruly Problem' (1969) 19 *DePaul Law Review* 217 at 222–223.

[60] On the two accounts of the social contract, see Matravers, above n 17.

[61] Hobbes, above n 17, and in modern scholarship by Gauthier, above n 20 ch 6.

[62] Beccaria, above n 1 at 10.

[63] J Rawls, *A Theory of Justice* revised edition (Oxford University Press, Oxford, 1999) 10.

[64] Kant, above n 34 at 83.

Duff and Marshall suggest that one reading of Beccaria is that

> the contract that binds Turkish citizens together is surely as valuable, as worthy of being upheld, as that which binds French citizens together; it would be odd, indeed outrageous, for a legislature to declare that a breach of the French social contract is a criminalisable wrong, but that a violation in Istanbul of the Turkish social contract is not a wrong ...[65]

That is indeed the likely conclusion from Beccaria's approach to the social contract. But under an approach that views the social contract as a mutually enforceable moral code, it is not at all outrageous for one state to think that a breach of the criminal laws of another state in that state is not in fact a wrong.[66] Instead, this becomes a question of whether the particular offence the other state seeks to enforce, in the particular circumstances of its enforcement, accords with the moral code that underpins the social contract.

Where does this leave us with respect to the offence of treason? In respect of the Hobbesian version of the social contract, it leaves us with unresolved doubts: if the social contract is a valid justification for the criminalisation of treason, the requesting state (say, Turkey) has as much right to enforce its social contract as the extraditing state (for example, France). It would be inconsistent to deny that. So, if states are indeed justified in refusing extradition for treason under the political offence exception, then the social contract, at least in its Hobbesian version, does not provide a good justification for this offence – which in turn must make us doubt whether the Hobbesian social contract can provide us with any foundation for the criminal law at all. If, however, the social contract is normative (Kantian), based on a set of constitutional principles such as justice, human rights and the rule of law, the inconsistency disappears. Then states could legitimately assert that, although their own treason offence is justified, this is not necessarily the case in all other states, and that they are right to question extradition requests in light of these universal principles.[67]

In ordinary circumstances we are not able to determine how states view each other's criminal law and its underlying constitutional values, or whether they believe it is appropriate to pass judgement on other states' social contracts. But the situation changes when states are faced with a request for extradition. Then they simply cannot avoid making a decision one way or the other.

[65] RA Duff and SE Marshall, ch 3 in this volume.

[66] Indeed, the latest amendments to the Turkish Constitution (in as much as it is a tangible stand-in for the ephemeral social contract), giving more executive powers to the Prime Minister, leading to criticism of an authoritarian change, were criticised by both the EU and France, calling for an investigation of the referendum upon which it was based. See D Boffey, 'Turkey Should Investigate Referendum Vote Irregularities Says EU Commission' *The Guardian* (18 April 2017).

[67] A distinction between universal and parochial conceptions exists not only within social contract theories, but also within utilitarian ones. For an exploration of Bentham as a universalist or parochial utilitarian, see JH Burns, 'Happiness and Utility: Jeremy Bentham's Equation' (2005) 17 *Utilitas* 46.

Generally, there are good reasons for demanding that states do not actively interfere with the way other states impose their criminal law, even under a universalist approach to the ambit of the criminal law. It would be a grave interference in state sovereignty if states were to practically impose their own criminal law in the territory of another state, even when state B's laws are repugnant to the constitutional code of state A. Extradition requests place states in a different position, however.[68]

This is clearly the case between states that do not share constitutional values. Think of the request by Turkey in 2016 that the United States extradite Fethullah Gülen, the purported leader of the failed coup d'etat. The United States and Turkey have diplomatic relations. Let us assume that there exists evidence for this alleged leadership of the coup. (It was this alleged treasonous behaviour that was at the heart of the Turkish request, even though the charges stipulated were not treason.[69]) But the Turkish Government itself acted in a way considered unconstitutional in the United States, breaching values of freedom of speech and academic freedom.[70] The United States' refusal to extradite in this case is therefore explained very well by the Kantian understanding of the social contract as a moral code.

iii. States with Similar Constitutional Values and the European Arrest Warrant

The limitations of the Kantian social contract tradition to explain the law and practice of extradition become apparent, however, when examining extradition between states that have similar underlying constitutional principles. Even states with shared constitutional principles do not necessarily accept the extent to which each of them criminalises treason. Take, for example, the Member States of the European Union. These states can surely be considered to hold similar, albeit not identical, constitutional values. All these states are, by virtue of their EU membership, bound to principles of democracy, fundamental rights and the rule of law.[71] They are parties to the European Charter of Human Rights and to the European Convention on Human Rights, and are bound by other democratic standards of the European Union.[72]

With such cohesion of fundamental values, it would seem that extradition should be easier between these states than it is between states with diverging

[68] See more on this in RA Duff, *The Realm of Criminal Law* (Oxford, Oxford University Press, 2018) 103–107.

[69] The political offence exception does not apply if the suspect is accused of violent offences, such as in the case of a 'Shining Path' member from Peru whose extradition was requested from the United States in *Ordinala v Hackman*, 438 F 3rd 588 (2007).

[70] V Nanda, 'Extraditing Fethullah Gulen to Turkey Would Erode the Rule of Law' *Denver Post* (21 November 2019).

[71] Treaty on European Union [2012] OJ C326/17, Art 2.

[72] See further P Bárd et al, 'An EU Mechanism on Democracy, the Rule of Law and Fundamental Rights', *CEPS Papers in Liberty and Security in Europe 91* (April 2016).

constitutional norms. It is on that assumption that the European Arrest Warrant was instituted,[73] and indeed the European Arrest Warrant mechanism[74] does not make provision for a political offence exception to extradition.[75] Presumably, this is because EU states already adhere to common political and constitutional values. But even between these states with aligned constitutional values, the specific elements of the treason offence, that is what states consider legitimate to criminalise as treason, can differ from state to state.[76] A good illustration is the fate of the European Arrest Warrant issued by Spain for Charles Puigdemont, the dismissed President of Catalonia who fled to Belgium and Germany, charging him with rebellion for his role in the campaign for the region's independence from Spain.[77] The conduct constituting rebellion as charged by the Spanish authorities consisted of conducting an independence referendum that, in Spain's view, was unconstitutional.[78] But it is not obvious that another European state would, or should, view this conduct as undermining common constitutional values.

Conducting an unofficial referendum is not an obvious case of rebellion undermining democracy when there is no violent action involved. The constitutional principle undermined is that of the division of constitutional power between central and regional governments. There could be differing views among

[73] EU Council Framework Decision on the European Arrest Warrant and the Surrender Procedures Between Member States 2012/584/JHA. For discussion of its recent developments, see J Wouters & F Naert, 'Of Arrest Warrants, Terrorist Offences and Extradition Deals: An Appraisal of the EU's Main Criminal Law Measures against Terrorism after 11 September' (2004) 41 *Common Market Law Review* 909.

[74] Strictly speaking, this is a mechanism of foreign judicial enforcement rather than extradition, although often referred to as extradition.

[75] The grounds for non-execution are listed in Arts 3 and 4. None comprises an exception for political offences. The only relevant provision might be Art 1(3), affirming that the Framework Decision does not modify obligations to respect fundamental rights.

[76] Duff, above n 68 at 114 suggests that the European Union may already be a political community to which individual citizens are answerable as far as criminal law is concerned. The existence of the European Arrest Warrant mechanism would suggest that this is the direction in which the European Union is going, but the cases discussed here show that for now this is not how Member States view this relationship.

[77] Art 472 of the Criminal Code of Spain. For the purposes of our discussion we can assume that the rebellion offence is broadly equivalent to treason.

[78] Indeed, many Spanish jurists did not think the Catalan leader's actions were unconstitutional (see at www.omnium.cat/en/more-than-120-spanish-law-professors-call-for-the-release-of-those-catalan-leaders-being-held-in-pre-trial-detention-for-non-existent-crimes/). The leaders of the separatist movement who remained in Spain were acquitted of rebellion, as their actions were not sufficiently violent, but convicted of sedition, and were handed heavy prison sentences of between 9 and 12 years: R Rincón et al, 'Supreme Court finds jailed Catalan secession leaders guilty of sedition' *El Pais* English Edition (14 October 2019). The conviction of and heavy sentences given to his associates, for what by and large were not violent actions but the carrying out of a referendum not sanctioned by the Constitution, indicate that Puigdemont had good reasons to be apprehensive. It more generally shows us that treason and similar offences, even when committed through non-violent actions, can be viewed even by democratic states, *de facto* and not just in theory, as very serious offences.

liberal democratic states on the suitable division of power between central and regional governments in the state. Indeed, European states have arrangements varying from federalism,[79] via devolution[80] and limited regional autonomy,[81] to a unitary state structure.[82] The German court, despite the absence of a political offence exception in the European Arrest Warrant, denied extradition, basing its decision on a lack of double criminality, as in the factual circumstances of this case no offence would be committed under German law.[83] The court thus reached the same result as would have been reached had a political offence exception existed. The political value system in Germany was such that non-violent actions were not criminal rebellion, while the political value system of Spain was such that even non-violent actions against perceived state interests could be criminal rebellion.

It is significant that the legal differences that lead one Member State of the European Union to effectively refuse rendition to another do not concern a marginal offence but rather the most serious offence of each legal system. If such liberal democracies as Spain and Germany, which by virtue of their common membership of the European Union are committed to similar constitutional values, do not extradite treason suspects to each other, this signals that they have misgivings about the validity of the offence as it exists in the requesting state. Such mistrust even between states sharing common liberal values casts doubt on the possibility of justifying the political offence exception on the basis of either of the two conceptions of the social contract outlined above. Therefore, neither of the two conceptions of the social contract can provide a satisfactory basis for the law and practice on extradition for the offence of treason.

IV. COMMUNITY AND STATE

Examination of the offence of treason is useful for evaluating the explicative value of the social contract theory of criminal law. It can serve to differentiate between the implications for the criminal law of a social contract theory of criminalisation and other political theories of criminalisation, such as a communitarian theory.

Modern criminal law theorists espousing a theory of the criminal law grounded in communitarian thought have found justification for criminalisation

[79] As in Germany: German Basic Law, Arts 28–31.

[80] As in the United Kingdom: see the Scotland Act 1998, the Northern Ireland Act 1998 and the Government of Wales Act 2006.

[81] As in Spain: Constitution of Spain, Arts 137–158.

[82] As in France: Constitution of France, Art 3.

[83] The *Oberlandesgericht* for the State of Schleswig-Holstein decided that treason under German law (Criminal Code, section 81) requires use of force, which did not occur in this case. See press release dated 5 April 2018 on the court's website: www.schleswig-holstein.de/DE/Justiz/OLG/Presse/PI/201803Puigdemontenglisch.html.

in the cohesion of community values. Alan Brudner posits a community principle that, together with the complementary harm principle and sovereignty principle, completes his liberal theory of criminalisation.[84] Brudner's complementary principles of criminalisation in turn correspond to his three-pronged inclusive liberal constitutional theory, consisting of libertarian, egalitarian and communitarian conceptions of liberalism.[85]

Brudner finds the treason offence to be justifiable under the community principle of criminalisation. On this approach, the criminalisation of treason would be justified by a communitarian political theory. However, this is not the only possible perspective. Rather than treating the existence of the treason offence as a reason for adding a justifying principle (namely, the community principle) to the theory of criminalisation, the conclusion could be that the offence of treason without harm (which I called 'pure treason' elsewhere)[86] is simply unjustified under a liberal theory of criminalisation.

For RA Duff, the criminal law is primarily a system by which citizens call each other to account for breaches of the community's fundamental values.[87] The assertion of jurisdiction by state A over crimes committed in state A by perpetrators who are citizens of state B is treated by him as a marginal case that does not refute his primary thesis that criminal law is based on responsibility of citizens to other members of their political community (i.e. the state).[88]

An examination of the offence of treason both enhances and undercuts this theory. The treason offence enhances the communal theory of criminal law, because the dignity of citizenship accorded to each of us requires us to be loyal towards fellow citizens. The commission of treason is the most serious breach of this dignity of citizenship.

The communal theory of criminal law is, however, undercut by the existence of a treason offence, because political communities (the states whose betrayal this offence is predicated upon) are not identical to actual communities to which people identify themselves as belonging.[89] This is especially true in the case of members of religious, racial, national and ethnic minorities, who may feel that their real community is the one within which they live, whose moral edicts they follow and towards which they feel loyalty, rather than the

[84] A Brudner, 'The Wrong, the Bad, and the Wayward: Liberalism's Mala in Se', in F Tanguay-Renaud & J Stribopoulos (eds), *Rethinking Criminal Law Theory* (Oxford, Hart Publishing, 2012) 61.

[85] A Brudner, *Constitutional Goods* (Oxford, Oxford University Press, 2004); and see also the discussion in T Poole, 'The Devil's Account: Men, Morals and Constitutional Goods' *LSE Law, Society and Economy Working Papers 1/2009*.

[86] Scolnicov, above n 21.

[87] RA Duff, 'Answering for Crime' (2006) 106 *Proceedings of the Aristotelian Society* 87; Duff, above n 68.

[88] Duff, 'Answering' above n 88 at 96, in reference to universal jurisdiction, but a similar rationale would seem to apply to other extra-territorial or territorial jurisdiction for crimes.

[89] Duff anticipates this as one of the critiques that could be raised against his theory of criminalisation and attempts to answer it (Duff, above n 68 at 119).

political community embodied by the state.[90] In fact, as we know from many historical and contemporary examples, they may feel that these loyalties are in conflict with each other.

The notion of community should not be equated with the state. If community merely means the political community, that is the state, then nothing is added by introducing the concept of 'community' into a political theory or a theory of criminalisation. However, certainly in the current state of the world, the political (state) unit and the communal unit are not one and the same. The state does not represent community, and in most cases includes a variety of (sometimes overlapping) communities. Nowhere is that more obvious than in respect of treason. The criminalisation of treason is predicated on a shared protected social value (*Rechtsgut*, to use the German expression) of loyalty to the state. But communal loyalties, especially of national, linguistic or ethnic minorities, might actively contradict this expected loyalty to the state, undercutting the existence of the *Rechtsgut*.

There could be other legitimate reasons for demanding a minimal degree of loyalty as a duty attached to citizenship, and even for demanding some such loyalty from residents and even visitors who are in a sense 'temporary citizens', who by entrance into the country take upon themselves temporarily the social contract. But for members of minority groups and others who may have been born in the state but do not identify with it, this requirement is more difficult to explain. It might be justified to impose certain duties towards the state even on those who do not identify with it or do not want to be part of the state but merely live there. But describing this as arising from membership in a 'community' seems to be taking a step too far.[91]

A theory of the criminal law grounded in the social contract might be thought to support a communitarian political theory. Yet the treason offence shows just how far apart these views are. The offence of treason is a demand for loyalty to the state above personal or (sub-state) communal loyalties. While social contract theory has, as we saw, its own problems in justifying the criminalisation of treason, it is at least clear that the social contract in question is a political contract underpinning the state. Communitarian theory also has to contend with the conflicting loyalties citizens have between the state and other communities, and with those who reject membership of the state (political) community.

[90] This offence brings into sharp relief the arguments in Nicola Lacey's critique of *The Realm of Criminal Law* in N Lacey, 'Approaching or Re-thinking the Realm of Criminal Law?' (2020) 14 *Criminal Law and Philosophy* 307.

[91] The Israel Supreme Court, in its decision *Abu Arfa v Interior Minister* HCJ 06/7803, had to contend with this issue. It decided that the Interior Minister could not revoke the permanent residency status of East Jerusalem residents who were Hamas members based on their disloyalty to the State of Israel.

V. CONCLUSION

If the criminal law has a constitutional role in determining the relations between citizen and state, the offences of treason, and similar offences of sedition and rebellion, are particularly crucial to this role.

The various branches classical liberal political theory has sprouted – communitarianism, republicanism, feminism, social democracy, human rights, even Marxism – all mandate scepticism towards a demand of loyalty to the state backed by the criminal law.

Yet the offence of treason remains a serious crime on the statute books of all states, both liberal and illiberal, creating a serious conundrum for theorists seeking to explicate the moral and constitutional basis of the criminal law.

A social contract theory might go some way to explaining and justifying the existence of these offences, and therefore the relationship between citizen and state, but it does not provide a sufficient justification for these offences.

As an early utilitarian, Beccaria boldly attempted to reconcile utilitarianism with social contract theory. But the analysis in this chapter has shown why the two theories are essentially at odds with each other. Treason, the offence Beccaria himself regarded as the most important, is not sufficiently justified by a social contract theory of the criminal law. The law and practice of extradition for this offence undercuts Beccaria's conception of the social contract. His social contract theory is simply not capable of justifying the imposition of the criminal law by the state.

6

Beccaria's Secular Metaphysics: Pain, Time and State Authority

SHAI LAVI

What made Beccaria's theory of punishment so novel at its time and continues to draw contemporary thinkers today?

There are two common answers to this question. The first, a Whiggish history of penal law, celebrates Beccaria as a pioneer of humanism and rationalism. Voltaire was one of the first to articulate this view. In a letter dated 30 May 1768, he wrote to thank Beccaria

> with all my heart. These sentiments are those of the entire Europe … You toil on behalf of reason and humanity, both of which have been quashed for so long. You revive those two sisters, beaten for over sixteen hundred years. They are finally beginning to walk and talk; but as soon as they do, fanaticism again rears its ugly head.[1]

Beccaria's humanism and rationalism, revolutionary at the time, continue to serve as a compass for our age.[2]

The second, a critical appraisal that is commonly associated with the work of Michel Foucault but also appears in the writings of Ignatieff,[3] Rothman[4] and Dubber,[5] views Beccaria as equally revolutionary but for almost the opposite reason. Under this account, Beccaria produced the blueprint for modern penal control. Beccaria, along with Bentham and other architects of the modern penitentiary, replaced the physical pain of punishment with a more subtle, but no less invasive, penal control, in which discipline takes the place of corporal

[1] C Beccaria, *Scritti e lettere inediti* edited by E Landry (1910) 153–154 [Letter attributed to Voltaire] quoted in BE Harcourt, 'Beccaria's On Crimes and Punishments: A Mirror on the History of the Foundations of Modern Criminal Law' in MD Dubber (ed), *Foundational Texts in Modern Criminal Law* (Oxford, Oxford University Press, 2014) 39 at 42.

[2] On Beccaria's reception, see Harcourt, above n 1.

[3] M Ignatieff, *A Just Measure of Pain: The Penitentiary in the Industrial Revolution, 1750–1850* (New York, Pantheon Books, 1978).

[4] DJ Rothman, *The Discovery of the Asylum: Social Order and Disorder in the New Republic* (Boston MA, Little, Brown and Company, 1971).

[5] MD Dubber, *The Dual Penal State: The Crisis of Criminal Law in Comparative-Historical Perspective* (Oxford, Oxford University Press, 2018).

punishment and total institutions substitute for public gallows. More than a quarter of a millennium later, Beccaria's proposed penitentiary system is still the most prevalent penal institution, and its critical appraisal is today as relevant as ever.

In this chapter, I wish to offer a third line of critical inquiry. I will argue that a key element necessary for deciphering the importance of Beccaria's treatise is his post-Christian secularism. His theory of punishment, I will argue, cannot be properly understood outside of his polemic against Christianity, and specifically against Catholicism.[6] His aversion to Christian metaphysics led Beccaria to draw far-reaching conclusions concerning penal justice, so much so that his theory can be seen as a mirror image of Christian penology. The consequences of his confrontation with Christianity, however, go well beyond his wish to separate religious and secular authority. Specifically, as we shall see, his confrontational approach led Beccaria to a radical transformation of two important elements of punishment: the morality of pain and the temporality of punishment.

Though Beccaria attempted to escape the metaphysics of Christian penology, his anti-Christian theory of punishment is impregnated with metaphysical thinking. While his eighteenth-century quibbling with Christian authorities is of less interest to contemporary penologists, his radical transformation of penal theory continues to hover over our thinking today. How to make sense of the morality of pain and the temporality of punishment are problems that Beccaria identified and strived to resolve but that are still with us today.

First, I wish to explore Beccaria's polemic against Christian penology and its role in *On Crimes and Punishments*.[7] Two aspects of his theory are of special importance – the authority of penal justice and its substantive justifications (section I). Second, I will show how Beccaria developed his own theory of punishment as a mirror image of Christian metaphysics and, specifically, his understanding of the morality of pain and the temporality of punishment. I will argue that Beccaria's polemical secularism does not free him from metaphysical assumptions but, quite to the contrary, entangles him in post-Christian metaphysics (section II). The chapter concludes by revisiting Beccaria's importance for contemporary penologists.

[6] I will refer interchangeably to Christianity and Catholicism, since in the Italian context in which Beccaria operated Christianity meant the Catholic Church. Interestingly, Beccaria uses neither term and rather speaks of 'religion'.

[7] Unless otherwise specified, all quotations from *On Crimes and Punishments* in this chapter are taken from one of the early English-language translations of Beccaria's work, *An Essay on Crimes and Punishments translated from the Italian of Marquis Beccaria with The Commentary by Voltaire translated from the French* 5th edition (London, printed for HD Symonds, 1804). The first English translation under this title appeared as early as 1767. This old translation gives present-day readers a more accurate sense than do modern translations of how Beccaria's text would have appeared to his contemporaries. When this edition is quoted, the chapter numbers are given in Roman numerals, as their order can differ from modern critical editions.

I. BECCARIA'S POST-CHRISTIAN SECULARISM

To point out Beccaria's secularism may seem, on first impression, to be either misguided or trivial. Beccaria was not a secularist if 'secularism' signifies atheism. Beccaria acknowledges in his writings the existence of God, and his theory of punishment pays due respect to religious authority. If, however, by 'secularism' one means a separation of religion as an otherworldly realm of authority and morality from this-worldly affairs, then Beccaria was no doubt a secularist, but so were most Enlightenment scholars, who were committed Deists. Even if he was one of the first scholars in modern times to develop a secularist theory of punishment, he was certainly not the last. How can such a broad characterisation help shed light on the distinctness of Beccaria's work and its relevance to our time?

In what follows, I argue that Beccaria's secularism, or, more accurately, his post-Christian secular stance, is central to his work and goes to the heart of his argument and to its lasting legacy. Beccaria strived to liberate the authority of penal justice from religion, to free punishment from its theological underpinnings and to cleanse penal theory from metaphysical residues. In doing so, however, he accomplished more than what an objection to Christian dogma would call for. He transformed punishment and its justification well beyond his initial disagreement with Christian theology.

Beccaria's secularism operates on two levels. The first concerns the authority of penal law. Whence comes the binding power of penal justice? What are the legitimate sources of penal sanctions? What implications does the authority of penal law have for the administration of penal justice? Beccaria's rejection of divine authority, natural rights and clerical administration of civic justice are central, as we shall see, to the formation of his own penology.

The second concerns the substantive justification for punishment. What are the aims of penal sanctions? How can the pain and suffering inherent in punishment be justified? What is the distinction between punishment and revenge? What role, if any, might penance have in an enlightened penal system? Here, too, Beccaria rejects the common answers that Christian tradition has provided, specifically the purging power of pain and the redeeming power of punishment.

Taken together, Beccaria's opposition to the authority of the Church and to its substantive understanding of punishment moves him to develop his own counter-theory of penal law. While the drive to develop his theory begins with a hostility to Christian authority and theology, it does not end there. Beccaria's thoughts take him much further than his initial counter-clerical impetus, but in the same direction. It is in this sense that his theory is not simply non-Christian but anti-Christian, or, more accurately, post-Christian. His secularism bears within it – albeit by way of stark opposition – the imprint of its Christian point of departure.

A. The Secular Authority of Penal Justice

The first and most apparent tension between Beccaria's penal theory and religion concerns the authority of penal sanctions. Beccaria seeks to ground punishment in human reason, in the social contract, and in utilitarian thinking rather than in divine revelation, natural law, religious tradition or clerical authority. Beccaria must have known that in promoting his ideas he was entering on to a collision path with Christian theologians and with Church authority, a confrontation that – as we shall see – came to pass shortly after the publication of his essay.

In the spirit of eighteenth-century European Enlightenment, however, Beccaria did not openly reject religion but insisted that it should have no bearing on civic affairs. The authority of punishing worldly crimes, he contended, cannot be resolved by turning to natural law or to divine revelation. In a key passage, Beccaria explains why the two sources of authority – human and divine – should not be confused, and why humans should not strive to punish religious sins. It is worth quoting the passage at length, as it clearly demarcates and contrasts the two spheres of divine and human justice.

> [O]thers have imagined that the greatness of the sin should aggravate the crime. But the fallacy of this opinion will appear on the slightest consideration of the relations between man and man, and between God and man. The relations between man and man are relations of equality. Necessity alone hath produced, from the opposition of private passions and interests, the idea of public utility, which is the foundation of human justice. The other are relations of dependence, between an imperfect creature and his Creator, the most perfect of beings, who has reserved to himself the sole right of being both lawgiver and judge; for he alone can, without injustice, be, at the same time, both one and the other. If he hath decreed eternal punishments for those who disobey his will, shall an insect dare to put himself in the place of divine justice, or pretend to punish for the Almighty, who is himself all-sufficient, who cannot receive impressions of pleasure or pain, and who alone, of all other beings, acts without being acted upon? The degree of sin depends on the malignity of the heart, which is impenetrable to finite beings. How then can the degree of sin serve as a standard to determine the degree of crimes? If that were admitted, men may punish when God pardons, and pardon when God condemns; and thus act in opposition to the Supreme Being.[8]

The passage contains a few key distinctions: man and God, crime and sin, equality and dependence, necessity and (implicitly) freedom, public utility and malignity of the heart, passive bearers of pain and all-sufficient agency. Beccaria weaves these distinctions together and creates two diametrically opposed realms of legitimate penal authority – secular and religious. He does not reject divine authority but demarcates its reach.

While the 25-year-old author tried to tread carefully, his caution did not immunise him from clerical attacks. As Aaron Thomas pointed out, '[r]eaction

[8] Beccaria, ibid at 26–27 (ch VII).

to the pamphlet was swift and widespread'.[9] Indeed, as early as 27 August 1764, the Venetian Inquisition blocked the importation of *On Crimes and Punishments* into Venetian territory. The Catholic Church shunned the book and placed it on the Index of Prohibited Books in 1766.[10]

Similarly, Ferdinando Facchinei, a monk from Vallombroso in Venetian territory, one of the first reviewers of the essay, criticised the work on numerous accounts. In his *Notes and Observations on the Book Entitled 'On Crimes and Punishments'*,[11] published in 1765, he indicted the then still anonymous author of the book on six charges of sedition and 23 of impiety. Most of his concerns went to the grounding of penal authority in human reason and to the general egalitarian spirit that Beccaria advocates: 'And it contains all of the greatest and most blasphemous sedition ever encountered against the sovereign rulers and against the Christian religion from the most impious heretics and from all the irreligious, ancient and modern alike,'[12] wrote the Catholic monk.[13]

The Verri brothers, Beccaria's intellectual patrons, immediately set out to defend him against Facchinei's accusations. Since Beccaria had published his essay anonymously, their response was likewise published anonymously, and they used the first person singular to give the impression that it had been written by the author of the impugned book himself.[14] They wrote on Beccaria's behalf: 'In my entire book I always spoke of crimes, never of sins …'[15] Defending Beccaria against his alleged critique of Catholic princes' authority to punish heresy, the Verri brothers quoted a passage from *On Crimes and Punishments*

[9] A Thomas, 'Preface', in C Beccaria, *On Crimes and Punishments and Other Writings* edited by A Thomas and translated by A Thomas & J Parzen (Toronto, Toronto University Press, 2008) xxiii.

[10] DB Young, 'Let Us Content Ourselves with Praising the Work While Drawing a Veil over its Principles: Eighteenth-Century Reactions to Beccaria's On Crimes and Punishments' (1984) 1 *Justice Quarterly* 155 at 158–159. The reaction of the Church more generally is addressed in A Bondolfi, 'Beccaria et la religion: la réaction de Facchinei et du saint-office' in P Audegean & L Delia (eds), *Le moment Beccaria: naissance du droit pénal moderne (1764–1810)* (Liverpool, Liverpool University Press, 2018) 33.

[11] F Facchinei, *Note ed osservazioni sul libro intitolato 'Dei delitti e delle pene'* (Venice, 1765), translated in Beccaria, above n 9 at 89.

[12] Ibid at 98.

[13] For an interesting argument that Beccaria and Facchinei shared key assumptions about the social conditions in which punishment would have to operate, placing them closer to each other in their general outlook on society than many of Beccaria's admirers were to him, see DB Young, 'Alternative Ideologies of Law: Traditionalists and Reformers in Eighteenth-Century Lombardy' (1989) 34 *McGill Law Journal* 264.

[14] P Verri & A Verri, 'Riposta ad uno scritto che s'intitola Note ed osservazioni sul libro "Dei delitti e delle pene"', excerpts translated as 'From "Response to a Writing Entitled Notes and Observations on the Book 'On Crimes and Punishments'", in Beccaria, above n 9, at 102. The 'Riposta' was added to the 3rd edition (1765) of Beccaria's book. When Beccaria later added his own note 'To the Reader' to the 5th edition (1766), he referred to the 'Riposta' as if it had also been written by him. See GR Newman & P Marongiu, 'Endnotes', in C Beccaria, *On Crimes and Punishments* edited and translated by GR Newman and P Marongiu (New Brunswick, Transaction Publishers, 2009) 127 note 22.

[15] Verri & Verri, above n 14 at 105.

that conceded the worldly authority of religion, as long as it remains outside the realm of civic law:

> I am speaking only of the crimes that arise from human nature and from the social pact, and not of sins, whose punishments – even in this world – should be regulated by principles other than those of a limited philosophy.[16]

Beccaria adopted many of these arguments in his impassioned note 'To the Reader', which was appended to subsequent editions of *On Crimes and Punishments*.[17] 'It would be mistaken, just because someone is discussing social conventions and their consequences, to attribute to him any opposition to the principles of natural law or revelation, because these are not what he is talking about,' writes Beccaria, adding that '[i]t is for theologians to chart the boundaries of the just and the unjust, insofar as the intrinsic good or evil of an action is concerned; but it is for the student of law and the state to establish the relationship between political justice and injustice …'[18]

Possibly in anticipation of such accusations, Beccaria had already devoted some of his argument in *On Crimes and Punishments* to refuting religious allegations of blasphemy. 'I do not, by any means,' he wrote there, 'speak of the justice of God, which is of another kind, and refers immediately to rewards and punishments in a life to come'.[19] In his note 'To the Reader', he explains:

> There are three sources from which the principles of morals and politics which guide men are drawn: revelation, natural law and the conventions arrived at by society. … As soon as these essentially distinct principles are confused, all hope of thinking clearly about public affairs is lost.[20]

Beccaria's demarcation of divine and human punishment may seem as benign as similar calls at the time (and still today) to separate the state from religion. No doubt this is one way of understanding Beccaria's penal enterprise. But it is important to note that Beccaria did not develop a general theory of state and religion, and that his main interest was in punishment. It is civic punishment that must be clearly separated from the logic of divine punishment.

[16] Ibid. For the quoted passage, see Beccaria, above n 9 at 77 (ch 39).

[17] C Beccaria, 'To the Reader', in C Beccaria, *On Crimes and Punishments and Other Writings* edited by R Bellamy and translated by R Davies (Cambridge, Cambridge University Press, 1995) 3 (and see ibid xli–xlii on the genesis of that Note). Young, above n 13 at 284, notes that the Verri brothers' 'Riposta' also deftly – and counterfactually – denied that the book claims that the sovereign has no right to punish by death; a point on which Beccaria's own 'To the Reader' does not follow the 'Riposta' but which Young considers was a 'strategic retreat' necessary to keep public and official sympathies with Beccaria, as the victim of apparently unreasonable accusations and as no challenger of sovereign authority: 'they realized how much support they would lose if Facchinei's interpretation were accepted' (ibid).

[18] Beccaria, above n 17 at 5.

[19] Beccaria, above n 7 at 9 (at the end of ch II 'On the Right to Punish').

[20] Beccaria, above n 17 ('To the Reader') at 4 and 5.

Beccaria, and this is a crucial point, did not make the more limited argument, one that Kant and many other thinkers would go on to make, that law differs from morality and that the inner realm of the human soul should be brought before the tribunal of one's own conscience and not before a public court of justice. Beccaria's novelty lies in singling out civic punishment from all other forms of punishment and attributing to it a distinct logic. Unlike most classic theories of punishment (Christian, or going back to Greek and Roman times), which assumed that different forms of punishment – parental, civic and divine – share a core logic, it is central to Beccaria's argument that civic punishment has a distinct aim and a distinct set of justifications. Civic punishment and punishment generally are mere homonyms. We shall see the implications of this radical rupture in the history of punishment in the following sections. It was a necessary precondition that allowed Beccaria to transform in fundamental ways the morality of pain and the temporality of punishment.

B. The Political Theology of Penal Law

Beccaria's challenge to religious penal authority is only one aspect of his secularism. Equally significant are his efforts to create a new and secular moral language for penal law. Here, too, Beccaria's essay is replete with references to the dangers of confusing the temporal and divine realms of punishment, and to the limitations of religious belief to curtail crime.

Throughout the essay, Beccaria highlights the shortcomings of a religiously based penal system. For example, in his famous opposition to the death penalty, Beccaria writes:

> Religion then presents itself to the mind of this lawless villain, and, promising him almost a certainty of eternal happiness upon the easy terms of repentance, contributes much to lessen the horror of the last scene of the tragedy.[21]

Similarly, in the chapter on oaths, Beccaria writes:

> The motives which religion opposes to the fear of impending evil, and the love of life, are too weak, as they are too distant, to make any impression on the senses. The affairs of the other world are regulated by laws entirely different from those by which human affairs are directed ...[22]

But Beccaria goes much further in his polemic against Christianity, and this is where his novelty lies. He seeks to cleanse civic institutions from core Christian, or more accurately Catholic, concepts, including sin, infamy and purgatory.

[21] Beccaria, above n 7 at 107 (ch XXVIII).

[22] Ibid at 69–70 (ch XVIII). Similar misgivings with religion also appear in Beccaria's discussion of the superstitious nature of witchcraft offences and ordeals, and of the punishment of suicide.

In a pivotal and one of the most insightful passages of the essay, Beccaria writes:

> It is not difficult to trace this senseless law to its origin; for an absurdity, adopted by a whole nation, must have some affinity with other ideas, established and respected by the same nation. This custom seems to be the offspring of religion, by which mankind in all nations, and in all ages, are so generally influenced. We are taught by our infallible church, that those stains of sin, contracted through human frailty, and which have not deserved the eternal anger of the Almighty, are to be purged away, in another life, by an incomprehensible fire. Now infamy is a stain, and if the punishments and fire of purgatory can take away all spiritual stains, why should not the pain of torture take away those of a civil nature? I imagine, that the confession of a criminal, which in some tribunals is required, as being essential to his condemnation, has a similar origin, and has been taken from the mysterious tribunal of penitence, where the confession of sins is a necessary part of the sacrament. Thus have men abused the unerring light of revelation; and, in the times of ignorance, having no other, they naturally had recourse to it on every occasion, making the most remote and absurd applications.[23]

Beccaria could not state his position more clearly. The argument is revealing and goes to the heart of Beccaria's critical stance toward the dominance of Christian penology. The problem with contemporary justifications of punishment is that they conflate the logic of religious punishment with the logic of secular punishment. The confusion, Beccaria argues, is not coincidental. The structure of Christian penology forms the basic matrix of civic sanction. The problem, as he understands it, is the continuous influence of Christian theology on civic law: sin transforms into crime, infamy turns into blameworthiness, and the purging fire of purgatory is replaced by the painfulness of the gallows. The concepts change, but their underlying significance remains the same. Civic law must free itself from its foundational Christianity in order to take on a rational and humanistic form. Beccaria, in other words, criticises the political theology of criminal law and seeks to replace its Christian grounding with sound reason.

In his attempt to free criminal law from its Christian baggage, however, Beccaria not only secularises penal law but also seeks to transform its fundamental grammar. This has far more wide-reaching implications than his polemic against religious authority. Put differently, one may accept Beccaria's wish to separate religion from state, crime from sin, law from morality, outward culpability from internal blameworthiness, and not draw the radical conclusions that Beccaria draws from his contra-Christian penology.

[23] Ibid at 57–58 (ch XVI). On the process of 'sacralisation' of punishment, especially of public executions, that took place during the late Middle Ages, see P Spierenburg, 'The Green, Green Grass of Home: Capital Punishment and the Penal System from a Long-Term Perspective' in A Sarat & J Martschukat (eds), *Is the Death Penalty Dying? European and American Perspectives* (Cambridge, Cambridge University Press, 2011) 17 at 22–28.

Beccaria's stance toward religious authority and religious morality is crucial for understanding his point of departure, but not his conclusions. It captures all that Beccaria condemns, but not what he accepts. And yet Beccaria's constructive contribution to penal theory continues exactly from the same point on which his critique ends. Christian penology is Beccaria's arch rival not because of its other-worldliness, nor because of its focus on the inner soul. It is the theological understanding of pain and temporality that Beccaria opposes and seeks to counter and reverse.

II. A NEW METAPHYSICS OF PAIN AND TIME

Within Catholic theology, as we have just seen, pain has a positive moral value. It can lead one to repent and has the power to purge the wrongdoers of their sins. Consequently, the temporality of punishment is not only forward-looking; it is also backward-looking. Punishment can undo the crime and cleanse the wrongdoers of their wrong. It is these two fundamental assumptions that Beccaria rejects outright and seeks to reverse. For him, there is no positive value in pain; pain is an evil that leads every person to recoil. Similarly, the aim of punishment is to influence the future, as the past cannot be changed. Beccaria seeks to invert the Christian morality of pain and the temporality of punishment and to develop a diametrically opposed penology.

In a key section of his essay, 'Of the Intent of Punishments', Beccaria highlights the radical shift that his theory offers. 'From the foregoing considerations,' the Italian reformer writes, 'it is evident, that the intent of punishments, is not to torment a sensible being, nor to undo a crime already committed'.[24] In this single sentence, Beccaria captures the heart of his opposition to Christian penology and the crux of his own argument. Beccaria rejects the two elements that previous theories of punishment had taken for granted: the power of the pain of punishment to induce penance and negate the crime.

For Beccaria, pain is a self-evident evil. So much so that his theory is premised on the assumption that (taken on its own) the pain of punishment inflicted on the criminal is morally equivalent to the pain of the crime. Both have equal weight in the calculus of pain. Similarly, punishment cannot undo the crime. It is senseless to believe that punishment has the power to cleanse the crime, or that inducing any backward-looking response – guilt, regret, penance or atonement, or balancing the scales of justice – may have any significance for penal justice.

Beccaria turns the guiding principles of Catholic penology on their head and transforms them from a problem into a solution. It is precisely because pain is negative and its effects future-oriented that punishment can be justified. It is this

[24] Beccaria, above n 7 at 41 (ch XII).

trans-valuation of Christian values that leads Beccaria to develop his alternative approach:

> The end of punishment, therefore, is no other than to prevent the criminal from doing further injury to society, and to prevent others from committing the like offence. Such punishments, therefore, and such a mode of inflicting them, ought to be chosen, as will make the strongest and most lasting impressions on the minds of others, with the least torment to the body of the criminal.[25]

Beccaria's understanding of the morality of pain and the temporality of punishment are rooted in deep, one might say metaphysical, presuppositions about the nature of pain and time. It is worthwhile examining more closely these presuppositions, especially those that concern pain, on which Beccaria elaborates at some length.

Beccaria's post-Christian secularisation of pain takes place on three levels: ontological, moral and epistemic. First, on an ontological level, he clearly distinguishes between sensual pain and other forms of suffering. The pain of punishment, specifically of corporal punishment, is for him sensual and cannot have any other effect or signification. This ontological distinction allows him, on a second level, to reject physical pain as senseless and morally worthless, while at the same time leading him to promote the value of imagined pain, that is, the threat of expected or imagined pain, as a deterrent force. Beccaria captures this distinction in his discussion of torture. He asks, rhetorically, 'Can pain, which is a sensation, have any connection with a moral sentiment, a matter of opinion?'[26] Once pain is understood merely as a sensation, it is obvious that it cannot have any bearing on morality. But the conclusion is based on the controversial assumption that physical pain and moral suffering are separable, and that the pain of punishment is not always an attempt to combine both as in Christian penology.

Beccaria not only rejects the moral value of pain (i.e., physical pain); on a third level, he also denies its epistemic power. Once again in the section on torture, Beccaria explains why torturing a person will not lead to the revelation of truth:

> Besides, it is confounding all relations, to expect that a man should be both the accuser and accused; and that pain should be the test of truth, as if truth resided in the muscles and fibres of a wretch in torture.[27]

We can only appreciate Beccaria's contribution to the history of penology if we do not accept his position as self-evident. In fact, for most of Western history, there was never a clear separation between physical, emotional and moral pain. Furthermore, pain was thought of as having the redeeming power to induce

[25] Ibid at 41–42.
[26] Ibid at 57 (ch XVI).
[27] Ibid at 56.

regret and to expiate sin. And, finally, torture was seen as a reliable way of attaining truth. The pain of torture, which was never understood to be purely physical, had the power to remove any obstacle that stood in the way of truth, to free the criminal from their attachment to lies, and release truth from the bonds of self-interest. For Beccaria, in contrast, pain is wrong in a dual sense of wrong: it is a self-evident moral wrong, and it is also a self-evident epistemic wrong.

Beccaria's reversals of the Catholic teachings on the temporality of punishment and the morality of pain mark the importance of his contribution to the history of penology. His nascent utilitarianism and his reliance on social contract theory are important but secondary. While the latter are broad conceptual frameworks to which Beccaria may have contributed, his revision of penal theory is far-reaching and original. It is this revaluation of Christian values that paves Beccaria's intellectual path. While Beccaria seeks to free penal justice from Christian metaphysics, ultimately he fails. His theory is the reverse image of Christian teachings, and in that sense brands his secularism as post-Christian.

III. CONCLUSION

Where do we, contemporary readers, stand vis-à-vis Beccaria's post-Christian penology? In the final analysis, Beccaria captures better than most writers before or after him the challenges facing punishment today. Punishment, if one may concede to a skeletal definition, is a negative reaction to the violation of the law. This basic definition, however, contains within it the paradox that Beccaria was perhaps the first to fully recognise and try to overcome. If punishment is by definition a negative response, how can it be morally positive? If punishment is always a reaction to a crime performed, that is, backward-looking, how can it change the future?

The old answers to these questions, which the Catholic doctrine had offered, were no longer attainable for Beccaria and are no longer attainable for us, inhabitants of a secular modern public. The redemptive power of pain and the metaphysics of soul searching did not convince the *philosophes*. Beccaria led the way in the opposite direction by embracing the negative and non-redeeming nature of pain and confidence in a better and progressive future.

In the final analysis, Beccaria's importance does not lie in his contribution to solving the riddle of punishment. Rather, he is the one who has put the problem on the table with all its force. His solution is hardly convincing, but the problem he identified emerged in his time and should continue to challenge contemporary thinkers.

7

Public Institutions without Public Offices: Beccaria's Use of Political Theory in the Reform of Criminal Justice

MALCOLM THORBURN

CESARE BECCARIA WROTE *On Crimes and Punishments* in order to change the world, and he did. At the time of its publication, Beccaria was a shy young man of 25, living far from the centres of European intellectual life. But with the publication of this little book, the reform of criminal justice institutions along the lines Beccaria proposed took European intellectual life by storm. It is no great exaggeration to refer to the half-century or so after the book's publication as the 'Beccaria moment'.[1] His influence on Bentham is well known,[2] he was also an important influence on Voltaire,[3] on Blackstone[4] and on penal reformers across Europe,[5] as well as the object of pointed attacks from Kant,[6] among others. What is more, a great many of the reforms to criminal justice he proposed – the elimination of the death penalty and torture; the

[1] P Audegean & L Delia (eds), *Le moment Beccaria: naissance du droit pénal moderne (1764–1810)* (Liverpool, Liverpool University Press, 2018).

[2] HLA Hart, 'Bentham and Beccaria' in *Essays on Bentham: Jurisprudence and Political Theory* (Oxford, Oxford University Press, 1982) 41.

[3] C Cave, 'Voltaire lecteur de Beccaria, Le commentaire sur le livre Des délits et des peines', in P Audegean et al (eds), *Le Bonheur du plus grand nombre: Beccaria et les lumières* (Paris, ENS editions, 2017) 257.

[4] S Stern, 'Blackstone's Criminal Law: Common-Law Harmonization and Legislative Reform', in MD Dubber (ed), *Foundational Texts in Modern Criminal Law* (Oxford, Oxford University Press, 2014) 61.

[5] These influences are detailed in a number of essays in Audegean & Delia (eds), above n 1 and Audegean et al (eds), above n 3.

[6] I Kant, *Metaphysics of Morals* revised edition edited by L Dennis and translated by M Gregor (Cambridge, Cambridge University Press, 2017) 117. See also BE Harcourt, 'Beccaria's On Crimes and Punishments: A Mirror on the History of the Foundations of Modern Criminal Law', in Dubber (ed), above n 4, 39.

abolition of a variety of crimes against religion; public trials; codification and the reduction of judicial and administrative arbitrariness; the elimination of class distinctions in criminal matters; and much else[7] – have become received wisdom among enlightened criminal justice thinkers to this day.

Centuries later, now that these reforms have long since taken place, is there still good reason to read *On Crimes and Punishments*? Does it contain insights that transcend the law reform projects of its time and speak to us still? Michael Oakeshott warns that books aimed mostly at reform, like Beccaria's *On Crimes and Punishments*, are not usually sites of deep and lasting philosophical reflection. '[W]hat in speculation is always the most influential in practical life,' he writes, 'is something half thought-out, something hazy, indefinite and confused. It is not the philosopher, the victim of thought, who influences our practical conduct of life, but the philophaster, the *philosophe*.'[8] Given Beccaria's clear desire to bring about change in penal practices and his warm reception from the leading *philosophe* of them all – Voltaire – one might be wary of Beccaria's book for just that reason.

In this chapter, I argue that Beccaria's *On Crimes and Punishments* is, indeed, the work of someone Oakeshott would call a 'philophaster', someone who engages with ideas primarily to bring about effects in the world, rather than to deepen our understanding of them. Like Kant and others after him, Beccaria is interested in the social contract theory developed before him by writers such as Hobbes, Locke and Rousseau. But unlike these more systematic theorists, Beccaria's primary interest is in *using* the idea of the social contract as a weapon with which to attack the injustices he sees in the criminal justice institutions of his day. And like Bentham after him, Beccaria is interested in the utilitarian theory developed before him by Helvétius. But, once again, Beccaria has little interest in generalising and systematising the theory, as Bentham did. His interest is purely practical: he uses the utilitarian concern with the maximisation of happiness of the greater number as a tool for attacking criminal justice institutions and practices he sees as in need of reform.

For all that, though, Beccaria's *On Crimes and Punishments* is a book that is still very much worth our attention. It is true that the arguments he marshals on important topics are often somewhat thin and flimsy, and in some cases lead to deeply misleading and unproductive conclusions. Nevertheless, there are important insights at the core of the book that have eluded generations of criminal justice theorists before and since.

[7] Although Beccaria's rejection of gun control for reasons that come straight out of the NRA's playbook would worry most modern progressives: see C Beccaria, *On Crimes and Punishments and Other Writings* edited by R Bellamy and translated by R Davies (Cambridge, Cambridge University Press, 1995) 101 (ch 40).

[8] M Oakeshott, 'The New Bentham' in *Rationalism in Politics and Other Essays* (Indianapolis IN, Liberty Fund, 1991) at 150.

The argument of this chapter is in three sections. In the first section, I consider and reject a variety of attempts over the years to turn Beccaria into a consistent follower of one of the many schools of thought from which he borrows. He is not a consistent follower of Rousseau, of Montesquieu, or of Helvétius. In the second section, I consider Beccaria's insight on a central question of criminal justice: his subtle and thoughtful understanding of the distinctively *political* nature of criminal justice and punishment. Unlike so many of his contemporaries and ours, Beccaria is well aware of the fact that criminal punishment cannot be understood in isolation from the rest of the political order. It is not just a tool either for giving wrongdoers their due or for maximising happiness. Its defining purpose, Beccaria makes clear, is fundamentally supportive, ensuring the continued authority of public institutions.

In the third section, I consider the two most prominent examples of Beccaria's failings as a political theorist, and the consequences of those failings for criminal law theory to this day. The first of these is his invocation of hypothetical consent as a measure of criminal justice policy. Although his treatment of the idea of a social contract is surprisingly thin, the practical use he makes of the idea is sweeping. Whereas more systematic thinkers had already produced a variety of accounts of how a social contract might justify the existence of political authority, Beccaria uses the idea on a retail level, measuring a wide variety of criminal justice policies by considering whether free persons would consent to be governed by such rules. We may fairly lay at Beccaria's feet much of the blame for the misguided efforts of so many criminal justice scholars today using some extra-legal yardstick such as hypothetical consent by which to evaluate specific criminal justice policies. Next, I consider one very important place where Beccaria's theoretical flimsiness leads him to unproductive, even absurd, conclusions: his treatment of judicial discretion. One of the best-known arguments in *On Crimes and Punishments* is Beccaria's invocation of the rule of law and the separation of powers to attack the widespread discretion at work in the operation of criminal justice institutions (then, as now). It is here, I argue, that Beccaria's shallow treatment of the subject leads him dangerously astray. Although he was surely right in pointing out the dangers of unbridled discretion in public office – and the abuse of such discretion by many officials of his time – the flimsiness of his theoretical arguments leaves him without the intellectual resources to make proper sense of the situation. Beccaria's solution to the problem of judicial discretion is to do away with official discretion altogether. Without a conception of public office, Beccaria insists that all officials must be reduced to mechanical tools for giving effect to the law, without the need for the exercise of judgment. A richer understanding of public authority – and, in particular, an understanding of public office – would have allowed Beccaria to follow up his powerful critique of unbridled judicial discretion with a plausible alternative. But without the concept of office to give structure to the exercise of public authority, Beccaria is forced into an implausible account not only of judicial decision-making, but of the rule of law more generally.

I. BECCARIA'S HETEROGENEOUS PRACTICAL PHILOSOPHY

What is Beccaria's overarching philosophy of criminal justice? Many scholars claim that Beccaria's arguments are best understood as the working out of some important figure's views within the context of criminal justice. At the time of its publication, for example, it was widely believed that the book simply drew out the implications of Rousseau's *Social Contract* in the field of criminal justice. One of the leading journals of his day described Beccaria's book in this way: 'Son ouvrage … n'est qu'un recueil des principales maximes du *Contrat social*, appliquées par l'Auteur à son sujet et dirigés à sa manière.'[9] Or, as another contemporary commentator put it, 'Il aspire à être considéré comme le Rousseau des Italiens.'[10] But that view – that Beccaria was a devoted follower of Rousseau, working out the implications of Rousseau's understanding of the social contract in the context of criminal justice – is quite clearly wrong. Although Beccaria makes much of the social contract foundations of the state's right to punish, his use of the social contract is radically different from Rousseau's in several fundamental respects. As I will set out in more detail below, Beccaria is at odds with Rousseau on perhaps the two most fundamental aspects of the social contract. First, he favours the Lockean view that we enter into a social contract to 'sacrifice a part of … freedom in order to enjoy what remains in security and calm'.[11] Rousseau, by contrast, famously insisted that under the social contract, 'each, uniting with all, nevertheless obey[s] only himself and remain[s] as free as before'.[12] Second, Beccaria insists that 'the general will … is the aggregate of individual wills'.[13] But for Rousseau, '[t]here is often a considerable difference between the will of all and the general will: the latter looks only to the common interest, the former looks often to private interest and is nothing but a sum of particular wills'.[14]

Another reading of Beccaria – one that Beccaria himself encourages[15] – is that his book is a working out of Montesquieu's *Spirit of the Laws* in the context of criminal law and punishment.[16] On a number of fronts, Beccaria

[9] *Gazette littéraire de l'Europe* (13 February 1765) 301–302.

[10] F Facchinei, 'Note ed osservazioni sul libro intitulato Dei delitti e delle pene' [1765] 188 quoted in D Ippolito, 'Contrat social et peine capitale: Beccaria contre Rousseau' in P Audegean, M Campanini & B Carnevali (eds), *Rousseau et L'Italie: Littérature, morale et politique* (Paris, Hermann, 2017) 147 at 148.

[11] Beccaria, above n 7 at 9 (ch 1).

[12] J-J Rousseau, *The Social Contract and Other Later Political Writings* 2nd edition edited by Victor Gourevitch (Cambridge, Cambridge University Press, 2019) 51–52.

[13] Beccaria, above n 7 at 66 (ch 28).

[14] Rousseau, above n 12 at 61–62.

[15] Beccaria, above n 7 at 8 ('Introduction') refers to 'the immortal Président Montesquieu', and he writes that 'indivisible truth' had compelled him 'to follow in the enlightened footsteps of that great man'.

[16] See DW Carrithers, 'Montesquieu's Philosophy of Punishment' (1998) 19 *History of Political Thought* 213; C Larrère, 'Droit de punir et qualification des crimes de Montesquieu à Beccaria', in M Porret (ed), *Beccaria et la culture juridique des lumières* (Geneva, Librairie Droz, 1997) 89.

does indeed follow Montesquieu's policy-level views, at least in outline:[17] the importance of codification and of constraining judicial discretion; the importance of restraint in punishment and of an ordered proportionality between crime seriousness and sentence severity, and so on. But even on the level of policy recommendations, Beccaria differs significantly from Montesquieu on several crucial matters – a point that Beccaria himself signals when he writes 'the thinking men for whom I write will know how to distinguish my steps from his'.[18] He rejects Montesquieu's defence of the power of executive or judicial clemency in criminal justice; he rejects Montesquieu's defence of shaming penalties; and he insists, *pace* Montesquieu, on public trials and on the equality of nobles and commoners before the criminal courts. Although these are mostly matters of doctrinal specifics rather than theoretical foundations, they reflect a deeper difference between Montesquieu's account and Beccaria's. Whereas Beccaria turns to the social contract and the limits of hypothetical consent to evaluate the legal order generally and criminal justice in particular, Montesquieu ignores such modern abstractions and turns instead to the laws of nature and the appropriateness of the law to the particular people over whom it governs.[19]

Perhaps the most common reading of Beccaria's philosophical significance – particularly in the English-speaking world – is that he was a great utilitarian theorist: an inspiration to Bentham, a true heir to Helvétius[20] and so on. But here, too, we encounter difficulties right away. First, although Beccaria appears to suggest that laws should be evaluated on the basis of whether they 'conduce to *the greatest happiness shared among the greater number*',[21] he does so not as a general declaration of his utilitarian principles but rather as a way of attacking laws that were quite explicitly tools for the oppression of the majority by a powerful minority. In Beccaria's hands, the utilitarian principle is not a general yardstick for measuring social policy; it is instead a means for attacking specific laws and practices that disregard the happiness of some people almost entirely.

There are precious few places in the work as a whole where utility does any argumentative work at all. For Beccaria, unlike for Helvétius or Bentham, utility was a principle of quite limited application. The right to punish does not descend from the principle of utility, according to Beccaria,[22] and neither does

[17] Most of Montesquieu's most important insights into criminal law are set out in book 6 of *De l'esprit des lois* [1748] (all references to this book are from the Pléiade edition: Montesquieu, *Oeuvres Complètes* vol 2 edited by R Caillois (Paris, Gallimard, 1951)).

[18] Beccaria, above n 7 at 8 ('Introduction').

[19] When discussing positive law, Montesquieu insists that 'le gouvernement le plus conforme à la nature est celui dont la disposition particulière se rapporte mieux à la disposition du people pour lequel il est établi' (Montesquieu, above n 17 at 237). But Montesquieu's method is notoriously opaque. He does not argue for a position so much as guide the reader through a series of considerations and historical developments, allowing her to draw her own conclusions.

[20] G Francioni advocates for this Helvétius-inspired utilitarian reading of Beccaria in 'Beccaria, philosophe utilitariste' in Audegean et al (eds), above n 3, 23.

[21] Beccaria, above n 7 at 7 ('Introduction') (emphasis in original).

[22] For the retributivist connotations of tracing the right to punish to an original contract, see DB Young, 'Cesare Beccaria: Utilitarian or Retributivist?' (1983) 11 *Journal of Criminal Justice* 318.

justice or the dignity of individual persons.[23] Beccaria insists that states must make laws to ensure conditions of general peace, but he does not insist that all such laws must serve only the maximisation of happiness. He does sometimes use language that strongly suggests that his account of criminalisation is utilitarian. For instance, he writes that 'the one true measure of criminality is the damage done to the nation',[24] and that 'the true measure of crime is … *harm to society*'.[25] Nevertheless, it is clear from the ensuing discussion that Beccaria's understanding of harm to society is not a simple tabulation of pleasure and pain. The most serious crimes deserving of the most severe punishments, he insists, are those that 'directly destroy society or its representative … which are called *lèse majesté* or sedition'.[26] The seriousness of crime has more to do with the seriousness of its attack on the legal order, rather than of the particular harms that it might impose upon particular victims. In this way, Beccaria's use of utilitarianism in his law-reform efforts is an excellent example of a phenomenon to which Michael Oakeshott draws our attention. He writes:

> The principle of utility performed wonders in the reform of the law, or rather wonders were performed in its name, but this was possible only because the inherent fallacies which lie at the root of [this] principle were unappreciated or neglected. The principle, for the purpose of reform, was a mere *obiter dictum* …[27]

Finally, one might try to suggest that the structure of the book is evidence of Beccaria's thorough-going utilitarianism. *On Crimes and Punishments* begins with two short preliminary sections that seem, at first glance, to be oriented toward utilitarianism. But upon closer inspection, it quickly becomes clear that these are just exercises in throat-clearing before the real argument begins. In the note to the reader, Beccaria insists that his account concerns 'political justice', which is to be distinguished from divine revelation and natural law. He goes on to say that this is all about 'what is socially useful and what is harmful'.[28] He then follows this with an introduction in which he sets out his famous formulation of '*the greatest happiness shared among the greater number*'.[29] All this talk of what is socially useful and of maximising happiness among the greater number might seem to set down a clear utilitarian agenda for the book as a whole. In fact, however, the note to the reader is a defensive argument written at a time and in a place where charges of blasphemy were dangerous. Beccaria is simply insisting that his arguments about how governments ought to make penal policy are not at odds with dominant views about natural law and divine revelation; they are simply two different domains of reasoning.[30] And the introduction, in which he

[23] See Hart, above n 2 at 50–51.
[24] Beccaria, above n 7 at 22 (ch 7).
[25] Ibid at 24.
[26] Ibid at 24–25. For discussion, see Scolnicov, ch 5 in this volume.
[27] Oakeshott, above n 8 at 148.
[28] Beccaria, above n 7 at 5 ('To the Reader').
[29] Ibid at 7 ('Introduction').
[30] On the fundamental reorientation for criminal justice policy that this entails, see Lavi, ch 6 in this volume.

sets out his famous 'greatest happiness' maxim, is designed simply to get certain worries out of the way before the argument begins. He is interested in pointing out that the laws that European countries have inherited from earlier times did not take seriously the basic claim of justification that any legal order must face. That is, they were quite clearly just the private preserve of a small governing élite, not even trying to serve the whole people over whom they ruled. Beccaria's emphasis is not on aggregate utility maximisation; his emphasis, instead, is on the distribution of benefits (*any* benefits) to the *greater* number, as opposed to the *lesser*. This argument is not a specifically utilitarian one; it is simply an argument that legal systems cannot just be tools to 'distribute benefits in the hands of a few';[31] they must be answerable to all those over whom they claim authority.

It is remarkable just how distinctly un-utilitarian Beccaria's starting point is when he begins his positive argument in earnest, in chapter 1. For a true utilitarian like Jeremy Bentham, the social contract is a distraction from the one true justifying principle, which is utility. For Bentham, the entire practice of threatening and carrying out criminal punishment is justified as a means of maximising the happiness of the greatest number. 'The general object which all laws have, or ought to have, in common,' Bentham insists, 'is to augment the total happiness of the community'.[32] For Bentham, laws are justified where they aim to maximise aggregate happiness, whether or not those subject to the laws consented to them or to the authority of those who drafted the laws. By contrast, Beccaria's argumentative starting-point is (as is typical of most political theorists of the eighteenth century) the wild, lawless freedom of all persons in the state of nature. The fundamental normative question for Beccaria in making sense of political authority is how states could come to have legitimate public authority over hitherto free persons. And the answer Beccaria comes up with is: through the consent of the governed. That is, the most normatively significant feature of persons is their freedom, and the only way to justify their subjection to public authority is through an exercise of that freedom in granting consent to the authority of the state over them.[33]

II. BECCARIA'S GREAT INSIGHT

Beccaria, it is clear, is not a fully paid-up follower of any of the leading camps of political thought of his time. He borrows from Rousseau and the broader social contract tradition, from Helvétius's utilitarianism, from Montesquieu and from others as needed to bolster his calls for criminal justice reform. However,

[31] Beccaria, above n 7 at 7 ('Introduction').

[32] J Bentham, 'Principles of Morals and Legislation' in his *A Fragment on Government with an Introduction to the Principles of Morals and Legislation* edited by W Harrison (Oxford, Basil Blackwell, 1948) at 281.

[33] For ways of developing this position into guarantees of fundamental rights, see Gur-Arye and Sebba and Er'el, chs 12 and 13 in this volume respectively.

Beccaria is happy to diverge from each orthodoxy as his argument requires. If *On Crimes and Punishments* remains relevant to us today, it is not as a repository of theoretical insights into any of these broader theoretical approaches. Beccaria, it is clear, keeps his eyes trained on object-level criminal justice reform at all times, and makes use of political theorising as the need arises.

Beccaria's focus on the reform of criminal justice institutions prompts him to pay careful attention to their proper place within the larger political order. In contrast to so many[34] political theorists of his day – and in contrast to most criminal justice theorists even today – he is remarkably clear-eyed about this. As Bernard Harcourt puts it, 'Beccaria was one of the first theorists who treated punishment as a matter of state legitimacy and political obligation, rather than from a moral or religious point of view – what evil people or sinners deserve.'[35] We should add that Beccaria avoids not only the moralist account of criminal punishment; he also avoids the thoroughgoing utilitarian account of criminal punishment, as well – and for the same reason. For both the moralist and the utilitarian assume that there is some good state of affairs (or some set of right relations) that the state may bring about through criminal justice – be it giving retribution to moral wrongdoers, maximising utility, or what have you: for moralists such as Michael Moore, criminal punishment secures the good of retributive justice;[36] for thoroughgoing utilitarians like Jeremy Bentham, criminal punishment serves to maximise aggregate happiness in the community. In short, on all these accounts, there is a valuable task calling out for someone – anyone – to carry it out. But for distinctly political accounts of criminal punishment like Beccaria's, it is an irreducibly *relational* idea: criminal punishment must come from the state because it is, first and foremost, about the relationship of political authority that obtains between the state and its subjects. And that relationship can only be preserved through the use of coercion of one kind or another. 'What were wanted,' Beccaria writes, 'were sufficiently tangible motives to prevent the despotic spirit of every man from resubmerging society's laws into the ancient chaos. These tangible motives are the punishments enacted against law-breakers.'[37] The state's role is not simply to enact laws, but also to see to it that they are effective in governing the conduct of its subjects.[38]

At the core of Beccaria's account of criminal justice is his understanding of criminal wrongdoing itself, which he refers to as 'the private usurpations of each individual'.[39] His point is that particular laws may aim at a variety of goods, but

[34] One notable exception is Rousseau, who anticipates Beccaria on this point. He writes: 'criminal laws … are not so much a specific kind of law as they are the sanction for all the others' (Rousseau, above n 12 at 83).

[35] Harcourt, above n 6 at 45.

[36] MS Moore, *Placing Blame: A Theory of Criminal Justice* (Oxford, Oxford University Press, 1997) 33.

[37] Beccaria, above n 7 at 9 (ch 1).

[38] For Kant, the very definition of law is set out in these terms: 'The lawgiving which is juridical … is a lawgiving which constrains, not an allurement, which invites.' Kant, above n 6 at 24 [6:219].

[39] Beccaria, above n 7 at 9 (ch 1).

the aim of punishment for their violation is always the same: to ensure that the laws remain effective so that they can provide a set of norms that apply in the same way to all, thereby avoiding the problems of the state of nature. In short, *pace* contemporary utilitarian *and* retributivist accounts, Beccaria insists that the criminal law has *no* freestanding purpose of its own; its purpose is ancillary to the value of the rest of the legal system. Put another way, Beccaria anticipates the 'political turn' in criminal law theory that has dominated discussion in the English-speaking world in the last few years.[40]

Once we see that the purpose of criminal punishment is the upholding of the law, it becomes clear that criminal law is but one of several ways of ensuring the law's effectiveness that are at the state's disposal. Beccaria anticipates several centuries of 'police science' with an extended discussion of the value of police measures such as street lighting, the posting of guards, public admonitions to keep the peace, and the like.[41] The point is that if punishment is a mechanism for ensuring the effectiveness of the state's laws, this end may be served as well or (often) better by non-punitive pre-emptive police mechanisms. In a more modern vein, we could add to Beccaria's list a variety of other measures that can be justified in part as instruments to diminish the incidence of various forms of criminal activity: economic redistribution, public education and health services, and the like.[42] In short, once we see the point of criminal law and punishment as concerned with ensuring the effectiveness of the laws, we can see that in most cases this end can be served as well or better by policing and other measures. This is true whether or not one takes a distinctly utilitarian approach to government. For whoever takes the effectiveness of laws seriously – be they utilitarians, strict Kantians, Thomist natural lawyers, or anyone else – can see that there are a variety of measures besides criminal punishment that may ensure that the laws will actually govern the relations among people in the jurisdiction.

III. BECCARIA'S DARKER LEGACY

A. Beccaria on Hypothetical Consent

Although Beccaria's insight into the supportive role of criminal justice was largely ignored by contemporary Anglo-American criminal law theory, Beccaria's

[40] I have argued for a 'political' turn of this sort in criminal law theorising for some time. See M Thorburn, 'Criminal Law as Public Law' in RA Duff & SP Green (eds), *Philosophical Foundations of Criminal Law* (Oxford, Oxford University Press, 2011) 42; 'Punishment and Public Authority' in A du Bois-Pedain, M Ulväng & P Asp (eds), *Criminal Law and the Authority of the State* (Oxford, Hart Publishing, 2017) 7; 'Criminal Punishment and the Right to Rule' (2020) 70 *University of Toronto Law Journal, Supplement 1* 44.

[41] Beccaria, above n 7 at 29 (ch 11).

[42] This is a point that Vincent Chiao emphasises in *Criminal Law in the Age of the Administrative State* (Oxford, Oxford University Press, 2018). See also Duff and Marshall, ch 3 in this volume.

invocation of an extra-legal standard by which to evaluate criminal law, institutions and practices has been widely emulated. For Beccaria, that standard is one of hypothetical consent to the terms of a social contract. Beccaria's account of the social contract is sketchy in the extreme: he develops it over just less than one paragraph of text. He seems to develop it simply as a winding up of the account of criminal law and punishment, which is the main object of his interest. What is clear even from the tiny fragment of an argument Beccaria provides, however, is that his understanding of the social contract sees it as a sort of bargain that can be made on fair or on unfair terms. In this manner, Beccaria's account is more reminiscent of Locke's understanding of the social contract than Rousseau's. Like Locke, Beccaria insists, first, that the social contract is something we enter into by choice and for good prudential reasons and, second, that the social contract only empowers the state to act for what is actually to the benefit of its members. Beccaria makes clear that entering into the social contract is a choice each of us makes for the sake of our private benefit: 'Wearied by living in an unending state of war and by a freedom rendered useless by the uncertainty of retaining it, they sacrifice a part of that freedom in order to enjoy what remains in security and calm.'[43] In this, Beccaria echoes Locke's famous phrase that 'The great and *chief end* therefore, of Men's uniting into Commonwealths, and putting themselves under Government, *is the Preservation of their Property*.'[44]

Beccaria had practical reasons for following Locke's account of the social contract over Rousseau's. For Rousseau, the idea of an original contract is a way of making sense of how a public authority can justifiably impose demands upon hitherto free persons. Referring to the present arrangement of states and laws, Rousseau famously asserted 'How did this … come about? I do not know. What can make it legitimate? I believe I can solve this question.'[45] That is, Rousseau employs the social contract to solve a highly abstract question: How is it possible for states to wield legitimate authority over free persons? If they are genuinely free, then how could they ever fall under an unwaivable obligation to do as states require them to do through their laws? The mere giving of consent will not do, for states do not merely offer a good bargain that we should keep to if we know what is good for us (or that we have some moral reason to keep to on grounds of 'fair play'). Instead, they claim to hold coercive authority over their subjects come what may: it is not open to us to say that we are no longer obligated by our state's laws, or to say that we have decided no longer to abide by them. And that is fundamentally at odds with the consent theory, for it is a standard part of voluntarily granting consent to someone or something that we can withdraw

[43] Beccaria, above n 7 at 9 (ch 1).

[44] J Locke, *Two Treatises of Government* edited by P Laslett (Cambridge, Cambridge University Press, 1988) 350–351.

[45] Rousseau, above n 12 at 43. (The expression Rousseau uses that is translated as 'I do not know' – 'je l'ignore' – might also be translated as 'I ignore it'. That would reinforce my point here even more strongly.)

that consent at some future time. This is why Rousseau sets aside talk of consent as a ground of the state's authority. It is not whether we did consent – or even whether it would have been *reasonable* to consent had we been asked – that matters. All that matters for Rousseau is whether the state's laws could have been the object of a general will – whether they have the formal generality and substantive aim toward the common good.[46]

It is important to see just how different Beccaria's argument is from that of many others in the social contract tradition such as, say, Rousseau or Kant or Hobbes. For each of these writers, the social contract provides a normative ground for the rights of states to make laws and to enforce them with coercion. What they do not provide, however, are strict limits on the rights of states to punish based on the limits of consent. For Rousseau, famously, we give up everything to the public authority by joining the social contract. 'Just as nature gives each man absolute power over his members,' Rousseau writes, 'the social pact gives the body politic *absolute power* over all its members …'.[47] And, most extremely, Rousseau insists that 'the Citizen is no longer judge of the danger the law wills him to risk … *his life is* no longer just a bounty of nature *but a conditional gift of the State*.'[48] That is, the social contract for Rousseau (as for Kant), is not a commercial transaction entered into in order to improve our empirical conditions; it is a way of understanding the legitimacy of the power structure under which we must live.[49] So, too, with Hobbes (with the exception that on his account, we may not consent to be killed).

If we start with this very different idea of the social contract, a wholly different way of thinking about the limits of legitimate state coercion arises. State coercion is necessary, on this account, insofar as it serves to put in place a rightful condition. Insofar as it goes beyond that purpose, however, it no longer conforms to the ideal of what public authority is supposed to be doing. This does not, in itself, give us the right to ignore the state's laws. It is still of paramount importance that we live under laws so that the basic problem of the state of nature can be solved. But it means that there is a meaningful standard (a 'regulative ideal') by which we may evaluate the workings of a given state. In many modern constitutional states – from Germany to Canada, Israel to South Africa – that regulative ideal has been given constitutional status and has been coupled with the power of constitutional judicial review. But that strategy for understanding the limits of legitimate state coercive power is part of a very different understanding of the social contract. It is not open to Beccaria.

[46] Ibid at 59.
[47] Ibid at 63.
[48] Ibid at 66 (emphasis added).
[49] 'By the well-being of a state must not be understood the welfare of its citizens and their happiness; for happiness can perhaps come to them more easily and as they would like it to in a state of nature …' (Kant, above n 6 at 103 [6:318]).

Beccaria, by contrast, sees the social contract as a strictly limited affair. As with Locke, the limits on legitimate state action derive from the limits of what it would be rational for persons to agree to when entering civil society from the state of nature. From this premise, Beccaria insists that state power is severely constrained to act only for the benefit of the law's subjects: '[N]one wished to surrender to the public repository more than the smallest possible portion [of freedom] consistent with persuading others to defend him. ... Any punishment that goes beyond the need to preserve this bond is unjust by its very nature.'[50] It is from this crucial premise about the nature of the social contract that Beccaria derives his principle of necessity in punishment, which plays such an important role in his policy recommendations later in the book: 'every act of authority between one man and another which is not derived from absolute necessity is tyrannous'.[51] In this way, Beccaria sets in place a pattern that will dominate centuries of criminal law thinking. Instead of inquiring as to the foundations of public authority (in the manner of Rousseau and Kant) and allowing democratic deliberation within the limits set by that account to determine the content of the criminal law, most modern criminal law theorists have followed Beccaria. Like him, they have sought some sort of yardstick outside of the arena of political debate by which to evaluate criminal laws, institutions and practices. Some have looked to moral wrongdoing as their guide; others have looked to the maximisation of utility; yet others have insisted that JS Mill's harm principle would provide a good guide to criminalisation. But whatever the particular principle that criminal law theorists have embraced, most of them have followed Beccaria's general approach and insisted that there is some correct answer to the question of what should and should not be criminally prohibited, how severely each crime should be punished, what procedures should be followed in the investigation and prosecution of criminal wrongdoers, etc. For better or for worse, Beccaria set the course of criminal law theorising in this way for centuries to come.

B. On Offices and the Rule of Law

Along with the evaluation of criminal justice practices according to a standard of hypothetical consent, Beccaria's most lasting contribution to criminal justice thinking is his critique of judicial discretion. It is here that he sounds most like Montesquieu, with his emphasis on constraining administrative and (especially) judicial discretion through codification. But unlike Montesquieu, the roots of Beccaria's argument are squarely in the social contract. Whereas Montesquieu

[50] Beccaria, above n 7 at 11 (ch 2).
[51] Ibid at 10 (ch 2).

simply asserts that fixed laws are characteristic of republican forms of government and the absence of written law is typical of tyrannical ones,[52] Beccaria insists that the need for fixed, codified law and the elimination of judicial discretion arises from the social contract:

> [L]aws alone can decree punishments for crimes … this authority resides only with the legislator, who represents the whole of society united by the social contract. No magistrate (who is a member of society) can justly establish of his own accord any punishment for any member of … society.[53]

As a result, Beccaria insists that '[n]or can the authority to interpret the laws devolve upon the criminal judges, for the same reason that they are not legislators'.[54]

Beccaria's argument from the social contract to the constraint on judicial discretion is not fully worked out, but the outline, at least, is clear. He insists that the social contract gives rise to a special entity that is entitled to speak on behalf of all – and this, Beccaria insists, is what he calls 'the sovereign', for it is 'the sovereign [who is] the repository of the current will of all'.[55] Beccaria understands that there is something very important about the standing of a public authority to speak in the name of all and that the sovereign – and *only* the sovereign – can claim that standing. The legal order, on his account, is made up of a law-making sovereign that represents the society as a whole and then many private persons who must abide by its laws. Now, what he means by 'sovereign' in this context is the power that makes the general laws that bind everyone in the jurisdiction. On Beccaria's understanding, judges and magistrates who interpret the laws, sheriffs who enforce the laws, and all other public officials are all just what he calls 'members of society'; accordingly, every time we are subject to their discretion, we have fallen victim to a 'petty tyranny'.[56]

The only way to ensure that we are subject only to the general will, rather than the petty tyrannies of individual 'members of society', according to Beccaria, is to do away with any sort of discretion in the application of the law. At every stage, the laws must be explicit and capable of being applied to a given factual situation mechanically, without any exercise of judgement. He writes:

> When a fixed code of laws, which must be followed to the letter, leaves the judge no role other than that of inquiring into citizens' actions and judging whether they conform or not to the written law … then the subjects are not exposed to the petty tyrannies of the many individuals enforcing the law …[57]

[52] Montesquieu, above n 17 at 311: 'Plus le gouvernement approche de la république, plus la manière de juger devient fixe … Dans les États despotiques, il n'y a point de loi …'

[53] Beccaria, above n 7 at 12 (ch 3).

[54] Ibid at 14 (ch 4).

[55] Ibid.

[56] Ibid at 15 (ch 4).

[57] Ibid.

This is a peculiar understanding of the rule of law, to say the least. According to Beccaria's vision, the sovereign (by which he seems to mean the lawgiver) has the authority to make laws over us because this body (be it an enlightened monarch or an elected body) is genuinely representative of us. *In what way* the lawgiver represents the general will, Beccaria does not make clear. A modern reader might assume that he is identifying the sovereign with the legislature that has democratic legitimacy because its members have been chosen by the society as a whole (and can be removed by the society as a whole if they misstep). If so, that would seem like a deeply voluntarist – dare one say 'populist'? – account of public authority. But there are good reasons to suppose that Beccaria – who seems to have been writing with Habsburg emperors in mind – is not focused on a democratic idea of legitimacy here. Accordingly it is not clear what is driving his argument about the limits of adjudication.

On many accounts of the rule of law, what is most important is that those who exercise public authority do so not in their private capacity (as a matter of their private right) but from a public office. Public office, as I have explained elsewhere,[58] is a way of solving the very problem that Beccaria confronts: squaring the coercive power of one person over another with an assertion of the equal claim of each person to independence. The solution that the idea of office presents is that it collects together a set of rights, liberties and powers as exercisable for the sake of some defining public purpose. The office of judge gives its occupant the power to impose a final resolution over a dispute, but it does not give this power to the occupant as a private right. Instead, the occupant of an office must act according to the reasons that define the office – for although the judge is the one to make the decision, it is not *her* decision to make on the basis of whatever reasons might suit her fancy. The judge (or the occupant of any public office) may make authoritative decisions about certain matters, but she may not make those decisions for her own private reasons; she must do so only as someone dutifully carrying out the purpose of the office.

Now, if we come to the problem of adjudicating criminal law cases with this idea of office in mind, the puzzle that Beccaria thought he faced quickly disappears. Judges are not simply private persons (or what he calls 'members of society') acting as they see fit. They are public office holders whose reasoning is constrained by the demands of their office. Although they make decisions under the law, they do so for public reasons that define their office, not for their own private reasons. It is for this reason that the decisions of public office holders must be subject to review: where they act for the wrong reasons, they have not carried out the function of the office; they have simply usurped the public office for their own private purposes. Further, if their understanding of the office's

[58] M Thorburn, 'Policing and Public Office' (2020) 70 *University of Toronto Law Journal, Supplement* 2 248.

public purpose is unreasonable, then we may say that their decision was a private one, peculiar to the occupant in her private capacity, and not attributable to the public office.[59] If judicial discretion is a serious problem in eighteenth-century Milan or elsewhere,[60] the solution is not to do away with judges altogether; it is to ensure that those who occupy a public office act according to the constraints of that office and to put in place mechanisms – appeal against judicial decisions, judicial review of administrative discretion, and the like – to ensure that those who occupy public office are actually limited in their decision-making by those constraints.

It is no great surprise to find Beccaria trying to make sense of the social contract tradition without any idea of public office. The idea of public office requires us to distinguish between the private purposes of individuals and the public purposes that we share as a society. Put another way, it requires that we distinguish sharply between the general will (which is concerned with the common interest) and the will of all (which is simply an aggregation of individuals' private purposes). And we have seen[61] that this is a distinction that Beccaria is unwilling to draw. On Rousseau's account, we can make sense of collective entities and their special will that takes their common interest as its object, and distinguish them from the specific wills of the individuals who make them up. On Beccaria's account, however, there is only ever the specific wills of individuals, either separate or aggregated. When judges are asked to adjudicate a case according to the law, on Beccaria's account, they can only ever apply their own private will to the problem, imposing their 'petty tyranny' over the criminal accused. They can never occupy a distinct position of public office, aimed at a public purpose and distinct from the pursuit of their own private ends. Any time a public official exercises discretion, Beccaria seems to suggest, there is nothing the law can have to say about the legality of its exercise. Or, put in the pointed and direct language of Richard Nixon, 'when the President does it, that means that it is not illegal'.[62]

[59] T Hobbes, *Leviathan* edited by Richard Tuck (Cambridge, Cambridge University Press, 1996) 231: 'The Office of sovereign, consisteth in the end, for which he was trusted with the sovereign power, namely the procuration of the safety of the people …' It is on the basis of this structure of office that we distinguish 'the king's two bodies' in English law; it is on the basis of this distinction that we distinguish the decisions of the President of the United States from the criminal designs of private citizen Richard Nixon; and it is on this basis that we have distinguished the rule of law from the tyranny of one person over another at least since the time of Hobbes.

[60] On this descriptive point, Beccaria was surely right. At the time of publication, many judicial offices in Continental Europe were inherited titles treated as a sort of private possession, much like titles of nobility. Indeed, in Ancien régime France, holders of inherited judicial offices were referred to as the '*noblesse de robe*'. See A Cremer, 'La genèse de la notion de noblesse de robe' (1999) 16 *Revue d'histoire moderne et contemporaine* 22.

[61] See n 13 and accompanying text.

[62] 'Excerpts from Interview with Nixon about Domestic Effects of Indochina War' *New York Times* (20 May 1977) A16.

IV. CONCLUSION

Beccaria's *On Crimes and Punishments* was a work of tremendous influence across eighteenth-century Europe. Its greatest accomplishment was to awaken philosophers, lawmakers and the broader reading public to the fact that criminal law and punishment are political institutions that must be justified as such. Mere facts about the law-breakers themselves – that they have done moral wrongs and that they deserve to be punished – will never be sufficient to justify the state's taking it upon itself to punish them. What we need is a relational account that explains the state's standing to sit in judgment and exercise coercive authority over criminal wrongdoers. Framing the debate in these terms was precisely what was required in the mid-eighteenth century. It is exactly what contemporary criminal law theory – dominated for so long by moralists and strict utilitarians – needs as well.

Beccaria's particular account of the political justification of criminal law and punishment, however, leaves much to be desired. In this chapter, I have drawn attention to two features of his account that stand out as particularly problematic. The first of these is Beccaria's account of the limits of the state's right to punish as based on the limits of what the parties to the social contract would consent to. Not only is this an implausible foundation for the limits of state power, it also displaces a more promising account based on the internal regulative principle of public authority. The second problem to which I have drawn attention is Beccaria's insistence that the lawgiver is the only public office and that judges must either apply laws mechanistically or else impose their private views on the parties. This account denies the possibility of a judicial office that makes it possible for its occupant to adjudicate disputes from a public point of view, without merely imposing her private will on the parties. As such, Beccaria's account simply does not countenance the possibility of public authority as expressed through a multitude of public offices: legislative, judicial, administrative and the like. This collapse of public offices into private interests not only makes it difficult for Beccaria to make sense of adjudication and administrative discretion in criminal justice; it seems to collapse the very idea of the rule of law itself.

8

Realism and the Rational Administration of the Law in Beccaria

VINCENT CHIAO

THE REPUTE OF Cesare Beccaria's *On Crimes and Punishments* is matched only by the terseness of its chapters. The entire treatise runs to a scant 80 pages in the David Young translation; the Richard Davies translation is slightly longer, but still only just exceeds 100 pages. The brevity of Beccaria's text is all the more notable when considered in light of the broad range of topics he discusses, from duelling to the death penalty, from how to prove crime to how to treat nobles, from a rudimentary psychology to the basic principles of the social contract. At the level of textual argument, Beccaria's writing is often elusive, couched in generalities and ambiguous as to its sources and targets.[1] Add Beccaria's frequently assertoric mode of presentation – often forgoing arguments in favour of bold conclusions – and *Of Crimes and Punishments* easily comes across as a Rorschach test, notable as much for what is read into it as for what is actually there.[2]

Certain broad themes are unmistakably part of Beccaria's treatise. For instance, as Bentham well recognised, a proto-utilitarian dimension is clearly evident in Beccaria's thinking: the first formulation of the utilitarian idea that law should seek to secure 'the greatest happiness of the greatest number' occurs in the introduction, and Beccaria attended to the relation between the certainty

[1] Piers Beirne suggests that Beccaria deliberately 'employed an array of devious textual practices', motivated by 'the cautious dictum that it is better to be a secret witness of Enlightenment than a posthumously acknowledged martyr' ('Inventing Criminology: The Science of Man in Cesare Beccaria's *Dei delitti e delle pene*' (1991) 29 *Criminology* 777 at 786). The organisation of the chapters appears to be due largely to the efforts of Pietro Verri, one of Beccaria's primary interlocutors, rather than to Beccaria himself. See ibid at 780 note 5; G Newman & P Marongiu, 'Penological Reform and the Myth of Beccaria' (1990) 28 *Criminology* 325 at 331.

[2] It is, Raymond Paternoster observes, 'thin with respect to any developed theory of crime or criminal conduct' ('How Much Do We Really Know about Criminal Deterrence' (2010) 100 *Journal of Criminal Law & Criminology* 765 at 770).

and severity of punishment centuries before Gary Becker. Beccaria was, as Raymond Paternoster puts it, the 'original deterrence theorist', emphasising that 'the self-interest to commit crime has to be thwarted by legal punishment that is certain, proportional, and swift'.[3] Philippe Audegean has noted Beccaria's insistence that 'the law does not bestow virtue upon any form of violence': punishment is, as Bentham would later argue, in all cases an evil that should be tolerated only insofar as necessary to secure other aims.[4] Just as clearly, however, there is a proto-contractualist line of thought in the volume, evident in the very first chapter, in which Beccaria insists that a sovereign's power is grounded in its citizens' decision to voluntarily alienate some portion of their pre-existing liberty in the name of preserving the remainder in 'security and calm'.[5]

How is the utilitarian aspect of Beccaria's thinking related to his concern with the conditions of political legitimacy? Beccaria's answer is succinct:

> [E]very act of authority between one man and another which is not derived from absolute necessity is tyrannous. Here, then, is the foundation of the sovereign's right to punish crimes: the necessity of defending the repository of the public well-being from the usurpations of individuals. The juster the punishments, the more sacred and inviolable is the security and the greater the freedom which the sovereign preserves for his subjects.[6]

The idea is that because private citizens are jealous of their liberty, they agree to alienate only so much as is necessary to safeguard their peace and security; insofar as safeguarding peace and security involves encroaching upon a person's liberty, the sovereign must act as the utilitarian social planner would, choosing the least restrictive means possible. This would seem to rule out purely expressive punishments, or indeed any punishment at all when peace and security can be purchased more cheaply. But why must citizens be so single minded about liberty? Why would they not also want the sovereign to uphold values, or condemn wrongdoers? And even if they do value liberty above all else, might we not regard those who prey on others as having forfeited their claims to liberty, at least to some (proportionate) degree? In that case, the appeal to the utilitarian social planner is otiose at best; perhaps even misguided, since by economising on punishment, the planner may be led to ignore the claim of the innocent to have their rights vindicated. Moreover, what if the citizens do not agree among themselves as to just how much peace and security they would like to purchase? Or what if they disagree whether it is fair to require a greater sacrifice from some,

[3] Ibid at 769.

[4] P Audegean, 'Cesare Beccaria's *On Crimes and Punishments*: the meaning and genesis of a jurispolitical pamphlet' (2017) 43 *History of European Ideas* 884 at 885.

[5] C Beccaria, *On Crimes and Punishments and Other Writings* edited by R Bellamy and translated by R Davies (Cambridge, Cambridge University Press, 1995) 9 (ch 1). See M De Caro, 'Utilitarianism and Retributivism in Cesare Beccaria' (2016) 2 *Italian Law Journal* 1.

[6] Beccaria, above n 5 at 10 (ch 2).

the easily protected, to subsidise the protection of others, whose security comes at a dearer price? Beccaria does not consider, much less answer, these questions.[7]

While I do not question this way of framing Beccaria – *On Crimes and Punishments* undoubtedly does feature elements of what we would today regard as contractarian and utilitarian political philosophy – my objective in this chapter is to consider two different, and perhaps less well-appreciated, ways of reading Beccaria's treatise. The first is in juxtaposition with a certain strand of American legal realism. The second is as a prophet of the administrative state, especially in connection with Weber's account of bureaucratic modes of social organisation. Re-reading Beccaria in these two frames reveals, I suggest, Beccaria's continuing salience for contemporary discussions of criminal law and policy.

I. REALISM

The 'core claim' of American legal realism, Brian Leiter has argued, is that judges (especially appellate judges) decide cases by attending to the particular facts of a given case, even when those facts are not decisive, or even relevant, under the acknowledged legal rules.[8] Law is indeterminate, in the sense that legal reasons fail both to uniquely explain or uniquely justify the decisions that judges make.[9] Legal rules are less authoritative than they might appear. One might read Beccaria's well-known distrust of judges in this light, particularly in passages in which Beccaria suggests that open-ended judicial discretion to apply law makes legal decisions subject to

> the good or bad logic on the part of the judge and of the state of his digestion, and would depend on the turbulence of his emotions, on the weakness of the aggrieved party, on the judge's relations with the plaintiff and on all those tiny pressures which, to the wavering mind of man, change the appearance of every object.[10]

Yet it would be misleading to read Beccaria as presaging the realists' scepticism about formalistic modes of legal reasoning. For starters, Beccaria did not regard untrammelled judicial discretion as an inevitable feature of legal reasoning. On the contrary, Beccaria's reason for distrusting judges was that he thought that a

[7] Though for a contrary view, see P Audegean, *La philosophie de Beccaria: savoir punir, savoir écrire, savoir produire* (Paris, Vrin, 2010). Audegean provides a detailed reconstruction of Beccaria's political philosophy, and concludes that Beccaria did not perceive a conflict between utilitarianism and contractualism because he believed that their conclusions would inevitably converge. In Beccaria's eyes, Audegean claims, 'les conséquences empiriques confirment toujours les principes de justice, qui peuvent donc être déduits ou justifiés aussi bien par leur rationalité intrinsèque que par leurs effets' (ibid at 167).

[8] B Leiter, 'American Legal Realism', in M Golding & W Edmundson (eds), *The Blackwell Guide to the Philosophy of Law and Legal Theory* (Oxford, Blackwell, 2005) 50 at 52–53.

[9] Ibid at 51.

[10] Beccaria, above n 5 at 15 (ch 4).

formal approach to legal interpretation law could rein in the excessive powers of the judiciary. In other words, the basis for Beccaria's distrust of judges was not that law cloaked what is in fact the arbitrary exercise of power; rather, it was that judges do not feel themselves sufficiently constrained by law. It is for this reason that Beccaria excoriated judges for ignoring the letter of the law in favour of 'the spirit of the laws'. '[T]he authority to interpret the laws,' Beccaria warned, cannot 'devolve upon the criminal judges, for … they are not legislators'. Instead of interpreting the law, judges should be limited to reasoning in a formal and syllogistic manner: 'the major premise should be the general law; the minor, the conformity or otherwise of the action with the law; and the conclusion, freedom or punishment'.[11] Ultimately, Beccaria's distrust of judicial discretion leads him to a rather extreme form of legal formalism, realism's traditional *bête noire*.

Nevertheless, despite Beccaria's faith in a formalistic mode of legal interpretation, there is an important affinity between *On Crimes and Punishments* and certain strands of American legal realism. To appreciate this requires a brief foray into realism. Scholars have emphasised that the realists did not regard the claim that legal reasons often do not point to a single uniquely correct solution as leading to wholesale scepticism about legal reasoning. Jerome Frank's focus on the idiosyncratic psychology of judges aside, few realists claimed that judicial behaviour was in principle inexplicable or indefensible.[12] Insofar as there is a single unifying thread in American legal realism, Priel has recently pointed out, it is in their resistance to the 'autonomy of law'. That is, the realists resisted the idea that manipulation of abstract legal concepts is sufficient to account for (or defend) legal reasoning.[13] Legal reasoning could not afford to focus solely on formal reasoning while neglecting what officials and judges do with those legal rules and concepts. As Llewellyn saw it, realists were concerned to describe and predict the effects of law on the community:

> 'Law' without effect approaches zero in meaning … To know law, then, to know anything of what is necessary to judge or evaluate law, we must proceed into these areas which have traditionally been conceived (save by the historical schools) as not-law. Not only what courts do instead of what courts say, but also what difference it makes to anybody that they do it.[14]

The realists' attack on the autonomy of legal reasoning, and their insistence that law be evaluated in terms of its observable effects, was not novel: 'All this is nothing new in social science … The only novel feature is the application to that

[11] Ibid at 14 (ch 4).
[12] Leiter, above n 8 at 54.
[13] D Priel, 'The Return of Legal Realism', in MD Dubber & C Tomlins (eds), *The Oxford Handbook of Legal History* (Oxford, Oxford University Press, 2018) 457 at 465.
[14] K Llewellyn, 'Some Realism About Realism – Responding to Dean Pound', reprinted in WW Fisher, M Horwitz & T Reed (eds), *American Legal Realism* (Oxford, Oxford University Press, 1993) 68 at 74.

most conventionalized and fiction-ridden of disciplines, the law.'[15] Felix Cohen was blunter, opining that '[t]he age of the classical jurists is over'. In Cohen's view,

> [t]he vested interests of our law schools in an 'independent' science of law are undermined by every advance in our knowledge of the social antecedents and consequences of judicial decisions ... [L]egal science necessarily involves us in psychology, economics, and political theory ... For the lawyer, no less than for the legal scholar, handling of materials hitherto considered 'non-legal' assumes increasing importance.[16]

On this account, the realists were not committed to the claim that legal reasoning is fatally indeterminate; they were committed to the claim that formal legal reasoning is enthymematic. The validity of legal arguments depends upon suppressed premises. While the realists were heterogeneous when it came to specifying what types of premises would make legal reasoning sound, they were unified in the belief that those premises were not describable purely in terms of abstract doctrinal concepts.

However, once law's autonomy is called into question, so too is its authority: if law cannot claim the mantle of scientific objectivity and expertise, what reason do laypeople have for deferring to the opinions of judges and lawyers? Perhaps, just as liberty requires dispelling the power of the priests, so too it requires disenchanting the social status of judges. From a critical point of view, the realists' attack on the autonomy of law was tantamount to pointing out the emperor's new clothes – or, perhaps, the judge's new robes. Yet, as Priel has emphasised, this is not where the realists left matters.

The realists were not of one mind about their positive agenda. Priel distinguishes between traditional and scientific realists. Traditional realists, most prominently Llewellyn, turned to the organic values of the community to supply the needed premises: even if law cannot claim objectivity in the abstract, it can nevertheless claim a kind of legitimacy insofar as it draws upon a community's own standards of decency and fair dealing. As Priel puts it, supplementing abstract legal concepts with a concrete community's values and traditions showed that 'the law was fairly determinate, that judges were not free to decide cases any way they wanted, and when legal materials are properly analyzed, they reveal the law'.[17]

In contrast, scientific realists, such as Holmes and Felix Cohen, charted a different route by turning to the empirical sciences. Legal reasoning on its own could not claim the mantle of science, but it could be shaped, and remade, in the

[15] K Llewellyn, 'A Realistic Jurisprudence – The Next Step', reprinted in Fisher, Horwitz & Reed (eds), above n 14, 53 at 57.

[16] FS Cohen, 'Transcendental Nonsense and the Functional Approach', reprinted in Fisher, Horwitz & Reed (eds), above n 14, 212 at 218. In Cohen's view, law has more in common with history and social science than with mathematics and logic (ibid at 224).

[17] Priel, above n 13 at 466.

light of the findings of empirical science, as Holmes famously suggested in 'The Path of the Law'. From the perspective of scientific realism,

> [l]aw is an instrument for improving the lives of people, and its legitimacy depends on its ability to *actually* achieve that goal. ... Law understood as a science in this sense could only have a place in the university not by isolating itself from other disciplines, but by incorporating their insights.[18]

Priel's distinction sheds considerable light on the affinity between Beccaria and the realists – the scientific realists in particular. It is important to appreciate that although Beccaria espoused a formalistic mode of legal reasoning, this was not because he subscribed to the formalist's view of law as an autonomous science. Beccaria's formalism is quite differently motivated than that of the nineteenth-century academic lawyers to whom the realists were responding. (Or, for that matter, the twenty-first-century formalists inspired by Weinrib's approach to private law.) As we have seen, Beccaria's argument for formalistic legal reasoning was based on his belief that unconstrained judges would run roughshod over the liberty of a state's citizens, claiming for themselves the sovereign's prerogative to make law. Interpretation of the laws in cases of doubt is a task for the sovereign, 'the legitimate repository of the current sum of the will of the whole of society', rather than the judge, 'whose task is merely that of enquiring whether a given man has committed an unlawful act or not'.[19] Beccaria's appeal to an interpretation-free, syllogistic legal reasoning does not rest on an optimistic view of law as an autonomous *Wissenschaft*, but rather on a division of labour: the sovereign makes the law, whereas judges merely apply it. Since law's authority arises out of the consent of the governed, it is necessary to keep judges on a tight leash in order to prevent them from arrogating to themselves (e.g., under the guise of interpreting the 'spirit of the laws') power that is only legitimately wielded by the sovereign as the representative of the people.[20] In short, Beccaria's argument for restricting judicial power is based on his conception of law's authority as resting in the sovereign (the 'current sum of the will of the whole of society') rather than any kind of faith in the power of abstract legal concepts to determine cases in a neutral, apolitical manner. What separates Beccaria from Felix Cohen is not faith in what Cohen mocked as the 'heaven of legal concepts', but rather the degree to which each thought ethical controversy could be separated out for legislative rather than judicial resolution. What unifies them is the shared suspicion that the use of traditional legal concepts – what Cohen jeeringly referred to as

[18] Ibid at 474.

[19] Beccaria, above n 5 at 14 (ch 4).

[20] Though it would be anachronistic to read Beccaria as a democrat; for Beccaria, the contrary force to aristocratic elites is not representative democracy but rather the sovereign monarch. See Audegean, above n 7 at 136 note 2.

'transcendental nonsense' – 'hides … the ethical character of every judicial question, and thus serves to perpetuate class prejudices and uncritical moral assumptions'.[21]

Seen in this light, while Beccaria's formalism is of course anathema to the realists, Beccaria shared with the realists the scepticism that the confident assurances of judges – law's high priests – could be sufficient to account for law's authority. In this regard, Beccaria is closer to Justice Scalia than to the formalists. Like Scalia, Beccaria insisted that certain, determinate law protects individuals from arbitrary power – a 'solid shield of a firm, clear principle enunciated in earlier cases', as Scalia put it.[22] In claiming that judicial interpretation in the absence of a 'solid textual anchor or an established social norm … appears uncomfortably like legislation', Scalia might just as well have cited Beccaria's dictum that judges are not to interpret criminal law, as that is a properly legislative function.[23] If anything, Beccaria articulates a more extreme view than Scalia. Scalia did not deny that judges must inevitably interpret the law, nor, as the passage just cited indicates, did he doubt that judicial interpretation could at times go beyond the text and rest on an 'established social norm'. In contrast, Beccaria insisted that 'a fixed code of laws, which must be followed to the letter', would protect people from the 'petty tyrannies of the many individuals enforcing the law'.[24] Civilian and common lawyers may have differing views about just how seriously we should take Beccaria's rhetoric in such passages but, be that as it may, Beccaria and Scalia are both clearly concerned to restrict the power of judges to impose their will on citizens in ways that go beyond what the citizens themselves have authorised. In short, strict application of the law as written is valued on *political* rather than *legal* grounds.

Beccaria is thus not obsessed with rules for their own sake. He is convinced that open-ended discretion results in the arbitrary power of some over others – in petty (and perhaps not-so-petty) tyranny.[25] In this respect, the concern shared by Beccaria and Scalia to tie the hands of the judiciary via strict interpretation of the law reflects a republican conception of liberty, in the sense of an individual's independence from the arbitrary will of others.[26] For Beccaria, the lack of security in the state of nature is what justifies the transition to civil order, in which freedom is made meaningful insofar as each is protected from the arbitrary will of others, private citizens and public officials alike.[27] Strict interpretation

[21] Cohen, above n 16 at 221.

[22] A Scalia, 'The Rule of Law as the Law of Rules' (1989) 56 *University of Chicago Law Review* 1175 at 1180.

[23] Ibid at 1185.

[24] Beccaria, above n 5 at 15 (ch 4).

[25] Ibid at 29 (ch 11): '[I]f the magistrate implements laws which are arbitrary and not set down in a code which is diffused among all the citizens, then the door is open to tyranny, which always hems in political liberty.'

[26] 'Liberté comme sûreté', as Audegean puts it: see Audegean, above n 7 at 130–134. See also P Pettit, *Republicanism: A Theory of Freedom and Government* (Oxford, Oxford University Press, 1999).

[27] Audegean, above n 7 at 56–60.

is grounded not in a Platonic view of law, but rather in a concern to protect secure expectations of non-interference (what Beccaria calls 'certainty') from unlicensed meddling by public officials.[28]

Yet while Beccaria's grounds for a strict mode of judicial interpretation more closely resemble Scalia's than the formalists', there is nevertheless an important divergence between the two. Priel's distinction between traditional and scientific realisms is once again instructive. For while Scalia's reference to 'established social norm[s]' is a nod toward Priel's conception of traditional realism, it is the scientific realists who are Beccaria's spiritual heirs. Beccaria's treatment of penal policy in *On Crimes and Punishments* is of a piece with Holmes' famous paean to the 'man of statistics and the master of economics'.[29] Beccaria's view that crimes are to be assessed in terms of their harm to society (in chapter 7); that proof of crime be viewed probabilistically (chapter 9); that even the suffering of the guilty is to be minimised (chapter 19); that the severity of punishment is inversely related to its certainty, that its expected value is to be assessed against the expected advantage of a criminal act, and that increasing punishment severity on other grounds is 'tyrannical' (chapter 27); that capital punishment is relatively ineffective (chapter 28); as well as his focus on preventing, rather than punishing crime (chapters 31 and 41), and on education and knowledge as a means of crime prevention (chapters 42 and 45), all point toward a scientific, rather than traditional, view of penal law and its administration. The sovereign's right to legislate is conditioned on our confidence that its exercise of that right is calculated to maximise our liberty, by ensuring that each exercise of penal power is narrowly tailored; and, perhaps more importantly, called upon only when other means of preventing crime more cheaply have failed. Neither community tradition nor the oracular pronouncements of judges (or other social elites) can fill that role; instead, law's legitimacy rests on its soundness as policy.[30] In the context of contemporary debates about criminal justice, Beccaria's vision of a penal law grounded on social science rather than tradition, as well as his endorsement of an assertively reformist view of penal policy, lives on most clearly in proponents of so-called 'harm reduction', who advocate for a more empirically grounded, and less overtly moralistic, approach to crime and punishment; and more generally in champions of 'evidence-based policy'.

As I see it, the main alternative to a Beccarian social scientific approach to criminal justice lies in the efforts, by theorists such as Duff and Kleinfeld, to motivate a methodology of 'rational reconstruction' in the criminal law.[31] As Duff explains it, rational reconstruction 'reconstructs what the practice or

[28] Ibid at 134–140.

[29] OW Holmes, 'The Path of the Law', reprinted in (1998) 78 *Boston University Law Review* 699 at 708.

[30] Audegean, above n 4 at 894–895. See also Thorburn, ch 7 in this volume.

[31] RA Duff, *The Realm of Criminal Law* (Oxford, Oxford University Press, 2018) ch 1; J Kleinfeld, 'Reconstructivism: The Place of Criminal Law in Ethical Life' (2016) 129 *Harvard Law Review* 1485.

institution in question must, in terms of the values intrinsic to it, aspire to be'.[32] In this respect rational reconstruction is aligned with formalist approaches to law, in that both emphasise that the concepts and principles they seek to elucidate are drawn from the law itself, rather than imposed on it from outside, whether by legislation, political philosophy, critical sociology or any other allegedly 'extrinsic' set of values. That makes it a reconstructive, rather than simply critical, methodology: the concepts and principles that the theorist uses to assess some area of law are 'discerned within, or excavated from' that area of law 'as it actually is'.[33] Yet rational reconstruction in the criminal law, at least as practised by Duff and Kleinfeld, is also distinct from the neo-formalism of the Weinrib school in private law. As Duff makes clear, the social practice he seeks to reconstruct is contingent and historically formed. The concepts and principles immanent in that practice are thus 'local or parochial'.[34] For Duff and Kleinfeld alike, rational reconstruction is not a matter of retrieving criminal law's alleged One True Essence, but rather of reconstructing the meaning of criminal law for a particular community, in a particular social, historical and political context. In this respect, Duff and Kleinfeld are more closely aligned to traditional realism than they are to formalism, in either its classical or contemporary versions.

It is notable, however, that neither custom nor conceptual analysis figures in any substantial way in Beccaria's thinking about crime and punishment. *On Crimes and Punishments* is a model of critical, rather than conventional, moral reasoning. Rather than criminalising actions simply because they violate traditional social norms, whether actions are to be deemed crimes should depend on their injury to society. In contrast to reconstructivists, Beccaria's argument is, in effect: even though we signed up for a social contract authorising a sovereign to criminalise and punish, in so doing we did not consent to criminalisation and punishment of 'vices and sins' generally, but only of the 'unjust privileges' which accrue to those who 'satisfy their own desires at the expense of others'.[35] Beccaria's approach to crime and punishment, as well as his evident concern to limit the power of judges, thus has more in common with the theorists of the administrative state than with the conservatism of rational reconstruction.[36] At the same time, Beccaria's critical methodology leads him to ground

[32] Duff, above n 31 at 13.

[33] Ibid.

[34] Ibid at 4. As Kleinfeld puts it, '[e]mbodied ethical life is inscribed in custom' (above n 31 at 1552).

[35] Audegean, above n 4 at 888.

[36] Compare Kleinfeld: 'Reconstructivism is thus conservative … in the small-c, Burkean sense: the reconstructive spirit is animated by respect for evolved moral culture and skeptical of projects in social reform by means of criminal law' (above n 31 at 1555) versus James Landis: 'Judicial interpretation suffered not only from inexpertness but more from the slowness of that process to attune itself to the demands of the day … To lodge a great, interpretative power in the judiciary involved the risk that a policy, which initially was given to the administrative to formulate, might be thwarted at its most significant fulcrum by judgments antagonistic to its own …' J Landis, *The Administrative Process*, reprinted in Fisher, Horwitz & Reed (eds), above n 14, 159 at 162.

the normativity of the law in a rudimentary theory of representative government (the sovereign being the representative of the popular will), rather than in an appeal to local or parochial values. Rational reconstructivists, in contrast, have greater difficulty explaining the normativity of a particular community's values, not only because the values themselves (however refined) might well be oppressive, but also because 'communities' are often pluralistic rather than solidaristic in character, resulting in conflict and competition between a community's values.[37]

II. THE RATIONAL ADMINISTRATION OF THE LAWS

I have briefly sketched how one might read *On Crimes and Punishments* as foreshadowing the debate in modern legal thought between formalists and realists, and suggested that Beccaria's superficial formalism disguises a deeper set of what we might regard, if anachronistically, as proto-scientific realist commitments. To this framing I now append a second, and equally anachronistic, frame: Beccaria as a prophet of the modern administrative state. More specifically, Beccaria's remarks on crime and punishment reveal an attitude toward law as instrumental and bureaucratic, largely sceptical of case-by-case discretion and optimistic about the power of scientific administration. These are themes most fulsomely developed by Weber. It is by reading Beccaria as a precursor to Weber's account of bureaucratic rationality that, I shall suggest, the ground-breaking character of *On Crimes and Punishments* is best appreciated. This framing runs somewhat against the grain of Beccaria's text, as it draws attention not so much to the particularities of Beccaria's account of crime and punishment as to the rationalist picture of public administration underlying that account.[38] There is, however, an historical basis for regarding the power to punish as broadly continuous with the powers of public administration more generally.[39]

Beccaria, as we have seen, emphasises the importance of certainty in punishment, especially when contrasted to the uncertainty of judicial discretion. An important dimension of Beccaria's concern with certainty is his insistence

[37] I have raised these issues in relation to Kleinfeld's 'reconstructivism' elsewhere. See V Chiao, 'A Response to Professor Kleinfeld's *Reconstructivism: The Place of Criminal Law in Ethical Life*' *Harvard Law Review Forum* 120 (April 2016) 258.

[38] Others have pointed out that Beccaria's approach to punishment stands in for a novel approach to government generally: see B Harcourt, 'Neoliberal Penality' (2010) 14 *Theoretical Criminology* 74 at 82 ('Under Beccaria's influence, the field of public economy would colonize the penal domain and impose the same logic of measured and proportional responses to the same problem of man's natural tendency to deviance. In the penal sphere – just as in the economic domain – the solution Beccaria proposed was to properly administer a rational framework of tariffs and prices.')

[39] MD Dubber, *The Police Power: Patriarchy and the Foundations of American Government* (New York, Columbia University Press, 2005); M Hildebrandt, 'Justice and Police: Regulatory Offenses and the Criminal Law' (2009) 12 *New Criminal Law Review* 43.

that law should not remain a domain of oracular pronouncements by aristocratic elites – a 'cloud of specious reasoning, seductive eloquence and diffident doubt' – but should be transformed into the object of scientific subject and 'mathematical rigour'.[40] The radicalness of Beccaria's position should not be understated. Beccaria included even such morally freighted questions as the use of capital punishment and torture as topics to be decided scientifically, rather than through emotion or tradition. Even today, outside some departments of criminology and economics, few are uniformly enthusiastic about 'evidence-based' criminal justice policy. Crime and punishment remain emotionally charged topics on which laypeople feel qualified to opine at length, and with great passion; they are not regarded as subjects best left to the experts, as is the case with monetary policy, environmental regulation, taxation and other technical fields.

For this reason, while Beccaria is frequently remembered as a proto-utilitarian theorist about crime and punishment (even if with some contractualist overtones), perhaps his more prophetic insights lie in his anticipation of the modern administrative state, both in terms of its bureaucratic organisation (abstracting, of course, from significant variations) and in terms of its claim to technical expertise and competence. Beccaria's vision of a just and rational approach to crime and punishment required that the laws are rationally calculated to achieve independently specified ends, rather than merely reflecting longstanding tradition or aristocratic values, and that officials are strictly bound by law, rather than operating in a purely discretionary or case-by-case manner. Weber, a century and a half later, saw more clearly that this vision renders law an essentially bureaucratic institution: impersonal, instrumentally rational and rule-bound.

One might suspect criminal law, and criminal justice policy more generally, to be one of the least instrumentally rational areas of governance. It deals with emotionally fraught issues, touches on fundamental values and is subject to vast swings in policy orientation as the public's mood changes. It is common to regard criminal justice policy, from three strikes laws to capital punishment and drug policy, as insufficiently 'evidence-based', ineffective and irrationally subject to popular emotion. It is rather less common to criticise criminal justice policy as being *too* instrumentally rational or too firmly grounded in sound empirical research and expertise. Rhetorically, critiques of this kind are usually couched in terms of 'democratic values', local community standards or individualised justice.[41]

Nevertheless, it is clear that even in common law jurisdictions, criminal law and criminal justice have become vastly more bureaucratic and professionalised than Beccaria could have imagined. Indeed, the bureaucratisation of criminal

[40] Beccaria, above n 5 at 30.

[41] For a thorough-going critique of this trend, see J Kleinfeld, 'Manifesto of Democratic Criminal Justice' (2017) 111 *Northwestern University Law Review* 1367.

law has been underway for centuries, starting (at least) with the advent of Crown prosecutors in political trials in the eighteenth century, as well as the eventual diffusion of both Crown prosecutors and defence counsel later in the eighteenth and nineteenth centuries. The prosecutorial function has largely been taken over by full-time civil servants trained in law, who typically profess adherence to norms of impartiality and professionalism.[42] The trial has consequently become subject to pervasive legal regulation at almost every step. Trials are no longer confrontations between an accused and a victim in front of a self-informing jury – a morality play in miniature – but have become technical, lengthy and often exceedingly boring presentations of evidence to anonymous decision-makers. Bureaucratisation and professionalisation are not merely an effect of increased reliance on lawyers. The kinds of scientific qualifications on modes of proof that Beccaria advocated have long since become *de rigueur*, with parties often competing to see whose experts or evidence are more credible. Over the course of the late nineteenth and early twentieth centuries, professional police forces became commonplace, displacing informal and community-based modes of social control. Additionally, the administration of punishment has become more private, less emotional and more calculated, largely thanks to the increasing bureaucratisation of jails and prisons.[43]

Although criminal justice policy is hardly a model of scientific rationality, particularly in countries like the United States that have long traditions of popular control over day-to-day government activities, it has generally become much more subject to bureaucratic rationality – that is, 'certain' in the sense of rule-bound, objective and specialised. One might argue that the bureaucratisation of criminal law remains incomplete and less effective than in other areas of public administration that are generally perceived as the domain of experts, such as public health or management of the economy. Even so, it is undeniable that the administration of criminal justice has not been immune from the long-term trend toward bureaucratisation and professionalisation.

The central advantage of a bureaucratic form of organisation, Weber insisted, is its technical superiority. It achieves this through specialisation: functionaries have specific tasks for which they have specialised training and deep experience, allowing them to make decisions 'precisely, unambiguously, continuously and with as much speed as possible'.[44] Bureaucracies, in other words, give pride of place to expertise and technical knowledge, thereby allowing for a more efficient and consistent processing of information than would be possible in a

[42] The United States is an outlier in this regard, as many prosecutors are subject to political rather than professional oversight.

[43] The classic treatment is M Foucault, *Discipline and Punish: The Birth of the Prison* translated by A Sheridan (New York, Pantheon, 1977).

[44] M Weber, *From Max Weber: Essays in Sociology* new edition edited by HH Gerth and C Wright Mills (Abingdon, Routledge, 1991) 215. See also Landis, above n 36 (defending the advantages of professional expertise in administration.)

purely case-by-case approach. 'The "objective" discharge of business primarily means a discharge of business according to *calculable rules* and "without regard for persons".'[45] A perfect bureaucracy, as Weber (and Kafka) observed, is one that has completely extirpated elements of 'love, hatred, and all purely personal, irrational, and emotional elements which escape calculation'.[46] Weber writes:

> The reduction of modern office management to rules is deeply embedded in its very nature. The theory of modern public administration ... assumes that the authority to order certain matters by decree – which has been legally granted to public authorities – does not entitle the bureau to regulate the matter by commands given for each case, but only to regulate the matter abstractly.[47]

Beccaria would have agreed. Recall Beccaria's rejection of mercy as a virtue in the application of the law. In Beccaria's eyes, mercy at the point of law application bespeaks arbitrariness and impunity; it is only when the laws are themselves barbaric and absurd that mercy has a role as a second-best corrective. First-best is that the rules themselves be humane and rational; if they are, they should be applied 'inexorabl[y]'.[48] Beccaria's rejection of mercy as a judicial virtue is of a piece with his rejection of open-ended modes of legal interpretation; in both cases, the administration of justice would depend upon the idiosyncrasies of a particular human, and his or her dispositions at a particular point in time.

A central feature of bureaucracy is impersonality. This portends not only the prevalence of a coolly calculating instrumental rationality, but also that bureaucracies are structured in terms of officially defined roles rather than in terms of personal relationships. Within a bureaucracy, loyalty is owed to the office, rather than to the person occupying the office. Instead of serving merely as a source of rents, a reward for loyal service, or as an inherited status, an office is 'an acceptance of a specific obligation of faithful management in return for a secure existence'.[49] Bureaucracies thus foster a kind of social levelling, one that favours the 'specialist type of man' as against the 'cultivated man' of earlier, more aristocratic eras.[50] As a result of their impersonality, rule orientation, and preference for specialised and technical knowledge, bureaucratic social organisation promotes a kind of formal equality. Not, to be sure, in a particularly

[45] Weber, ibid at 215.
[46] Ibid at 216.
[47] Ibid at 198.
[48] Beccaria, above n 5 at 112 (ch 46). For a contemporary account of mercy's role as a second-best response to barbaric and absurd law, see C Steiker, 'Criminalization and the Criminal Process: Prudential Mercy as a Limit to Penal Sanctions in an Era of Mass Incarceration', in RA Duff et al (eds), *The Boundaries of the Criminal Law* (Oxford, Oxford University Press, 2010) 27. Mary Sigler's defence of 'equity' in lieu of mercy, although framed as a response to Steiker, might itself be viewed as an expression of Beccaria's insistence that penal law be humane and rational but applied uniformly and, indeed, 'inexorably'. See M Sigler, 'Equity, Not Mercy', in C Flanders & Z Hoskins (eds), *The New Philosophy of Criminal Law* (Lanham MD, Rowman & Littlefield, 2015) 231.
[49] Weber, above n 44 at 199.
[50] Ibid at 243.

substantive sense – bureaucracies are, as Weber notes, and as anyone who has ever interacted with one will observe, quite value-neutral – but in the sense of imposing a norm of 'abstract regularity' on government.[51] A norm of abstract regularity resists purely case-by-case decision-making in favour of operating by general rules, which tends to limit the influence of the identity of both the decision-maker and the affected party.

Impersonal decision-making and non-domination share a central impulse, which is to limit the degree to which the idiosyncrasies (the 'whims' or 'arbitrary caprice') of decision-makers and parties influence how they are treated. A mode of decision-making that operates substantially by general rules, known in advance, of reasonably clear and determinate meaning is a mode of decision-making in which the parties will typically know where they stand relative to each other. Consequently, the underlying commitments that animate Beccaria as much as contemporary republican theorists – to oppose or undercut practices of currying favour, showing obeisance and other signs of pervasive status hierarchy – weigh in favour of bureaucratic modes of social organisation. A high point of *On Crimes and Punishments* is surely Beccaria's insistence that the criminal law should make no distinction between noble and commoner, and should instead operate by general rules designed to fairly accommodate the interests of all.[52] Beccaria's egalitarian instincts are clearly connected to his defence of subordinating criminal justice to general rules; both, I suggest, provide a basis for replacing traditional and personality-driven (what Weber might call 'charismatic') forms of authority with more legalistic and rule-bound forms.

Nowhere is the connection between bureaucratic impersonality and opposition to status hierarchy more clearly in evidence than in void-for-vagueness doctrine, in which the Supreme Court has invalidated US State laws and local ordinances as overly vague. Despite the ostensible focus on the formal language in the statute, the underlying concern is that such language will be ineffective in controlling the arbitrary exercise of state power.[53] That was a theme in two of the most famous American vagueness cases, *Papachristou* and *Morales*.[54] In both of those cases, majorities on the Supreme Court rejected statutory delegations of power to the police as too undefined, and hence too permissive of

[51] Ibid at 224; on value-neutrality, see ibid at 229.

[52] Beccaria, above n 5 chs 3 and 21.

[53] As Edward Rubin puts it, '[t]he doctrinal basis of vagueness' is the 'requirement that governmental agents cannot make certain significant decisions about individuals by acting in their unfettered discretion'. E Rubin, 'Law and Legislation in the Administrative State' (1989) 89 *Columbia Law Review* 369 at 408.

[54] *Papachristou v City of Jacksonville* 405 US 156 (1972); *City of Chicago v Morales* 527 US 41 (1999); *Kolender v Lawson* 461 US 352, 357–361 (1983). This is not idiosyncratic to American courts; see eg, *R v Nova Scotia Pharmaceutical Society* [1992] 2 SCR 606 (articulating concern that vague legislation creates excessive uncertainty and grants officials excessive enforcement discretion).

oppressive or biased application. The idea is that undefined power – the opposite of bureaucratic power – is irrational power. Perhaps in more solidaristic societies, this idea would seem dubious; in a diverse society with a history of severe racial antagonism, it seems unsurprising.

The statutes in *Papachristou* and *Morales* arguably differed along the substance-procedure axis. *Papachristou* concerned a statute that purported to criminalise 'vagrancy' – that is, conduct engaged in by private citizens. In contrast, the municipal ordinance at issue in *Morales* created a power on the part of Chicago police to order loitering groups to disperse. However, this division is plainly artificial, as empowering police is tantamount to restricting the conduct of private citizens; just as obviously, restricting the conduct of private citizens, as the *Papachristou* statute attempted to do, amounts to empowering the police (and prosecutors and judges).

Interestingly, the *Morales* ordinance also criminalised failure to comply with a police officer's order to disperse. This makes it somewhat odd from the point of view of vagueness. After all, once an officer invokes the statute to order people to disperse, the law has become about as clear as law ever is. Indeed, an offence under the ordinance required proof of direct and specific notice to the accused. In this respect, the ordinance provided far more notice, and is far more specific, than most criminal offences. The Supreme Court's concern, rather, was that the statute failed to adequately define the power of the police to order people to disperse.[55] It is not difficult to see how such unfettered discretion on the part of the police could easily facilitate subordinating relationships between police and civilians. In this respect, *Morales* stands as an exemplar of the bureaucratic turn in policing: a turn, that is, away from the image of the friendly neighbourhood officer walking the beat, relying on personal relationships, common sense and informal justice; and toward the image of the officer as a professional, guided by a thicket of technical rules and regulations, who stands at arm's length from the people and communities she polices.

The main exception in many otherwise thoroughly rule-oriented jurisdictions is sentencing, which often remains an overwhelmingly discretionary affair. Under highly discretionary sentencing regimes, the specific identity of the judge, along with the baggage of his or her value orientations, policy preferences, experience, and other psychological and social predictors, looms large. In at least some instances, courts defend their sentencing powers against incursion by legislators on grounds of individualistic, intuitive moral values, such as proportionality. For instance, the Supreme Court of Canada has been consistently opposed to attempts to impose structure on sentencing. This includes not just a recent line of cases striking down mandatory minimums enacted by Parliament, but also mandatory maximums enforced by lower courts, as well as

[55] *City of Chicago v Morales*, above n 54 at 58.

attempts (driven by judicial initiative) to set defeasible starting points.[56] There is no sentencing commission, nor are there uniform sentencing guidelines. There is a smattering of mandatory minima, some maxima, and rules developed by provincial prosecution agencies related to positions they will take for particular types of offences, such as driving while under the influence of alcohol.[57] Local lore – about which courts, or even which judges, are 'better' for this or that type of offence – predominates.

What is perhaps of most interest in this connection is that discretionary sentencing may nevertheless yield stable and predictable patterns of outcomes. There is some reason to believe that the bureaucratic organisation of the judiciary may serve much the same role as explicit legal rules in securing stability in sentencing practice. Tatjana Hörnle, for instance, has argued that German sentencing judges – who, like their Canadian counterparts, are only loosely governed by law – are disciplined by a culture of consensus and deference to local norms among their colleagues. Sentencing practice in Germany remains very much influenced by the experience of the lawyers and informal consultation among junior and more senior judges.[58] What explains this stability, Hörnle suggests, is that the judiciary is staffed by career judges, who are professionally, rather than politically, appointed, and the 'corporatist spirit' of the judiciary, in which the individuality of the particular judge is subsumed to adherence to 'established principles and values that are … part of [the judiciary's] professional self-understanding'.[59] In short, it is conformity to widely held norms within a bureaucracy, rather than public law per se, that, on Hörnle's view, explains why sentencing is not completely arbitrary.[60]

Sentencing in Canada parallels Hörnle's account of sentencing practice in Germany. Although there are important differences (for instance, in how judges are appointed), nevertheless in broad strokes the picture is similar. Perhaps public quiescence reflects an implicit appreciation of Hörnle's point: the particular reasons judges give to defend their sentencing decisions are ultimately not that important; what is more important is the perception of judges as members of a respectable, consensus-oriented profession.

More surprisingly, the case of sentencing may suggest that guidance by rules is less central to bureaucratic organisation than Weber intimated, at least

[56] See *R v M(CA)* [1996] 1 SCR 500 (rejecting a judicially created sentencing ceiling); *R v McDonnell* [1997] 1 SCR 948 (rejecting a judicially created starting point within broadly defined sentencing range); *R v Smith* [1987] 1 SCR 1045 (rejecting a statutory minimum); *R v Nur* [2015] 1 SCR 773 (same); *R v Lloyd* [2016] 1 SCR 130 (mandatory minimum for drug offences).

[57] See Ministry of the Attorney-General (Ontario), Crown Policy Manual D18, available at www.ontario.ca/document/crown-prosecution-manual/d-18-impaired-driving.

[58] T Hörnle, 'Moderate and Non-Arbitrary Sentencing Without Guidelines: the German Experience' (2013) 76 *Law & Contemporary Problems* 189 at 201.

[59] Ibid at 207–208.

[60] Ibid.

when that bureaucracy exhibits sufficient conformity in attitudes and outcomes. Similarly, Beccaria's analysis arguably misses the sociological dimension of bureaucratic organisation; that is, the patterns of deference to internal hierarchy and resistance to outside influence that Weber would later emphasise. Beccaria's writing betrays a degree of rule-fetishism: he failed to appreciate how bureaucratic modes of organisation, even when given fairly free rein in terms of governing legislation, can nevertheless serve much the same aims that he assigned to the rule of law proper, namely, curbing arbitrariness in interpretation and enforcement. Moreover, as Weber emphasised, bureaucratic modes of organisation can also serve to counteract the influence of inherited privilege and status, given the insular and technical orientation of professional administrators. A major objective of *On Crimes and Punishments* was precisely to 'discredit the legal understanding' that legitimated the rule of the Milanese aristocracy, and to present Beccaria and his collaborators as an enlightened alternative to Milan's Habsburg rulers.[61] It is, of course, perfectly understandable that Beccaria would emphasise the importance of faithful adherence to laws based on careful, scientific and rational study as a means of criticising the power of inherited elites. Whether a public bureaucracy that resists guidance by rules in favour of case-by-case judgments is consistent with the rule of law is, unfortunately, a question that will have to be taken up on another occasion.

III. CONCLUSION

The significance of *On Crimes and Punishments* in both the social contract and utilitarian philosophical traditions has been well studied. In contrast, the consilience between Beccaria's critical, scientific, reform-minded approach and American legal realism has been less noted. Like the realists, Beccaria was sceptical that law could be treated as an internally closed system of concepts. That image of law, for Beccaria, served only the interests of the ruling class. Beccaria positioned himself as an advocate of a more rational and scientific approach to law, thereby presaging the challenge to the formalists' distinction between law and policy mounted by realists, particularly those such as Holmes and Cohen, who placed great faith in what we might now, somewhat anachronistically, refer to as 'evidence-based policy'.

Similarly, it is not hard to see Beccaria's defence of the values of impersonality, rule-abidingness and instrumental rationality as a defence of a bureaucratised mode of government. The professionalisation of criminal justice, nascent in Beccaria's time, took firm root in the decades after the publication of *On Crimes and Punishments*, with the criminal process becoming increasingly, ultimately

[61] For an overview of the political context in which Beccaria was operating, see Audegean, above n 4 at 891 ff.

almost exclusively, the domain of licensed professionals raising technical arguments rather than a locus for moral confrontation between victim and accused. More generally, the values of impersonality, rule-abidingness and instrumental rationality, to say nothing of claims to technical competence and even-handed application of law, are firmly associated with bureaucratic modes of social organisation, as opposed to more informal and decentralised, thickly normative, religious or charismatic modes.

For this reason, I have suggested that one might sensibly regard Beccaria as a prophet of the modern administrative state, with its armies of functionaries, administrators and bureaucrats devoted to 'best practices' of measurement, evaluation, prediction, prevention and enforcement related to a dizzying array of legal and regulatory objectives. Ironically, Beccaria's emphasis on the sovereign's role in ensuring the rational administration of the law takes on a different significance after the emergence of powerful executive branch bureaucracies in modern administrative states in the early to mid-20th century. Beccaria may have defended the values that later became associated with administrative bureaucracy, but he did not foresee the degree to which those bureaucracies, and the values of administrative governance they embody, would come to pose a challenge to his still formalistic conception of the rule of law.[62]

[62] See A Vermeule, *Law's Abnegation* (Cambridge MA, Harvard University Press, 2016).

Part II

Locating Beccaria in Present-Day Discourses on Criminal Justice

9

Beccaria Now: (Re)reading On Crimes and Punishments

PAUL ROBERTS

> Well may it be said of the Marquis di Beccaria, looking at these results of his 'Essay', that it is indeed one of the most important Works that has ever been written, and that he, by writing, has contributed towards the enduring happiness of nations.[1]

> Beccaria's classic study *On Crimes and Punishments* belongs to the category of works which are much cited and little read.[2]

I. INTRODUCTION: BECCARIA THEN AND NOW

I CANNOT RECALL ever citing 'Beccaria's classic study *On Crimes and Punishments*', but I know I had never read more than a few quoted snippets of the text before participating in this project. Beccaria was introduced to me as a postgraduate student in Criminology, alongside Bentham, as a leading light and torchbearer of the 'classical school' of criminology. The classical school stood for individualism, personal responsibility for criminality and deserved punishment, and as I was learning this from Marxist-inspired and other left-leaning sociologies,[3] this 'classical' orientation was mostly bad – a foil against which to react, if not an intellectual foe to be vanquished. Criminological

[1] TR Bridgwater, 'The Great Jurists of the World VIII – Cæsar Bonesana, Marquis Di Beccaria' (1907) 8 *Journal of the Society of Comparative Legislation* 219 at 228.

[2] R Bellamy, 'Introduction', in C Beccaria, *On Crimes and Punishments and Other Writings* edited by R Bellamy and translated by R Davies (Cambridge, Cambridge University Press, 1995) ix.

[3] Including J Young, 'Thinking Seriously about Crime: Some Models of Criminology', in M Fitzgerald, G McLennan & J Pawson (eds), *Crime and Society: Readings in History and Theory* (Abingdon, Routledge & Kegan Paul, 1981); I Taylor, P Walton & J Young, *The New Criminology: For a Social Theory of Deviance* (Abingdon, Routledge & Kegan Paul, 1973).

theory has come a long way since the early 1990s,[4] let alone 1764 – the year *On Crimes and Punishments* was published.

We can be confident that neither Beccaria nor Bentham ever regarded themselves as part of any 'school' of criminology, classical or otherwise, even though Bentham had plainly read *On Crimes and Punishments* and was significantly influenced by it.[5] One reason is that the academic field of Criminology was not invented for another century, with the advent of positivist social science in the late nineteenth century.[6] But another, more profound reason is that the allocation of key thinkers and their ideas to particular 'schools' is a (frequently anachronistic) reconstruction of the past from the vantage point of a contemporary perspective and framed by the inquirer's current preoccupations. Conceptual issues of definition and taxonomy are bound up with analytical purpose and method, constituting the triadic structural logic of any intellectual inquiry.[7] Modelling and marshalling the history of ideas, and thereby in some respects rewriting that history, in this way inevitably answers to modern motivations and agendas. It follows that the historiographically astute[8] question is not 'What is the meaning and significance of *On Crimes and Punishments*?' *tout court*, but rather 'What does *On Crimes and Punishments* mean and signify *for us today*?' Each new generation will have its own Beccaria, or plural Beccarias ranged across disciplinary and jurisdictional boundaries. Who, then, is ours? Or perhaps one should say, who is *mine*? What follows is an unabashedly personal reading by a legal scholar specialising in criminal procedure.

One, non-trivial answer to these inquiry-framing questions might be, who cares? It does not follow from the possibility that old texts can be given new, contemporary meaning that exhumation and revivification would be worth the effort. The fact that Beccaria is still sporadically cited and discussed, sometimes in terms of 'lost history'[9] or 'forgotten influence',[10] constitutes at least prima

[4] Now see P Roberts, 'Thinking Through Critical Criminology', in A Amatrudo (ed), *Social Censure and Critical Criminology: After Sumner* (London, Palgrave Macmillan, 2017) 1.

[5] P Schofield, '"The First Steps Rightly Directed in the Track of Legislation": Jeremy Bentham on Cesare Beccaria's *Essay on Crimes and Punishments*' (2019) 4 *Diciottesimo Secolo* 65; HLA Hart, *Essays on Bentham: Jurisprudence and Political Theory* (Oxford, Oxford University Press, 1982) 40 at 42.

[6] D Garland, 'Of Crimes and Criminals: The Development of Criminology in Britain', in M Maguire, R Morgan & R Reiner (eds), *The Oxford Handbook of Criminology* (Oxford, Oxford University Press, 1994) 7.

[7] See P Roberts, 'Interdisciplinarity in Legal Research', in M McConville & WH Chui (eds), *Research Methods for Law* 2nd edition (Edinburgh, Edinburgh University Press, 2017) 90 (elucidating the eternally triangular relationship of 'What?', 'Why?' and 'How?' questions in research).

[8] Generally, see RJ Evans, *In Defence of History* revised edition (London, Granta, 2000); EH Carr, *What Is History?* 2nd edition edited by RW Davies (London, Penguin, 1987); RG Collingwood, *The Idea of History* revised edition (Oxford, Oxford University Press, 1994).

[9] 'Beccaria inexplicably fails to make the list of great economists, even in a book highlighting *fifty* influential economists … Today, most people around the world still know little, if anything, about Beccaria or his life, though his ideas – like Adam Smith's – continue to shape twenty-first century thought, just as they shaped the Enlightenment': JD Bessler, 'The Economist and the Enlightenment: How Cesare Beccaria Changed Western Civilization' (2018) 46 *European Journal of Law and Economics* 275 at 276, 281.

facie grounds for greater curiosity. But are these historical traces really anything more than habituated genuflection to the founding fathers or cheap pretension to intellectual gravitas? Does Beccaria really still speak of matters and in a language capable of resonating with a twenty-first-century audience? And if so, what is he saying?

For those (like me) who knew Beccaria only by popular reputation and criminological gossip, the couple of hours that it takes to read *On Crimes and Punishments* confound lazy expectations. For one thing, the text is mostly not about punishment per se, nor even concerned with what we would regard today as 'penological' issues. A great deal more attention is devoted to questions of criminal evidence and procedure than I anticipated, and these institutional and jurisprudential issues will be examined in some detail later. If forced to place *On Crimes and Punishments* into a disciplinary pigeonhole, I would describe it as a work of political theory. This classification, I think, is quite instructive and teaches a salutary lesson for modern penal theorising about the potential costs of progressively narrowing disciplinary specialisation. Before getting to the politics of *On Crimes and Punishments*, however, some more general observations about the book's structure, style and argumentation will help to set the scene.

II. BECCARIA'S ENLIGHTENED METHOD: SCIENTIFIC RATIONALISM AS PROTO-PENAL THEORY

There is more than one way in which a text can be informative or valuable, beyond the salience and quality of its content. The style of the text, its organisation, the type of arguments it deploys, what it omits, its epistemological assumptions and methodological protocols – all of this and more can be highly revealing, sometimes in ways unnoticed or entirely inaccessible to the author.

On first impression, *On Crimes and Punishments* is a slim volume of only a little over 100 pages, being divided into 47 sections ('chapters') of varying length, but often no more than a paragraph or two. The style is, possibly self-consciously,[11] literary – though one cannot fairly judge stylistic merit in

[10] See, eg, JD Bessler, 'The Italian Enlightenment and the American Revolution: Cesare Beccaria's Forgotten Influence on American Law' (2016) 37 *Mitchell Hamline Journal of Public Policy and Practice* 1; G Sween, 'Texas Ain't Tuscany: How A Truism Might Further Invigorate Contemporary "Cost Arguments" for Death-Penalty Abolition' (2014) 41 *American Journal of Criminal Law* 151 (*pace* Sween at 154, describing Beccaria as 'a relatively obscure Enlightenment thinker from Tuscany', Milan is in Lombardy); DS Nagin, 'Deterrence in the Twenty-First Century' (2013) 42 *Crime and Justice* 199; JD Bessler, 'Revisiting Beccaria's Vision: The Enlightenment, America's Death Penalty, and the Abolition Movement' (2009) 4 *Northwestern Journal of Law & Social Policy* 195.

[11] It is said that Beccaria was 'far from being insensible to glory; he recognised that a literary reputation, liberty for himself, and a compassion for the misfortunes of mankind, were in him three sentiments equally alive': Bridgwater, above n 1 at 221.

translation. It has the appearance of a loosely connected set of penseés, reminiscent of Michel de Montaigne's *Essais*,[12] but any superficial comparison to Montaigne quickly becomes a sharper contrast. Where Montaigne is reflective, inward-looking and haunted by existential doubt,[13] Beccaria is self-confidently and, often, peremptorily didactic. This is a book designed to tell policymakers, in no uncertain terms, what they should do. A better comparator, then, might be Machiavelli's *The Prince*; and Beccaria shares some of Machiavelli's republican spirit[14] too, as we shall see. Whereas Montaigne and Machiavelli are Renaissance figures, however, Beccaria is writing well into the European Enlightenment and under the mantle of the scientific revolution. A century after Descartes, Locke, Pascal, Newton and Leibniz, he was an historical contemporary of Rousseau, Hume and Kant. As the work of an educated and well-read man of affairs, we must assume that *On Crimes and Punishments* takes the form it does because Beccaria deliberately wanted it that way.[15] It is a book bursting with ideas, but not directly encouraging thought or fastidious argumentation. It is more in the nature of a political tract than a philosophical treatise (and, again, Beccaria must have known the difference). Some commentators attribute the book's immediate popularity and far-flung practical influence on eighteenth- and nineteenth-century law reform and penal discourse[16] partly to these stylistic choices.[17] As contemporaries such as Diderot appreciated, a dose of sentimentality is sometimes more rhetorically effective in motivating social progress than the cold calculation of unremittingly logical argument.[18]

[12] M de Montaigne, *The Complete Essays* [1580] translated and edited by MA Screech (London, Penguin, 2003).

[13] S Bakewell, *How to Live: A Life of Montaigne in One Question and Twenty Attempts at an Answer* (London, Vintage, 2011).

[14] M Viroli, *Machiavelli* (Oxford, Oxford University Press, 1998).

[15] Beccaria's text was chopped and changed around by French and English translators, but the Bellamy version (above n 2) restores the original Italian format.

[16] BE Harcourt, 'Beccaria's *On Crimes and Punishments*: A Mirror on the History of the Foundations of Modern Criminal Law', in MD Dubber (ed), *Foundational Texts in Modern Criminal Law* (Oxford, Oxford University Press, 2014) 39; A Cadoppi, 'Cesare Beccaria, John Bessler and the Birth of Modern Criminal Law' (2015) 3 *University of Baltimore Journal of International Law* 1 (noting at 5 that 'the views of the first four American presidents – George Washington, John Adams, Thomas Jefferson and James Madison – were shaped by Beccaria's writings', and that Beccarian thinking also underpins pan-European codification of criminal law during the late 18th and early 19th centuries); AJ Draper, 'Cesare Beccaria's Influence on English Discussions of Punishment, 1764–1789' (2000) 26 *History of European Ideas* 177; T Cizova, 'Beccaria in Russia' (1962) 95 *Slavonic and East European Review* 384.

[17] '*Dei delitti e delle pene* was written in an accessible style – one highly readable by lawyers and non-lawyers alike. Its style, no doubt, is partly what made it so appealing and successful': Bessler, above n 9 at 287.

[18] See F Venturi, *Utopia and Reform in the Enlightenment* (Cambridge, Cambridge University Press, 1971) 107–108. An Italian jurist concurs that 'though Beccaria's little book was probably not the product of a refined juridical mind, sometimes jurists are not so convincing when their arguments get too-hair-splitting … [W]e must recognise that *On Crimes and Punishments* is also a literary work full of sentiment and passion, and this has probably been another key of [its] enormous success': Cadoppi, above n 16 at 27, 29.

One point that should be immediately conceded to Beccaria is his clear-eyed realisation that a work such as *On Crimes and Punishments* cannot hope to be completely comprehensive, and in particular cannot be expected to trace each of its philosophical commitments back to primary sources and first principles. As Beccaria fairly remarks (twice), if he had tried to say everything he would have ended up saying nothing. This is a methodological prescription for effective argumentation that never goes out of date. Any theorist who does not learn to 'bracket' effectively and build on reasonable shared assumptions will very soon find themselves trapped in the intellectual maze of radical (and for most purposes, self-defeating) scepticism.

Read as a single continuous work, the text appears very badly organised, lacking sustained narrative arc or logical structure. Beccaria hops from one topic to another, and with many digressions and loops. He openly confesses to digressing but, like another notable contemporary – Tristram Shandy[19] – does it anyway, and the reader will just have to keep up. Disorganisation in the text is not simply a matter of failing to link topics together in an orderly sequence exhibiting logical narrative progression. Organisational laxity leaks into loose conceptual thinking and unreflective classification, inevitably detracting from the clarity and coherence of the book's central arguments. In some measure, lack of taxonomical refinement is a symptom of the absence of modern academic 'subjects' and their institutionalised disciplinary schemas, simultaneously the liberation and the curse of the intellectual pioneer. Beccaria is not hidebound by disciplinary tradition or the institutionalised group-think of academic tribes, and if he had been born two centuries later he would presumably have been a staunch proponent of interdisciplinarity.[20] But lacking the conceptual precision demanded of modern theoretical scholarship, he does not clearly differentiate related, but distinct, questions, and consequently runs together arguments and conclusions that more profitably could have been kept apart. By today's standards, *On Crimes and Punishments* would not stand up as a work of analytical penal theory. Conceptual rethinking and renewal in disciplinary classifications remain, to be sure, unfinished business for contemporary criminal jurisprudence,[21] but *On Crimes and Punishments* is taxonomy soup. Its pioneering,

[19] L Sterne, *The Life and Opinions of Tristram Shandy, Gentleman* (1759–67) (London, Penguin, 2003).

[20] Beccaria insisted that 'whoever restricts himself within the confines of his science and ignores similar and neighbouring sciences will never become great and famous in his own. An immense network links all truths, and they are more varying, uncertain and confused the more cramped and limited they are; becoming simpler, grander and more dependable only as they expand into a wider space and raise themselves to a higher point of view': 'Inaugural Lecture', in Beccaria, above n 2 at 132.

[21] In relation to criminal procedure and evidence, see P Roberts, 'Adrian Zuckerman's New Evidence Scholarship', in R Assy & A Higgins (eds), *Principles, Procedure, and Justice: Essays in Honour of Adrian Zuckerman* (Oxford, Oxford University Press, 2020) ch 4; J Jackson & P Roberts, 'Beyond Common Law Evidence: Reimagining, and Reinvigorating, Evidence Law as Forensic

if more rudimentary, methodological contributions lie in conspectus and synthesis, collecting together a set of questions, issues and arguments pertaining to the specifically penal mode of governance.

Beccaria is first and foremost a methodological rationalist. His principal weapon is the persuasive force of argument, and he wields it like an English broadsword rather than an Italian stiletto. There is none of the wit of Voltaire or the allegorical satire of Swift (two more rough contemporaries). Particularly striking, because somewhat discordant, for the modern reader are Beccaria's circumspection in making himself amenable to the religious authorities and his sycophantic overtures to the local prince. Right at the beginning of *On Crimes and Punishments* Beccaria assures his readers that he does 'not, by any means, speak of the justice of God, which is of another kind'.[22] Later he reiterates that 'My topic is solely those crimes which arise from human nature and the social compact, and not those sins whose punishments, even in this life, ought to be regulated by principles other than those of a limited philosophy.'[23] Beccaria's prophylactic self-insurance against accusations of blasphemy is, to my mind, one of his most ingenious arguments:

> If He has laid down eternal punishments for those who disobey His Omnipotence, what manner of insect will dare to add to divine justice, will seek to avenge the Being Who is sufficient unto Himself, Who cannot be affected with pleasure or pain by anything, and Who, alone among beings, acts without fear of any reaction? The gravity of a sin depends on the inscrutable malice of the heart, which finite beings cannot know without special revelation. How, then, could it be used as a guide for the punishment of crimes? If such a thing were tried, men could punish when God pardons and pardon when God punishes. If men can run counter to the Almighty by blaspheming against Him, then they can do so also by punishing on His behalf.[24]

So Beccaria's humanistic preoccupation with secular crimes and punishments is rooted in profound piety, whereas those who would accuse of him of laxity are the real blasphemers! Conflict with churchmen was less perilous in Beccaria's day than it was for his countryman Galileo in the previous century, but not without risk.[25] Besides, an effective reformer intent on challenging traditional habits and

Science', in DK Brown, JI Turner & B Weisser (eds), *The Oxford Handbook of Criminal Process* (Oxford, Oxford University Press, 2019) ch 35; P Roberts (ed), *Theoretical Foundations of Criminal Trial Procedure* (Farnham, Ashgate, 2014); P Roberts, 'Rethinking the Law of Evidence: A Twenty-first Century Agenda for Teaching and Research' (2002) 55 *Current Legal Problems* 297.

[22] Beccaria, above n 2 at 11 (ch 2).

[23] Ibid at 100 (ch 39).

[24] Ibid at 23 (ch 7).

[25] In a letter to his French editor, André Morellet, of 26 January 1776, Beccaria confides concern for his personal safety and the need for circumspection: 'I had before me the examples of Machiavelli, Galileo and Giannone. I could hear the rattling chains of superstition and the howls of fanaticism stifling the faint moans of truth. It was this that caused me – forced me – sometimes to veil the light of truth in a pious shroud. I wished to defend humanity without becoming a martyr to it' ('To André Morellet', ibid 119 at 121).

embedded social privilege would have been well advised to burnish and advertise their religious orthodoxy, just as modern US presidents must sincerely implore that 'God bless America'. Establishment figures such as Blackstone apparently saw no difficulty in accommodating their criminal jurisprudence with religious conviction,[26] whilst the atheist Bentham hurled a hundred argumentative brickbats from the sidelines but made little tangible progress in law reform.[27] Beccaria's anticipatory *tu quoque* defence of his tract's foundational secularism implied that he, and his readers, could have their confessional cake and eat it. 'For thousands of years sin and crime, guilt and offence to society, had been tied together in an intricate knot', marvelled the twentieth-century Italian historian Franco Venturi. 'It was now cut in one blow by Beccaria. … Penal law was to lose all its sacred content. Beccaria's radical thinking, implicitly but nonetheless definitively, denied every religious conception of evil …'[28]

Beccaria displays an unwavering commitment to treating criminal justice reform as a problem of public administration susceptible of rational analysis and (a more capacious adjective in Romance languages than in modern-day English) *scientific* solutions. The law-reformer, Beccaria tells us, is a kind of engineer, constructing social institutions to contend with the forces of (human) nature. 'And the legislator behaves like the skilled architect, whose task is to counteract the destructive forces of gravity and to exploit those forces that contribute to the strengthening of the building.'[29] Just as buildings are designed to incorporate protective hard materials without showering stone and glass on their occupants' heads, criminal punishments must 'eliminate [the] … evil effects [of private interests], without destroying the … sensibility inalienable from man's nature'.[30] The 'legislator' Beccaria has in mind are potentates of Italian city states and the

[26] At the pinnacle of the hierarchy of criminal offences presented in Blackstone's *Commentaries* are offences against God: W Blackstone, *Commentaries on the Laws of England*, bk IV: *Public Wrongs* (Oxford, Clarendon Press, 1765–1769) ch 4 at 42–43 (presenting a fivefold taxonomy of municipal crime, comprising 'first, those which are more immediately injurious to God and his holy religion; secondly, such as violate and transgress the law of nations; thirdly, such as more especially affect the sovereign executive power of the state, or the king and his government; fourthly, such as more directly infringe the rights of the public or common wealth; and, lastly, such as derogate from those rights and duties, which are owing to particular individuals, and in the preservation and vindication of which community is deeply interested'). Also see JW Cairns, 'John Millar's Lectures on Scots Criminal Law' (1988) 8 *Oxford Journal of Legal Studies* 364.

[27] It cannot have helped, either, that Bentham was witheringly defamatory about judges and lawyers. Although Bentham's intellectual influence on penal philosophy was profound and enduring, the Benthamite law reform project was pursued more successfully by juristic insiders such as Brougham, Macaulay and Stephen: see KJM Smith, *Lawyers, Legislators and Theorists* (Oxford, Oxford University Press, 1998); G Binder, 'Foundations of the Legislative Panopticon: Bentham's *Principles of Morals and Legislation*', in Dubber (ed), above n 16 at 80; and MO DeGirolami, 'James Fitzjames Stephen: The Punishment Jurist', in Dubber (ed), above n 16 at 184; R Cross, 'The Making of English Criminal Law: (5) Macaulay' [1978] *Criminal Law Review* 519; and 'The Making of English Criminal Law: (6) Sir James Fitzjames Stephen' [1978] *Criminal Law Review* 652.

[28] Venturi, above n 18 at 100.

[29] Beccaria, above n 2 at 19–20 (ch 6).

[30] Ibid at 19.

incumbent Habsburg Holy Roman Empress Maria Theresa (ruling 1745–1780), and it is to them and their councils of advisors that *On Crimes and Punishments* is principally addressed. Beccaria takes it as read that enlightened rulers share his own Enlightenment rationalism and philosophy (literally, 'love of wisdom/ reason'):

> The great monarchs, the human benefactors who rule us, love the truths which are expounded by humble philosophers with an unfanatical zeal directed exclusively against those who, eschewing reason, rely on force or machination.[31]

And this indubitably being the case, the princes must be provided with an alibi for the recalcitrant failings of their current administrations, which are laid at the door of unenlightened (and conveniently mute and undefended) tradition:

> [T]he history of mankind gives the impression of a vast sea of errors, among which a few confused truths float at great distances from each other. … How happy humanity would be if laws were being decreed for the first time, now that we see seated on the thrones of Europe benevolent monarchs, inspirers of the virtues of peace, of the sciences, of the arts, fathers of their peoples, crowned citizens. Their increased power serves the happiness of their subjects because it removes that crueller, because more capricious intermediary despotism, which choked the always sincere desires of the people which are always beneficial when they may approach the throne! If they leave the ancient laws in place, I say, it is because of the endless difficulty of removing the venerated and centuries-old rust. That is a reason for enlightened citizens to wish all the more fervently for their authority to continue to increase.[32]

Is Beccaria sincere in his oily sycophancy? Was this blatant sucking-up a successful strategy for exploiting the vanity of princes? To the modern ear, this passage has all the authenticity of a smirking Francis Urquhart drawling '*You* might think that, *I* couldn't possibly comment'.[33] But these must have been more ardently expressive, less cynical times, and Beccaria needed enthusiastic patrons to implement his reformist programme. Twenty-five years before most of the French nobility was despatched for an audience with Madame Guillotine, the notion – or implicit threat? – that rulers were merely 'crowned citizens' striving to combat tradition's follies, and being loved all the more fervently for it by their grateful citizen-subjects, might well have found favour at the doge's palace.[34]

[31] Ibid at 3 ('To the Reader').

[32] Ibid at 71–72 (ch 28).

[33] M Dobbs, *House of Cards* (New York, HarperCollins, 1989) & BBC (1990), screenplay by Andrew Davies and Michael Dobbs.

[34] A modern equivalent might be Call-me-Dave Cameron, professing to support a football team so that he would not seem too posh to be British prime minister: see D Boffey, 'David Cameron Blames "Brain Fade" for Getting his Football Team Wrong' *The Guardian* (25 April 2015). Gary Lineker tweeted, 'David Cameron has forgotten which Football Club he supports. Aston Villa last week, West Ham this. Burnley next?' (the joke being that only a handful of English football league teams play in claret and sky blue; and only a shirt colour enthusiast could have confused Villa with the east London 'Hammers', whereas genuine football supporters would be more likely to forget their own name than their team's).

Beccaria did in fact greatly influence Joseph II of Austria and Leopold, Grand Duke of Tuscany, in their successful criminal law reforms of the 1780s,[35] and was fêted by Russian Empress Catherine the Great – with minimal practical impact.[36] At all events, *On Crimes and Punishments* is written *for* enlightened rationalists *by* one, and nobody else is at the races.

Beccaria reserves his most developed and concerted arguments for his discussions of capital punishment and judicial torture; to which, indeed, *On Crimes and Punishments* owes much of its contemporary renown and enduring influence. On both topics Beccaria is a liberal progressive. According to the stick-person models of 'theories of punishment' taught to students, utilitarians are supposed to be in favour of interrogational torture and judicial execution, at least in principle and subject to empirical contingencies. Many latter-day utilitarians adopt such positions, 'out-Smarting'[37] their deontological opponents by embracing the intended *reductio*.[38] Earlier utilitarians preferred to argue that utility generally favours the more humane policy, either because harsh punishments do not deter more effectively than milder ones (and are consequently gratuitously painful and pointless) or on more specific grounds, e.g. because convict labour is more socially productive than execution, or in a world in which everybody lives in peril of being tortured, even if innocent, pervasive fear would generate massive disutility (a standard manoeuvre I call, not entirely neutrally, 'the empirical dodge' because such counterfactual speculations are largely immune to empirical falsification). Bentham, contrary to widespread misapprehensions, opposed the death penalty,[39] and was barely lukewarm on the practice of torture, albeit refusing to rule it out as a theoretical possibility.[40] Viewed in historical context, and mindful of the tendentiousness and anachronism in classifying Beccaria

[35] Cadoppi, above n 16 at 9–10. For details on these reforms, see also Du Bois-Pedain, ch 14 in this volume.

[36] Cizova, above n 16 at 392, pronounced it 'quite clear that the ideas expressed in *On Crimes and Punishments* could not have any practical application in Russia, regardless of whether Catherine or her successors were sincere', owing to the absence of effective legal and social order and the countervailing force of nobles' traditional privileges and entrenched illiberal institutions, including serfdom.

[37] Named in honour of JJC Smart, a celebrated pioneer of this manoeuvre. See D Dennett & A Steglich-Petersen, *The Philosophical Lexicon* (2008) available at www.philosophicallexicon.com/#O: '**outsmart**, v. To embrace the conclusion of one's opponent's *reductio ad absurdum* argument. "They thought they had me, but I outsmarted them. I agreed that it *was* sometimes just to hang an innocent man".'

[38] See, eg, M Bagaric and J Clarke, 'Not Enough Official Torture in the World? The Circumstances in Which Torture is Morally Justifiable' (2005) 39 *University of San Francisco Law Review* 581; CR Sunstein & A Vermeule, 'Is Capital Punishment Morally Required? Acts, Omissions, and Life-Life Tradeoffs' (2005) 58 *Stanford Law Review* 703.

[39] HA Bedau, 'Bentham's Utilitarian Critique of the Death Penalty' (1983) 74 *Journal of Criminal Law and Criminology* 1033.

[40] WL Twining & PE Twining, 'Bentham on Torture' (1973) 24 *Northern Ireland Legal Quarterly* 305; R Morgan, 'The Utilitarian Justification of Torture: Denial, Desert and Disinformation' (2000) 2 *Punishment & Society* 181.

as a 'utilitarian' at all,[41] it should not be very surprising to find *On Crimes and Punishments* ranging its most forceful arguments *against* capital punishment and judicial torture. Given the prevalence of routine judicial torture in the Continental criminal process of Beccaria's day,[42] and the sanguinary nature of eighteenth-century European penal codes,[43] the abolitionist ethical positions staked out in *On Crimes and Punishments* were radically humane. Yet these arguments are presented in the form of a cumulative list rather than an integrated package. The impression is somewhat scattergun. Certain points are well judged and forcefully made, whilst others are dubious or transparent makeweights. For Bentham (according to Hart), such sloppiness was symptomatic of 'rather a lazy man' who 'shrank from … laborious and infinitely detailed tasks'.[44] Yet in the longer run a humane, if theoretically muddled, liberalism may have wider appeal and greater longevity than Bentham's unflinching intellectual rigour.[45] Beccaria may have the last laugh in penal theory, just as Mill's conceptually unstable compromise with individual rights makes his version of utilitarianism more normatively attractive than Bentham's, notwithstanding its theoretical equivocations.[46]

A recurrent methodological issue pervading *On Crimes and Punishments* is the absence of any empirical basis for many of the claims and assumptions Beccaria makes about social order, the impact of regulation and potential lawbreakers' personal motivations. Beccaria proceeds by introspection, knowledge of general experience and commonsense speculation, which are perfectly legitimate sources of epistemic warrant for many purposes[47] but have obvious limitations in philosophical argument and policy analysis. The absence of secure

[41] Indeed, it has been suggested that even Bentham was not a utilitarian in the sense that 20th-century moral philosophers and their critics co-constructed: Binder, above n 27. In that case, Bentham was not a Utilitarian before Marx was not a Marxist.

[42] M Damaška, 'The Death of Legal Torture' (1978) 87 *Yale Law Journal* 860; JH Langbein, *Torture and the Law of Proof: Europe and England in the Ancien Régime* (Chicago IL, Chicago University Press, 1977).

[43] Including the English: this was the period of the Hanoverian 'bloody code' and the notorious Waltham Black Act (albeit that English penal law's bark was far worse than its bite, since many capital sentences were actually commuted): see EP Thompson, *Whigs and Hunters: The Origin of the Black Act* (London, Penguin, 1977); VAC Gatrell, *The Hanging Tree: Execution and the English People 1770–1868* (Oxford, Oxford University Press, 1994); P Linebaugh, *The London Hanged: Crime and Civil Society in the Eighteenth Century* (Cambridge, Cambridge University Press, 1992). On Habsburg-Austria during Maria Theresa's reign, see Du Bois-Pedain, ch 14 in this volume.

[44] Hart, above n 5 at 49.

[45] This was Hart's assessment, ibid at 50–51: '[I]f Beccaria was a utilitarian his utilitarianism was qualified in ways which Bentham thought absurd. … I think that very often where Bentham and Beccaria differ in detail this is traceable to Beccaria's conviction that what may be done in the name of utility should be limited by consideration of what befits the dignity of a man. … [A]t the root of their divergencies lie very different conceptions of the idea of justice.'

[46] R Crisp, *Mill on Utilitarianism* (Abingdon, Routledge, 1997); CL Ten, *Mill on Liberty* (Oxford, Oxford University Press, 1980).

[47] G Gigerenzer, *Rationality for Mortals* (Oxford, Oxford University Press, 2008); W Twining, 'Narrative and Generalizations in Argumentation about Questions of Fact' (1999) 40 *South Texas Law Review* 351.

empirical moorings for his normative arguments is all the more incongruous because Beccaria is fond of mathematical – especially geometrical – metaphors (which in themselves sound forced and not very successful to modern ears) and flaunts his familiarity with the latest scientific thinking. Clearly, the methodological protocols and epistemological expectations of modern social science – let alone psychology – lay in a still undreamt future for Beccaria. Evidence-based policymaking[48] this is not:

> Although men, who always suspect the voice of reason and respect that of authority, have not been persuaded by the experience of centuries, during which the ultimate penalty has never dissuaded men from offending against society, nor by the example of the citizens of Rome, nor by the twenty years of the reign of the Empress Elizabeth of Muscovy, in which she set the leaders of all peoples an outstanding precedent, worth at least as much as many victories bought with the blood of her motherland's sons, it will suffice to consult human nature to be convinced of the truth of my claim.[49]

Notwithstanding the shaky epistemological status of numerous assertions appearing in *On Crimes and Punishments*, Beccaria's commitment to rationality in political argument and penal policymaking is unwavering. He repeatedly asserts the absolute necessity of designing policy programmes and conducting government on the basis of enlightened reason rather than blind tradition. These were themes to which Beccaria returned in his inaugural lecture as Professor of Cameral Sciences at the Palatine School in Milan, delivered on 9 January 1769. In this rousing oration, in which Beccaria commits himself to 'the sacred duty of those responsible for public instruction of always speaking the truth clearly, simply and vigorously', he promises to 'try to steer clear of all sterile and abstract speculation and from that sort of impressive apparatus of scientific terminology which makes all the sciences seem mysterious and inaccessible'.[50] His method is essentially Aristotelian in elucidating 'a chain of reasoning and of orderly deductions of one truth from another' and 'bring[ing] forth warrant for what we say by breaking complex notions down into their elements and by giving an orderly deduction form the simplest propositions to the most general and complicated truths'.[51] And Beccaria warns:

> No one should believe that blind experience and mechanical habit can take the place of sure principles and of reasoned maxims in confronting unexpected political

[48] Admittedly, 'evidence-based policymaking' is not entirely unproblematic, notably in its susceptibility to ironic inversion as 'policy-based evidence-making': cf R Walters, 'Government Manipulation of Criminological Knowledge and Policies of Deceit', in T Hope & R Walters (eds), *Critical Thinking about the Uses of Research* (London, Centre for Crime and Justice Studies, 2008) 7; House of Commons Science and Technology Committee, *Scientific Advice, Risk and Evidence Based Policy Making*, HC 900-I, Seventh Report of Session 2005–06. But as a general methodological proposition, the demand for pertinent data to supplement and sometimes correct philosophical speculation is a fair expectation of rational argument.

[49] Beccaria, above n 2 at 67 (ch 28).

[50] 'Inaugural Lecture', ibid 129 at 139.

[51] Ibid at 134, 139.

circumstances. Nor is it enough to have general truths without descending to particulars, since theory … often has to be profoundly and substantially modified in the light of attempts to apply it to individual cases. … It is characteristic of human beings to throw themselves blindly into their present and immediate concerns, neglecting the future; they love variety and change, but only within familiar surroundings, which exercise a stronger influence than any reasoning; they wish to do much, but with the least possible effort …[52]

As Brexit slides inexorably from tragedy to farce, and with a gameshow host recently resident in the White House, it is hard not to read this passage and think that today's beleaguered democracies would benefit from a strong dose of Beccaria's passionate rationalism.[53] Yet I would say that in some respects Beccaria overdoes his critique of tradition, finding nothing in it other than habit and superstition. I will later suggest that in theorising and curating complex human institutions like criminal justice, respect for tradition may have its proper place, whereas hyper-rationalism and its fellow traveller scientism[54] are intellectual vices with the capacity for precipitating appalling maladministration.[55] Beccaria's vulnerability to this methodological criticism is noteworthy, partly because his liberal instincts generally[56] save him from any corresponding dogmatism at the substantive level of practical ethics and policy choice.

How should we judge the overall quality of Beccaria's normative argumentation? By modern standards, he is only a ß+ student. In addition to being no great shakes as a philosopher, Beccaria's jurisprudence is crude and naive in many respects. The third section of this chapter will substantiate this accusation through critical examination of Beccaria's remarks on detailed points of criminal procedure and evidence. Here, I briefly mention Beccaria's blanket condemnation of judicial discretion, which follows logically enough from his foundational commitment to the rule of law[57] but tempts Beccaria into a very

[52] Ibid 130–131.

[53] Developing this theme, see eg R Peston, *WTF?* (London, Hodder & Stoughton, 2017); AC Grayling, *Democracy and Its Critics* (London, OneWorld, 2017); M Lilla, *The Once and Future Liberal: After Identity Politics* (New York, HarperCollins, 2018).

[54] S Haack, *Defending Science – Within Reason: Between Scientism and Cynicism* (Amherst NY, Prometheus Books, 2003); T Sorell, *Scientism: Philosophy and the Infatuation with Science* (Abingdon, Routledge, 1994).

[55] Soviet agronomy is the stock illustration: see N Roll-Hansen, 'The Lysenko Effect: Undermining the Autonomy of Science' (2005) 29 *Endeavour* 143. Another, lesser-known example is described by J Chang & J Halliday, *Mao: The Unknown Story* (London, Vintage, 2007) ch 40: 'The Great Leap: "Half of China May Well have to Die" (1958–61)'.

[56] Not always. He has some peculiar things to say about censuring 'parasites', for instance: Beccaria, above n 2 ch 24.

[57] Set out ibid at 12 (ch 3), 14 (ch 4), 90 (ch 34). *Le gouvernement des juges* remains to this day a *bête noire* of French legal and political thought: see J Hodgson, *French Criminal Justice* (Oxford, Hart Publishing, 2005) 16–22.

crude version of logico-deductive legal positivism[58] foreclosing the possibility of valid judicial precedent.[59] This position is both theoretically unsustainable and a poor guide to policymakers, who would be better advised to try to channel, delimit and infuse professionals' discretionary decision-making with ethical guidance[60] rather than pursuing the fool's errand of seeking to abolish discretion in the administration of criminal justice. *On Crimes and Punishments* is heading in the right direction on many practical issues and has a sound commitment to rationality, but the execution is patchy, often question-begging and ultimately unpersuasive. Of course, this is an outrageously anachronistic judgement that singularly fails to do justice to the historical significance of Beccaria's writing in his own day and its enduring legacy. *On Crimes and Punishments* was an instant critical success, 'an event',[61] 'a European sensation'.[62] Multiply reissued and translated, it was admired by Voltaire and Diderot, and enthusiastically consulted by European sovereigns and law reformers. For a time Beccaria became a (reluctant) celebrity. Certainly, Beccaria's style and approach mark him out as an unmistakably modern, Enlightenment writer rather than a Renaissance (let alone medieval) thinker. He is seeking to persuade his readers through the force of argument, not – for example – by amassing authoritative anecdotes, quoting Scripture, or recycling the sayings of prophets in the style of casuistical instruction (in which, so critics say, 'arguments' are merely paraded as *ex post* rationalisations and *ad hoc* excuses).[63]

Glancing back from a remote twenty-first-century posterity, any authentic sense of *On Crimes and Punishments*' contemporary impact and significance must remain elusive, at least without extended historical digressions. Beccaria's celebrated tract has been described as 'the crown jewel of the Italian

[58] Cf J Gardner, 'Legal Positivism: 5½ Myths' (2001) 46 *American Journal of Jurisprudence* 199; AJ Sebok, 'Misunderstanding Positivism' (1995) 93 *Michigan Law Review* 2054.

[59] 'The judge should construct a perfect syllogism about every criminal case: the major premise should be the general law; the minor, the conformity or otherwise of the action with the law; and the conclusion, freedom or punishment. Whenever the judge is forced, or takes it upon himself, to construct even as few as two syllogisms, then the door is opened to uncertainty.' (Beccaria, above n 2 at 14 (ch 4)). The logico-deductive model of statutory interpretation continued to be influential long after Beccaria's time, especially in civilian jurisprudence and law-school pedagogy: see further, R Grote, 'Comparative Law and Teaching Law Through the Case Method in the Civil Law Tradition – A German Perspective' (2005) 82 *University of Detroit Mercy Law Review* 163; E Hondius, 'Precedent in East and West' (2005) 23 *Penn State International Law Review* 521; J Bell, 'Comparing Precedent' (1997) 82 *Cornell Law Review* 1243. There is even a – now largely forgotten – Anglophone variant of logico-deductive legal science, built on judicial precedent rather than legislation: see MH Hoeflich, 'Law and Geometry: Legal Science from Leibniz to Langdell' (1986) 30 *American Journal of Legal History* 95.

[60] For detailed elucidation and case-studies, see J Hunter, P Roberts, SNM Young and D Dixon (eds), *The Integrity of Criminal Process* (Oxford, Hart Publishing, 2016).

[61] Bridgwater, above n 1 at 220.

[62] Bessler, above n 9 at 283.

[63] For a more sympathetic reading, see AR Jonsen & S Toulmin, *The Abuse of Casuistry: A History of Moral Reasoning* (Berkeley CA, University of California Press, 1990).

Enlightenment and a classic text of modern penality'[64] that 'changed Western civilization'.[65] More sober reflection has it that this 'slim but potent book was a success primarily because it advocated changes deemed desirable and supported by public opinion. ... There are reasons for believing that the essay would have failed to impress or to have attracted but passing attention had it not appeared when it did. Europe was ready for it in 1764'.[66] Another possibility is that *On Crimes and Punishments* contains such a rich and varied cornucopia of themes, digressions, intuitions and arguments that contemporary readers were sure to find morsels to their taste and were able to cherry-pick according to personal predilection.[67] Since my topic is 'Beccaria *now*', more charitably contextual readings can safely be deferred to better qualified historians.

III. A POLITICAL THEORY OF CRIMINAL JUSTICE

Beccaria, like Bentham, visualises criminal justice as a problem of government. At least since Hobbes, government has posed the question of the legitimacy of political authority and its claimed entitlement to the use of coercive force. Beccaria (drawing directly on Rousseau) easily adopts the liberal assumption that liberty is the natural state of being and 'every act of authority between one man and another which is not derived from absolute necessity is tyrannous'.[68] That necessity is found, pretty much where Hobbes left it, in the need to preserve 'the public well-being from the usurpations of individuals'.[69] Natural freedom, being coarse and precarious,[70] is rationally traded for an enlarged and more bounteous liberty under fair and effective government. Questions of crime and punishment are already close at hand. Punishment is a tool of government to force those inclined to subordinate the public interest to their own desires to think again or behave differently. It is far from being the only, the main, or the first means of persuasion or restraint in government's playbook, but it is sometimes the most efficient regulatory technique and stands as the ultimate guarantor of governmental authority when nothing else will serve. Crimes are

[64] Harcourt, above n 16.

[65] Bessler, above n 9 at 291.

[66] E Monachesi, 'Pioneers in Criminology IX: Cesare Beccaria (1738–1794)' (1955) 46 *Journal of Criminal Law, Criminology and Police Science* 439 at 448. Monachesi adds 'Without such perspective the present-day reader of Beccaria's essay is quite apt to see little that is new or striking in the essay, since what Beccaria proposed and so ably argued for in 1764 has been in great part achieved in the modern world.'

[67] Cf Draper, above n 16 (describing Blackstone's studiously selective reliance on Beccaria).

[68] Beccaria, above n 2 at 10 (ch 2).

[69] Ibid.

[70] Beccaria calls it 'the old state of unsociability' (ibid at 11), echoing Hobbes' aversion to a life 'solitary, poore, nasty, brutish and short'. On Hobbes' – largely neglected – contributions to theorising penal regulation, see A Ristroph, 'Hobbes on "Diffidence" and the Criminal Law', in Dubber (ed), above n 16 at 238.

then defined as those assaults on the common public interest that should, in principle, attract punishment.

These parsimonious elements, already well-established in eighteenth-century political theory and widely popularised, are sufficient to enable Beccaria to construct a fairly sophisticated conception of criminal justice that is rationalist, secular, liberal, humane and justified by its instrumental contribution to legitimate government. Parallels to Benthamite utilitarianism are almost irresistible, not merely because Beccaria occasionally refers to 'utility', but more substantially owing to overlapping theoretical foundations and congruent policy prescriptions.[71] It is essential to grasp that Beccaria conceives his political argument as *the measure of penal justice*, rather than punishment being justified by some external or free-standing deontological criterion such as moral desert or unfair advantage-taking:

> [B]y 'justice' I mean nothing other than the restraint necessary to hold particular interests together, without which they would collapse into the old state of unsociability. Any punishment that goes beyond the need to preserve this bond is unjust by its very nature.[72]

Structurally, this parallels the classical utilitarian's insistence that utility just *is* the measure of justice, displacing all other measures of moral performance. However, Beccaria insists that only genuine vices may be criminalised, lest penal regulation in the service of the general welfare become perversely self-defeating: 'To forbid a large number of trivial acts is not to prevent the crimes they may occasion. It is to create new crimes, wilfully to redefine virtue and vice, which we are exhorted to regard as eternal and immutable.'[73] It seems here as though the scope of the criminal law is answerable to standards of vice and virtue anterior to any utilitarian calculation. The logic of this moralised consequentialism unfolds and extends into various discrete principles of criminalisation and penal policy, prominently including the following five.

First, crimes are to be defined in terms of attacks on the collective public interest, rather than as private wrongs. Beccaria informs us that 'the one true measure of criminality is the damage done to the nation'.[74] Consequently, '[t]he right to have someone punished does not belong to any individual; it is the right of all the citizens and of the sovereign'.[75] Second, punishment can be tolerated

[71] Close textual reading of archival material supports the conclusion that 'Bentham's debt to Beccaria was profound and extensive, but that, as he established a reputation as a major jurist in his own right, he believed that his own work had superseded that of the Italian jurist … Bentham drew explicitly on Beccaria in some instances, and yet rejected other elements in his thought': Schofield, above n 5 at 66, 69.

[72] Beccaria, above n 2 at 11 (ch 2).

[73] Ibid at 103 (ch 41).

[74] Ibid at 22 (ch 7).

[75] Ibid at 75 (ch 29).

only to the extent that it does good, that is, penal consequentialism. The good of punishment, moreover, cannot be cashed out in terms of penitential suffering or moral nullification: these benighted notions belong to primitive philosophy. '[T]he purpose of punishment is not that of tormenting or afflicting any sentient creature, nor of undoing a crime already committed,' Beccaria assures us, and adds with a rhetorical flourish 'Can the wailings of a wretch, perhaps, undo what has been done and turn back the clock?'[76] Third, the primary modality of punishment is general deterrence. This accords with rational liberal governance, inasmuch as prevention is far better, and cheaper, than cure. The very best punishments are those that are so effective in motivating compliance that they never, or hardly ever, have to be imposed.[77] Fourth, forms of punishment should be devised and calibrated so that they achieve optimal deterrence with maximal efficiency.[78] As well as delegitimating penal excess,[79] this precept recommends exploiting the psychological impact of penal symbolism to inflict punishments calculated to 'make the most efficacious and lasting impression on the minds of men with the least torment to the body of the condemned'.[80] Fifth, Beccaria's penal philosophy is encapsulated in a powerful idea of *proportionality*:

> It is in the common interest not only that crimes not be committed, but that they be rarer in proportion to the harm they do to society. Hence, the obstacles which repel men from committing crimes ought to be made stronger the more those crimes are against the public good and the more inducements there are for committing them. Hence, there must be a proportion between crimes and punishments.[81]

Proportionality is a thoroughly modern penal notion, and Beccaria's advocacy of this 'fixed proportion' marks him out, possibly above all else, as a prophet of future penal theory and policymaking. In later twentieth-century thinking, proportionality is of course associated with 'just deserts' neo-retributivism,[82] but in England and Wales we know from experience that 'proportionality' itself is a malleable and capacious concept. Everything turns on *what* is being held in

[76] Ibid at 31(ch 12). The latter seems to be an anticipatory rejection of the symbolic nullification argument advanced by Hegel: see P Nicholson, 'Hegel on Crime' (1982) 3 *History of Political Thought* 103.

[77] Beccaria, above n 2 at 103 (ch 41).

[78] This productive furrow qualifying Beccaria as the godfather of modern Law and Economics scholarship: Harcourt, above n 16 at section 4.

[79] '[I]f it could be shown that the extreme severity of some punishments … is merely useless, even then, it will be contrary … to … beneficent virtues …' (Beccaria, above n 2 at 13 (ch 3)); 'If a punishment is to be just, it must be pitched at just that level of intensity which suffices to deter men from crime' (ibid at 68 (ch 28)).

[80] Ibid at 31 (ch 12).

[81] Ibid at 19 (ch 6).

[82] See, eg, A von Hirsch, *Deserved Criminal Sentences* (Oxford, Hart/Bloomsbury, 2017); MJ Fish, 'An Eye for an Eye: Proportionality as a Moral Principle of Punishment' (2008) 28 *Oxford Journal of Legal Studies* 57; A von Hirsch & A Ashworth, *Proportionate Sentencing: Exploring the Principles* (Oxford, Oxford University Press, 2005); A von Hirsch, *Censure and Sanctions* (Oxford, Oxford University Press, 1993).

proportion to penal treatment. For example, if crimes against God are infinitely evil, eternal damnation and roasting in hellfire[83] are not necessarily *disproportionate* (whatever other objections might be levelled against them as criminal punishments). More prosaically, once it is said that punishment is meted out in proportion to wrongdoing, culpability *and general deterrence*,[84] the structural capacity of the concept to limit unwarranted punishments is, for retributivists, fatally compromised. In many of his specific recommendations for penal policy, as well as in his more speculative forays into general theorising, Beccaria certainly sounds like a utilitarian *avant la lettre*. Principles of efficacy, frugality and exemplarity in punishments are all familiar Benthamite themes,[85] and the following summary of principle might have been penned by Old Father Utility himself:

> It is better to prevent crimes than to punish them. This is the principal goal of all good legislation, which is the art of guiding men to their greatest happiness, or the least unhappiness possible, taking into account all the blessings and evils of life.[86]

[83] The relevant Quranic verse runs 'The punishment of those who wage war against Allah and His messenger and strive to make mischief in the land is only this, that they should be murdered or crucified or their hands and their feet should be cut off on opposite sides or they should be imprisoned; this shall be as a disgrace for them in this world, and in the hereafter they shall have a grievous chastisement …' Or as Exodus 21:24–27 proximately has it, 'Eye for eye, tooth for tooth, hand for hand, foot for foot, burning for burning, wound for wound, stripe for stripe. If any man strike the eye of his manservant or maidservant, and leave them but one eye, he shall let them go free for the eye which he put out. Also if he strike out a tooth of his manservant or maidservant, he shall in like manner make them free.'

[84] See *R v Cunningham* [1993] 1 WLR 183, (1993) 14 Cr App R (S) 444, CA, where Lord Taylor CJ at 186 and 447 unhesitatingly declared that 'The purposes of a custodial sentence must primarily be to punish and to deter. Accordingly, the phrase "commensurate with the seriousness of the offence" [in the Criminal Justice Act 1991, s 2(2)] must mean commensurate with the punishment and deterrence which the seriousness of the offence requires.' The dilution of just deserts proportionality by other penal aims is, unwittingly, laid bare in the Halliday Review preceding the Criminal Justice Act 2003, where it was stated that 'The principle of proportionate punishments ("just deserts") needs to be sustained. … The question is: proportionate to what? … Clarification needs to be based on a clear presumption that sentence severity should increase as a consequence of sufficiently recent and relevant previous convictions. The justification for this modified principle is two-fold. A continuing course of criminal conduct in the face of repeated attempts by the State to try to correct it, calls for increasing denunciation and retribution, notwithstanding that earlier crimes have already been punished. In addition, persistent criminality justifies the more intensive efforts to reform and rehabilitate which become possible within a more intrusive and punitive sentence.' Home Office, *Making Punishments Work: Report of A Review of the Sentencing Framework for England and Wales* (July 2001) paras 2.6–2.7.

[85] J Bentham, *An Introduction to the Principles of Morals and Legislation* [1789] edited by JH Burns & HLA Hart (Oxford, Oxford University Press, 1996) chs 13–15. Of 'exemplarity' (and its first-cousin, 'characteristicalness'), the least intuitive of the three, Bentham (ibid 178–179), advised that 'there is not any means by which a given quantity of punishment can be rendered more exemplary, than by choosing it of such a sort as shall bear an *analogy* to the offence … Retaliation, therefore, in the few cases in which it is practicable, and not too expensive, will have one great advantage over every other mode of punishment.'

[86] Beccaria, above n 2 at 103 (ch 41).

As commentators have noted, however, many of Beccaria's other statements break with Benthamite orthodoxy, and hint at a more nuanced, pluralistic and humane – if under-developed – penal philosophy. Towards the end of *On Crimes and Punishments* Beccaria declares 'it is a false idea of utility to sacrifice the thing to the name and to separate the public good from the good of each individual.'[87] This remark, I think, lends the lie to Bentham's assumption that Beccaria was just muddled, or intellectually lazy, whenever he failed to follow through on the unflinching logic of utility maximisation.[88] Read in conjunction with several other intriguing observations scattered throughout the text, it is not tendentious to interpret Beccaria's rejection of 'false idea[s] of utility' as rooted in a conception of political authority that is both more respectful of individual rights and more robustly democratic than even Mill's revisionist utilitarianism. Thus, in a passage that might be read as anticipating twentieth-century ideas of human dignity as the basis for universal human rights,[89] Beccaria dramatically announces:

> There is no freedom when the laws permit a man in some cases to cease to be a *person* and to become a *thing*.[90]

The clear implication is that legitimate political authority is, at least,[91] side-constrained by a conception of the person mandating respect for individual rights. This very unBenthamite sentiment is consistent with passages in which Beccaria seems to be signalling, quite explicitly, that maximising aggregate social welfare ('happiness') is *not* the sole criterion of justice.[92] The following quotations synthesise this broader conception of legitimate political authority with Beccaria's foundational methodological commitment to rational public administration and more granular principles of penal minimalism:

> [I]f it could be shown that the extreme severity of some punishments … is merely useless, even then, it will be contrary not only to those beneficent virtues which arise from an enlightened reason which prefers to govern happy men [rather] than a herd of slaves … but also be contrary to justice and to the very nature of the social contract.[93]

[87] Ibid at 102 (ch 40).

[88] Also see DB Young, 'Cesare Beccaria: Utilitarian or Retributivist?' (1983) 11 *Journal of Criminal Justice* 317 (contending that '[c]ontrary to common opinion, … Beccaria was basically a retributivist, quite close at many points to Kant and Hegel').

[89] See further G Kateb, *Human Dignity* (Cambridge MA, Harvard University Press, 2011); M Dan-Cohen, 'Dignity, Crime and Punishment: A Kantian Perspective', in Dubber (ed), above n 16 at 101.

[90] Beccaria, above n 2 at 50 (ch 20).

[91] On a stronger view, respect for human dignity is partly *constitutive* of legitimate political authority, not merely a side-constraint on governmental policy. But *On Crimes and Punishments*' implicit political theory is too fragmentary to support confident exegesis.

[92] See, eg, Beccaria, above n 2 at 58 (ch 25) (stating that 'a punishment is just not simply because it produces some good, but because it is necessary. Even a useful injustice cannot be tolerated by a lawgiver').

[93] Ibid at 13 (ch 3).

> If a punishment is to serve its purpose, it is enough that the harm of punishment should outweigh the good which the criminal can derive from the crime, and into the calculation of this balance, we must add the unerringness of the punishment and the loss of the good produced by the crime. Anything more than this is superfluous and, therefore, tyrannous.[94]

So the enlightened sovereign governs in the name of happiness *and* freedom; and freedom from *slavery* at that. Virtuous citizenship is cultivated, reciprocally, 'by the creed [that] liberates and invigorates the spirit and enlightens the mind' and 'knows no fear', a condition of liberty Beccaria sharply differentiates from mere 'pliant prudence which is fitting only to those who have to live a precarious and uncertain existence'.[95] It is difficult to see how servile contentment could be felicific for this Beccaria, though the empirical reality of (some) happy slaves is a notorious fact of classical civilisations. There is more than a distant historical echo of modern conceptions of republican freedom.[96] The implication, according to *On Crimes and Punishments*, is that the ruler who opts for penal excess becomes *a tyrant*, not merely an incompetent calculator of maximal social utility. Strict limits on the scope and implementation of penal law, underpinned by rights, are characterised as 'a sacred creed, without which there cannot be a legitimate society', being reckoned 'a just recompense for men's sacrifice of that universal power over all things common to all sentient creatures'.[97]

Further clues to Beccaria's morally pluralistic conception of legitimate government can be found in some of his rather flamboyant endorsements of political equality. Beccaria has absolutely no truck with aristocratic privilege:

> [P]unishments ought to be the same for the highest as they are for the lowest of citizens. To be legitimate, every distinction whether of honour or wealth presupposes an antecedent equality based on the laws, which treat every subject as equally subordinate to them.[98]

Formal equality before the law is presented as part of a package of ideas directly anticipating more fully elaborated modern conceptions of the rule of law:[99]

> Do you want to prevent crimes? Then make sure that the laws are clear and simple … that the laws favour individual men more than classes of men. … Make sure that men fear the laws and only the laws.[100]

[94] Ibid at 64 (ch 27).
[95] Ibid at 25 (ch 8).
[96] See, eg, P Pettit, *Republicanism: A Theory of Freedom and Government* (Oxford, Oxford University Press, 1997) (citing Cicero, Machiavelli, Montesquieu and Rousseau as key historical thinkers in the republican tradition; Beccaria is not mentioned).
[97] Beccaria, above n 2 at 25 (ch 8).
[98] Ibid at 51 (ch 21).
[99] Generally, see BZ Tamanaha, *On the Rule of Law: History, Politics, Theory* (Cambridge, Cambridge University Press, 2004); Lord Bingham, 'The Rule of Law' (2007) 66 *Cambridge Law Journal* 67; RS Summers, 'The Principles of the Rule of Law' (1999) 74 *Notre Dame Law Review* 1691; J Raz, 'The Rule of Law and its Virtue' (1977) 93 *Law Quarterly Review* 195.
[100] Beccaria, above n 2 at 104 (ch 41).

Here we see again *On Crimes and Punishments*' now familiar conjunction of penal policy and broader theory of government. Although the policy issue is framed as a question of crime prevention, Beccaria's answer comes in the form of a meditation on general techniques of legal regulation and the values underpinning it. In this comprehensive reconstruction, punishment is only one chapter of a more holistic criminal jurisprudence, which is itself an applied extrapolation from political morality.

Beccaria's writings frequently return to class interests and the need for greater social equality. His critique of the potentially corrupting influence of financial leverage or preferment is almost Marxian in its denunciation of the propertied interest and – a more specific target for Beccaria – the idleness of inherited wealth:

> [T]he rich and the powerful should not be able to put a price on assaults on the weak and the poor; otherwise wealth, which is the reward of industry under the protection of the laws, feeds tyranny.[101]

Yet if Beccaria was a kind of proto-socialist, his own privileged background[102] perhaps inevitably marks him out as one of the champagne fraternity. Even when he is trying to be sympathetic and humanitarian, Beccaria's tendency is to look down on the ignorant proles and patronise the populism of 'the mob', as in the following passage:

> Who can fail to feel himself shaken to the core by the sight of thousands of wretches whom poverty, either willed or tolerated by the laws, which have always favoured the few and abused the masses, had dragged back to the primitive state of nature ... or found guilty only of nothing but being faithful to their own principles, and are then torn apart with premediated pomp and slow tortures by men with the same faculties and emotions, becoming the entertainment of a fanatical mob?[103]

Elsewhere, Beccaria assures his genteel readers that he 'know[s], that self-analysis is a skill which we acquire with education'; before lamenting – in another presentiment of Marx – the currency of the warped logic commending criminality when 'religion comes into the mind of the ruffian ... offering an easy repentance and near-certainty of eternal bliss'.[104] Still, Beccaria should be credited with trying to think clearly and seriously about the rationality of motivation from the perspective of those most likely to be tempted into a life of crime. His imaginative reconstruction of 'the reasoning of a robber or assassin'

[101] Ibid at 50 (ch 20).

[102] See Monachesi, above n 66 (noting that '[b]oth his father and mother were members of the aristocracy and amongst his ancestors were persons who had achieved distinction in various fields of endeavor').

[103] Beccaria, above n 2 at 64–65 (ch 27).

[104] Ibid at 69 (ch 28).

along the following lines has an enduring, even endearing, resonance down the centuries:

> What are these laws which I have to obey, which leave such a gulf between me and the rich man? He denies me the penny I beg of him, brushing me off with the demand that I should work, something he knows nothing about. Who made these laws? Rich and powerful men, who have never condescended to visit the filthy hovels of the poor, who have never broken mouldy bread among the innocent cries of starving children and a wife's tears. Let us break these ties, which are pernicious to most people and only useful to a few and idle tyrants; let us attack injustice at its source … [P]erhaps the day for suffering and repentance will come, but it will be brief, and I shall have one day of pain for many years of freedom and pleasure. … I shall put to rights the iniquities of fortune, and I shall see these tyrants blanch and cower at one whom they considered, with insulting ostentation, lower than their horses and dogs.[105]

It would be another two centuries before the rationality of criminal motivations would become a serious topic for Criminology, notably in those theories and associated policy programmes that seek to recalibrate the opportunity structure through situational crime prevention, 'designing out crime', 'target-hardening' and the like.[106] Some of the proponents of these theories like to (re)claim 'classical criminology' as part of a respectable intellectual heritage.[107] Whether or not such elective ancestry can survive charges of anachronism or wishful thinking, Beccaria's evident compassion for the downtrodden and dispossessed is more progressive than certain segments of modern penal discourse that, in my professional lifetime, have demonised juvenile offenders as hyenas[108] and vermin.[109] Besides, Beccaria would hardly be the last left-leaning thinker to prefer the abstract concept of the workers (eg as an historical agent of revolutionary socialism) to the filthy, coarse, diseased, risky, violent and prejudiced realities of much working-class life later documented by Engels, Orwell[110] and – in more recent decades – Bea Campbell.[111]

[105] Ibid.

[106] Generally, see A Bottoms, 'Developing Socio-Spatial Criminology', in M Maguire, R Morgan & R Reiner (eds), *The Oxford Handbook of Criminology* 5th edition (Oxford, Oxford University Press, 2012) 450.

[107] See, eg, B McCarthy & AR Chaudhary, 'Rational Choice Theory and Crime', in G Bruinsma & D Weisburd (eds), *Encyclopedia of Criminology and Criminal Justice* (New York, Springer, 2014) 4307; M Felson & MA Eckert, *Crime and Everyday Life* 6th edition (Thousand Oaks CA, Sage, 2018).

[108] 'The "Hyena" campaign was launched in 1992 – with the long-term objective of making car crime socially unacceptable. The campaign likens car criminals to scavenging hyenas, and encourages the public to collectively deter offenders': www.nationalarchives.gov.uk/films/1979to2006/filmpage_crime.htm (including the original film).

[109] 'Court Traps "Ratboy" after Six-year Crime Spree' *Independent* (2 April 1997); T Wilkinson, 'Teenage Criminal Known as "Ratboy" Grows Up – But He's Back Behind Bars' *Independent* (30 August 2013).

[110] As Orwell chides in *The Road to Wigan Peer*, 'You cannot have affection for a man whose breath … habitually stinks': see R Colls, *George Orwell – English Rebel* (Oxford, Oxford University Press, 2013) chs 1 and 2.

[111] B Campbell, *Goliath: Britain's Dangerous Places* (London, Methuen, 1993).

Reading *On Crimes and Punishments* straight through at a single, concentrated sitting leaves the abiding impression that Beccaria has no sense of penal theory as being isolated from political morality in general, or of penal policy as being a discrete area of lawmaking and administration demarcated from other dimensions of government. This holistic vision, long pre-dating modern disciplinary taxonomies, is a major theoretical strength in my estimation and vindicates Beccaria's status as an intellectual pioneer. Having studied aspects of penology twice, first as a law undergraduate and subsequently as part of a criminology masters, I gradually formed the impression that penal theory had somehow come adrift of the philosophical mainland and was in danger of becoming a stagnant and uninviting backwater. The same well-rehearsed arguments were being recycled and repackaged for new (student) audiences, with minimal theoretical innovation or novel criticism but growing ennui. Happily, the last two or three decades have witnessed major theoretical renewal in penal theory, the infusion of much new blood (especially from US grad schools) and a rapidly expanding literature. Two characteristic features of this renaissance are essentially methodological. The first is a concerted attempt to reunite and reintegrate penal theorising with more general philosophical inquiries.[112] The second is greater attention to political theory,[113] balancing up a quite pronounced bias towards moral theory (aka ethics, practical ethics) and metaphysics (questions of agency, action, causation and intentionality) in large swathes of criminal-law theorising of the 1990s and early 2000s.[114] As we have seen, Beccaria was already fully engaged in both projects two centuries earlier. Perhaps more intimate acquaintance with the contents of *On Crimes and Punishments* might have prevented normative theorists[115] from forgetting about the politics of punishment, or cured their amnesia sooner.

[112] Trail-blazing texts with broader philosophical ambitions include J Braithwaite & P Pettit, *Not Just Deserts: A Republican Theory of Criminal Justice* (Oxford, Oxford University Press, 1990); and N Lacey, *State Punishment: Political Principles and Community Values* (Abingdon, Routledge, 1988).

[113] See further, eg, A du Bois-Pedain, M Ulväng & P Asp (eds), *Criminal Law and the Authority of the State* (Oxford, Hart Publishing, 2017); M Thorburn, 'Criminal Law as Public Law', in RA Duff & SP Green (eds), *Philosophical Foundations of Criminal Law* (Oxford, Oxford University Press, 2011) 42; G Binder, 'Punishment Theory: Moral or Political?' (2002) 5 *Buffalo Criminal Law Review* 321.

[114] For plausible overviews, see eg M Davis, 'Punishment Theory's Golden Half Century: A Survey of Developments from (about) 1957 to 2007' (2009) 13 *Journal of Ethics* 73; L Alexander, 'The Philosophy of Criminal Law', in J Coleman & S Shapiro (eds), *The Oxford Handbook of Jurisprudence and Philosophy of Law* (Oxford, Oxford University Press, 2002); GP Fletcher, 'The Fall and Rise of Criminal Theory' (1998) 1 *Buffalo Criminal Law Review* 275.

[115] I am not overlooking an unbroken tradition of critical criminological literature on crime and punishment. However, this work mostly eschews normative ambitions, denying the relevance of philosophical theorising or simply presupposing its own ethical mandate and arguing by stipulation or assumed self-evidence. As Stan Cohen noted (before giving up Criminology to tackle human rights and the politics of global justice), '[t]he great unwritten book in criminology is a serious examination of the basic principles of liberalism': S Cohen, *Against Criminology* (New Brunswick NJ, Transaction Books, 1988) x.

IV. REINVENTING CRIMINAL PROCEDURE

Beccaria wrote *On Crimes and Punishments* at a pivotal moment in the historical development of European criminal procedures. Reform was already in the air, and would sweep the European continent within half a century: albeit that Napoleon's armies would have an as great, or a greater, causal role to play in that unfolding drama as did the conquering force of reason. It is hard to know how much of the detailed argumentation of *On Crimes and Punishments* was genuinely novel, or might be perceived as such by its intended readership. It seems likely that Beccaria was channelling the progressive mood of the times and reflecting it back, pithily encapsulated, as reformism's prevailing wisdom. At all events, much of what is written in *On Crimes and Punishments* would come to be endorsed as the enlightened common sense of modern Continental criminal procedure. Beccaria's forceful criticism of judicial torture is only the most obvious illustration of the text's progressive procedural modernism.

The starting point is a thoroughgoing critique of the unreformed inquisition, which operated without any institutional division of forensic labour, effective constraints on destructive sovereign power, or mechanisms of oversight to ensure judicial accountability. '[T]he whole arrangement of the criminal law,' Beccaria complains, '[is] centred on a confession of guilt' to be extracted from the suspect's person, by force or guile:

> [T]he judge takes possession of the criminal's body and, with methodical formalities, tears it apart, to draw from it, as from some capital he has earned, all the profit he can. … The judge becomes the enemy of the accused … and he does not seek for the truth of the matter, but only for the crime in the prisoner; he sets traps for him, and if they do not succeed, he feels it as a personal failure … The judge has in his power the evidence which leads to the arrest. If anyone is to prove himself innocent, he must first be declared to be guilty …[116]

This 'offensive trial' model of criminal justice, in which the judge levies war on presumed enemies of the people, should be replaced, insists Beccaria, by a rational procedure orientated towards truth-finding. This arrangement would better befit the government of citizens who possess inherent dignity and do not cease to be right-holders when accused of crimes. According to Beccaria, even soldiers and sultans embrace rational inquiry, whilst 'criminal proceedings almost everywhere in the enlightened Europe of the eighteenth century' remain captives of medievalism:

> The true trial, the *informative*, which consists in the impartial search for the facts, which is what reason demands, what martial law implements, and what even Asiatic despotism employs in peaceful and unimportant cases, is very little in evidence in

[116] Beccaria, above n 2 at 45–46 (ch 17).

> European courts. What an involuted maze of strange illogicalities, which no doubt a happier future will find incredible![117]

Structural reorientation of criminal adjudication towards rational fact-finding is envisaged as being complemented by intelligent normative constraints on judicial inquiry. Beccaria specifically mentions numerous procedural or, as we might say, 'due process' guarantees with direct modern counterparts, including many now enumerated in core human rights instruments such as Article 6 (fair trial) of the European Convention on Human Rights (ECHR).[118] These include the right to know the charge and to a public trial and verdict,[119] adequate time to prepare a defence,[120] expeditious trial (and punishment, if convicted),[121] and rudimentary versions of the presumption of innocence and the privilege against self-incrimination.[122] Beccaria adds, tantalisingly if somewhat noncommittally:

> The law according to which every man should be tried by his peers is a very useful one, because, when a citizen's freedom and fortune are at stake, the sentiments inspired by inequality should be silenced.[123]

As it would for the French revolutionaries of the later eighteenth century, mid-nineteenth-century Russian reformers, and the Spanish and Russians again in the twentieth century,[124] trial by one's peers has a pleasant savour of liberal democracy, especially to those who have not had much of either in recent memory. Everyone has long since forgotten that the original reference to trial by peers, in King John's Magna Carta, had nothing to do with either liberalism or democracy. Legal traditions vary enormously in the extent to which lay involvement in criminal adjudication is regarded as desirable, or even permissible. Anglophones tend to regard the uninformed citizen jury as a peculiarly, if not exclusively, common law phenomenon, but in fact many modern European legal systems utilise lay juries or assessors in one form or another.[125] Nonetheless,

[117] Ibid at 46 (ch 17) (emphasis original).

[118] Generally, see JD Jackson & SJ Summers, *The Internationalisation of Criminal Evidence* (Cambridge, Cambridge University Press, 2012); S Trechsel with SJ Summers, *Human Rights in Criminal Proceedings* (Oxford, Oxford University Press, 2005).

[119] 'Verdicts and the proof of guilt should be public … Secret denunciations are an obvious abuse … Who can defend himself against false accusation when it is guarded by tyranny's strongest shield, *secrecy*?' Beccaria, above n 2 at 36–37 (ch 15) (emphasis original).

[120] '[T]he laws ought to establish a certain amount of time for preparing both the defence and the prosecution …' Ibid at 76 (ch 30).

[121] 'In order that punishment should not be an act of violence perpetrated by one or many upon a private citizen, it is essential that it should be public, speedy, necessary, the minimum possible in the given circumstances, proportionate to the crime, and determined by the law.' Ibid at 113 (ch 47).

[122] 'No man may be called guilty before the judge has reached his verdict … I believe that it is a wilful confusion of the proper procedure to require a man to be at once accuser and accused …' Ibid at 39 (ch 16).

[123] Ibid at 35 (ch 14).

[124] R Vogler, *A World View of Criminal Justice* (Farnham, Ashgate, 2005) ch 12; SC Thaman, 'Europe's New Jury Systems: The Cases of Spain and Russia', in N Vidmar (ed), *World Jury Systems* (Oxford, Oxford University Press, 2000) ch 9.

[125] See *Taxquet v Belgium* (2012) 54 EHRR 26 (GC) at [46]–[47] (identifying 10 Council of Europe states in which common law-style juries are employed, and a further two dozen with mixed panels).

trial by jury has never been elevated to the status of a European (let alone global) human right, and it is not entirely clear that the traditional English jury practice of delivering unreasoned general verdicts specifying only 'guilty' or 'not guilty' is fully compliant with ECHR Article 6.[126] It seems that Beccaria's enigmatic remarks on the nature and rationale of trial by peers presage the ambivalence of modern-day European jurisprudence on this issue.

Twenty-first century readers looking to *On Crimes and Punishments* for emphatic endorsements of robust principles of presumption of innocence and privilege against self-incrimination are destined for disappointment. We need to proceed with caution, however, because these ideas are generally underspecified, and their protean malleability sometimes attracts unreasonable expectations.[127] Commentators often find modern jurisprudence, including decisions of the European Court of Human Rights, similarly disappointing. Beccaria evidently thinks that detailed accusations backed by evidence call for a response,[128] and that failure to provide excuse or exculpation indicates there is none:

> [O]ne who under examination obstinately refuses to answer the questions put to him, deserves a penalty which should be fixed by law, and be of the severest kind, in order to prevent men from avoiding their public duty in this way. … [However,] a confession is superfluous when other evidence proves an individual's guilt. This last is usually the case, because experience shows that on the whole the guilty deny everything.[129]

Many common lawyers would be scandalised by Beccaria's apparent nonchalance in this passage. A fairly orthodox retort would be that the presumption of innocence entitles the accused to sit back, say nothing and put the prosecution to full proof; whilst the blithe assumption that the guilty generally lie to save their hides itself constitutes a serious procedural irregularity, insofar as the presumption of innocence also requires factfinders to keep an open mind and return a verdict based only on evidence adduced in the trial. But the orthodoxy here is strictly doctrinal. Everybody knows, as a matter of ordinary commonsense inference, that silence in the face of compelling evidence of guilt is tantamount

[126] See P Roberts, 'Does Article 6 of the European Convention on Human Rights Require Reasoned Verdicts in Criminal Trials?' (2011) 11 *Human Rights Law Review* 213; JC Smith, 'Is Ignorance Bliss? Could Jury Trial Survive Investigation?' (1998) 38 *Medicine, Science and the Law* 98. Cf J Jackson, 'Unbecoming Jurors and Unreasoned Verdicts: Realising Integrity in the Jury Room', in Hunter et al (eds), above n 60, 281; M Coen & J Doak, 'Embedding Explained Jury Verdicts in the English Criminal Trial' (2017) 37 *Legal Studies* 786.

[127] See further, P Roberts, 'Presumptuous or Pluralistic Presumptions of Innocence? Methodological Diagnosis towards Conceptual Reinvigoration' (2021) 198 *Synthese* 8901; RL Lippke, *Taming the Presumption of Innocence* (Oxford, Oxford University Press, 2016); P Roberts, 'The Right of Silence, Socio-Legal Research and Law Reform Politics (and Brexit)' (2019) 23 *International Journal of Evidence and Proof* 330.

[128] At least one influential modern commentator might be sympathetic: cf RA Duff, *Answering for Crime: Responsibility and Liability in the Criminal Law* (Oxford, Hart Publishing, 2007). Also see A Duff et al, *The Trial on Trial* vol 3: *Towards a Normative Theory of the Criminal Trial* (Oxford, Hart Publishing, 2007).

[129] Beccaria, above n 2 at 98 (ch 38).

to throwing in the forensic towel. As I understand it, fact-finding by Continental judiciaries and mixed panels proceeds essentially on this basis to this day. The accused enjoys a notional 'right of silence' (not least because Strasbourg insists on it),[130] but he is expected to speak up for himself at trial or be treated as having nothing pertinent to say.[131] English law is a more recent convert to this way of proceeding, albeit within slightly stricter normative parameters.[132] If there is a problem with this approach in principle (i.e. ignoring contingent deficiencies in particular legislative schemes),[133] it is not that traditional jurisprudence necessarily trumps the logic of inference in criminal adjudication. The problem would be that the distinctly non-prosaic, minutely stage-managed environment of the adversarial criminal trial is not as safe for commonsense inferential reasoning as unsophisticated critics (such as Bentham)[134] tend to presume.

Beccaria's position on inferences from silence is underpinned by a more general, positive commitment to 'freedom of proof', which became an article of faith in European procedural reform and remains a cornerstone of modern Continental criminal procedure.[135] This is a point on which Beccaria's views cohere substantially with Bentham's advocacy of the 'natural system of procedure':[136]

> Where the laws are clear and precise, the judge's task is merely to discover the facts. But, if the search for the evidence of a crime calls for skill and ability, if the

[130] *Saunders v UK* (1996) 23 EHRR 313; *Murray v UK* (1996) 22 EHRR 29; *Funke v France* (1993) 16 EHRR 297 (interpolating into the text of Art 6 'the right to remain silent under police questioning and the privilege against self-incrimination [as] generally recognised international standards which lie at the heart of the notion of a fair procedure').

[131] G van Kessel, 'European Perspectives on the Accused as a Source of Testimonial Evidence' (1998) 100 *West Virginia Law Review* 799; JK Walker, 'A Comparative Discussion of the Privilege Against Self-Incrimination' (1993) 14 *New York Law School Journal of International and Comparative Law* 1; B McKillop, 'Readings and Hearings in French Criminal Justice: Five Cases in the *Tribunal Correctionnel*' (1998) 46 *American Journal of Comparative Law* 757; M Moskovitz, 'The O.J. Inquisition: A United States Encounter with Continental Criminal Justice' (1995) 28 *Vanderbilt Journal of Transnational Law* 1121; MR Damaška, 'Evidentiary Barriers to Conviction and Two Models of Criminal Procedure: A Comparative Study' (1973) 121 *University of Pennsylvania Law Review* 506.

[132] Criminal Justice and Public Order Act 1994, ss 34–38.

[133] For telling criticisms of English law, see J Hall, 'Simplifying the Adverse Inference Direction' [2019] *Criminal Law Review* 684; AL-T Choo, *The Privilege Against Self-Incrimination and Criminal Justice* (Oxford, Hart Publishing, 2013) ch 5; H Quirk, 'Twenty Years On, The Right of Silence and Legal Advice: The Spiralling Costs of Unfair Exchange' (2013) 64 *Northern Ireland Legal Quarterly* 465; M Redmayne, 'English Warnings' (2008) 30 *Cardozo Law Review* 1047; I Dennis, 'Silence in the Police Station: the Marginalisation of Section 34' [2002] *Criminal Law Review* 25; JD Jackson, 'Silence and Proof: Extending the Boundaries of Criminal Proceedings in the United Kingdom' (2001) 5 *The International Journal of Evidence and Proof* 145; D Birch, 'Suffering in Silence: A Cost-Benefit Analysis of Section 34 of the Criminal Justice and Public Order Act 1994' [1999] *Criminal Law Review* 769.

[134] MA Menlowe, 'Bentham, Self-incrimination and the Law of Evidence' (1988) 104 *Law Quarterly R* 286.

[135] MR Damaška, 'Free Proof and its Detractors' (1995) 43 *American Journal of Comparative Law* 343.

[136] Generally, see W Twining, *Theories of Evidence: Bentham & Wigmore* (London, Weidenfeld, 1985) ch 2.

> presentation of the result calls for clarity and precision, then forming a judgement on the basis of this resulting evidence requires only simple and ordinary good sense, which is less misleading than the learning of a judge who is accustomed to wanting to find criminals and who reduces everything to an artificial system derived from his studies. It would be a happy nation in which the law were not a learned profession![137]

Conversely and consistently, Beccaria is contemptuous of the canon law formalism of 'half guilt' as a basis for authorising judicial torture:

> [H]ard crimes to prove, are precisely those in which, according to the received views, the tyrannical presumptions of the *nearly proofs* and *half-proofs* are admitted (as if a man could be *half-innocent* or *half-guilty*, that is *half-punishable* or *half-acquittable*) ...[138]

Beccaria here targets a notorious corruption of civilian procedure, and its erosion of the presumption of innocence firmly embedded in Romanist legal tradition,[139] which had been widely condemned by civilian jurists in earlier centuries.[140] Quasi-mathematical approaches to juridical proof are today regarded as the epitome of medieval scholasticism in jurisprudential thinking.[141] Beccaria naturally positions himself on the modernist side of this tectonic intellectual fissure. But he is not quite able to stay in character for the entire performance, and the mask occasionally slips to reveal a mind not fully liberated from medieval concepts.

Common lawyers would be puzzled by Beccaria's attachment to a general principle of corroboration, the need for which he seems to regard as almost self-evident: 'More than one witness is needed, because, so long as one party affirms and the other denies, nothing is certain and the right which every man has to be believed innocent preponderates.'[142] The Roman law principle of *unus testis, nullus testis* survives in pockets of modern Continental jurisprudence,[143] though its currency and force are greatly diminished.[144] English law,

137 Beccaria, above n 2 at 35 (ch 14).

138 Ibid at 79–80 (ch 31) (emphasis original).

139 JC Cascarelli, 'Presumption of Innocence and Natural Law: Machiavelli and Aquinas' (1996) 41 *American Journal of Jurisprudence* 229.

140 M Damaška, 'The Quest for Due Process in the Age of Inquisition' (2012) 60 *American Journal of Comparative Law* 919.

141 An accessible and entertaining historical overview is provided by J Franklin, *The Science of Conjecture: Evidence and Probability before Pascal* (Baltimore MD, Johns Hopkins University Press, 2002).

142 Beccaria, above n 2 at 32.

143 Notably, under Art 342.2 of the Dutch Criminal Procedure Code the testimony of one witness is not a sufficient basis for conviction; see, eg, C Brants, 'Wrongful Convictions and Inquisitorial Process: The Case of the Netherlands' (2012) 80 *University of Cincinnati Law Review* 1069 at 1087 ('[E]vidence requires other evidence as corroboration. A conviction may not rest on the statement of a defendant alone, on that of a single witness, or on anonymous testimony'). For general theoretical discussion, see Á Paúl, 'Sana Crítica: The System for Weighing Evidence Utilized by the Inter-American Court of Human Rights' (2012) 18 *Buffalo Human Rights Law Review* 193.

144 In Scotland, with its curious blend of common law evidentiary rules and civilian-inspired criminal procedure, abolition of the general corroboration requirement is a centrepiece of – controversial – recommendations for procedural reform: see P Duff & PR Ferguson (eds), *Scottish*

too, maintains residual corroboration requirements, but only as marginal exceptions to the general expectation that any source or type of evidence is capable, in principle, of satisfying the standard of proof for criminal conviction if it has sufficient probative value on the facts. When it operates categorically, *unus testis* is plainly a significant derogation from what modern civilian jurists call 'free proof'.[145] Whilst the notion of epistemic safety in numbers has ancient roots,[146] everyday commonsense reasoning does not routinely demand corroboration as a prerequisite to arriving at and acting on inferential conclusions. Only in particular situations where mistakes are very costly and/or easily remedied (eg 'measure twice, cut once') does the always desirable presence of confirmatory evidential warrant become mandatory. If corroboration requirements are ever truly warranted in criminal adjudication, it can only be for some 'artificial' jurisprudential or normative reason rather than on strictly epistemic grounds.

Beccaria rationalises *unus testis* in terms of sceptical doubt and the presumption of innocence. The connections may seem intuitive, but in fact both of these suggestions are dead ends. To point out, correctly, that 'nothing is certain' is merely to sigh at the human condition, but says nothing about how we should actually go about reasoning and acting under inescapable uncertainty. Accepting the plausible and widespread assumption that the presumption of innocence implies *in dubio pro reo*, it does not follow that a single testimony is always, or even normally, incapable of dispelling reasonable – that is, practically salient – doubt about the accused's guilt. English law came to regard corroboration requirements, in the main, as artificial fetters on the logic of proof. Part of the problem was that English law adopts a strict definition of 'corroboration' with a robust independence requirement.[147] My suspicion – suggesting a nice experimental hypothesis for an enterprising socio-legal researcher – is that *unus testis* lingers in Continental jurisprudence, to the residual extent that it does,[148]

Criminal Evidence Law: Current Developments and Future Trends (Edinburgh, Edinburgh University Press, 2017).

[145] Damaška, above n 135.

[146] Cf Deuteronomy 19:15 (KJV): 'One witness shall not rise up against a man for any iniquity, or for any sin, in any sin that he sinneth: at the mouth of two witnesses, or at the mouth of three witnesses, shall the matter be established'; Franklin, above n 141 at 4–5, 18–22; JA Makdisi, 'The Islamic Origins of the Common Law' (1999) 77 *North Carolina Law Review* 1635 at 1688.

[147] *R* v *Baskerville* [1916] 2 KB 658 (CCA).

[148] Cf *Prosecutor* v *Tadić*, ICTY Case No IT-94-I-T, Trial Chamber Judgement, 7 May 1997, [535]–[539] (pointing out, in response to defence counsel's argument for its application in the instant case, that *unis testis* no longer applies as a general principle in France, Belgium, Germany, Spain, former Yugoslavia or China, and is interpreted narrowly in the Netherlands). *Unus testis* has been rejected in international criminal law and in international human rights law, partly owing to the practical obstacles it would create in proving typically clandestine crimes including torture and sexual violence: L Talsma, 'UN Human Rights Fact-Finding: Establishing Individual Criminal Responsibility?' (2012) 24 *Florida Journal of International Law* 383; CB Coan, 'Rethinking the Spoils of War: Prosecuting Rape as a War Crime in the International Criminal Tribunal for the Former Yugoslavia' (2000) 26 *North Carolina Journal of International Law and Commercial Regulation* 183; R Mary & M Wierda, 'Trends in International Criminal Evidence: Nuremberg, Tokyo, The Hague, and Arusha' (1999) 37 *Columbia Journal of Transnational Law* 725.

because judges, as the principal or dominant factfinders, are prepared to 'find' corroboration whenever their intuitive appraisal of the evidence impels them to convict.[149]

Beccaria's brief observations on evidential sufficiency and the standard of proof reflect the jurisprudential thinking of his day, without doing much to clarify, let alone advancing, legal theory. The schoolmen's standard was 'moral certainty'.[150] Of this, Beccaria opines:

> [M]oral certainty is, strictly speaking, nothing but a probability, though a probability of such a sort as to be called certainty because every reasonable man necessarily assents to it out of force of habit born of the need to act and antecedent to any theorising. Therefore, the certainty which is called for to establish that a man is guilty is the same as that which guides men in the most important enterprises of their lives.[151]

Perhaps sensing the opacity of these ruminations and apprehending the wisdom of hedging his bets, he also warns 'it is easier to feel the moral certainty of evidence than to define it exactly'.[152] To this day, the subjective test of *intime conviction* remains the official standard of proof in Continental criminal proceedings,[153] provoking outrage and dismay amongst rationalists everywhere.[154] Beccaria's conflation of probability, certainty and reasonableness is conceptually shaky, and its attribution to 'force of habit' is unhelpfully misdirected. His better thought is that 'the need to act' demands a practically achievable level of evidential sufficiency, which – we can add – must take the human epistemic condition as given and work around it. This truism holds not merely 'antecedent to any theorising', but after as much philosophical speculation as you might care to attempt. It is very much to Beccaria's credit that he is asking the right questions on this topic: the correctness of any answers is still hotly debated between theorists and

[149] Damaška (who, intriguingly, characterises quantitative standards of evidentiary regulation as a distinctively *common law* technique in modern jurisprudence) anticipated this speculation many years ago: 'Corroboration rules would be termed by continental scholars *negative*, as opposed to *positive*, rules of legal proof … [T]he former require the factfinders not to convict, irrespective of their convictions, before certain kinds of evidence are gathered … Whether all vestiges of the negative rules of legal proof have disappeared from continental law is, however, not altogether clear. It is, for instance, a hotly debated issue whether a judgment of conviction can rest solely on the defendant's confession, although the judge is thoroughly convinced of its verity. *In practice, of course, at least a modicum of corroboration is always found*': Damaška, above n 131 at 531 note 51 (emphasis added).

[150] JQ Whitman, *The Origins of Reasonable Doubt: Theological Roots of the Criminal Trial* (New Haven CT, Yale University Press, 2008); BJ Shapiro, '"To a Moral Certainty": Theories of Knowledge and Anglo-American Juries 1600–1850' (1986) 38 *Hastings Law Journal* 153.

[151] Beccaria, above n 2 at 34 (ch 14).

[152] Ibid at 35 (ch 14).

[153] KM Clermont, 'Standards of Proof Revisited' (2009) 33 *Vermont Law Review* 469.

[154] See, eg, L Laudan, 'Is Reasonable Doubt Reasonable?' (2003) 9 *Legal Theory* 295 at 321 (contending that '[t]he key point is that the question: How strongly does the evidence support the theory of guilt? is an *objective* question about logical relations between events, not merely or primarily a question about the subjective state of the jurors' minds').

a source of controversy in practical jurisprudence.[155] English law dabbled with a jury direction explicitly drawing analogies to important decisions in life, but soon abandoned it as capricious.[156] Beccaria, however, is not offering practical advice to English policymakers or jurists on how to direct juries. He is trying to give a theoretical explanation of evidential sufficiency; and the underlying contention that standards of proof in criminal adjudication should be indexed to the animating purpose and values of practical human affairs is essentially sound.

In other passages, Beccaria lapses back into the formalist medieval mindset of categories and quantitative measures of proof. He asserts, for example, that:

> We may distinguish between perfect and imperfect pieces of evidence for a crime. Those which exclude the possibility that a given man is innocent I call perfect; and those which do not exclude that possibility, imperfect. Of the former, even a single piece is sufficient to obtain a conviction ...[157]

To preserve *unus testis* and save Beccaria from self-contradiction, we must infer that witness testimony is never 'perfect evidence'. But since evidence 'which exclude[s] the possibility that a given man is innocent' is an impossible fiction, incompatible with the contingency of all empirical knowledge, we cannot save Beccaria from the charge of spinning meaningless evidentiary classifications. It gets worse. In relation to 'imperfect evidence', Beccaria informs readers:

> [W]e need as many pieces as are necessary to make up one perfect piece of evidence; that is to say, if, relative to each of the pieces taken alone, it is possible that a man should be innocent, then relative to them jointly, it is impossible that he should be.[158]

Beccaria the modern penal rationalist has suddenly become possessed by the spirit of a medieval canon lawyer! Talk of adding up atomistic 'pieces' of evidence to form 'one perfect piece of evidence' belongs with angels-dancing-on-pinheads fairy tales. The only mitigating circumstance is that Beccaria is evidently worried about bogus 'proofs' of witchcraft and other 'fantastical crimes', and brings to the problem a modern proto-scientific sensibility about

[155] See, eg, A Keane & P McKeown, 'Time to Abandon "Beyond Reasonable Doubt" and "Sure": the Case for a New Direction on the Criminal Standard and How it Should be Used' [2019] *Criminal Law Review* 505; KN Kotsoglou, 'Proof Beyond a Context-Relevant Doubt: A Structural Analysis of the Standard of Proof in Criminal Adjudication' (2020) 28 *Artificial Intelligence and Law* 111; F Picinali, 'The Threshold Lies in the Method: Instructing Jurors about *Reasoning* Beyond Reasonable Doubt' (2015) 19 *The International Journal of Evidence and Proof* 139; S Sheppard, 'The Metamorphoses of Reasonable Doubt: How Changes in the Burden of Proof have Weakened the Presumption of Innocence' (2003) 78 *Notre Dame Law Review* 1165; LM Solan, 'Refocusing the Burden of Proof in Criminal Cases: Some Doubt about Reasonable Doubt' (1999) 78 *Texas Law Review* 105.

[156] See AAS Zuckerman, *The Principles of Criminal Evidence* (Oxford, Oxford University Press, 1989) 131–132.

[157] Beccaria, above n 2 at 34–35 (ch 14).

[158] Ibid at 35 (ch 14).

the fallibility of evidence, worrying, for example, that 'words remain only in the hearers' memory, which is generally unreliable and often imposed upon'.[159] But it is bad, self-defeating strategy to fight one set of irrationalities by advancing another set, as though fake news could be combatted by making more things up. Beccaria is tempted into overgeneralising contingent evidential weaknesses into implausible evidentiary maxims such as '[a] witness's credibility noticeably diminishes as the enormity of the crime … increase[s]' and 'when the crime is verbal, the credibility of witnesses is virtually nil'.[160] One only has to imagine what the implications for prosecuting sexual offences would be if these maxims were generally followed by our police and prosecutors to appreciate their epistemic and normative unacceptability. (Adopting the reverse policy of always *believing* complainants is also very problematic, in my opinion, but that is another story.[161]) Part of the problem is that Beccaria is confusing *witness credibility* with *the sufficiency of proof* to sustain a criminal conviction. Witness testimony may be entirely credible but still unable to provide adequate epistemic warrant for criminal conviction and punishment, for a variety of reasons (uncertainty, ambiguity, misperception, incompleteness, inconsistency with other evidence, inherent implausibility, untested rival hypotheses, residual lurking doubt, etc).

Two further, more specific criticisms can be made of Beccaria's treatment of the related ideas of presumption of innocence, probability of facts and sufficiency of proof. First, Beccaria stumbles into the vicinity of what we know today as the 'conjunction paradox'. He states:

> There is a very useful theorem for calculating the certainty of a matter, such as the evidence for a crime. When the pieces of evidence for some matter are interdependent, that is, when the pieces of evidence cannot be tested except against each other, then, the more evidence is adduced, the less credible is the matter in question, because anything which would make the earlier parts fail will make the later parts fail too.[162]

Beccaria cannot mean only that subsequently-acquired or presented evidence can undermine, contradict or falsify evidence in-hand, because nobody would need a 'useful theorem for calculating' such an elementary commonsense precept. He must have in mind something more *axiomatic*; and entirely in keeping with his penchant for mathematical thinking.[163] Yet anybody who has not already been bamboozled by elementary probability theory ought to be baffled by the

[159] Ibid at 33 (ch 13).

[160] Ibid at 32–33 (ch 13).

[161] Part of it is narrated by R Henriques, *From Crime to Crime* (London, Hodder & Stoughton, 2020) ch 17 ('The Review of Operation Midland').

[162] Beccaria, above n 2 at 34 (ch 14).

[163] 'In Parma he was nicknamed "the little Newton" ("il Newtoncino") because of his skills in mathematics. He probably applied his talents in logics and mathematics in writing his little book': Cadoppi, above n 16 at 29.

proposition that 'the more evidence is adduced, the less credible is the matter in question'. That proposition encapsulates the supposed paradox; but the result is not paradoxical at all when the evidential dynamics are properly understood. The conjunction problem attracted the attention of the Oxford philosopher LJ Cohen, who showed that it arises from applying the classical probability calculus (which Cohen dubbed 'Pascalian' or 'mathematicist') to multiple pieces of evidence for some proposition.[164] When individual items of evidence are *independent*, their compound probability is given by the multiplication rule, that is, by multiplying together the probabilities for each piece of evidence. But given that the probability with which each piece of evidence establishes the proposition in issue will necessarily be less than 1 (i.e., no piece of evidence warrants a factual conclusion with mathematical certainty), every time a new piece of evidence is added the compound probability of the expanded corpus of evidence for the proposition will go *down*, not up. Beccaria, in announcing 'a very useful theorem for calculating the certainty of a matter', appears to be thinking along these Pascalian lines.[165] The conjunction problem encountered in relation to *independent* pieces of evidence is only exacerbated when evidence is not independent – the scenario of *inter*dependency Beccaria hypothesises – because dependencies will reduce the compound probability of each evidential item even further.[166] Having diagnosed the source of the paradox, Cohen proposed a radical solution that few commentators accept. But one thing Cohen was definitely right about is that factfinders in criminal trials are never asked to 'calculat[e] the certainty of a matter' using the classical probability calculus, and this very prosaic fact about adjudication ought to make us wary of anybody proffering supposedly 'useful theorem[s]' for prosecuting an altogether different kind of business. To cut a rather long – and mostly boring[167] – story short, it is possible to model conditional dependencies between items of evidence without violating classical probability axioms or producing any paradoxical results

[164] L Jonathan Cohen, *The Probable and the Provable* (Oxford, Oxford University Press, 1977) ch 5. Also see RJ Allen, 'The Nature of Juridical Proof' (1991) 13 *Cardozo Law Review* 373.

[165] He is also anticipating a theoretical problem that behavioural scientists still employ today to demonstrate the (supposed) irrationality of commonsense reasoning: see D Kahneman, *Thinking, Fast and Slow* (London, Penguin, 2011) ch 15.

[166] On a 'Pascalian' approach, conditional probabilities merely 'internalise' the conjunction paradox to individual pieces of evidence. For example, the compound probability of guilt conditioned on 'recovering an authentic fingermark at the crime scene *and* matching it to the accused' will necessarily be smaller than the frequentist probability of guilt conditioned only on 'matching a fingermark to the accused', whenever the probability of 'recovering an authentic fingermark at the crime scene' is less than certain (<1) – which it always is, for *all* empirical contingencies. A mathematically rigorous dissolution of the 'paradox' would not be widely known until after the (posthumous) publication of Thomas Bayes' celebrated *Essay Towards Solving a Problem in the Doctrine of Chances* in December 1763, just four months before *On Crimes and Punishments* itself appeared in print. These interpretations are highly speculative. Beccaria (above n 2 at 34, ch 14) seems to think that the problem he identifies affects 'interdependent evidence' exclusively, which only serves to accentuate the inscrutability of his intentions and the obscurity of his 'useful theorem'.

[167] Because it involves a great deal of repetition and talking at cross-purposes: cf JA Michon, 'The Time has Come to Put this Debate Aside and Move on to Other Matters' (1997) 1 *The International Journal of Evidence and Proof* 331.

using Bayes' Theorem.[168] Beccaria was right to worry about hidden conditional dependencies, because treating interdependent items of evidence as though they are independently mutually corroborative involves illegitimate double-counting and risks miscarriages of justice.[169] But he was wrong to think that we need a 'theorem' to 'calculate' this important caveat – it can be explained clearly in a sentence or two – and the proposition that 'the more evidence is adduced, the less credible is the matter in question' is a fine illustration of how half-baked ideas can educate people stupid.[170]

A second granular criticism is more jurisprudential than probabilistic. Beccaria is exercised by the practical problem of dealing with apparently dangerous individuals against whom there is insufficient evidence to sustain moral certainty of guilt. It is essentially the same problem that the UK Government has been grappling with for the last two decades in relation to those suspected of terrorist activities or intentions in the absence of concrete proof of criminality.[171] This is Beccaria's proposed solution:

> It seems as if those who have been accused of a terrible crime and who are very likely, but not certainly, guilty, ought to be banished. ... The evidence would have to be more persuasive in the case of a citizen than in that of a foreigner, and in the case of a person of good record than in that of a frequent offender.[172]

Can this be the same Beccaria who fulminates against 'tyrannical presumptions of the *nearly proofs* and *half-proofs* ... as if a man could be *half-innocent* or *half-guilty*, that is *half-punishable* or *half-acquittable*'? If there is not here a glaring contradiction it must be because Beccaria does not regard banishment as a criminal penalty or in any way equivalent to official procedures exposing individuals to the risk of judicial torture. I have no difficulty with the idea that, in principle, governments may take life-changing decisions on the basis of information falling well short of proof beyond reasonable doubt: the unaccountably widespread notion that the consequences of criminal penalties are always, or even typically, more serious than other types of official intervention, affecting wealth, health, family and freedom, etc, is demonstrably false. Yet in the circumstances posited by Beccaria, banishment certainly looks like a half-punishment for a half-proved crime; and it is a racing certainty that it would be interpreted as a penal measure by the Strasbourg Court applying ECHR

[168] B Robertson, GA Vignaux & CE Berger, *Interpreting Evidence: Evaluating Forensic Science in the Courtroom* 2nd edition (Chichester, Wiley, 2016); C Aitken, P Roberts & G Jackson, *Fundamentals of Probability and Statistical Evidence in Criminal Proceedings* (London, Royal Statistical Society, 2010); RO Lempert, 'Analyzing Relevance' (1977) 75 *Michigan Law Review* 1021.

[169] A notorious real-world illustration is *People v Collins*, 68 Cal 2d 319 (1968). See LH Tribe, 'Trial by Mathematics: Precision and Ritual in the Legal Process' (1971) 84 *Harvard Law Review* 1329.

[170] Cf RD Friedman & RC Park, 'Sometimes What Everybody Thinks They Know is True' (2003) 27 *Law and Human Behavior* 629.

[171] Even 'criminality' of the sort that seriously stretches the boundaries of the criminal law: cf J Hodgson & V Tadros, 'How to Make a Terrorist Out of Nothing' (2009) 72 *Modern Law Review* 984.

[172] Beccaria, above n 2 at 56–57 (ch 24).

Article 6's 'autonomous concept' of a criminal charge.[173] This, then, is further evidence of Beccaria's rudimentary grasp of the presumption of innocence. Some might argue that treating prior record as salient information also, and independently, violates the presumption of innocence.[174] I agree that it *might* do so if the use of prior record were tantamount to double jeopardy, but I do not think that the presumption of innocence precludes drawing epistemically well-warranted inferences from a person's previous behaviour.[175] Whether or not such information should be admissible in criminal trials, irrespective of the presumption of innocence, is a complex and controversial issue. Character evidence is routinely admitted in Continental criminal proceedings,[176] and nobody seemingly bats an eyelid. English law has lately abandoned the common law's presumptive exclusion of bad character evidence, especially in terms of propensity reasoning,[177] and to this extent has moved closer to the modern civilian norm anticipated by Beccaria. Whether this legislative break with procedural tradition represents an undiluted triumph of modernist law reform is a question awaiting a definitive verdict in England and Wales, partly because a great deal turns on how prosecutors, defence lawyers and first-instance judges understand and apply the legislation in practice.

Beccaria, as we have seen, regarded tradition as the implacable foe of enlightened reason. He laments that 'reason has almost never been the lawgiver to nations',[178] and ascribes this rationality bypass to 'the prejudice of ages, the voluminous and impressive tomes of innumerable commentators, the staid paraphernalia of endless procedural formalities, the support of the most fawning and least feared semi-literates'.[179] Although he is not nearly as rude or direct as Bentham, Beccaria's pen portrait of previous generations of jurists and lawyers is hardly flattering. Moreover, says Beccaria, common sentiment is the prisoner of '[t]he barbaric notions and fierce ideas of our ancestral northern huntsmen'

[173] See, eg, *Han v Customs and Excise Commissioners* [2001] 1 WLR 2253, [2001] EWCA Civ 1040; applying *Oztürk v Germany* (1984) 6 EHRR 409; *Bendenoun v France* (1994) 18 EHRR 54; and *Engel v The Netherlands (No 1)* (1976) 1 EHRR 647.

[174] This connection is made, eg, in *S and Marper* v *UK* ECtHR (GC) (2009) 48 EHRR 50 at [114], [122]. A more general objection is developed by DT Wasserman, 'The Morality of Statistical Proof and the Risk of Mistaken Liability' (1991) 13 *Cardozo Law Review* 935; A Pundik, 'Statistical Evidence and Individual Litigants: A Reconsideration of Wasserman's Argument from Autonomy' (2008) 12 *International Journal of Evidence and Proof* 303.

[175] P Tillers, 'If Wishes Were Horses: Discursive Comments on Attempts to Prevent Individuals from being Unfairly Burdened by their Reference Class' (2005) 4 *Law, Probability and Risk* 33; M Redmayne, *Character in the Criminal Trial* (Oxford, Oxford University Press, 2015).

[176] S Field, 'State, Citizen, and Character in French Criminal Process' (2006) 33 *Journal of Law and Society* 522.

[177] Which is now expressly permitted by Criminal Justice Act 2003, ss 101(1)(d) and 103. It is widely believed, on the strength of authorities such as *DPP v Boardman* [1975] AC 421 (HL) and *Makin v AG for New South Wales* [1894] AC 57 (PC), that the common law precluded 'the propensity inference'. But I have my doubts: cf *R v Ball* [1911] AC 47 (HL), *Thompson v R* [1918] AC 221 (HL) and – ultimately the leading English case at common law – *R v P* [1991] 2 AC 447 (HL).

[178] Beccaria, above n 2 at 79 (ch 31).

[179] Ibid at 111 (ch 46).

and contemporary laws and customs are 'always a hundred years behind a given nation's stage of goodness and enlightenment'.[180] The reformer's task almost appears hopeless in the face of popular ignorance and hostility, and Beccaria sometimes gives the impression of writing only for posterity:

> [M]en ... always suspect the voice of reason and respect that of authority ... [T]he history of mankind gives the impression of a vast sea of errors, among which a few confused truths float at great distances from each other. ... Great truths ... last but a flash compared with the long and dark night which engulfs mankind. The happy time has not yet begun in which the truth, like error hitherto, is the property of the many. ... The voice of a philosopher is too weak against the uproar and the shouting of those who are guided by blind habit.[181]

Nor should the embattled philosopher expect any gratitude for his selfless and courageous service to his tribe (no good deed must go unpunished, after all):

> This country is still buried under the prejudices which its ancient masters left it. The Milanese do not forgive those who wish them to live in the eighteenth century. In a capital of 120,000 inhabitants, there are hardly twenty individuals who desire to instruct themselves and who devote themselves to truth and virtue.[182]

Beccaria was evidently locked in a personal tussle with the forces of reaction and emotionally quite incapable of ascribing any value to historical traditions embedded in existing institutional practices. I think he is mistaken in this, if understandably so. Beccaria barely lived long enough to see the French Revolution disintegrate into terror and dictatorship, and could not have begun to imagine what radical programmes of legal and social reform might look like as the handiwork of a Lenin, Hitler or Mao. Burkean conservatism appears much more attractive when the alternatives are chaos and perdition. The best theory of criminal justice does not need to be a paragon, it just needs to be better than any viable alternative (including giving up on the enterprise entirely, if that is considered viable). Appropriate regard for procedural tradition will probably feature in any sound justificatory theory of criminal justice, if only because the enterprise of legislating criminal offences and punishing offenders (typically with punishments of extended duration) requires considerable temporal stability in normative frameworks. Institutional conservatism is the cultural ballast of criminal law and the social anchor of its legitimacy. Beyond these structural dynamics, legal systems and cultures vary in the extent to which they invest in tradition. Common law systems are traditional in this sense, and the English is the oldest and one of the most traditional. English lawyers will invoke Magna Carta at the drop of a hat, and invented fictions like 'time immemorial' because no actual date could be made to sound sufficiently ancient and venerable.[183]

[180] Ibid at 74 (ch 29).
[181] Ibid at 67, 71 (ch 28).
[182] 'To André Morellet', ibid 119 at 123.
[183] Time immemorial is defined at English common law as 'time whereof the memory of men runneth not to the contrary' (*Bryant v Foot* (1866–67) LR 2 QB 161, 173, Blackburn J citing Littleton),

It will not enlighten anybody to point out that these institutional memories are mythologised. What is significant is that the myth *matters* so much to those who live in and by it, irrespective of whether this or that piece of the institutional embroidery faithfully memorialises the historical facts.

Beccaria's unflinching rationalism is set on a collision course with the circumscribed, path-dependent rationality of procedural tradition. Although *On Crimes and Punishments* is alive to the importance of symbolism in penal practices, Beccaria does not seriously entertain the idea that the legitimacy of criminal verdicts might in some degree be rooted in venerated procedural traditions that have come to be invested with particular cultural resonances and institutional functions. A common lawyer will perhaps feel this deficit more keenly, given that the common law itself is comprised of a set of traditional cultural (legal-professional) practices sanctifying hierarchies of authority and juridically cognisable forms of argument. At any rate, recognising the normative force of tradition would put a crimp on the more reductive and universalistic ambitions of theories of criminal procedure, and open up a legitimate space for 'the fact of reasonable pluralism'[184] in the design and practices of criminal adjudication. Pluralism in criminal procedure, informed by local traditions but constrained by an increasingly robust cosmopolitan framework of fundamental (human) rights supervised by supranational judicial institutions, has served European democratic politics fairly well in the past and present,[185] but it may need more attentive curation than ever in our increasingly diverse, fragmented and fractious societies of the unfolding future.

V. CONCLUSION: BECCARIA NOW AND THEN

Beccaria is through and through the modern rationalist penal reformer, arguably the first[186] and the one who led the way. He championed the secular logic

and has an actual date for the purposes of fixing prescriptive rights: 6 July 1189, marking the accession of Richard I.

[184] Extrapolating from J Rawls, *Political Liberalism* (New York, Columbia University Press, 1996).

[185] For broader intellectual, institutional and geopolitical context, see J Habermas, *The Crisis of the European Union: A Response* (Cambridge, Polity, 2012); A Giddens, *Turbulent and Mighty Continent: What Future for Europe?* (Cambridge, Polity, 2014). For detailed illustrations of what I mean by a cosmopolitan criminal jurisprudence, see P Roberts, 'Normative Evolution in Evidentiary Exclusion: Coercion, Deception and the Right to a Fair Trial', in P Roberts & J Hunter (eds), *Criminal Evidence and Human Rights: Reimagining Common Law Procedural Traditions* (Oxford, Hart Publishing, 2012) ch 7; P Roberts, 'Comparative Criminal Justice Goes Global' (2008) 28 *Oxford Journal of Legal Studies* 369; P Roberts, 'Comparative Law for International Criminal Justice', in E Örücü & D Nelken (eds), *Comparative Law – A Handbook* (Oxford, Hart Publishing, 2007) ch 15.

[186] One early-20th-century commentator hails Beccaria as 'the first systematic modern criminal law reformer', and compares his contribution to criminal jurisprudence to the pioneering work of Bacon in experimental science and Descartes in philosophy: C Phillipson, *Three Criminal Law Reformers: Beccaria, Bentham, Romilly* (London, JM Dent & Sons, 1923) 100.

of argument over religious authority and blind tradition. He could not reasonably be expected to match the technical finesse of twenty-first-century analytical philosophy or the methodological rigour of modern empirical social science, nor did he. Beccaria's trail-blazing approach to penality was holistic. He conceived crime and punishment as part of the more general problem of enlightened liberal government. This was an illuminating lesson that many subsequent penal theorists forgot, rediscovering only relatively recently vital connections between their studies and more general considerations of political morality. In criminal procedure, Beccaria anticipates the central tenets of what became, during the nineteenth-century reforms and ever after, orthodox civilian criminal process. His commentaries on the more specifically evidentiary aspects of criminal adjudication are patchy, underdeveloped and antiquated in ways that Beccaria the arch-modernist would have been mortified to realise; though a common lawyer, educated to regard the Law of Evidence as a major and voluminous disciplinary specialism,[187] might think twenty-first-century Continental jurisprudence comparably rudimentary in our time.

Beccaria was fond of modish scientific ideas and idioms, and this sometimes misfires in his clunky metaphors and contorted applications of probability calculations to judicial evidence. Scientific fashions change. At the beginning of the twentieth century another notable Italian would claim to have superseded 'the Classical School of Penal Jurisprudence, of which Beccaria was the founder' and replaced it with '[t]he Modern School ... founded on a new science'.[188] The problem with Beccaria's 'classical' approach, announced Lombroso, was that it 'based its doctrines on the assumption that all criminals, except in a few extreme cases, are endowed with intelligence and feelings like normal individuals'.[189] This is not the only striking instance where Beccaria's 'mistakes' have stood the test of time far better than the ideas of those who sought to correct him. *On Crimes and Punishments*' intermittent and qualified references to utility, which Bentham may have taken for lapses of concentration, capitulation to sentiment or want of intellectual rigour, were in reality an expression of Beccaria's deeper commitments to human dignity, individual rights and responsible limited government. These normative intuitions have eclipsed utilitarian calculation in their enduring

[187] JB Thayer, 'The Present and Future of the Law of Evidence' (1898) 12 *Harvard Law Review* 71; E Swift, 'One Hundred Years of Evidence Law Reform: Thayer's Triumph' (2000) 88 *California Law Review* 2437.

[188] G Lombroso-Ferrero, *Criminal Man, According to the Classification of Cesare Lombroso* (New York, GP Putnam & Sons, 1911) 1.

[189] Ibid. The object of the new science of Criminal Anthropology was said to be to cure rather than punish 'the born criminal', but the policy implications soon became entangled with other agendas: see T Morris, 'British Criminology: 1935–48' (1988) 28 *British Journal of Criminology* 20 at 26–27; GQ Battaglini, 'Eugenics and the Criminal Law' (1914) 5 *Journal of the American Institute of Criminal Law and Criminology* 12.

contributions to enlightened penal philosophy. In summary, it would be difficult to improve on Radzinowicz's affectionate encapsulation:

> Beccaria's language is non-technical and forceful; he combined eloquence of expression with strictly logical reasoning. But far above these accomplishments of form stands his profound humanity, his ardent belief in human reason and the perfectibility of social institutions which he instilled into everything he wrote, and which make his book such inspiring reading. … His faith in progress was intense. From every page of his book flows that serene and confident hope of which Europe was then so much in need.[190]

If Beccaria's Whiggish optimism is irretrievably lost to us, knowing what we now know about the double-edged nature of civilisational 'progress' and technological solutions to problems of social organisation,[191] and his rationalism was at times over-extended and reductively dogmatic, his passionate humanism continues to inspire whilst his far-sighted policy and law reform agendas remain global works in progress.

[190] L Radzinowicz, *A History of English Criminal Law* vol I: *The Movement for Reform* (London, Stevens & Sons, 1948) 280 (footnote omitted).

[191] Z Bauman, *Modernity and the Holocaust* (Cambridge, Polity, 1989); J Glover, *Humanity: A Moral History of the Twentieth Century* (London, Pimlico, 2001).

10

Should Murder be More Difficult to Prove than Theft? Beccaria and Differential Standards of Proof

AMIT PUNDIK

I. INTRODUCTION

SHOULD MURDER BE more difficult to prove in criminal proceedings than theft? Nowadays, if one sought to advocate higher standards of proof for graver crimes, one common argument would probably be made along the following lines: the graver the offence, the greater the harm from convicting an innocent defendant (in terms of both criminal punishment and social stigma). Hence, more precautions should be taken before convicting someone of a grave offence, and that higher level of care should be effected (inter alia) through a higher standard of proof, against which the prosecution's allegations should be tested.[1] Such an argument would be open to the immediate objection that the standard of proof does not correspond only to the risk of false convictions, but also to the risk of false *acquittals*.[2] The graver punishment and stigma not only increase the harm caused by convicting the innocent, but also indicate the greater harm caused by acquitting the guilty of these graver offences (in terms of deterrence, prevention and distress to the victims of the offence). Consequently, this argument for higher standards of proof in graver offences succeeds only if the ratio between the harm of falsely convicting the innocent and the harm of falsely acquitting the guilty is higher in graver offences than in less serious offences – something that, to date, has not been established in the literature.

In his essay *On Crimes and Punishments*,[3] Beccaria provides a different argument to support the claim that a graver crime should be more difficult to prove.

[1] See, eg, L Laudan, *Truth, Error, and Criminal Law* (Cambridge, Cambridge University Press, 2008) 54–56.

[2] J Kaplan, 'Decision Theory and the Factfinding Process' (1968) 20 *Stanford Law Review* 1065 at 1073–74; E Lillquist, 'Recasting Reasonable Doubt: Decision Theory and the Virtues of Variability' (2002) 36 *University of California Davis Law Review* 85 at 105–111.

[3] C Beccaria, *On Crimes and Punishments and Other Writings* edited by R Bellamy and translated by R Davies (Cambridge, Cambridge University Press, 1995).

Instead of referring to the consequences of false convictions (or acquittals), he takes a more empiricist approach and suggests that the graver a crime is, the less common it is, and hence the more likely it is that the accused is innocent. In chapter 13 ('Of Witnesses'), Beccaria states that 'A witness's credibility noticeably diminishes as the enormity of the crime or the unlikeliness of its circumstances increase.'[4] In chapter 30, he links these two factors again, and states that 'the likelihood of a crime is in inverse proportion to its seriousness'.[5] In both cases, a simplified version of Beccaria's stance is that a graver crime should be harder to prove, because the accused is empirically less likely to have committed such a crime to begin with.

At first glance, Beccaria's claims and contemporary scholarship on differential standards of proof seem to yield similar consequences. Holding fixed the evidence available in the case, assessing this evidence while taking into account the relatively low frequency of graver offences would achieve a similar effect to that of raising the standard of proof. Under both rationales, it would become more difficult to convict a person of a graver offence.

However, closer scrutiny reveals that the different claims would lead to *opposite* conclusions in cases of graver offences that are nevertheless more frequent. Beccaria's factual assertion that graver crimes are less frequent is clearly false in some cases. Most notably, while rape is one of the most serious offences in the book,[6] it is unfortunately more common than traditionally thought,[7] and certainly more common than some esoteric minor offences that are still in force, such as wearing armour in Parliament[8] or firing a cannon within 300 yards of a house.[9] However, it is probably correct in other cases, such as the example with which this chapter began. If murder is less frequent than theft, as it is to be hoped it is, then according to the logic underlying Beccaria's claims, it should be harder to prove. More importantly, even if graver offences are not generally less

[4] Ibid at 32.

[5] Ibid at 77. Beccaria's psychological argument for why the gravity of the crime makes it less probable is also set out here: 'The safety of one's own life is a natural right, the protection of property is a social right. The number of motives which impel men to overstep the natural feelings of pity is far fewer than the number of motives which impel them by the natural desire to be happy to violate a right which they do not find in their hearts but in social conventions. The vastness of the difference in probability of these two classes of crimes requires them to be regulated by different principles.'

[6] In the United Kingdom, a man guilty of rape is liable to imprisonment up to life: Sexual Offences Act 2003, s 1(4). Under United States Federal Law, the offence of sexual abuse is also punishable by up to life imprisonment. See 18 USC §§ 2242 (for the law in specific US States, see National District Attorneys Association, 'Sexual Assault Statutes in the United States Chart' (2016) available at https://healthdocbox.com/Sexuality/78759471-Sexual-assault-statutes-in-the-united-states-chart.html.

[7] See, eg, *The National Intimate Partner and Sexual Violence Survey (NISVS): 2010 Summary Report* (Atlanta GA, National Center for Injury Prevention and Control, Centers for Disease Control and Prevention) 20.

[8] Bearing of Armour or Coming Armed to Parliament Act 1313.

[9] Metropolitan Police Act 1839, s 55.

frequent, Beccaria's claims could be easily amended to a more general form: *the lower the frequency of a given crime, the stronger the proof required for conviction should be.* The less frequent the alleged crime is, the stronger the evidence against the accused should be; and, by inference, the more frequent the alleged crime is, the more willing the fact-finder should be to convict (henceforth, this will be referred to as 'Beccaria's argument').

In this chapter, I assess Beccaria's argument by suggesting two possible interpretations. According to the first interpretation, the frequency of the alleged crime is but one example of the statistical variables (or base-rates) that should be taken into account when assessing the accused's guilt. Here, to properly assess the evidence available in the case, Beccaria's logic should be applied not only to the type of crime but also to any other statistical variable that could help us accurately calculate the initial (prior) probability that the accused committed the alleged crime. In other words, to arrive at a more accurate result, the proof required for conviction should be *individualised* as much as possible according to the specific circumstances of each case. The implication of this interpretation is that statistics on the frequency of the alleged crime in *similar circumstances* should also be calculated and adduced as evidence in criminal proceedings. In particular, the prosecution should be permitted to present statistical evidence on the high frequency of the alleged crime among people who are similar to the accused to support its allegation that the accused has committed that crime. This first interpretation of Beccaria's argument is therefore a call to use such evidence (also known as 'naked statistical evidence') in criminal proceedings. As such, it should be assessed using the contemporary literature on this issue (for any sound argument against the use of such evidence in criminal proceedings would also apply to Beccaria's argument under this interpretation).

My proposed alternative interpretation of Beccaria's argument holds that the prosecution should *not* be permitted to use the (relatively high) frequency of the alleged crime as evidence to support their claim that the accused committed the crime, but the defence *should* be permitted to refer to the (relatively low) frequency of the alleged crime to support their claim that the accused is innocent. Based on my previous work,[10] I contend that the use of high frequency evidence by the prosecution is problematic, because it involves *contradicting presuppositions* about the individual's conduct. In this chapter, I seek to show that this objection does not apply to the use of low frequency evidence by the defence. I proceed by drawing on the conceptual distinction between causes and enablers (or conditions), to offer a more nuanced analysis of the divergent roles of statistical evidence in arguments for the prosecution and defence.

[10] A Pundik, 'Freedom and Generalisation' (2017) 37 *Oxford Journal of Legal Studies* 189.

II. THE INDIVIDUALISED PROOF INTERPRETATION

According to the first interpretation of Beccaria's argument, the way in which the fact-finder assesses the available evidence should be *individualised* to the specific circumstances of each case. Ideally, the evidence should be assessed while taking into account all the information that is relevant for determining the frequency of the specific allegation, including the frequency of the alleged crime among people who are similar to the accused. To illustrate this point, consider the following non-legal case, in which a man goes to see his doctor about an abdominal pain. The doctor needs to decide whether to send him for a certain test that diagnoses a rare cancer that is consistent with such pain, but which would expose the patient to potentially harmful radiation. Applying Beccaria's argument to this scenario, it sounds intuitively right: when assessing the available evidence, surely the doctor needs to bear in mind the low frequency of the suspected cancer as a consideration *against* sending the patient for the test?

Furthermore, the doctor should not stop at the frequency of that cancer within the *general* population, but rather assess this probability using the frequency of this cancer within a population *similar to the patient*. If the patient presents risk factors that are known to be correlated with this cancer (for example, he is overweight, male, a heavy smoker and has relatives who suffer from this disease), his complaints should be assessed differently from those of a patient who does not present these risk factors. If the frequency of the rare cancer among people with these risk factors is high enough, the doctor should send him for the test despite the risk associated with the radiation, even if it should usually be avoided by other people who report the same symptoms. Returning to criminal proceedings, if Beccaria is right that the frequency of the alleged crime should affect the assessment of the available evidence, there seems to be no good reason to take into account the frequency of the alleged crime *in the general population*. Instead, the frequency of the crime should be *individualised* to the accused by reference to the group of people to whom the accused is most similar.

To individualise the standard of proof according to the frequency of the alleged crime among people who are similar to the accused, the fact-finder would need some statistical evidence to establish what this frequency is (henceforth, 'crime-rate evidence'). However, such base-rates are usually excluded from criminal fact-finding,[11] and their use for the purpose of conviction also seems *intuitively inappropriate*. For example, using the high rate of crimes involving illegal firearms in a certain neighbourhood to support the conviction of an individual resident of a crime involving an illegal firearm seems highly objectionable. The objection to crime-rate evidence is not only aimed at its sufficiency (on the grounds that crime rates are insufficient on their own to prove that

[11] JJ Koehler, 'When Do Courts Think Base Rate Statistics Are Relevant?' (2002) 42 *Jurimetrics Journal* 373.

the individual is guilty). The objection also requires that such evidence should not be used at all in determining the individual's guilt – namely, it should be *inadmissible* in criminal proceedings.[12]

Note that the inadmissibility of such individualised crime-rates could not be justified by invoking the problem of the reference class.[13] There is a question that haunts every attempt to infer the probability of a certain event from the frequency of this event within a certain population: what is the most appropriate group of cases in which this frequency should be measured? One could take a sceptical approach (as Allen and Pardo seem to)[14] and hold that the most appropriate group either does not exist or cannot be identified, thus concluding that inferences that require a reference to a group should never be used in criminal proceedings. However, the challenge that the sceptic faces is to explain how inferences of this sort can be drawn at all. For example, one would have to explain how the above-mentioned doctor should reach a decision without taking into account the frequency of the cancer within a population more refined than the general population. More generally, it seems that every factual inference relies on a generalisation, which is a form of reference to a group.[15] Be that as it may, I only assume that some reference classes are more appropriate than others (consider patients who smoke heavily versus patients who wear red shirts), so the problem of the reference class cannot be the reason why crime rates should be inadmissible.

Note also that it is difficult to justify the inadmissibility of individualised crime rates on grounds of practicality. In the age of big data, I believe it is easier than ever to identify the variables that are correlated with specific crimes and to calculate their exact frequency among people who are most similar to the accused. And even if there are practical constraints on the definition of the population, the definition that could be used to calculate the frequency is arguably more fine-grained than just the type of crime.

However, the implications of this interpretation of Beccaria's argument seem to be both counterintuitive and reformative, requiring a radical change in our current legal fact-finding practices. That does not necessarily make Beccaria's argument wrong, but it does mean that accepting his argument would require us to reject the various accounts that seek to justify why crime-rate evidence should

[12] This intuitive objection to admissibility distinguishes this example from the lottery and prefaces paradoxes in epistemology and the gate-crasher and prisoner paradoxes in legal theory. I have argued elsewhere that the latter are confusing and unhelpful – see Pundik, above n 10 at 192–193.

[13] For a general discussion of this issue in the context of evidence law, see the compilation entitled 'Special Issue on the Reference Class Problem' (2007) 11 *International Journal of Evidence and Proof* 242.

[14] RJ Allen & MS Pardo, 'The Problematic Value of Mathematical Models of Evidence' (2007) 36 *Journal of Legal Studies* 107.

[15] Schauer, for example, holds that 'the avoidance of generalizations is, with few or no qualifications, simply not possible at all'. F Schauer, *Profiles, Probabilities and Stereotypes* (Cambridge MA, Belknap Press, 2003) 101.

not be used in criminal fact-finding.[16] Instead of examining whether any of these accounts offer a sound enough argument for rejecting Beccaria's argument so interpreted, I would like to take a different path. In the next section, I propose an alternative interpretation that does not license the use of crime-rate evidence against the accused and yet illuminates a specific context in which crime-rate evidence should nevertheless be made admissible.

III. THE ASYMMETRICAL INTERPRETATION

Beccaria's argument could be interpreted as accepting that crime rates should not be used by the prosecution to support their contention that the accused has committed the alleged crime, while drawing attention to an important defence claim that could nevertheless be established using this evidence. In proposing this interpretation, I rely on an account that I have developed elsewhere to justify why predictive evidence such as crime rates should not be used in criminal proceedings to establish the accused's guilt.[17]

A. The Culpability Account

According to my 'culpability account', predictive evidence supports the prosecution's claim that the accused committed the alleged crime only if the accused's conduct was determined by a certain *causal* factor that rendered their conduct unfree. Yet, in the context of attributing culpability, it is necessary to presuppose the exact opposite: that the accused *was* free to determine their own conduct. Using predictive generalisations to determine culpability is objectionable, because it involves *contradicting* presuppositions about the individual's conduct.[18]

My culpability account assumes that criminal law seeks to avoid punishing those who are not culpable for their actions and, hence, that criminal

[16] For critical surveys of these accounts, see F Schoeman, 'Statistical vs. Direct Evidence' (1987) 21 *Noûs* 179; M Redmayne, 'Exploring the Proof Paradoxes' (2008) 14 *Legal Theory* 281; A Pundik, 'What is Wrong with Statistical Evidence? The Attempts to Establish an Epistemic Deficiency' (2008) 27 *Civil Justice Quarterly* 461.

[17] Pundik, above n 10. The term 'predictive evidence' is based on Uviller's distinction between trace and predictive evidence: the former results from a past event that leaves some traces in the present (such as eye-witnesses or fingerprints), while the latter 'looks forward from an established event or trait to predict the likely repetition of its occurrence'. See R Uviller, 'Evidence of Character to Prove Conduct: Illusion, Illogic, and Injustice in the Courtroom' (1982) 130 *University of Pennsylvania Law Review* 845 at 847.

[18] That determining culpability should not be based on contradictory presuppositions should not be confused with the stronger claim that *every* case of practical decision-making is subject to *all* epistemic norms – a claim I do not endorse. Nor is it assumed that holding contradictory beliefs is, in itself, morally wrong – only that it is wrong to rely on contradictory beliefs to treat someone as culpable.

punishment is constrained by culpability. This constraint does not imply retributivism – namely, that punishment is inflicted because it is deserved. Instead, any theory of punishment that considers culpability to be a *constraint* on other legitimate goals of punishment should refrain from knowingly convicting non-culpable persons.[19] I also assume, like most theorists of free will, that acting freely is a necessary condition of culpability.[20] While some hold that our practices of attributing culpability do not require the metaphysical question of free will to be settled,[21] I share the position that the distinction between justified and unjustified attribution of culpability – which any theory of culpability needs to make – is likely to rely on (or bring through the back door) notions very similar to 'freedom' and 'control'.[22]

My culpability account first argues that inferences about human conduct require reliance on *causal* generalisations – that is, generalisations that reflect a causal connection between the type of fact from which the inference begins and the type of fact the inference seeks to establish. If an inference is based on a non-causal generalisation, a mere correlation, it is unlicensed and thus invalid.[23] The causal relation that the generalisation reflects can operate either directly or through a common cause. For example, inferring that a smoker is likelier to contract cancer than a non-smoker is based on a causal generalisation that smoking is a cause of (lung) cancer. By contrast, inferring that a Coca-Cola drinker is likelier to contract cancer than a non-drinker might involve a causal generalisation that reflects a common cause: living in a hot country might be the common cause of both Coca-Cola drinking and (skin) cancer. The culpability account does not require that the (direct or indirect) causal generalisation be *specified*, but only that it be accepted that, for the inference to be valid, the *existence* of such a causal generalisation must be presupposed.[24]

[19] One notable example is Hart's mixed theory of punishment, which accepts the retributivist constraint ('only those who have broken the law – and voluntarily broken it – may be punished') while rejecting retributivism as the 'General Justifying Aim of the system' in HLA Hart, *Punishment and Responsibility* 2nd edition (Oxford, Oxford University Press, 2008) 9. Hart acknowledges his debt to Beccaria, who in his *On Crimes and Punishments* has already offered a similar mixed theory of punishment. See 'Bentham and Beccaria', in HLA Hart, *Essays on Bentham: Studies in Jurisprudence and Political Theory* (Oxford, Oxford University Press, 1982) 40 at 50–52.

[20] A notable exception is semi-compatibilist theories, such as J Fischer & M Ravizza, *Responsibility and Control: A Theory of Moral Responsibility* (Cambridge, Cambridge University Press, 1998) 31–34.

[21] PF Strawson, 'Freedom and Resentment' (1962) 48 *Proceedings of the British Academy* 1.

[22] V Tadros, *Criminal Responsibility* (Oxford, Oxford University Press, 2005) 69.

[23] This claim is part of the Common Cause Principle. See H Reichenbach, *The Direction of Time* 2nd edition (Berkeley CA, University of California Press, 1991) 158–159; F Arntzenius, 'The Common Cause Principle' (1992) 2 *PSA: Proceedings of the Biennial Meeting of the Philosophy of Science Association* 227.

[24] I object to the opposite stance, according to which a mere correlation between the two types of fact can suffice to infer an unknown from a known fact, since this stance faces difficulty in rejecting *spurious correlations* (such as the statistically-significant correlation between the number of people who drown by falling into a swimming pool and the number of films featuring Nicholas Cage; see T Vigen, 'Spurious Correlations', available at www.tylervigen.com). For more detail on this point, see Pundik, above n 10 at 199.

Given that inferences about human conduct require reliance on causal generalisations, my culpability account proceeds to argue that free actions cannot be proved with such generalisations, for their use in criminal proceedings relies on contradictory presuppositions. On the one hand, this use presupposes that the accused's conduct was caused by factors outside their control, thereby presupposing that their conduct was unfree and hence non-culpable. On the other hand, convicting the accused of the alleged crime presupposes the exact opposite: that they were free to determine their own conduct.[25]

Starting with a simple example, assume that Richard is exposed to radiation of a particular kind, which affects his nervous system, resulting in blotches all over his skin and an irresistible urge to attack everyone around him. Assume further that *every* person exposed to this radiation develops these symptoms and subsequently attacks everyone around them uncontrollably. When Richard is admitted to hospital, it seems unproblematic to infer from the blotches that, given the opportunity, he will go berserk and should therefore be restrained. However, inferring from these marks that a violent action that had taken place before Richard arrived at the hospital was committed by him, for the purpose of convicting him of a violent offence, seems intuitively problematic.

This inference should not be used for the purpose of determining culpability, because it is based on contradicting presuppositions. To infer from Richard's skin marks that he had acted violently, it is necessary to presuppose a *causal* generalisation, according to which either one caused the other or they both had a common cause. In this example, the radiation caused both Richard's blotches and his violent conduct. However, Richard's acting violently may be culpable only if he acted *freely*. Establishing Richard's guilt by inferring from his skin marks that it was he who acted violently is contradictory, because his conduct is treated as free and unfree at the same time. This example also explains why the very same inference seems unproblematic when restraining him in the hospital, because, in the medical context, it is not necessary to presuppose that Richard's violent conduct will be free and culpable.

Moving to probabilistic generalisations, consider the following variation on the previous example. Assume that Stephen is exposed to another type of radiation, which affects the nervous system and always causes certain skin blotches but triggers an irresistible urge to attack others, when the opportunity arises, in only 80 per cent of cases. According to the subjective interpretation of probability,[26] which is commonly considered the most suitable for legal

[25] Notably, I assume here a libertarian theory of free will. I sketch this theory in A Pundik, 'Predictive Evidence and Unpredictable Freedom' (2020) 40 *Oxford Journal of Legal Studies* 238, where I also discuss the application of the culpability account under other theories of free will, particularly compatibilist and semi-compatibilist theories.

[26] For the application of the culpability account under the objective interpretation, see Pundik, above n 10 at 204–205.

purposes,[27] probabilistic generalisations reflect the limited state of our knowledge rather than the true nature of the world. While the generalisation about the radiation is probabilistic, it imperfectly reflects a reality that may be deterministic. If the world is indeed deterministic, Stephen belongs to one of two possible sub-groups. He may belong to the sub-group of people who possess an extra unknown variable, which, together with the radiation, determines that they will go berserk. Or he may belong to the sub-group of people who do not possess the extra variable, in which case exposure to the radiation will not cause them to go berserk.

Supporting Stephen's conviction by inferring from the blotches on his skin that he was (80 per cent) likely to have acted violently is problematic. If Stephen does indeed possess the extra variable, then – similarly to Richard – this inference leads to a contradiction: his conduct is taken to be both free (in order to be culpable) and unfree (as, together with another unknown variable, his violent actions were determined by the radiation). If Stephen does not possess the extra variable, then inferring from his skin marks that he acted violently is mistaken and misleading, because the radiation did not cause him to act violently; therefore, the probability that he acted violently is not affected by exposure to the radiation. In sum, this inference is either contradictory, because it requires inconsistent presuppositions, or misleading, because it is mistaken and yet is presented as informative.

My culpability account is able to justify the hostility of criminal fact-finding toward predictive evidence. Predictive evidence should not be used by the prosecution to support their contention that the accused committed the alleged crime, because such evidence can be probative of the accused's conduct only if it reflects a causal generalisation that also rendered their conduct unfree and thus non-culpable. Consequently, inferring from crime rates that a certain resident was likelier to have committed a crime involving an illegal firearm requires presupposing that there is a causal generalisation that makes the resident's conduct predictable to some extent – for instance, the dangerous character of the neighbourhood or its socio-economic conditions. Such causal factors are outside the resident's control, and therefore the inference from crime rates to the resident's committing the alleged crime is either inconsistent with their being culpable or mistaken.

[27] For criminal law, see L Alexander & KK Ferzan with S Morse, *Crime and Culpability: A Theory of Criminal Law* (Cambridge, Cambridge University Press, 2009) 31; for tort law, see S Perry, 'Risk, Harm, and Responsibility', in DG Owen (ed), *Philosophical Foundations of Tort Law* (Oxford, Oxford University Press, 1995) 321 at 333–335; for health and safety regulation, see MD Adler, 'Against "Individual Risk": A Sympathetic Critique of Risk Assessment' (2005) 153 *University of Pennsylvania Law Review* 1121 at 1247.

B. The Defence's Use of Predictive Evidence

Interestingly, the objection of the culpability account to predictive evidence does not arise when the evidence is used by the defence. This is because the defence are not committed to the presupposition of free will: whenever they claim that the accused did not act as the prosecution allege, they imply that the accused did something else instead, but it is immaterial to the defence's case whether the alternative course of action was performed freely or not. Consequently, the defence may allege (or imply) a causal connection between being a member of the group and the accused's action *even if* this action was caused by antecedent factors that rendered it unfree and non-culpable. Only the prosecution are committed to the presupposition that the accused acted freely, because only the prosecution need to prove that the accused acted *culpably*. It is hence only the prosecution's use of predictive evidence that is objectionable, because the evidence supports the contention that the accused committed the alleged crime at the price of conceding that their conduct was caused by a certain factor that they share with the group and is outside their control – which renders their conduct unfree and non-culpable. The culpability account could therefore support an asymmetrical interpretation of Beccaria's argument, according to which crime rates *could* be used by the defence to establish the *low* frequency of a certain crime among similar people.

Consider the Israeli case of Nissim Hadad,[28] in which a man was charged with sexually assaulting an 18-month-old boy whose mother he was dating. There was no direct evidence of the assault, but serious injuries were found to the infant's rectum after the accused had been alone with him.[29] The defence called Dr Landa, a forensic psychiatrist, who testified that sexual assaults on infants rarely include penetration. According to Dr Landa, the rarity of such a phenomenon is 'astronomical', if it exists at all.[30] In addition, the psychiatrist insisted that people with this form of paraphilia (known as 'infantophilia' rather than 'paedophilia') almost always possess paraphilic material, such as photos or videos, none of which was found in the accused's possession. The defence claimed that Hadad should not be convicted on the basis of a scenario that neither the medical sciences nor the legal scholarship had ever encountered.[31]

The court diverged in its assessment of this evidence. Justice Jubran rejected the claim that the rarity of the alleged crime should, on its own, lead to the conclusion that the accused could not be guilty of the alleged crime.[32] This is

[28] *Nissim Hadad v State of Israel* CrimA 2697/14 (2016).

[29] Hadad was accused of sodomy under Penal Law 5737–1977, § 347(b), with the aggravating circumstance of the victim being a helpless person under the accused's responsibility, Penal Law 5737–1977, § 351(a).

[30] *Hadad*, above n 28 at para [78].

[31] Ibid at para [78].

[32] Ibid at para [79].

because, had direct evidence of the alleged crime been available, it could have proved Hadad's guilt despite the rarity of this phenomenon. Nevertheless, Justice Jubran accepted that the rarity of the alleged crime constituted circumstantial evidence that should affect the assessment of the incriminating evidence available in the case. Justice Amit, on the other hand, dismissed the significance of the rarity of such a crime, because the defence failed to show that one of its theories for the potential cause of the injury, the mother's insertion of her finger into the infant's rectum, was more frequent.[33] Hadad was eventually acquitted, after Justice Mazuz joined Justice Jubran in accepting that the rarity of the alleged crime supported the finding of a reasonable doubt about Hadad's guilt.[34]

The asymmetrical interpretation of Beccaria's argument supports Justice Jubran's judgment. Similarly to Beccaria's claim in chapter 13 that the low frequency of the crime should affect the fact-finder's evaluation of the witness's credibility,[35] Jubran relied on the rarity of the alleged crime – particularly among people who exhibit no other symptoms of the alleged paraphilia, such as possession of infantophilic material – when assessing the incriminating evidence and subsequently reaching the conclusion that Hadad's guilt was not proved beyond reasonable doubt. According to the asymmetrical interpretation, the defence were seeking to adduce the rarity of the alleged crime to support the claim that Hadad did not commit that crime. The evidence submitted for this claim was that virtually no one – not even an infantophile – acts in the manner attributed to Hadad by the prosecution. The defence presupposed a certain unspecified causal mechanism that leads all human beings to avoid acting in the manner alleged by the prosecution. While such an inference may presuppose that Hadad's avoidance was caused by something outside his control and was therefore unfree, this assumption poses no difficulty for the defence, which need not assume his alleged avoidance to be free.[36]

The asymmetrical interpretation also supports the common law's traditional suspicion of previous convictions,[37] and yields some criticism of recent reforms in this area of law. The rules and case law governing the admissibility of previous convictions are vast and complex, and I cannot provide here a comprehensive analysis of them. However, the issue of previous convictions for child molestation is one useful example. Such convictions are admissible in both the

[33] Ibid at para [7].

[34] Ibid at para [11].

[35] Beccaria, above n 3 at 112–113.

[36] A similar 'defence' claim could be made by the prosecution whenever they seek to prove that another potential suspect (eg the infant's mother) did *not* commit the crime. This is because the prosecution are not committed to the assumption that the other suspect acted freely, since the prosecution do not allege that the other suspect acted culpably.

[37] 'English law's suspicion of bad character and extraneous misconduct evidence has been cultivated for many centuries. It is deeply embedded in English judicial culture and institutions, and has frequently been actively propounded and celebrated.' P Roberts & AAS Zuckerman, *Criminal Evidence* 2nd edition (Oxford, Oxford University Press, 2010) 586.

United Kingdom and the United States.[38] While the admission of such previous convictions has been criticised on various grounds, such as being unconstitutional,[39] unfair[40] and even truth-suppressing,[41] the connection to the issue of free will seems to have gone unnoticed. The culpability account would draw attention to the importance of identifying the exact generalisation involved and considering whether using it for conviction conflicts with other presuppositions made in criminal proceedings. Like any inference about human conduct, inferring from the accused's previous convictions that they are likelier to have committed the alleged similar offence(s) relies on a causal generalisation. These previous convictions may be probative because they indicate that the accused suffers from a condition, such as perversion, illness or addiction, that raises the probability of reoffending. According to the culpability account, if these previous convictions do indeed support the prosecution's contention that the accused committed the alleged crime, it might only be at the price of conceding that the accused's conduct was unfree and thus non-culpable. Previous convictions of child molestation may only be used to refute the accused's claims that they lacked any reason to commit such crimes (because they lack such sexual desire, for instance).

However, it is interesting to note that, even when existing rules of evidence exclude previous convictions, they still allow the defence to use their absence to establish that the accused has a 'clean record'.[42] The asymmetrical interpretation explains and justifies this exception. Even if the lack of previous convictions supports the accused's claim that they did *not* act as the prosecution alleged only if a causal generalisation is presupposed, this is not a problem for the defence, which need not establish that the accused's conduct was culpable (and thus free).

Lastly, the asymmetrical interpretation could explain why Beccaria only claims that the low frequency of the crime should render the witness less credible *without* making the 'vice versa' claim, namely, that the high frequency of a crime should render the witness more credible.[43] It is thus possible to interpret Beccaria's discussion of crime rates as aligning with the rest of his humanist

[38] For the United Kingdom, see Criminal Justice Act 2003, s 103; for the United States, see Federal Rules of Evidence, r 414.

[39] MA Sheft, 'Federal Rule of Evidence 413: A Dangerous New Frontier' (1995) 33 *American Criminal Law Review* 57.

[40] JL McCandless, 'Prior Bad Acts and Two Bad Rules: The Fundamental Unfairness of Federal Rules of Evidence 413 and 414' (1997) 5 *William & Mary Bill of Rights Journal* 689 at 694.

[41] M Cowley & JB Colyer, 'Asymmetries in Prior Conviction Reasoning: Truth Suppression Effects in Child Protection Contexts' (2010) 16 *Psychology, Crime & Law* 211.

[42] This exception is usually known by the permission it provides the prosecution to admit previous convictions to dispute such a defence claim. For the United Kingdom, see Criminal Justice Act 2003, s 101(1)(f); for the United States, see Federal Rules of Evidence 2014, r 404(a)(2)(A).

[43] Beccaria nevertheless makes the vice versa claim in his chapter 30, when referring to 'time for inquiry and justification', but these issues relate to criminal procedure and are thus outside the scope of this chapter.

essay: rather than advocating a counter-intuitive reform that would allow the prosecution to infer the high likelihood of the accused's committing the alleged crime from their group membership, predictive evidence could be used only as a shield but not as a sword.

However, while the defence's lack of commitment to the assumption that the accused acted freely provides the basic logic underlying the asymmetry between the different uses of statistical evidence by prosecution and defence, it is unable to provide a comprehensive account of when statistical evidence should, or should not, be used. In particular, this lack of commitment is unable to explain and justify why the defence cannot rely on crime rates *at the conviction stage* to establish that the accused committed the actions alleged by the prosecution but did so *unfreely* and should therefore be acquitted.[44] Consider again the crime rates scenario, in which there is a high rate of crimes involving illegal firearms in a certain neighbourhood. If the defence are not committed to the presupposition that the accused acted freely, it is unclear why they cannot rely on the crime-rate evidence to claim that the accused performed the *actus reus* of a crime involving an illegal firearm, but they did so *unfreely* because their conduct was caused by a characteristic that is shared by the other residents and is outside their control (for example, the socio-economic conditions of the neighbourhood). Yet such a generic argument is not accepted in criminal proceedings.[45]

To provide a more nuanced analysis of how statistical evidence is used in different inferences, I would suggest integrating into the culpability account the distinction between causes and enablers (or conditions). Enablers are necessary for the effect to occur, but do not amount to causes themselves (for example, the presence of a murder victim at the crime scene may be a necessary condition of the death, but is not its cause). There are several attempts, in various fields, to distinguish between causes and enablers, or between causes and conditions, and these attempts involve various criteria, such as abnormality, degree of probability and the context of inquiry.[46] My argument in this chapter does not hinge on accepting any specific distinction, but only on accepting that causes could somehow be separated from enablers (or conditions). However, for illustrative purposes, I would like to describe one possible distinction between causes and

[44] The defence may use such evidence at the sentencing stage, when asking for mitigation of sentence. However, as I argued elsewhere, such a claim does not necessarily rest on the same objectionable causal generalisation as the claim mentioned above, according to which the accused is not guilty at all. See A Pundik, 'Rethinking the Use of Statistical Evidence to Prove Causation in Criminal Cases: A Tale of (Im)Probability and Free Will' (2021) 40 *Law & Philosophy* 97 at 121–122.

[45] Duress and cultural defences might raise different issues from that of free will, because they do not necessarily rely on factual inferences from how similar people tend to act in similar situations (rather, they might rely on normative claims regarding, for example, how a person is *permitted* to act in such a scenario).

[46] For a critical survey of the different attempts to distinguish between causes and enablers, see PW Cheng & LR Novick 'Causes versus enabling conditions' (1991) 40 *Cognition* 83 at 85–94. Cheng and Novick develop their account ibid at 94–108.

enablers, proposed by Laurence Lombard.[47] In his work on the counterfactual analysis of causation, Lombard addresses a known problem that haunts this area.[48] According to the counterfactual analysis, which also underlies the legal test of *causa sine qua non*, C is a cause of E if, and only if, had C not occurred, E would not have occurred.[49] While this analysis has an intuitive appeal, the problem it faces is that, according to this test, a person's birth is their cause of death, because had this person not been born, they would not have died. To address this counterintuitive outcome, Lombard distinguishes between 'causes' and 'enablers'. Causes are *events* that 'make things happen'.[50] In other words, they bring about effects that did not exist before, and are thus *changes*. Lombard assumes that 'there are to be no temporal gaps between causes and their effect that are not filled by intermediary causes and effects'.[51] By contrast, enablers are not events but 'conditions or states the obtaining of which merely makes it possible for one event to cause another'.[52] For example, the oxygen is not a cause of a fire that was initiated with a match, even though it is true that, had the oxygen not been present, the fire would not have started. This is because there was a gap between the oxygen's presence and the lighting of the match, and the oxygen only made it possible for another event, the striking of the match, to cause the fire.

To make the distinction more precise, Lombard distinguishes between *primary* and *secondary* capacities. A primary capacity is the capacity of an object to be changed in a certain way if acted on in a certain way. For instance, the capacity of a dry match to light up is a primary capacity because the match will light up when struck. By contrast, a wet match has a secondary capacity to light up. If it is struck, it will *not* light up; but if it dries out, it will acquire the primary capacity to ignite when struck. According to Lombard, causes are activators of primary capacities, while enablers are activators of secondary capacities.[53] Blowing hot air on a match and drying it out would therefore

[47] Readers who prefer another theoretical basis for this distinction (or hold that it is so obvious that it requires no such basis) could skip the following two paragraphs.

[48] LB Lombard, 'Causes, Enablers and the Counterfactual Analysis' (1990) 59 *Philosophical Studies* 195.

[49] The counterfactual analysis of causation is subject to numerous scholarly discussions. For a detailed introduction, see J Collins, N Hall & LA Paul, 'Counterfactuals and Causation: History, Problems, and Prospects', in J Collins, N Hall & LA Paul (eds), *Causation and Counterfactuals* (Cambridge MA, MIT Press, 2004).

[50] Lombard, above n 48 at 201.

[51] Ibid.

[52] Ibid.

[53] Lombard holds that there is still a difference between remote causes and enablers. Pushing the first domino *causes* the 14th domino to fall, but it is *not an enabler*: it does not make it possible for the 14th domino to fall. It does not change the 14th domino's capacities so as to allow another event to occur and cause the 14th domino to fall. It is a chain of events in which each event brings about a change in the world, which in turn brings about the following change. By contrast, placing the 14th domino after the 13th *is* an enabler. It only makes it possible for the 13th domino to cause the 14th to fall – that is, it merely gives the latter the primary capacity to be affected in a certain way.

amount to an *enabler* of the match's burning rather than its cause, because it only activates the match's primary capacity to light up when struck. To summarise, a cause initiates an immediate effect (or a chain of causes and effects), while an enabler merely allows another event to cause the effect.

When the distinction between causes and enablers is integrated into the culpability account, the role of the agent's subjective reasons in their free actions would amount to that of *enablers* of free decisions (rather than their causes). In free actions, reasons to act in one way are met with reasons to act in another way, thereby causing a torn decision *together*.[54] When the agent eventually makes their choice, that resulting action is *not* caused by any of these reasons, irrespective of their strength.[55]

The distinction between causes and enablers and the view of conflicting reasons as enablers of free actions explain why the culpability account may object to the defence's attempt to rely on crime-rate evidence to argue that the accused committed the *actus reus* of the crime unfreely. The defence may not use crime-rate evidence whenever it reflects enablers rather than causes because only the causal powers to which the accused was subjected would support the defence's claim that the accused's conduct was determined by antecedent factors outside their control. However, the prevalence of a crime within a certain population does not necessarily reflect any causal powers to which this population is exposed. Instead, it may reflect the prevalence of subjective reasons to commit that crime among this population – that is, the prevalence of enablers. For example, the high rate of crimes involving illegal firearms in a certain (poor) neighbourhood may reflect the fact that it is harder for residents to obtain firearms legally, or that the neighbourhood is unsafe, which results in more residents facing the choice of whether to commit these crimes. However, when these residents freely choose to commit crimes involving illegal firearms, these factors do not necessarily cause their conduct. Instead, these factors may merely enable them to choose freely how to act. Consequently, if the crime-rate evidence merely reflects the prevalence of enablers, such evidence does not support the defence's claim that the accused acted *unfreely*, and hence is irrelevant. Perhaps courts implicitly make a 'presumption of free will', so people are presumed to have acted freely until a freedom-undermining cause is proved. The courts' refusal to accept crime-rate evidence also from the defence exemplifies their general reluctance to accept that people are *caused* to act in a certain way by their socio-economic conditions, genetic make-up, etc.

[54] The term 'torn decision' is taken from M Balaguer, *Free Will as an Open Scientific Problem* (Cambridge MA, MIT Press, 2009) ch 3.

[55] For more detail on the role of subjective reasons in free actions according to the culpability account, see Pundik, above n 25 at 241–247.

IV. CONCLUSION

My reading of Beccaria's empiricist claims through the lens of the culpability account gives rise to an argument for requiring stronger proof for certain crimes that differs from contemporary arguments in both its theoretical foundations and practical implications. Theoretically, while contemporary scholarship addresses the issue of standards of proof, this argument is directed at how the fact-finder should assess the evidence available in the case. Practically, this argument would lead to the opposite conclusion to that of the existing arguments in cases of graver offences that are nevertheless frequent, such as rape (as well as in cases of less serious offences that are nevertheless infrequent). Re-reading Beccaria's work therefore may offer important contributions not only to penal theory and substantive criminal law, but also to the theory of evidence and proof.

Drawing conclusions from Beccaria's work to illuminate contemporary issues risks anachronism and may be subject to various objections. Nevertheless, I hope this chapter serves as a modest example of the thought-provoking claims *On Crimes and Punishments* contains, despite the many years that have passed since its publication.

11

Cesare Beccaria's Integrative Deterrence Approach

MORDECHAI KREMNITZER AND ADI GAL

I. INTRODUCTION

WHILE DETERRENCE CONSTITUTES a cornerstone of penological thought today, there are fundamental theoretical and empirical reasons to doubt that it can stand by itself as punishment's justification and as a sole criterion for sentence measurement. The moral difficulty of punishing someone who acted without guilt; the theoretical reliance on overly generalised assumptions such as the rationality of the offender; and the historical relocation of the punishing act from the town square to isolated prisons, are all grounds to contest the suitability of deterrence as a single rationale for modern legal systems. In this chapter we contend that Cesare Beccaria's understanding of deterrence, as presented in his stellar piece *On Crimes and Punishments*, is essential today, for it allows for an effective balancing of deterrence with various other punitive approaches, particularly with retributivism and expressivism (positive prevention).

The chapter is structured as follows. In section II we provide some historical background to Beccaria's *On Crimes and Punishments*; in section III we address the deontological objections Beccaria provoked and examine some difficulties in applying his approach today by focusing on four key elements of his theory – certainty, severity, speed, and publicity of punishment. We then move, in section IV, to suggest that Beccaria's deterrence approach and the principles he listed are not crude nor absolute. They should be read holistically – as part of his overall approach to criminal justice. We show how Beccaria sensitively integrates deterrence with considerations of justice, guilt and proportionality – notions that are usually attributed to retributivism and expressivism. Drawing on Beccaria's integrative approach, section V advances the claim that the principle of deterrence is an important and valuable tool that should not be marginalised. Instead – and provided that it is better implemented and integrated, based on guilt and limited by justice considerations – it should be combined with retribution, and given an important place in punishing particular types of crimes and certain types of perpetrators. This normative argument is illustrated by two examples: economic and white-collar crimes, and international criminal law. Finally, section VI provides concluding remarks.

II. BECCARIA'S DETERRENCE IN A NUTSHELL

Carlo Calisse asserted, in *A History of Italian Law*, that 'no book, indeed, upon penal law created a greater stir in Europe, was more read, or brought greater fame to its author than [*Dei Delitti e Delle Pene*] published in 1764 by Beccaria'.[1] Beccaria was in his mid-twenties when he wrote what was soon to become one of the most influential works in the history of criminal law literature. His views on deterrence developed, changed and affected both the theory and the practice of criminal law.[2] Many of his notions were revolutionary in his time, and are still considered viable today.[3]

During the eighteenth century, Italy – like the rest of the Continent at the time – still relied on a feudal and religious ethos of punishment. Impoverished individuals were frequently arrested without due process, judges enjoyed an almost unlimited discretion to convict and sentence, and punishments included horrendous tortures like amputations and death by burning.[4] Beccaria, a key figure in, and representative of, the Enlightenment era, condemned the cruelty and arbitrariness on which the legal system was based, and sought to instil it with justice and impartiality.[5] He believed that adherence to the notion of the social contract meant that citizens must relinquish some measure of their liberties, but no more than the bare necessary minimum, whereas the state must fearlessly protect the remaining freedoms of citizens.[6]

[1] C Calisse, *A History of Italian Law* translated by LB Register (Boston MA, Little, Brown & Co, 1928) 456, quoted in JD Bessler, 'The Long March toward Abolition: From the Enlightenment to the United Nations and the Death Penalty's Slow Demise' (2018) 29 *University of Florida Journal of Law & Public Policy* 1 at 25.

[2] For a broader discussion of Beccaria's extensive influence, see JD Bessler, 'The Economist and the Enlightenment: How Cesare Beccaria Changed Western Civilization' (2018) 46 *European Journal of Law and Economics* 275 at 281 (suggesting that Beccaria's 'writings on happiness and tyranny shaped the American Revolution and American constitutions and laws, and his writings on crime and punishment influenced declarations of rights and penal codes the world over'). See also J Hostettler, *Cesare Beccaria: The Genius of 'On Crimes and Punishments'* (Hampshire, Waterside Press, 2011) 129–136.

[3] S Eldar, 'Introduction', in C Beccaria, *Dei Delitti e Delle Pene* translated into Hebrew (Jerusalem, Shalem Press, 2018) at x–xi. See also Roberts, ch 9 in this volume.

[4] Eldar, above n 3 at xv.

[5] Ibid.

[6] Ibid at xvi. According to Bernard Harcourt, Beccaria echoed Thomas Hobbes' ideas in *Leviathan*, but while he accepted the Hobbesian notion that it was the need for security that inspired individuals to form a state, he rejected that they had relinquished *all* liberty to the Leviathan. See BE Harcourt, 'Beccaria's *On Crimes and Punishments*: A Mirror on the History of the Foundations of Modern Criminal Law', in MD Dubber (ed), *Foundational Texts in Modern Criminal Law* (Oxford, Oxford University Press, 2014) 39 at 44.

At the core of his theory was the view that punishment is not intended to torment the offender, to avenge the victim or to repair the damage done. Rather, its purpose is to deter the offender from returning to his or her bad ways (individual deterrence), and to deter others in society from following in the offender's footsteps (general deterrence).

> The purpose of punishment is not that of tormenting or afflicting any sentient creature, nor of undoing a crime already committed … The purpose, therefore, is nothing other than to prevent the offender from doing fresh harm to his fellows and to deter others from doing likewise.[7]

At the same time, proportionality must be maintained between the offence and the punishment prescribed and imposed. On the one hand, the sentence must create a strong and long-lasting impression on the offender and on the public; on the other hand, and given the state's commitment to the social contract and its citizens' liberty, the punishment should be the lightest of the appropriate sanctions:[8]

> Therefore, punishments and the means adopted for inflicting them should, consistent with proportionality, be so selected as to make the most efficacious and lasting impression on the minds of men with the least torment to the body of the condemned.[9]

Beccaria opposed severe punishment for offences that cause minor damage. He believed it sufficient for prevention that the harm caused to the offender by the sentence exceed the benefit that the offender derived, or intended to derive, from the offence.[10] This theory is based on the assumption that it is human rationality that leads a person to break the law. Hence, the most effective way to prevent crime is to change the calculation of benefits versus costs. Therefore, while the power of the state is not unlimited and must be consistent with the social contract, Beccaria also contends that 'the obstacles which repel men from committing crimes ought to be made stronger the more those crimes are against the public good and the more inducements there are for committing them'.[11] To this he adds a deterrence-based argument in favour of correlating the severity of the punishment directly with the severity of the crime, based on the greater interest society has in deterring more serious crimes: 'If an equal punishment is laid down for two crimes which damage society unequally, men will not have a stronger deterrent against committing the greater crime if they find it more advantageous to do so.'[12]

[7] C Beccaria, *On Crimes and Punishments and Other Writings* edited by R Bellamy and translated by R Davies (Cambridge, Cambridge University Press, 1995) 31 (ch 12).

[8] Eldar, above n 3 at xvii.

[9] Beccaria, above n 7 at 31 (ch 12).

[10] Eldar, above n 3 at xvi.

[11] Beccaria, above n 7 at 19 (ch 6). It should be noted that here Beccaria refers to the offender's motives for delinquency in a way that suggests a possible correlation with a Kantian approach. This aspect of his writing will be discussed in section IV.C.

[12] Ibid at 21. See also MD White, 'The Neglected Nuance of Beccaria's Theory' (2018) 46 *European Journal of Law & Economics* 315 at 318. According to White, modern economists should

III. BECCARIA'S APPROACH – THE CONDITIONS FOR ITS FEASIBILITY AND A REALITY CHECK

A. Retributive Objections

Beccaria's essay spurred immense interest and enthusiasm in Europe, England and America, the 'New World',[13] but it also encountered considerable resistance from philosophers and jurists.[14] Kant, in a passage that is often taken to enshrine the deontological-retributivist approach, famously argued:

> Punishment … can never be inflicted merely as a means to promote some other good for the criminal himself or for civil society. It must always be inflicted upon him only *because he has committed a crime*. For a human being can never be treated merely as a means to the purpose of another … He must previously have been found *punishable* before any thought can be given to drawing from his punishment something of use for himself or his fellow citizens.[15]

And Hegel criticised Beccaria,[16] stressing that to base the justification of punishment on threats 'is to treat a man like a dog instead with the freedom and respect due to him as a man'.[17]

Indeed, while deterrence focuses on consequences and results, and is by its nature forward-looking, retributivism is based upon duties and rights, and is backward-looking.[18] From a Kantian perspective, the only legitimate use of the

adopt Beccaria's nuanced deterrence, which includes 'relatively moderate endorsement of retributivist principles', for it might result in 'a richer and more humanistic economic approach to crime and punishment': ibid at 316, 328. While we certainly agree with White's reading of Beccaria's theory as multifaceted, we contend that his holistic approach can enrich penal law as a whole, and thus should be taken into consideration not only by utilitarians, but also by retributivists, as well as – and even more importantly – legislatures and judges.

[13] For further reading see DR Massaro, 'Cesare Beccaria – The Father of Criminal Justice: His Impact on Anglo-American Jurisprudence' (1991) 1 *The Digest: National Italian American Bar Association Law Journal* 19.

[14] Pierre-Francois Muyart de Vouglans referred to it as 'a pleading in favour of that miserable portion of the human species' and considered it a dangerous piece. See Harcourt, above n 6 at 41.

[15] I Kant, *The Metaphysics of Morals* [1797] edited and translated by M Gregor (Cambridge, Cambridge University Press, 1996) 105 (emphasis in original).

[16] See Eldar, above n 3 at xxxii.

[17] GWF Hegel, *The Philosophy of Right* [1821] translated by SW Dyde (London, George Bell, 1896; reprinted by Dover Publications, 2005) 36. Hegel explicitly rejected Beccaria's acceptance of the social contract, writing that 'the state is not a contract, nor, moreover, are the protection and security of the life and property of individuals in their capacity as separate persons, the unconditional object of the state's existence. On the contrary, the state is the higher existence, which lays claim to the life and property of the individuals and demands the sacrifice of them.' Ibid at 37. Similar observations with respect to the above segments of Kant and Hegel were made by White, above n 12 at 325. See also MA Pauley, 'The Jurisprudence of Crime and Punishment from Plato to Hegel' (1994) 39 *American Journal of Jurisprudence* 97 at 137–138, 142–143, who provides further reading on the differences between Beccaria, Kant and Hegel; and RL Christopher, 'Deterring Retributivism: The Injustice of "Just" Punishment' (2002) 96 *Northwestern University Law Review* 843 at 925–926.

[18] White, above n 12 at 324. For a critical analysis of both retributivism and deterrence, see MC Materni, 'Criminal Punishment and the Pursuit of Justice' (2013) 2 *British Journal of American Legal Studies* 263.

state's power to punish is retributive, and such use must proportionately reflect the guilt of the offender. Using state power for external purposes, deterrence included, deprives offenders of their dignity and is thus prohibited.[19] After all, if the sole purpose of punishment were to prevent future crimes, what would keep a state from imprisoning people who are inclined to commit a crime but have not yet done so?[20]

Modern authors like RA Duff likewise insist that punishing offenders *solely* to prevent them from committing further crimes, that is, relying entirely on individual deterrence, is treating them as if they are no longer members of society but rather 'dangerous enemies' from whom society must protect itself. Relying *only* on general deterrence, on the other hand, suggests that society consists of 'rational egoists' who avoid crime only to avoid punishment.[21] Both of these stances are problematic. As Duff rightly says, the law in a liberal political society

> must address its members in terms of the values which it embodies – values to which they should, as members of the community, already be committed: it portrays criminal conduct as wrongful in terms of those values; and the reasons which citizens have to refrain from such conduct, the reasons to which law refers and on which it depends, are precisely the moral reasons which make such conduct wrong.[22]

At the basis of the retributive approach, then, lies the idea that since the criminal conduct is the result of the perpetrator's choice, once she decides to violate her duty to obey the law, she bears a moral guilt that justifies a punitive response by the state. Her conduct attests to her failure to internalise the relevant social values protected by the norm. An additional educational effort may be needed but is insufficient at this stage. This retributive conception of punishment's

[19] M Kremnitzer, 'An Argument for Retributivism in International Criminal Law', in F Jeßberger & J Geneuss (eds), *Why Punish Perpetrators of Mass Atrocities? Purposes of Punishment in International Criminal Law* (Cambridge, Cambridge University Press, 2020) 161 at 163. The precise shape of Kant's theory of punishment is much disputed. Some scholars read Kant as a proponent of a mixed theory that draws on retributivism as well as on utilitarianism, eg BS Byrd, 'Kant's Theory of Punishment: Deterrence in Its Threat, Retribution in Its Execution' (1989) 8 *Law & Philosophy* 151; DE Scheid, 'Kant's Retributivism' (1983) 93 *Ethics* 262.

[20] We do not mean to suggest that 'pre-punishment' is a necessary or even a plausible implication of accepting deterrence as the sole aim of penal law. As Gideon Yaffe wrote, 'it appears that it is never justified to punish in advance. "Pre-punishment," as such a practice has been called, seems no better than punishing for something the person did not do. Because punishment of the innocent is so abhorrent, the first inquiry in any criminal trial is an inquiry about actual innocence: assuming there was a crime, is the defendant the very person who committed it? It does not do to show that the defendant will commit the crime in the future or commit it if not punished. Pre-punishment is no better than punishment of the innocent.' G Yaffe, 'Prevention and Imminence, Pre-Punishment and Actuality' (2011) 48 *San Diego Law Review* 1205 at 1206.

[21] RA Duff, 'Penal Communities' (1999) 1 *Punishment & Society* 27 at 34.

[22] Ibid. See also RA Duff, 'A Criminal Law We Can Call Our Own?' (2017) 111 *Northwestern University Law Review* 1491 (where he suggests a general ideal model for criminal law that could serve as means to achieve broader aims and values of a polity).

justification allows for a more sophisticated understanding of punishment's social purpose. The state, having failed in its primary duty to protect citizens from attacks, bears the ancillary duty to reduce the damage of its initial failure and to re-establish the validity of the violated norm.[23] The lack of a punitive response would enhance the crisis of validity of the norm caused by its violation. In order to protect the victim and society at large from additional attacks that are encouraged by the absence of a punitive response, punishment is needed to assure law-abiding citizens that the norms are taken seriously and that those who break them are not the 'winners' at the end of the day. Such an integrated moral approach cannot rely on deterrence alone. Relying on deterrence considerations, regardless of notions of guilt and positive prevention, is thus flawed, causes serious harm to human dignity and infringes on citizens' autonomy.

Apart from the deontological normative critique, other central elements of Beccaria's approach raise difficulties that support the conclusion that deterrence cannot hold as a sole justification for punishment.

B. Severity and Certainty

In the second half of the twentieth century, it was a popular assumption that severe punishments lead to greater deterrence. In the United States of America this widespread perception encouraged astronomical increases in incarceration.[24] It is only more recently that it has been recognised that severe punishments are not necessarily more effective than milder punishments at preventing recidivism and/or deterring members of the public, and they may even have criminogenic effects.[25]

[23] Kremnitzer, above n 19 at 164.

[24] See H Lernau, *Criminal Behavior and Law Enforcement* (Haifa, Pardes Press, 2016) (in Hebrew) 67. See also National Research Council, *The Growth of Incarceration in the United States: Exploring Causes and Consequences* (2014) 9, 13 (finding that '[a]fter decades of stability from the 1920s to the early 1970s, the rate of incarceration in the United States has increased to a rate more than four times higher than in 1972 … with nearly 1 out of every 100 adults in prison or jail', and warning that 'these high rates of incarceration themselves constitute a source of injustice and, possibly, social harm').

[25] See, eg, AN Doob & CM Webster, 'Sentence Severity and Crime: Accepting the Null Hypothesis' (2003) 30 *Crime & Justice* 143 at 143 (asserting that 'sentence severity has no effect on the level of crime in society'); DS Nagin & G Pogarsky, 'Integrating Celerity, Impulsivity, and Extralegal Sanction Threats into a Model of General Deterrence: Theory and Practice' (2001) 39 *Criminology* 865 at 883 (finding that 'the certainty main effect is far more robust than is the severity main effect'); J Fagan & TL Mears, 'Punishment, Deterrence and Social Control: The Paradox of Punishment in Minority Communities' (2008) 6 *Ohio State Journal of Criminal Law* 173 at 173 (stressing that 'recent experiments have shown that among persons of color, especially those who are poor or reside in poor neighborhoods, harsher punishment has produced iatrogenic or counterdeterrent effects'). It has been argued, however, that findings such as these might be more common in the United States, where sanctions are already very severe, whereas in other countries, with softer criminal sanctions, severity may carry greater weight: see SP Roche et al, 'Perceived Control, Severity, Certainty, and Emotional Fear: Testing an Expanded Model of Deterrence' (2019) 57 *Journal of Research in Crime and Delinquency* 493 at 521 note 1.

These findings would not have come as a surprise to Beccaria. When identifying and assessing the deterrent factors, he suggested that it was not (primarily) the *severity* of the punishment but rather its *inevitability* that generated the deterrent effect:

> [O]ne of the most effective brakes on crime is not the harshness of its punishment, but the unerringness of punishment ... The certainty of even a mild punishment will make a bigger impression than the fear of a more awful one which is united to a hope of not being punished at all.[26]

Beccaria, like modern adherents of the economic approach to punishment, here assumes that human beings are rational agents who seek to maximise their personal benefit. From that perspective, delinquent behaviour is a calculated choice, chosen amongst other possible modes of action.[27] The agent evaluates her expected gain as a derivative of the ratio between the profit she expects to derive from the offence (mainly economic but also emotional, psychological, etc) and the risk of being caught and punished. Increasing the probability of punishment will therefore markedly reduce the potential perpetrator's profit calculation, which factors in the risk of apprehension, and this will weaken or annihilate her incentive for committing the offence.[28]

This proposition about the deterrent effects of punishment's certainty, however, suffers from some noticeable deficiencies.

First and foremost, as von Hirsch et al explained, deterrence is subjective. It depends less on the objective certainty that punishment will indeed be endured by potential offenders than on whether or not they *believe* it will ensue.[29] Studies have shown that there is only a weak connection between the objective likelihood of punishment and the prevailing public assumptions (even among those with a criminal past) regarding the chances of getting caught and the severity of the punishment.[30] In addition, deterrence is largely subjective because it depends on how potential offenders *evaluate* their chances of succeeding or

[26] Beccaria, above n 7 at 63 (ch 27).

[27] Lernau, above n 24 at 61; Eldar, above n 3 at xxiv.

[28] Ibid at 55–56.

[29] A von Hirsch et al, *Criminal Deterrence and Sentence Severity: An Analysis of Recent Research* (Oxford, Hart Publishing, 1999) 6 (emphasising that even if the state decides to expand law enforcement, for marginal deterrence to succeed five conditions must be met: 'a potential offender must realize that the probability of conviction or the severity of punishment has changed ...; a potential offender must take these altered risks into account when deciding whether to offend ...; a potential offender must believe that there is a non-negligible likelihood of being caught ...; a potential offender must believe that the altered penalty will be applied to him if he is caught ...; a potential offender must be willing to alter his or her choices regarding offending in the light of the perceived change in certainty or severity of punishment ...').

[30] Lernau, above n 24 at 68 (citing FE Zimring & GJ Hawkins, *Deterrence: The Legal Threat in Crime Control* (Chicago IL, University of Chicago Press, 1973), EG Owens & SB Bushway, 'Framing Punishment: A New Look at the Incarceration and Deterrence' (Paper presented at the Cornell University Conference on Empirical Legal Studies, Cornell University, 2008); and G Kleck, 'Constricted Rationality and the Limits of General Deterrence', in TS Blomberg & S Cohen (eds), *Punishment and Social Control* (New York, Aldine De Gruyter, 2003) 291).

failing. Offenders often believe they can control the risk of apprehension, or they optimistically assume that this risk is negligible anyway.[31]

In short, deterrent effects depend on potential offenders' assessments of getting caught. These assessments, in turn, depend on the behavioural, psychological, cognitive and socio-economic characteristics of these individuals.[32] Thus, in order to create an effective deterrence system that will lead to changes in offender behaviour, these characteristics must be given due consideration, which renders the calculus for general deterrence extremely complex and difficult to make.

This deficit of certainty then pushes the pendulum back to the question of severity. Moreover, despite advances in technology and science over the years, such as new measures of documentation and surveillance that have increased the abilities to trace and collect evidence, enforcement is still imperfect. It is thus not irrational for potential offenders to assume that they can avoid consequences for their criminal behaviour. In order to mitigate that optimism, utilitarians then often return to the notion of severity to worsen the risk-benefit calculation on the part of potential offenders.[33] This tendency towards aggravation, however, may push for much harsher penalties than those deserved. Such a tendency is particularly problematic in cases of reduced guilt – for example, crimes committed under great temptation, grave pressure or strong mental impulse.[34]

C. Imminence of Punishment

Another prominent element Beccaria emphasised, which still constitutes an important aspect of deterrence theory, is that a sentence should be as prompt and immediate as possible (celerity):[35]

> [T]he stronger and more lasting the association in the human mind between the two ideas *crime* and *punishment* … [the more the] former will come to be sensed as the cause and the latter as the necessary, and inexorable effect.[36]

[31] A von Hirsch et al, above n 29 at 6; RT Wright et al, *Burglars on the Job: Street Life and Residential Break-Ins* (Boston MA, Northeastern University Press, 2011) 197–198. The problem of evaluating probability of risks produces various sorts of difficulties not only for potential offenders but also for regulators: see CR Sunstein, 'Probability Neglect: Emotions, Worst Cases, and Law' (2012) 112 *Yale Law Journal* 61.

[32] For example, street offences (including violent offences, drug and property-related offences) are usually committed by criminals who have grown up in a particular socio-economic environment, which often makes it difficult to make rational and calculated decisions. See Lernau, above n 24 at 67–68. To this, we should add the fact that these offences are often carried out impulsively, under social pressure or under the influence of substances such as alcohol or drugs, factors that weaken the rational agency of perpetrators and their susceptibility to deterrence.

[33] White, above n 12 at 320.

[34] Nussbaum takes this a few steps further, asserting that criminal justice systems should not neglect the particular circumstances of the offenders but rather follow the Greek principle of *epieikeia*, which she interprets as 'the ability to judge in such a way as to respond with sensitivity

At its core, celerity of punishment after the crime can be seen as enhancing the moralising effect that punishment of crime has on an offender: the sooner the punishment is endured, the deeper the impression it will have on her.[37]

Over the past few decades, it has been suggested that it is not immediate punishment that deters potential criminals but rather the lengthy and 'painful' process that leads to its imposition, and which involves a high degree of uncertainty.[38] But even if one accepts that celerity advances deterrence, enforcement limitations and due process requirements inevitably produce significant time gaps between the stages of offending, apprehension, trial and verdict. Moreover, there is usually a positive correlation between the severity of the punishment and the level of certainty in the guilt of the offender: the graver the potential sentence, the greater the caution needed before attributing the crime, which inevitably involves higher procedural barriers.[39] Since such barriers do not allow for speedy proceedings, they reduce the celerity of punishment, and thus decrease deterrence. Here again, the attempt to secure deterrence may take the shape of increased penalties to counteract the reduction in deterrent effect caused by the loss of immediacy. But, as we explained above, increases in severity bear their own difficulties.

D. Public Punishments

As mentioned in section III.B, a crucial element of deterrence is the impression and impact the punishment produces in people's minds. Indeed, the visual element of punishment during Beccaria's time must not be underestimated. In the eighteenth century, the offender's submission and humiliation were achieved by forms of punishment that had a direct and intimidating effect on the public. Executions and punishments such as public torture, amputation, disfigurement of the face or body, beatings, stoning, burning, crucifixion and other horrific

to all the particulars of a person and situation, and the "inclination of the mind" toward leniency in punishing – equity and mercy'. See MC Nussbaum, 'Equity and Mercy' (1993) 22 *Philosophy & Public Affairs* 83 at 85–86.

[35] According to HLA Hart, Bentham endorsed Beccaria's notion that punishment must be both speedy and certain for together they 'fortify the association of ideas between punishment and crime' (HLA Hart, 'Bentham and Beccaria', in his *Essays on Bentham: Jurisprudence and Political Theory* (Oxford, Clarendon Press, 1982) 40 at 47.

[36] Beccaria, above n 7 at 49 (ch 19).

[37] KC Kennedy, 'A Critical Appraisal of Criminal Deterrence Theory' (1983) 88 *Dickinson Law Review* 1 at 4 note 27.

[38] A Pathinayake, 'Should We Deter against General Deterrence' (2018) 9 *Wake Forest Journal of Law & Policy* 63 at 85, referring also to G Loewenstein, 'Anticipating and the Valuation of Delayed Consumption' (1987) 97 *The Economic Journal* 666.

[39] Lernau, above n 24 at 68, citing L Sebba, 'Relief of Punishment as a Means of Deterrence' (1979) 7 *Crime and Social Deviance* 125 (in Hebrew).

penalties were carried out in the city centres and served as a kind of a local carnival.[40]

In the violent atmosphere of a legal system based on brutal displays of cruelty for all to see, Beccaria denounced the widespread use of torture and the death penalty and presented convincing arguments for reducing them.[41] However, in order not to allow the powerful and rich to set a price for attacks against the weak and the poor, he argued that in contrast to crimes against property, crimes against the person must be punished, without exception, with corporal punishment (which for Beccaria included imprisonment and penal servitude).[42] Added to that, he asserted that the law ought to be evident and transparent in the public sphere. This should be achieved, he explained, both *ex ante* through clear legislative provisions, strictly applied,[43] and *ex post* by imposing public and visible punishments. Such transparency would expose the public to the criminal justice system, lead them to internalise the connection between crimes and punishments, and leave a long-lasting and daunting impression on both the offender and the public:[44]

> It is not the terrible but fleeting sight of a felon's death which is the most powerful brake on crime, but the long-drawn-out example of a man deprived of freedom, who having become a beast of burden, repays the society which he has offended with his labour.[45]

Today, not only are corporal punishment and penal servitude considered completely unacceptable and illegitimate in the majority of western democracies, but modern sentences are diverted from the public eye to isolated prisons. Sociologists have offered different explanations for the transition from public physical punishments to imprisonment as the primary mode of (serious) punishment, with, for example, Norbert Elias stressing the modern sensitivity to such severe violence and Michel Foucault suggesting that there is no longer a need for violent force to control the public.[46] Whatever the reasons, Beccaria's

[40] Lernau, above n 24 at 37–38. For a classic account of penal culture in Europe from the Middle Ages to the Enlightenment, see P Spierenburg, *The Spectacle of Suffering: Executions and the Evolution of Repression* (Cambridge, Cambridge University Press, 1984).

[41] Eldar, above n 3 at xv. See also Beccaria, above n 7 (ch 16).

[42] Beccaria, above n 7 at 50 (ch 20).

[43] Ibid at 17 (ch 5).

[44] Ibid at 31 (ch 12). Beccaria's opposition to judicial interpretation of the law is further discussed by Thorburn, ch 7 in this volume. Beccaria added that verdicts and proofs of guilt should also be made public. See Beccaria, above n 7 at 36 (ch 14).

[45] Beccaria, above n 7 at 67 (ch 28).

[46] AN Tennenbaum & S Levy, 'The Sweeping Transition from Physical Punishment to Imprisonment – Between Elias and Foucault and Future Implications', in D Han et al (eds), *Gabriel Bach Book* (Srigim Li-On, Nevo Publishing, 2011) 305 (in Hebrew). According to Foucault, technology has led to a new approach that enables the state to supervise and control the criminal not through physical means, but through 'a system of constraints and privations, obligations and prohibitions'. The weight had shifted from controlling the criminal's physical body to controlling and supervising the criminal's mind. See M Foucault, *Discipline and Punish: The Birth of the Prison* translated by A Sheridan (New York, Random House, 1979) at 11.

strong support for punishments that are open for all to see is utterly rejected and condemned in modern democracies, and consequently it could be suggested that removing the violent and the visual-public element from punishment, and placing the punishment act away from the public eye, weakens at least to some degree Beccaria's deterrence. In reply, it should be noted that Beccaria's primary aim was to mitigate the cruelty of the penal system. His notion of publicity of punishment did not involve aggravation of the punishments in use during his time, for they were already extremely public. Applying the demand of publicity to the punishments presently in use would, by contrast, exacerbate the severity of these punishments, and as such it is likely to have been rejected by Beccaria.

IV. SUGGESTION FOR AN INTEGRATIVE READING OF BECCARIA – A HUMANISTIC DETERRENCE

Singular principles aspire to their full implementation at the expense of other considerations; in the words of Judge Benjamin Cardozo, it is 'the tendency of a principle to expand itself to the limit of its logic'.[47] Not least to counteract this tendency, the balancing of various principles is likely to produce more reasonable and moderate results. In the present context, while it is widely recognised that deterrence is a centrepiece of our criminal justice system,[48] it is hardly disputable, as we have shown above, that there are solid empirical and normative reasons that make it difficult for this principle to operate as the sole justification and measurement for punishment.[49]

In any event it would be a mistake to read Beccaria's version of deterrence as crude or simplistic. His notions of certainty, severity, celerity and publicity were not intended to provide a list to be followed to maximise deterrence. They have to be seen, instead, as components of a broader humanistic theory of criminal law – one that provides a nuanced and delicate understanding of deterrence alongside the need to tame and curb it. While Beccaria had an immense influence on utilitarian philosophy and substantively affected Jeremy Bentham,[50]

[47] BN Cardozo, *The Nature of the Judicial Process* [1921] (New Haven CT, Yale University Press, 1968) 51.

[48] This is not to say, however, that there is consensus regarding the degree of deterrence the criminal rules provide. Robinson and Darley famously argued that while 'having a punishment system does deter … there is growing evidence to suggest skepticism about … the ability to deter crime through the manipulation of criminal law rules and penalties': PH Robinson & JM Darley, 'The Role of Deterrence in the Formulation of Criminal Law Rules: At Its Worst When Doing Its Best' (2003) 91 *Georgetown Law Journal* 949 at 951. Still, the general effectiveness of deterrence has been well recognised both by lawmakers and theorists: see von Hirsch et al, above n 29 at 1 (stating 'there are also good reasons for believing the criminal justice system as a whole exercises deterrence effect … To the question, "does deterrence ever work?" our answer is that it clearly does.').

[49] There are other difficulties that we did not address here, such as Beccaria's notion that the public good is the correct guide for scaling offences in terms of severity (see Beccaria, above n 7 at 22 (ch 7)).

[50] As Bentham wrote, 'It was from Beccaria's little treatise on crimes and punishments that I drew as I well remember the first hint of the principle by which the precision and clearness and

Gary Becker and Richard Posner, he was not purely committed to utilitarianism.[51] His perspective on deterrence was accompanied by considerations of equality, compassion and a clear aspiration for both penal and social justice.

By incorporating such further considerations into his approach, Beccaria cultivated a multifaceted outlook on deterrence; one that can, and should, be used as a source of inspiration in modern democratic criminal law systems. We will first outline these considerations and then show their relevance for present-day criminal justice.

A. A Quest for Social Justice

Beccaria, as a political philosopher, understood the limited role of punishment in reducing the crime rate and the deep roots of criminality in an unjust socio-economic reality. His quest to promote social justice is a central theme throughout the book.[52]

The first point that should be noted in this context is Beccaria's demand for equality in the rule of law:

> [P]unishments ought to be the same for the highest as they are for the lowest of citizens. To be legitimate, every distinction whether of honour or wealth presupposes an antecedent equality based on the laws, which treat every subject as equally subordinate to them.[53]

To suggest that the rich should be subject to the same methods of punishment as the poor was considered a rather new idea. But Beccaria did not stop there. He acknowledged that the possibilities of action facing criminals and the calculation of cost-benefit are affected by social conditions. A striking example of this can be found in his imagined monologue of a poor person who justifies his prohibited deed:

> What are these laws which I have to obey, which leave such a gulf between me and the rich man? He denies me the penny I beg of him, brushing me off with a demand that I should work, something he knows nothing about. Who made these laws? Rich and

incontestableness of mathematical calculations are introduced for the first time into the field of morals.' See in HLA Hart, above n 35 at 40, citing *The Works of Jeremy Bentham* III (11 vols, published under the superintendence of John Bowring, Edinburgh, 1838–1843).

[51] White, above n 12 at 316 (citing GS Becker, 'Crime and Punishment: An Economic Approach' (1968) 76 *Journal of Political Economy* 169; GS Becker, 'The Economic Way of Looking at Behavior' (1993) 101 *Journal of Political Economy* 385; and RA Posner, 'Retribution and Related Concepts of Punishments' (1980) 9 *Journal of Legal Studies* 71).

[52] For a more extensive reading on the role of equality in Beccaria's writing, see A Burgio, 'Introduction: Between Law and Politics – The Idea of Equality in *On Crimes and Punishments*', in C Beccaria, *On Crimes and Punishments* translated by A Thomas & J Parzen (Toronto, University of Toronto Press, 2009).

[53] Beccaria, above n 7 at 51 (ch 21).

> powerful men, who have never condescended to visit the filthy hovels of the poor, who have never broken mouldy bread among the innocent cries of starving children and a wife's tears. Let us break these ties, which are pernicious to most people and only useful to a few and to idle tyrants; let us attack injustice at its source. I shall return to my natural state of independence; for a while I shall live free and happy on the fruits of my courage and industry; perhaps the day for suffering and repentance will come, but it will be brief, and I shall have one day of pain for many years of freedom and pleasure. King of a small band of men, I shall put to rights iniquities of fortune, and I shall see these tyrants blanch and cower at one whom they considered, with insulting ostentation, lower than their horses and dogs.[54]

Beccaria also acknowledged the complexity of crimes committed by perpetrators who were themselves victims of unequal power relations. An instructive example of this can be seen in his chapter on 'Crimes Difficult to Prove', where he addresses one of the biggest taboos – a woman wanting to kill her child:

> Likewise, infanticide results from the unavoidable conflict in which a woman is placed if she has given in to weakness or violence. How could one who finds herself caught between disgrace and the death of a being unable to feel what harms it, not prefer the latter to the certain misery to which she and her unhappy fruit would be exposed? The best way to prevent this crime would be have effective laws to protect the weak against the tyranny which exacerbates those vices which cannot cover themselves with the mantle of virtue.[55]

He then goes on to say:

> I do not mean to belittle the just revulsion which these crimes deserve. But, having pointed out their sources, I think I am allowed to draw a general conclusion, which is that one cannot say that a punishment for a crime is exactly just (meaning necessary) until the law has instituted the best possible means in a given nation's circumstances for preventing such a crime.[56]

In 1768 Voltaire wrote in his commentary on *On Crimes and Punishments*, 'I should limit myself to hope that we all and often reread this great work by this lover of humanity'.[57] Indeed, Beccaria's recognition of the complex power relations that bring victims to become victimisers, his ability to put himself in the perpetrator's shoes, and his distinctly humanistic view that punishment will only be justified when society has done everything in its power to prevent the sources of crime are invaluable lessons that ought to shape policy today.

[54] Ibid at 69 (ch 28). Original emphasis omitted. Eldar offers a similar reading of this part, see above n 3 at xxx.

[55] Beccaria, above n 7 at 81 (ch 31).

[56] Ibid at 81–82 (ch 31).

[57] Voltaire, 'Commentaire sur le livre Des delits et des peines, par un avocat de province' in *Voltaire, Oeuvres completes* vol 5 (Paris, Houssiaux, 1853) 411, cited in Harcourt, above n 6 at 42.

B. Prevention through Education

Beccaria believed that constructing a just society is a more efficient means for preventing crime than relying on punitive deterrence. And he did not leave this notion as a general utopian proposition but suggested concrete steps to promote prevention through education, emphasising that

> the surest but hardest way to prevent crime is to improve education … it encourages virtue by the easy path of the feelings, and diverts men away from evil by the infallible method of alerting them to the necessary ill consequences it brings, rather than by the uncertain method of ordering them what to do, which gains only a feigned and fleeting obedience.[58]

This quotation shows his belief that the most effective way of preventing crime is not via commands but through attaining virtue – that is, through instilling moral obligations to obey the law.[59] This is a form of education that is aligned with the retributive approach.

It is true that incarceration allows prisoners to be offered education and rehabilitation, and the field of correctional education has been widely explored and developed.[60] Still, the conditions of imprisonment are far from being ideal circumstances for such efforts, and for many it might already be too late.[61] As Brinig and Garrison show, recent studies have demonstrated that good pre-school programmes and parent training are associated with a substantial decrease in criminal activity. Programmes meant to advance more calculated decision-making amongst underprivileged youth yield promising outcomes.[62] And these are but narrow segments of education.

Education provides individuals with tools of choice and reason that help them to choose paths compatible with the demands of the law (as well as tools of critique by which to identify when the law is no longer moral and just).

[58] Beccaria, above n 7 at 110 (ch 45).

[59] For a discussion of the tensions between Beccaria's commitment to limited government and his call for policies to encourage virtue, and for an interpretation of Beccaria's conception of virtue as civic virtue, see Duff and Marshall, ch 3 in this volume.

[60] See, eg, LM Davis et al, *Evaluating the Effectiveness of Correctional Education: A Meta-Analysis of Programs That Provide Education to Incarcerated Adults* (Santa Monica CA, Rand Corporation, 2013); NG Vandala, 'The Transformative Effect of Correctional Education: A Global Perspective' (2019) 5 *Cogent Social Sciences* 1 (both suggest findings that support the positive long-term effects of correctional education).

[61] This is perhaps mostly evident in the United States, where studies have shown that 'the lack of education among those who land on death row is striking': JD Bessler, 'Revisiting Beccaria's Vision: The Enlightenment, America's Death Penalty, and the Abolition Movement' (2009) 4 *Northwestern Journal of Law & Social Policy* 195 at 283 note 661 (referring to other studies that show that 'most individuals on death row fall below the poverty line, and many can neither read nor write').

[62] MF Brinig & M Garrison, 'The Invisible Prison: Pathways and Prevention' (2020) 95 *Notre Dame Law Review* 1439 at 1488 notes 218–221; B Duke, 'A Meta-Analysis Comparing Education Attainment Prior to Incarceration and Recidivism Rates in Relation to Correctional Education' (2018) 69 *Journal of Correctional Education* 44.

As Paternoster put it, Beccaria, in that sense, echoed Rousseau's Emile much more than Bentham's Panopticon.[63]

C. Proportionality and Guilt

As already mentioned at the beginning of section II, Beccaria sought to limit the use of force to the bare minimum necessary to achieve deterrence.[64] The punishment, he said, should be 'as lenient as possible on him who undergoes it'.[65] While supporters of the positive retributivist approach[66] would oppose this view, there is clearly common ground between this position and negative retributivist theory.[67] Indeed, unlike in the writings of contemporary utilitarian theorists, some essential retributivist principles can be identified in Beccaria's writings.[68]

This claim of ours might seem puzzling given that, in his chapter on 'Errors in the Measuring of Punishments', Beccaria explicitly rejects the view that 'the true measure of criminality lies in the malefactor's intention'.[69] He explains that given the varied dispositions of the mind and the 'very swift succession of ideas, emotions and circumstances', basing criminality on intention would make it necessary 'to frame not only a special code of laws for each citizen, but also a new law for each particular crime'.[70] And yet, when he expresses compassion towards a mother who 'has given in to weakness or violence' and must choose 'between disgrace and the death of a being unable to feel what harms it' – he accepts the retributivist perspective on the importance of motives;[71]

[63] R Paternoster, 'How Much Do We Really Know about Criminal Deterrence' (2010) 100 *Journal of Criminal Law & Criminology* 765 at 770.

[64] Beccaria, above n 7 at 31 (ch 12).

[65] Ibid at 48 (ch 19).

[66] White, above n 12 at 326, citing JL Mackie. Mackie first distinguished between positive and negative retributivism in JL Mackie, 'Morality and the Retributive Emotions' (1982) 1 *Criminal Justice Ethics* 1. At its core, positive retributivism holds 'the principle that one who is guilty ought to be punished', whereas negative retributivism maintains 'the principle that one who is not guilty must not be punished' (ibid at 4).

[67] From a practical point of view, there seems to be tension between the punishment that is intended to leave the strongest impression, and the choice of the mildest or most lenient punishment among the appropriate penalties. It is therefore doubtful whether the implementation of Beccaria's proposal would lead to the adoption of the more lenient punishment.

[68] White, above n 12 at 327. See also in M De Caro, 'Utilitarianism and Retributivism in Cesare Beccaria' (2016) 2 *The Italian Law Journal* 1 at 1 (stating that 'one should consider Beccaria as a forerunner of utilitarianism, but not an outright utilitarian').

[69] Beccaria, above n 7 at 22 (ch 7).

[70] Ibid. Discussed in S Eldar & E Laist, 'The Irrelevance of Motive and the Rule of Law' (2017) 20 *New Criminal Law Review* 433 at 435.

[71] According to Eldar, Beccaria's statement that '[t]here is no liberty whenever the laws permit a man in some cases to cease to be a person and to become a thing' resembles Kant's categorical imperative in his second formulation: 'Act in such a way that you treat humanity, whether in your own person or in the person of any other, never merely as a means to an end, but always at the same time as an end.' See Eldar, above n 3 at xxxii.

and unlike classical utilitarians, he opposes punishments that are unjust, even if their consequences are good or beneficial.[72] This is why John Bessler is correct in observing that 'Beccaria's philosophy certainly contains retributivist strains'.[73]

Beccaria's acknowledgement of the significance of guilt and proportionality, then, is an instructive example of his integrative approach to punishment. Essentially, he hoped for a just society, based on rationality and impartiality, and for that to be achieved – as he brilliantly understood – deterrence will not suffice.

V. PROPOSAL FOR INTEGRATIVE SENTENCING OF CRIMES

It has been suggested that a viable way to explain Beccaria's solid support of deterrence and his simultaneous genuine concern with proportionality and other justice considerations that resemble retributivism is to characterise his position as a version of what HLA Hart described as a *hybrid model* of punishment, in which punishment's justifying aim and the method of imposing and distributing it can differ.[74] This kind of analysis is definitely valuable for philosophers, but is perhaps less useful for practitioners.

We suggest, therefore, a different type of hybridity, namely, to maintain guilt as the basis for punishment while preserving the principle of deterrence, provided that it is tamed and limited by justice (retribution). Furthermore, following Beccaria, we contend that a distinction between different categories of crimes is required, or at least might be of help when considering the weight to be given to deterrence and retributivism respectively. To set out our argument, we use examples of economic crime, including political corruption, and crimes under international law. But first a few general comments should be made regarding the reciprocal relations between three central purposes of punishment. As can be seen, there are strong and significant interrelations between the various punishment considerations.

At the basis of retribution is the belief that a wrongful act ought to be punished proportionately. Thus, at its core, retributivism entails a strong element of condemnation.[75] Naturally, this condemnation creates a deterrent effect, which – as already mentioned briefly above – comprises both general and individual prevention. The former refers to punishment's intended effect of deterring the general public from committing crimes, whereas the latter

[72] Christopher, above n 17 at 867 note 128.

[73] Bessler, above n 61 at 282 note 656.

[74] See White, above n 12 at 327. Somewhat similarly, Christopher suggested that modern 'mixed' theories that integrate different theses of punishment – such as Hart's – are Beccaria's 'intellectual heirs' (above n 17 at 867).

[75] Kremnitzer, above n 19 at 161.

refers to its intended effect in steering the criminal away from recidivism.[76] Condemnation serves severity, certainty, publicity and – especially in a world of social media – celerity, and therefore enhances the effectiveness of deterrence. Another similarity between retribution and deterrence is the importance to both of the societal rejection of a crime, manifested by a calculated and well-thought-out punishment.[77] In contrast to Hegel's and Kant's criticism above, deterrence should not be reduced to intimidation; its effects arise from reinforcing, in the eyes of the offender and the whole of society, the validity of the norm the offender violated. Therefore, deterrence cannot be viewed simply as using persons as means; on the contrary – it conveys a clear message of reason. Instead of directing public anger to violence, a legal response, through the imposition of punishments, supports the prevention of crimes and strengthens the reinforcement of the rule of law and the public's pre-existing commitment to it. And it is this element of retribution (a deserved reaction to a committed crime, which upholds the rule of law) that corresponds to expressivism. Expressivism (which is also called positive prevention) sees criminal law as a system for the reinforcement of norms so that the public internalise them and then voluntarily comply with them.[78] The punishment is intended to validate the protected value of the attacked and violated norm,[79] so that the intentional suffering entailed in the punishment conveys a positive educational message. In this way, the public are expected to deduce the wrongfulness of the criminal action from the sentence imposed for it.

These tight interdependencies between retribution, deterrence and expressivism indicate that the perception that there is one, and only one, rationale for punishment leads to analytical and practical difficulties. However, this does not mean that there is no room for emphasising deterrence over retribution, or vice versa, for certain crimes, provided they are restrained by justice considerations and provided they continue to impose checks and balances on one another.

A. Economic Crime and Political Corruption

It has been widely contended that, unlike street crimes, which are often committed spontaneously, economic crimes are instrumental and calculated and thus more prone to be reduced by general deterrence.[80] In addition, in these kinds

[76] Ibid at 162.

[77] Ibid.

[78] Ibid (citing MA Drumbl, *Atrocity, Punishment, and International Law* (Cambridge, Cambridge University Press, 2007) 173–174).

[79] Ibid (citing J Andenaes, 'The General Preventive Effects of Punishment' (1966) 114 *University of Pennsylvania Law Review* 949 at 963).

[80] This conviction has been highlighted by the Israeli Supreme Court in various cases, eg CA 1656/16 *Davidovich v The State of Israel* (Published in Nevo, 20.03.2017) (in Hebrew) (where Justice Yoram Danziger wrote, at para 103, 'These offences are characterised, for the most part, by being inherently instrumental offences. They require planning, resourcefulness and creativity,

of cases deterrence also serves the need to convey an educational message of crime seriousness through severity of punishment.[81] This message is needed because the harm to society that results from many economic crimes, although very serious, is more abstract, less direct and, therefore, less obvious to the public at large. Offenders and their hired aides tend to contest the legitimacy of the prohibitions and alter their stigmatisation. This tendency is vivid in cases involving large multinational corporations, entities that often have greater financial resources and means of influencing public opinion than states, and which therefore can be powerful enough to ensure immunity for their activities. Dealing effectively with their criminality requires an analysis of the structural mechanisms, especially within corporations, that neutralise or diminish awareness of the nature and significance of criminal activity within the corporation. In another paper, one of us (MK) suggested that in order to overcome this problem without breaching the principle of culpability, criminal liability should be imposed on the corporation in addition to the individual criminal liability of the perpetrators.[82] Such imposition is intended to enable retribution to the full extent by making the corporation accountable for the mitigation of individual responsibility that results from its internal workings and messaging. The need to consider deterrence is enhanced by the positive bias towards offenders who are 'like us', or towards those ranking high in society (as opposed to the negative bias against blue-collar offenders, deemed 'different from us' and usually ranking low in society, that has to be offset in the opposite direction). Of course, the emphasis on deterrence does not, in any way, marginalise the requirement for guilt and proportionality.

and the main goal in front of the offender's eyes is to make a financial profit from committing the offence. Unlike other offences that may be committed in the heat of the moment, the perpetrator of an economic offence acts as a rational person calculating a profit of an offence against its loss.'); CA 677/14 *Dankner v The State of Israel* (Published in Nevo, 17.07.2014) (in Hebrew) (where Justice Elyakim Rubinstein emphasised, at para xxxviii, 'In my opinion, even those who do not believe that general deterrence, perhaps unlike individual deterrence, works in the "classic" crimes of murder, robbery and rape … might think it has a chance for economic offences, at least in "white collar" crimes. The one who plans an offence and hears that his sentence may be imprisonment, might think twice.').

[81] Some scholars have suggested that this trend (of aggravating punishment both by the Israeli Supreme Court and by the Israeli legislature in cases of economic offences) requires rethinking, both because the court and the public have already assimilated the seriousness of these crimes and because 'the adoption of a principled policy of punishment … may deviate from the unique features of the act and the individual defendant': G Eshet, 'Economic Offences in Israel', in O Gordon (ed), *Edmond Levy Book* (Srigim Li-On, Nevo Publishing, 2017) (in Hebrew) 485 at 520. Eshet refers to similar criticism which was made with respect to the US federal system's approach to economic crimes, eg ES Podgor, 'The Challenge of White Collar Sentencing' (2007) 97 *Journal of Criminal Law & Criminology* 731.

[82] M Kremnitzer, 'A Possible Case for Imposing Criminal Liability on Corporations in International Criminal Law' (2010) 8 *Journal of International Criminal Justice* 909. Among the arguments made to justify imposing criminal liability on corporations are, first, consistency (if the corporations is a bearer of rights and duties it should also be held accountable when it commits crimes); second, sometimes, imposing criminal liability on the corporation is the only way to enable accountability; third, similarly to the 'small fry' justification in international criminal law (see section V.B), when low-ranking officials are blamed whereas the corporations enjoy impunity, justice is undermined and lack of public trust in the legal system is increased.

A similar logic applies to political corruption. Politicians have an immense influence on public opinion. When suspected of political corruption, they often belittle and downplay the offences, attack the law enforcement agencies and claim that 'such are the ways of politics' or that all politicians act the same. As described by Beccaria:

> Attacks on citizens' security and freedom are among the greatest crimes, and into this class fall not only the murders and thefts practiced by common people, but also those of the nobility and magistrates, whose influence is wider and has a greater effect, destroying the subjects' faith in the ideas of justice and duty, and replacing it with the notion that might is right, which is as dangerous in him who adopts it as it is in him who suffers from it.[83]

Thus, the penal response to these offences ought to reflect their seriousness, as well as the integrity of and necessity for law enforcement.

B. International Criminal Law

In international criminal law (ICL), like domestic criminal law, punishments are typically justified by two rationales – retribution and prevention. Yet over the past two decades, the former has been heavily criticised for being a problematic justification in the international setting.[84] Nevertheless, there are two important reasons to favour retribution in ICL, provided that it is adjoined to and balanced with deterrence.[85]

First, from time immemorial, retribution, or in its ancient form 'an eye for an eye', has been strongly connected to the law's legitimacy for the general public, and it seems hard to even imagine our civilisation without it.[86] Thus, given the weakening legitimacy of ICL, especially in terms of adjudication, retribution has an important role in providing a strong moral ground in the face of increasing hesitancy and declining cooperation by states. Second, retribution, or more precisely its inherent principle of proportionality, assists in reducing two

[83] Beccaria, above n 7 at 25 (ch 8).

[84] Kremnitzer, above n 19 at 161 (citing MA Niggli, 'Security as a Goal of Criminal Justice', presented at the Asian Society's 4th Annual Conference, 20–22 August 2012, 1 at 4–5; K Günther, 'The Criminal Law of "Guilt" as Subject of a Politics of Remembrance in Democracies', in E Christodoulidis & S Veitch (eds), *Lethe's Law: Justice, Law and Ethics in Reconciliation* (Oxford, Hart Publishing, 2001) 3 at 4–5). See also Drumbl, above n 78. According to Koller, retribution arguments were criticised already at Nuremberg. See DS Koller, 'The Faith of the International Criminal Lawyer' (2008) 40 *New York University Journal of International Law & Politics* 1019 at 1026.

[85] Kremnitzer, above n 19 at 161. The argument that will be made here regarding the importance of retribution in ICL is developed in more detail in that article.

[86] Ibid at 163 (citing Aristotle, *The Nicomachean Ethics* translated by D Ross (Oxford, Oxford University Press, 2009) 1132b; Genesis 3:14–24; Epistle to the Colossians 3:23–25.) See also JR Steffen, 'Moral Cognition in Criminal Punishment' (2020) 9 *British Journal of American Legal Studies* 143 at 146 (citing Exodus 21:22–25).

major threats that cast their shadows over ICL – the risk of over-punishing the small fry, and despair at the limited prospects of arresting and sentencing the 'big fish'. And it is at this point where retribution and deterrence are adjoined to serve ICL.

In a recent paper, one of us (MK) proposed a 'principle of conservation of criminal energy',[87] meaning that when the criminal liability of the small fry, the subordinates, is reduced on account of their having acted under orders, or in conditions close to duress, it should not be 'lost' but rather attributed to the big fish. This theoretical move can be justified by three interrelated and widely acknowledged explanations: first, the small fry are not responsible for the initiating and the shaping of the overall criminal policy leading to the atrocities; they are merely screws in the machinery of evil. Second, those who did establish the criminal mechanisms and installed them in the domestic order should be held accountable for both their own and their subordinates' actions. Third, the right of victims to full legal relief for their suffering includes punishments that fully reflect the culpability of all offenders.[88]

This proposition correlates with both deterrence and prevention. In the absence of an international police force, an aggravated sentence serves both these rationales. If high-ranking officials are accountable not only for their own doings but also for what is done by their subordinates, it might increase their reluctance to act, or at least lead them to mitigate their actions. Such an argument assumes that the top-level perpetrators are rational and calculating (as, frighteningly, they indeed often are).[89] In contrast, when it comes to low-level perpetrators, deterrence and prevention might be less efficient, not only because of the threats they may be under and the limited control they hold over the situation, but also because they are often brainwashed into believing in the local criminal propaganda.[90]

At the same time, the difficulty of deterring crimes committed in such circumstances *ex ante* should not detract from the importance of punishing low-ranking officials who do not fall under one of the recognised excuses or defences.[91] A full excuse should apply only in appropriate cases; not every perpetrator who acted under orders should be automatically exempted.[92]

[87] Kremnitzer, above n 19 at 173.

[88] Ibid. This focus by the International Criminal Court, as well as other international criminal tribunals, on the big fish requires that similar attention be paid by state parties, and that every effort should be made to bring high-ranking perpetrators to an impartial trial. This includes making moral concessions (eg not holding the small fry accountable in exchange for charging evidence against the big fish).

[89] Ibid at 173 (citing J von Holderstein Holtermann, 'A "Slice of Cheese": A Deterrence-Based Argument for the International Criminal Court' (2010) 11 *Human Rights Review* 289).

[90] Ibid at 173–174.

[91] The most relevant for this discussion is duress, one of the grounds for excluding criminal responsibility in the Rome Statute (Art 31(d)).

[92] See Kremnitzer, above n 19 at 173–174.

Full exemption or near-complete mitigation should only be considered when low-ranking individuals were brainwashed or operated in extreme circumstances close to duress. Aside from that, some preventive measures are required. The preferable policy is to make the public aware of the gravity as well as the implications of the international crimes that are taking place. This educative method must take place in real time and through all available media forms to expand its reach. Enabling low-ranking perpetrators to gain access to this information can undermine the local propaganda that usually starts to stir the 'hate pot' before or in the early stages of the commission of the actual crimes. It is expressed by racist and 'patriotic' messages that demonise the targeted groups in order to justify the criminal acts that were launched or are soon to be launched against them.[93]

Thus, while we suggest that retribution is the predominant rationale for punishment in ICL in general, there also seems to be considerable room for deterrence with regard to the punishment of high-ranking perpetrators, provided that their punishment does not exceed what they deserve notwithstanding their aggravated liability. In contrast, in relation to the small fry, a deterrence rationale is weaker, whereas retributive considerations are salient.

VI. CONCLUDING REMARKS

People (including philosophers) tend to fall in love with their ideas, to stretch and follow them to their far end, blinded to their problematic and negative outcomes. Beccaria – to his great merit – was different. He was well aware of the downsides of the deterrence approach he was originating. He knew that the conditions for deterrence are hard to fulfil in real life and that deterrence may enhance cruelty in punishment. He therefore introduced proportionality, rational utility and leniency as curbing forces. He regarded criminal law as a heavy hammer. Since it is applied to humans, it must be used reluctantly, with care, prudence and moderation. He also understood that criminal law is not the real battlefield against criminality. The means for – and the challenges of – reducing crime are to bring about a just structure of society and good education. In this chapter we have sought to advance an integrative approach to punishment that draws on Beccaria's rich and multi-dimensional theory of deterrence. We have illustrated how deterrence should be adjoined to retribution and given an important role, without circumventing notions of justice and fairness, in respect of two distinct classes of crimes. But many other lessons can (and should) be learned from Beccaria. Among these is the need to approach crime in a calculated way. For example, following Beccaria and the utilitarian approach he developed,

[93] Ibid at 174.

a careful analysis of the use of prison sentences is required, given their proven negative consequences on the population of prisoners. Imprisonment should be viewed as a last resort, and alternatives, which do not involve the withdrawal of liberty in a closed institution, should be given priority and examined further.[94] It may well be the case that an emotional reaction to crime is unavoidable and perhaps even necessary, but any action in criminal law policy has to be dictated by rationality, knowledge and the modesty appropriate to what we, as jurists, do not know. In this respect, it was to Beccaria's advantage that he was looking at the criminal law from the external perspective of a philosopher attending to the prerequisites for a just society. Furthermore, Beccaria still sets an example of how social conventions ought not to be accepted as such but constantly re-examined and, when not found convincing, rejected.

Last but not least, the talent to write concisely should be cherished and even imitated by the sharpest minds.

[94] For such an argument that draws on Beccaria, see C Barker, 'The Certainty of Punishment and the Proportionality of Incarceration', in C Suprenant (ed), *Rethinking Punishment in the Era of Mass Incarceration* (Abingdon, Routledge, 2018) 69.

12

Human Rights and Criminal Law: From Beccaria's On Crimes and Punishments *to Modern Criminal Law*

MIRIAM GUR-ARYE

I. INTRODUCTION

BECCARIA PERCEIVED HIS essay *On Crimes and Punishments*[1] as a plea for the 'interests of humanity'[2] against 'the savagery and the disorderliness of the procedures of criminal justice'.[3] In arguing for a humane criminal law Beccaria relates to the 'rights of men'.[4] The role Beccaria attaches to the 'rights of men' resembles the role of human rights in modern criminal law – such as the right of due process[5] and the right not to be subjected to cruel, inhuman and degrading punishment[6] – which subjects modern criminal law to constitutional constraints. In this chapter I will discuss the importance attached by Beccaria to the 'rights of men' in different contexts of the criminal law, and will evaluate the relevance of Beccaria's discussions of these rights to modern criminal law. In doing so, I will focus on three different contexts discussed by Beccaria: the rule of law, torture, and the crimes of adultery and sodomy. In the concluding section, I will point out some of the lessons that modern criminal law may learn from Beccaria's discussion in these contexts.

[1] C Beccaria, *On Crimes and Punishments and Other Writings* edited by R Bellamy and translated by R Davies (Cambridge, Cambridge University Press, 1995).

[2] Ibid at 8 (Introduction).

[3] Ibid.

[4] Ibid at 30 (ch 11).

[5] The right of due process is guaranteed by various international documents. See Art 14 of the International Covenant on Civil and Political Rights (ICCPR), 999 UNTS 171; Art 6 of the Convention for the Protection of Human Rights and Fundamental Freedoms (European Convention on Human Rights; ECHR). See also the Fifth and Fourteenth Amendments to the Constitution of the United States of America (US Constitution).

[6] See Art 7 of the ICCPR, Art 3 of the ECHR; Eighth Amendment to the US Constitution.

II. THE RULE OF LAW

Beccaria discusses various aspects that fall under the modern notion of the rule of law.[7] According to him, 'laws alone can decree punishments for crimes, and ... this authority resides only with the legislator, who represents the whole of society united by the social contract'.[8] Therefore, 'a magistrate may not, on any pretext of zeal or concern for the public good whatsoever, increase the punishment laid down by law'.[9] Penal laws should not be obscure, 'written in a language which is not understood by the people'.[10] In interpreting penal laws judges ought not to take into account 'the spirit of the law';[11] judges should rather follow 'the letter' of the laws, which leaves them with 'no role other than that of enquiring into citizens' actions and judging whether they conform or not to the written law'.[12]

According to Beccaria, the various aspects connected with the rule of law are required to guarantee equality and to enhance liberty. Penal laws that are codified by the legislature and are interpreted strictly by the judiciary will bind equally 'the most elevated and the humblest of men'.[13] Penal laws that are written in a language known to the people will provide mankind with certainty[14] that will enable each person 'to evaluate exactly the drawbacks of wrongdoing [and] acquire a spirit of independence'.[15]

It should be noted, however, that in his report from 1787 on the Austrian criminal code,[16] which had been suggested as a model for the future code of Lombardy,[17] Beccaria deviated somewhat from his claim for equality in punishment. In that report, Beccaria – following a distinction made in the Austrian code – distinguishes between two kinds of crimes: genuine crimes tending towards the destruction of the social bond, punishment for which should aim to deter others from committing such crimes; and policy offences that consist of transgressions that undermine the needs of a particular society without destroying its bond, the punishment for which should aim to correct the individual transgressor.[18] Punishments for genuine crimes aimed at general deterrence should indeed

[7] Beccaria, above n 1 chs 3–5.
[8] Ibid at 12 (ch 3).
[9] Ibid.
[10] Ibid at 17 (ch 5).
[11] Ibid at 14 (ch 4).
[12] Ibid at 15 (ch 4).
[13] Ibid at 12 (ch 3).
[14] Ibid at 17 (ch 5). Beccaria regards uncertainty as the 'cruelest tormentor of the wretched'. See ibid at 8 (Introduction).
[15] Ibid at 16 (ch 5).
[16] On Joseph II's criminal code, see Du Bois-Pedain, ch 14 in this volume, section II.B.
[17] C Beccaria, 'Brevi riflessioni intorno al Codice generale sopra i delitti e le pene per quanto riguarda i delitti politici' in C Beccaria, *Opere* vol 2 edited by S Romagnoli (Florence, Sansoni, 1958) 705–718, here quoted as translated in Appendix 1 to this volume. This report is further analysed in Du Bois-Pedain, ch 14 in this volume, section IV.B. On the correct dating (June 1787), see Appendix 1 to this volume, n 2.
[18] Appendix 1 to this volume at [5]–[6].

be imposed equally on offenders of high and low rank.[19] However, punishments for policy offences aimed at correcting the individual should take into account the status of the convict in order to avoid inflicting greater suffering on a person of high standing than on an uneducated labourer. In Beccaria's own words:

> [F]logging, which might correct a coarse individual, demoralises and destroys a nobleman, an honest merchant, and any civilised person, and involves their whole family in the most miserable infamy. The punishment is no longer proportionate to the offence, but greater by far ...[20]

Beccaria's distinction between the two aims of punishment – general deterrence for genuine crimes and correction of the individual offender for minor violations – resembles the distinction between deterrence and rehabilitation in modern penal policy.[21] However, unlike Beccaria's view in this regard, the modern distinction between rehabilitation of the individual offender and general deterrence does not depend solely on the classification of the offence as either a major or a minor crime. The distinction depends rather on the assessment of the potential of successful rehabilitation, on the one hand, and the need to protect society from crimes, on the other. More importantly, modern punishment, which aims to correct/rehabilitate the individual offender, indeed takes into account the personal circumstances of the offender, including his socio-economic background. These personal circumstances and background are required in order to assess the forces that led the offender to commit the crime, and to identify the best way in which the offender can be helped to overcome these forces. Beccaria's proposal to take into account the status of offenders convicted of policy offences, on the other hand, is based on the assumption that a person of high standing suffers more than an uneducated labourer from being punished, due to the horrible shame he and his family would feel. Modern criminal law, committed to equality in punishment, would reject Beccaria's idea of proportionate punishment in this regard.[22]

Leaving aside the distinction between different classes of crimes, Beccaria's original claims with regard to the various aspects of the rule of law, which for their time were probably revolutionary, have been followed by modern penal laws and constitute one of the fundamental principles of criminal law: the principle

[19] Ibid at [20].

[20] Ibid at [21].

[21] See, eg, D Garland, *Punishment and Welfare: A History of Penal Strategies* (Aldershot, Gower, 1985); M Feeley & J Simon, 'The New Penology: Notes on the Emerging Strategy of Corrections and Its Implications (1992) 30 *Criminology* 449; B Hudson, *Justice Through Punishment: A Critique of the 'Justice' Model of Corrections* (London, Palgrave Macmillan, 1987); P Raynor & G Robinson, 'Why Help Offenders? Arguments for Rehabilitation as a Penal Strategy' (2009) 1 *European Journal of Probation* 3.

[22] It is interesting to note Beccaria's concern with regard to policy offences, defined by both the penal code and regulations outside the code, with different sanctions provided for each. Such a practice leaves too much discretion to the authorities as regards the question under which law to proceed. See Appendix 1 to this volume at [3].

of legality. The principle of legality serves as a basis for subjecting criminal law to constitutional constraints. Thus, for example, in various legal systems, crimes that are not defined with sufficient precision are considered unconstitutional. According to the US 'void-for-vagueness' doctrine,[23] crimes whose definition either fails to give 'fair notice' or is too wide to provide law-enforcement officials with guidance necessary to prevent discrimination, violate the constitutional right of due process and are, as such, unconstitutional.[24] Under German law, crimes whose definition does not provide fair notice violate human dignity and are therefore unconstitutional.[25]

It is safe to say that in Beccaria's time, his strong advocacy for the rule of law was needed in order to establish the monopolistic power of the legislator to make penal laws and to achieve equality before the law and certainty as a means to enhance liberty. However, notwithstanding the rise in the prevalence of the rule of law, modern criminal law often suffers from over-criminalisation[26] and harshness.[27] To protect individuals' liberty and autonomy from the intrusive power of the criminal law, modern criminal law should, and some legal systems already do, relax some aspects of the rule of law. A distinction between offences and defences, as well as a distinction between creating crimes and abolishing crimes, should be drawn within the various aspects of the rule of law. To demonstrate this, let me discuss these distinctions, with respect to the creation of new criminal law doctrines by the judiciary and in the context of the retroactive application of penal laws.

A. Creation of New Criminal Law Doctrines by the Judiciary

The rule of law, as discussed by Beccaria, prohibits the judiciary from creating offences, expanding liability or imposing punishment that exceeds the maximum punishment fixed for the offence. In all such instances the core

[23] See RC Post, 'Reconceptualizing Vagueness: Legal Rules and Social Orders' (1994) 82 *California Law Review* 491; OS Kerr, 'Vagueness Challenges to the Computer Fraud and Abuse Act' (2010) 94 *Minnesota Law Review*

[24] See *City of Chicago v Morales* 527 US 41, 56 (1999); *Coates v City of Cincinnati* 402 US 611, 616 (1971); *Giaccio v Pennsylvania* 382 US 399, 402 (1966).

[25] See M Gur-Arye & T Weigend, 'Constitutional Review of Criminal Prohibitions Affecting Human Dignity and Liberty: German and Israeli Perspectives' (2011) 44 *Israel Law Review* 63 at 65 note 4 and 70.

[26] See, eg, SH Kadish, 'The Crisis of Overcriminalization' (1968-69) 7 *American Criminal Law Quarterly* 18; D Husak, *Overcriminalization: The Limits of the Criminal Law* (Oxford, Oxford University Press, 2007).

[27] The harshness of the criminal justice system has mainly been noted in the United States; see the comparison of criminal punishments in the United States and Europe by JQ Whitman, *Harsh Justice: Criminal Punishment and the Widening Divide Between America and Europe* (Oxford, Oxford University Press 2003). The American Law Institute recommended creating 'a "second-look" process for sentence modification available to prisoners who have served exceptionally long terms'. The motivation for that proposal lies in the 'heavy use of lengthy prison terms' in the American justice system, 'dramatically more so than other Western democracies' (American Law Institute, *Model Penal Code*, Sentencing, §305.6).

values underlying the rule of law – certainty, as a means to enhance liberty, and equality – are violated. However, when a judge reaches a conclusion that a new criminal law defence is warranted, the judicial creation of such a defence does not infringe upon the defendant's liberty; on the contrary, the defence will grant the defendant freedom from conviction and punishment. 'Fair notice', which serves as a means to enhance 'liberty and independence', is not required in cases where the defendant's liberty is increased even by an *ex-post* judicial ruling. It is true that recognising the power of the judiciary to create a new criminal law defence will undermine the monopoly of the legislator to decide on the exact scope of criminal liability. However, as opposed to offences, the definition of which seeks to protect well-established interests, defences are exceptions often tailored to specific circumstances. As such, the need to grant a defence might arise only during the trial itself, and legislators are usually not quick to respond to such a need. Would the 'humanity' of the criminal law (pleaded for by Beccaria) be served by setting aside such a defence until the legislator enacts the new defence? Judicial creation of an *ex-post* defence might, additionally, undermine equality. However, as opposed to judicial discretion in sentencing, where discrepancies are not always easy to expose,[28] a new defence created by the judiciary is transparent; and once it is created, it will apply to similar cases as a precedent. Therefore, the risk of discrepancy with regard to defences is not that high.

Indeed, in some legal systems, including civil law systems that attach special importance to the principle of legality, the judiciary has the power to create new criminal law defences.[29] A well-known example is provided by a criminal

[28] Studies indicating disparities in modern criminal law focus mainly on the effect of race, ethnicity, gender and nationality on sentencing. Thus for example, in the United States, black defendants often receive harsher sentences than white defendants for similar offences: see JM MacDonald & EA Donnelly, 'Evaluating the Role of Race in Sentencing: An Entropy Weighting Analysis' (2017) 34 *Justice Quarterly* 1; X Wang & DP Mears, 'Sentencing and State-Level Racial and Ethnic Contexts' (2015) 49 *Law & Society Review* 883; J Ulmer, N Painter-Davis & L Tinik, 'Disproportional Imprisonment of Black and Hispanic Males: Sentencing Discretion, Processing Outcomes, and Policy Structures' (2016) 33 *Justice Quarterly* 642. Studies in Israel show a similar discrepancy in the sentencing of Jews, who make up Israel's majority, and Israeli-Arabs, a minority group comprising about 21% of the population. See A Rattner & G Fishman, *Justice For All? Jews and Arabs in the Israeli Criminal Justice System* (Westport CT, Praeger, 1998); YGA Rahav & Y Rabin, 'Disparities between Jews and Arabs in the Israeli Criminal Justice System' (2016) 13 *Ohio State Journal of Criminal Law* 233; O Gazal-Ayal & R Sulitzeanu-Kenan, 'Let My People Go: Ethnic in-Group Bias in Judicial Decisions – Evidence from a Randomized Natural Experiment' (2010) 7 *Journal of Empirical Legal Studies* 403.

[29] For the judicial power to create a new criminal law defence in Germany, see the example discussed in the text. In Israel, one can identify a more recent development in this regard. The Draft Bill of the New General Part of the Israeli Penal Law (Israeli Penal Law (The Preliminary and General Parts), Draft Bill, 1992) explicitly stated that 'there is no criminal law defence unless it has been defined by the legislator' (s 40). However, following a criticism against such a restriction, the new General Part of the Israeli Penal Law (Penal Law (Amendment No 39) (Preliminary and General Parts) 1994) does not included any restriction on the power of the judiciary to acknowledge new criminal law defences. For criticism of the ban on the judicial power to acknowledge criminal law

case decided in 1927 by what was then the highest German court, where the defendant, a surgeon, was charged with committing an abortion despite the fact that the abortion was needed to save the mother's life.[30] The defendant could not have taken advantage of the necessity defence, since this was defined in the German penal code at that time as a personal defence limited to cases of imminent danger to the life or bodily integrity of the actor himself. The German court interpreted necessity, as it was defined in the code, as an excuse, based on the unfairness of expecting those who find themselves in imminent and severe danger to obey the law and to avoid saving their own life or bodily integrity. The court ruled that necessity as a justification, based on the lesser of two evils, should also be acknowledged. The defendant was granted the justification on the basis that his choice to commit an abortion in order to save the mother's life was the right choice. Since then, the existence of two necessity defences – one as an excuse, the other as a justification – found its way into the German Penal Code of 1975.[31]

B. Retroactive Application of Penal Laws

Beccaria does not explicitly discuss the retroactive application of penal laws. But from his discussion of the various aspects of the rule of law, and the values underlying these aspects, it is clear that had he thought about it, he would have argued that criminal laws defining offences and punishments ought not to apply retroactively to acts committed before they were enacted. The retroactive application of these laws suffers from all the faults that Beccaria protested against and violates the core values underlying the rule of law. It enables discriminatory enforcement of crimes tailored *ex-post* for specific defendants and cannot provide 'fair notice'. Indeed, once the rule of law had been established, both international and domestic documents have granted constitutional protection to the ban on retroactive application of penal laws.[32] Such protection is required with regard to penal laws that either create new offences or aggravate punishments. By contrast, the retroactive applicability of laws that either abolish an offence or mitigate its punishments does not violate the various values underlying the rule of law. On the contrary, retroactive application of these

defences proposed by the Draft Bill, see M Gur-Arye, 'The Israeli Penal Law (The Preliminary and General Parts), Draft Bill, 1992' (1994) 24 *Mishpatim* 9 (in Hebrew). See also the references in n 30 below.

[30] Judgment of 11 March 1927, RGSt 61, 242. For discussion of that ruling, see G Fletcher, *Rethinking Criminal Law* (Boston MA, Little Brown & Co, 1978) 779–783.

[31] German Penal Code, ss 34 and 35.

[32] See Art 15(1) ICCPR; Art 7(1) ECHR; Art 9 of the American Convention on Human Rights (1969); Art 22(1) of the ICC Statute; Art 11 of the Universal Declaration of Human Rights, 10 December 1948; United Nations General Assembly Resolution 217 A(III). On the domestic level, see US Constitution, Art 1, s 9, cl 3 and s 10, cl 1; Basic Law (Constitution) of the Federal Republic of Germany, Art 103 (2); and German Penal Code, ss 1 and 2; Israeli Penal Law, s 3.

laws enhances the humanity of the criminal law. Take, for example, the legislative abolition of the death penalty for murder on the ground that it is a cruel and inhuman punishment. How could a court be asked to continue imposing the death penalty on defendants who had committed murder before the death penalty was abolished? Similarly, should a court be required to ignore a new more lenient punishment in cases where the legislator decided that the punishment for a specific offence had been too harsh, merely because the defendant committed the offence before the legislator mitigated the punishment for that offence?

Indeed, various legal systems do not require the judiciary to ignore such laws. Thus, for example, the Acts that abolished the death penalty for murder in the United Kingdom (1965)[33] and Israel (1954)[34] each explicitly stated that the Act applied to murder committed before it came into force, and that mandatory life imprisonment replaced the death penalty imposed on those who had already been convicted of murder but not yet executed. In the same spirit, according to the common law doctrine of amelioration, when the legislator reduces the maximum punishment for an offence after a defendant has committed the offence but before he is sentenced, the new, more lenient, maximum punishment will apply.[35] In view of Beccaria's claims against both the death penalty[36] and the 'useless severity'[37] of punishments, Beccaria might well have supported the retroactive application of penal laws that mitigate punishments.

According to the additional relaxation of the ban against retroactive application of the criminal law, penal laws that abolish *offences* should apply retroactively. Under the Israeli Penal Law, when the legislator abolishes an offence, the abolition affects all criminal proceedings for 'the offence' committed before it was abolished: criminal liability for that offence will not be imposed, convictions of those who have already been convicted of the offence will be erased, sentences will be terminated and no future consequences will derive from past convictions.[38] The underlying assumption is that the criminal law infringes upon the basic human rights of offenders. The general freedom to act as one pleases

[33] Murder (Abolition of Death Penalty) Act 1965.

[34] Penal Law Amendment (Abolition of Death Penalty for Murder) 1954.

[35] For the doctrine of amelioration, see ER Morrison, 'Resurrecting the Amelioration Doctrine: A Call to Action for Courts and Legislatures' (2015) 95 *Buffalo Law Review* 335; Comment, 'Today's Law and Yesterday's Crime: Retroactive Application of Ameliorative Criminal Legislation' (1972) 121 *University of Pennsylvania Law Review* 120. In the same spirit, at the international level, see ICC Statute, Art 24(1)–(2); Protocol Additional to the Geneva Conventions of 12 August 1949, and relating to the Protection of Victims of International Armed Conflicts (Protocol I) of 8 June 1977, 1125 UNTS 3, Art 75(4)(c). In Israel, the effect of statutory reduction of punishments is stronger. According to s 5(b) of the Penal Law, reduced punishments apply even to defendants whose sentences are already final, provided that the sentence modification does not require re-opening their case; their punishment is reduced to the new maximum punishment.

[36] Beccaria, above n 1 ch 28.

[37] Ibid at 8 (Introduction).

[38] Section 4 of the Israeli Penal Law. The only exception is that of temporary offences, the liability for which could be enforced even after they ceased to exist (s 6 of the Israeli Penal Law).

is infringed by criminal law prohibitions; dignity is infringed by the criminal law stigma attached to a conviction; the right of free movement is infringed by imprisonment. The infringement of these rights through the criminal law can be justified only so long as the interests protected by the prohibition of the offence are worthy of such protection. When the legislator decides that a specific interest should no longer be protected by the criminal law and therefore abolishes the offence, continuing to subject the individual to the intrusive power of the criminal law is no longer justified either. It is true that those who committed the offence before it was abolished broke, and were willing to break, the law. However, the law prohibiting the offence, as such, has no independent value; it has only an instrumental value in protecting social interests.

Would Beccaria, who insisted on the importance of the rule of law, have supported an approach that attaches merely instrumental value to the law prohibiting an offence?

III. TORTURE

Beccaria is a fierce opponent of torture.[39] He describes torture aimed at either extracting confessions or revealing accomplices during investigation and trial as a cruel, barbarous and abusive practice, 'worthy of a cannibal'.[40] Like the 'ancient and savage' practices of 'ordeal by fire, by boiling water',[41] torture is not a proper means of discovering truth: '[t]elling the truth in the midst of spasms and beatings is as little subject to our will as is preventing without fraud the effects of fire and boiling water'.[42] The gravamen of Beccaria's claims against torture focuses on torturing the innocent. He emphasises the importance of the presumption of innocence: 'No man may be called guilty before the judge has reached his verdict.'[43] So, too, he claims that '[i]f it is true that, from fear or from virtue, more men observe the laws than break them, the risk of torturing an innocent ought to be accounted all the greater, since it is more likely that any given man has observed the laws than that he has flouted them'.[44] He points out the unjust consequences of torturing the innocent: 'either he confesses the crime and is convicted, or he is acquitted and has suffered an unwarranted punishment'.[45]

Beccaria's strong objection against torture matches the absolute ban against torture laid down by modern international documents.[46] The absolute ban

[39] Beccaria, above n 1 ch 16.
[40] Ibid at 40.
[41] Ibid at 41.
[42] Ibid.
[43] Ibid at 39.
[44] Ibid at 40.
[45] Ibid at 43.
[46] See, eg, Art 3 of the ECHR; Art 7 of the ICCPR; and the Convention against Torture and other Cruel, Inhuman or Degrading Treatment or Punishment of 10 December 1984, UNTS 1465, 85.

on torture is based on its being an extreme violation of human dignity, in the Kantian sense. Forcing an interrogee to reveal information against his/her will instrumentalises the interrogee; he/she is being treated merely as an object.[47]

Beccaria does not rest his claims against torture on 'human dignity' in the Kantian sense. He emphasises the cruelty of torture,[48] the risk of torturing the innocent and the inability of torture to reveal the truth. Does the lack of explicit reference to human dignity undermine Beccaria's plea against torture? I think that it does. To show this, let me refer to the *Daschner* case.[49] In that case, during his interrogation, Gäfgen, a suspect in the abduction of a child, was shown a document by the local deputy chief of the police, Daschner, which stated that the deputy chief had authorised the use of means to inflict pain on him if he did not reveal the whereabouts of the child. Gäfgen gave in, delivered the necessary details, and the body of the child, who had been murdered by Gäfgen, was found. Beccaria would probably not have objected to the threat of torture in such a case. According to Beccaria, the cruelty of torture, its inability to discover the truth and the risk to the innocent involved in torture derive from the pain inflicted by torture. In the *Daschner* case, on the other hand, the threat of torture turned out to be an efficient means to discover the 'truth' – the whereabouts of the body of the child – without having to cause pain to the suspect. By contrast, both the German Court in the *Daschner* case[50] and the European Court of Human Rights in the case brought by Gäfgen against Germany[51] were of the opinion that the threat of torture violates human dignity, which prohibits forcing a suspect to reveal information against his own will, whether or not the information is extracted through the use of physical pain.[52]

The fact that Beccaria did not refer to human dignity in his discussion of torture is probably connected to his somewhat different perception of the Kantian notion of human dignity that prohibits treating human beings as mere

[47] See, eg, M Gur-Arye & F Jessberger, 'The Protection of Human Dignity in Interrogations: May Interrogative Torture ever be Tolerated? Reflections in Light of Recent German and Israeli Experiences' (2011) 44 *Israel Law Review* 229; S Levinson (ed), *Torture: A Collection* (Oxford, Oxford University Press, 2004).

[48] Beccaria's description of torture as a cruel, barbarous and abusive practice might be perceived as indicating a violation of human dignity in a different sense, that of freedom from humiliation. The notion of human dignity as a freedom from humiliation derives from A Margalit's book *The Decent Society* (Cambridge MA, Harvard University Press, 1996), according to which 'a decent society is one in which institutions do not humiliate people' (ibid at 1). For human dignity in this sense, see T Hörnle & M Kremnitzer, 'Human Dignity as a Protected Interest in the Criminal Law' (2011) 44 *Israel Law Review* 143.

[49] Frankfurt Regional Court, Judgment of 20 December 2004, [2005] *Neue Juristische Wochenschrift* 692. For an English translation, see A Cassese, 'Respect for Human Dignity in Today's Germany: Regional Court (Landgericht) of Frankfurt am Main, Decision of 20 December 2004, Daschner Wolfgang and E. Case' (2006) 4 *Journal of International Criminal Justice* 862.

[50] *Daschner* case, above n 49.

[51] *Gäfgen v Germany* (2011) 52 EHRR 1 (GC).

[52] 'The human being was not to be treated … as somebody having information that the state would wring out of him, even if for the purpose of serving justice': *Daschner* case, above n 49 at 863.

objects. In dealing with crimes of violence,[53] Beccaria claimed that crimes against the person ought to be punished corporally.

This support for corporal punishments within a plea for a 'humane criminal law' is surprising, especially when compared with Beccaria's fierce objection to torture that involves pain. One might have concluded that in supporting corporal punishment for crimes against the person, Beccaria was motivated by a retributive justification of punishments in its strict sense – *ius talionis* – which (20 years later) led Kant to support the death penalty.[54] However, according to Beccaria, punishments are justified solely by utilitarian considerations aimed at preventing crimes through deterrence.[55] As opposed to Kant, Beccaria contested the death penalty[56] on the grounds both that 'the punishment of death is not a matter of right … but is an act of war on the part of society against the citizen', and that it 'is neither necessary nor useful'.[57]

It is even more surprising to realise that Beccaria's support of corporal punishment is explicitly based on the claim that otherwise 'there is no freedom when the laws permit a man in some cases to cease to be a person and to become a thing'.[58] It follows that for Beccaria, the constraint on treating human beings as mere objects requires the state to impose corporal punishment.

Beccaria's support for corporal punishment for crimes of violence was probably motivated by his fear that monetary punishments would not deter the rich from physically harming the weak and the poor: 'the rich and the powerful should not be able to put a price on assaults on the weak and the poor'.[59] Such a fear is understandable (although not necessarily justified) in light of the use of imprisonment in Beccaria's time, when it was still mainly used for pre-trial detention and crimes of violence were standardly punished by either monetary or corporal sanctions. However, once imprisonment serves as a possible punishment for those convicted of violent offences, imprisonment, rather than corporal punishment, should be the typical sentence for violent crimes that would prevent the rich from setting a price on the bodily integrity of the poor.

[53] Beccaria, above n 1 ch 20.

[54] I Kant, *The Metaphysics of Morals* [1797] (Ak 6: 335) in *The Cambridge Edition of the Works of Immanuel Kant: Practical Philosophy* edited by A Wood and translated by M Gregor (Cambridge, Cambridge University Press, 1996) 476. For the view that Kant's embrace of the death penalty is not required by the fundamental tenets of Kant's moral and legal philosophy, see eg J-C Merle, 'A Kantian Critique of Kant's Theory of Punishment' (2000) 19 *Law & Philosophy* 311; NT Potter, 'Kant and Capital Punishment Today' (2002) 36 *Journal of Value Inquiry* 267. For the view that Kant presents a sound argument in support of the death penalty, see eg BS Yost, 'Kant's Justification of the Death Penalty Reconsidered' (2010) 15 *Kantian Review* 1.

[55] Beccaria, above n 1 ch 6.

[56] Ibid ch 28.

[57] Ibid at 66.

[58] Ibid at 55 (ch 20).

[59] Ibid.

IV. CRIMES OF ADULTERY AND SODOMY

Beccaria discusses adultery and sodomy under the chapter heading of 'Crimes difficult to prove'.[60] However, neither his discussion of these crimes nor his conclusion focus exclusively, or even principally, on the difficulties of proof. Adultery, according to him, 'is a crime which, viewed politically, is motivated and directed by two factors: the fluctuating laws of men and that very powerful attraction which urges one sex towards the other'.[61] It 'arises from the abuse of a constant and universal need in all mankind, a need antecedent to and, indeed, foundational of society itself'.[62] Homosexuality, which is 'so severely punished by laws and so easily subjected to the tortures which defeat innocence, has its foundation less in the needs of an isolated and free man, than in the emotions of a socialized and enslaved one'.[63] Youths who are sent to be educated at public seminars, where they are deprived of contact with the other sex, are pushed towards sodomy.

Beccaria's approach to adultery seems to be in line with the tendency of modern liberal states to refrain from using the criminal law in order to enforce common morality.[64] Beccaria even adopts in this context a principle similar to that of the harm principle, according to which the use of the criminal law will only be justified to prevent acts that are 'socially destructive'.[65] However, there is a significant difference between Beccaria's conclusion that both adultery and sodomy should not be punished by the criminal law and the tendency of modern liberal states to decriminalise these offences.[66]

[60] Ibid, ch 31.

[61] Ibid at 80.

[62] Ibid.

[63] Ibid at 81.

[64] The reluctance to enforce morality is connected with the harm principle (as first formulated by JS Mill, *On Liberty and Other Essays* edited by J Gray (Oxford, Oxford University Press, 1991) 13), which serves as a constraint on the state's power to use penal laws. For the harm principle as a constraint on criminalisation, see eg J Feinberg, *Harm to Others* (New York, Oxford University Press, 1984) 31–64; J Raz, 'Autonomy, Toleration, and the Harm Principle', in R Gavison (ed), *Issues in Contemporary Legal Philosophy: The Influence of HLA Hart* (Oxford, Clarendon Press, 1987) 313; J Kleinig, 'Crime and the Concept of Harm' (1978) 15 *American Philosophical Quarterly* 27; RE Epstein, 'The Harm Principle – And How It Grew' (1995) *University of Toronto Law Journal* 369.

[65] Beccaria, above n 1 at 80 (ch 31).

[66] In the United Kingdom, private homosexual activity between men over 21 years old was decriminalised in 1967 (Sexual Offences Act, 1967, s 1). In Israel, sodomy offences between consenting adults were abolished in 1988 (Penal Law (Amendment No 22) 1988). The Supreme Court of the United States ruled in 2003 that the offence of homosexual activity between consenting adults is unconstitutional (*Lawrence v Texas* 539 US 558 (2003)), and the European Court of Human Rights held that such laws violate Art 8 of the ECHR (see CB Rabinowitz, 'Proposals for Progress: Sodomy Laws and the European Convention on Human Rights' (1995) 21 *Brooklyn Journal of International Law* 425). Adultery has not been a crime either in the United Kingdom or in Israel. In various US States, adultery has been a crime (against morality), but many of these States have followed the American Law Institute in its Model Penal Code recommendations that adultery be decriminalised. See further JD Weinstein, 'Adultery, Law and the State: A History' (1986) 38 *Hastings Law Journal* 195.

According to Beccaria, punishment of both adultery and sodomy cannot be 'just (meaning necessary) until the law has instituted the best possible means in a given nation's circumstances for preventing such a crime'.[67] Alternative ways of preventing adultery and sodomy are rooted in Beccaria's implicit criticism against the social institutions of his time. Adultery could have been prevented had marriage been based on attraction between the parties rather than on 'ancestral prejudices [and] domestic power'.[68] Sodomy could have been prevented had the youth been able to have contact with the other sex during their studies.[69]

As opposed to Beccaria, who believed that both adultery and sodomy should be prevented by fixing social institutions, in modern criminal law both adultery and sodomy fall within the sexual autonomy of each individual that should only be restricted when it is not freely consented to.

It should be noted that in his 1787 report on the Austrian criminal code, mentioned in section II, Beccaria surprisingly changed his mind with regard to adultery.[70] In the Austrian penal code, adultery was classified as a policy offence rather than as a genuine crime. Beccaria, on the other hand, suggested that adultery be reclassified as a genuine crime – albeit of a minor kind – since it undermines the bond of marriage! Beccaria further suggested distinguishing between a man who commits adultery and a woman who does so. An adulteress may give her husband children that are not his; a man who commits adultery does not harm society in the same way. Therefore, a man who commits adultery deserves a lesser punishment than an adulteress! The difference between Beccaria's original views, that punishing adultery cannot be 'just (meaning necessary)' because it would have been prevented had marriage been based on attraction between the parties rather than on 'ancestral prejudices [and] domestic power', and his later view that adultery should be classified as a crime given that it undermines the marriage bond, is hard to understand. Moreover, Beccaria's later approach to adultery, according to which a man who has committed adultery should be punished more leniently than an adulteress, deviates from his plea for equality in punishments, and it leaves Beccaria far behind liberal penal laws.

V. LESSONS TO BE LEARNED

There are two lessons that modern criminal law may learn from the discussion of Beccaria's approach to the 'interests of humanity' in the area of criminal law.

First, Beccaria's concern with the cruelty of punishments and the irregularity of proceedings in criminal cases has been dealt with in modern criminal

[67] Beccaria, above n 1 at 82 (ch 31).
[68] Ibid at 80.
[69] Ibid at 81.
[70] See Appendix 1 to this volume at [27].

law by giving constitutional protection to the right of due process[71] and to the right against inhuman and cruel punishment.[72] However, in practical terms, much remains to be done in reducing both the harshness of sentencing and the discrimination against minorities in all stages of the criminal process,[73] and in guaranteeing the full spectrum of the right to a fair trial.

Second, Beccaria connected the issue of over-criminalisation with his criticism of social institutions. According to his original views in his essay *On Crimes and Punishments*, there would be no need to criminalise adultery and sodomy if marriage were based on attraction between the spouses rather than on status and additional monetary interests, and if youths were not separated from the other sex during their studies.[74] The issue of over-criminalisation is one of the main concerns of modern criminal law[75] and it cannot be remedied solely by reforming social institutions, as suggested by Beccaria. Over-criminalisation unduly infringes upon offenders' freedom and other basic rights. Therefore, modern criminal law should move towards subjecting the issue of criminalisation itself to constitutional control. Currently, one can identify a reluctance to do so, based on the dual function of the criminal law.

Criminal law aims to protect basic rights of the *victim*, such as the right to life, to bodily integrity and to property, or vital *public* interests. In so doing, the criminal law infringes upon the *offender's* basic rights: the prohibition of the offence infringes upon the freedom to act as one pleases, the stigma involved in criminal conviction infringes upon dignity, and the punishment infringes upon the right to free movement and additional rights. As a rule, modern criminal law balances the need to protect rights (of victims) with the infringement of rights (of offenders) by distinguishing between the criminal process and punishment, on the one hand, and criminalisation, on the other. Offenders' rights are guaranteed by the presumption of innocence and by constitutional right to both a fair trial and humane punishments; once these rights are guaranteed, the need to protect victims' rights prevails.

The German experience provides an interesting example of the tendency to prefer victims' rights, protected by the prohibition of the offence, over the offenders' rights that are infringed by the prohibition. The German Constitution includes various rights that could serve as a basis for constitutional control over crimes: dignity,[76] the right to develop one's personal life, interpreted to include the right to act as one pleases,[77] and the right to free

[71] See above n 5.
[72] See above n 6.
[73] See above nn 27–28.
[74] See above nn 68–69 and the accompanying text.
[75] See above n 26.
[76] Dignity, under Art 1(1) of the Basic Law of the Federal Republic of Germany, is 'inviolable', trumping all other rights and public interests.
[77] Art 2(1) of the Basic Law of the Federal Republic of Germany. For the interpretation of this provision to include the right to act as one pleases, see Gur-Arye & Weigend, above n 25 at 81.

movement.[78] As a rule, the German Constitutional Court exercises judicial review of the constitutionality of crimes on the basis of these rights. However, in almost all cases in which the constitutionality of an offence has been challenged, the constitutionality of the offence was approved. Thus, for example, in 1994, the German Constitutional Court approved the constitutionality of the prohibition on possession of marijuana,[79] and in 2008 the prohibition of incest between consenting adult siblings was held to be constitutional.[80] The tendency of the German Constitutional Court to uphold the constitutionality of criminal prohibitions is based on the doctrine of the margin of appreciation, which, according to the German Court, has special significance in criminal law – it is the prerogative of the legislator to decide which interests and rights should be protected by the criminal law, and what should be the scope of their protection.[81] However, in 1975, the German Constitutional Court imposed on the legislator a duty to criminalise abortion during the first trimester of pregnancy in order to protect the foetus's 'rights'.[82] This shows that the Court has been willing to interfere with the prerogative of the legislator in order to protect the interests or rights of victims, but has been reluctant to interfere in order to prevent undue infringement of offenders' rights.

The reluctance to exercise constitutional control over crimes stands in contrast to the willingness to exercise such control over the criminal process and punishment. The US Constitution provides an example of such a contrast. The 5th and the 14th Amendments to the US Constitution explicitly guarantee the right to due process, and the 8th Amendment guarantees the right against cruel and unusual punishments. By contrast, the rights on the basis of which constitutional control over crimes could have been exercised – such as the freedom to act as ones pleases, the right to free movement – are not listed in the US Constitution. In the rare cases in which the US Supreme Court has exercised constitutional control over crimes, the Court extended the constitutional right

[78] Art 11 of the Basic Law of the Federal Republic of Germany.

[79] BVerfGE 90, 145 (1994), discussed by Gur-Arye & Weigend, above n 25 at 81–83.

[80] BVerfGE 120, 224 (2008), criticised by T Hörnle, 'Consensual Adult Incest' (2014) 17 *New Criminal Law Review* 76.

[81] Gur-Arye & Weigend, above n 25 at 65, 71 and the references therein.

[82] BVerfGE 39, 1 (1975). For an English translation of the ruling, see JD Gorby & RE Jonas, 'West German Abortion Decision: A Contrast to *Roe v Wade*' (1976) 9 *John Marshall Journal of Practice & Procedure* 605. For discussion of the ruling, see Gur-Arye & Weigend, above n 25 at 66; A du Bois-Pedain, 'The Place of Criminal Law Theory in the Constitutional State', in AP Simester, A du Bois-Pedain & U Neumann (eds), *Liberal Criminal Theory: Essays for Andreas von Hirsch* (Oxford, Hart Publishing, 2014) 305 at 312–313. However, following the unification of Germany, and due to the practice of abortion that had prevailed in East Germany, in 1993 the German Constitutional Court ruled that the legislator could fulfil its duty to protect the foetus through an advisory regime rather than criminalisation: see BVerfGE 88, 203 (1993), the English translation of which can be found at www.bverfg.de/entscheidungen/fs19930528_2bvf000290en.html. For comparative analysis of the two rulings, see A Harel, 'The Duty to Criminalize' (2015) 34 *Law & Philosophy* 1; R Siegel, 'Constitutionalization of abortion', in M Rosenfeld & A Sajó (eds), *Oxford Handbook of Comparative Constitutional Law* (Oxford, Oxford University Press, 2012) 1057.

of due process so as to include substantive rights – 'substantive due process'.[83] The doctrine of 'substantive due process' allowed the US Supreme Court in 1965 to strike down a statute prohibiting any person from using 'any drug, medicinal article or instrument for the purpose of preventing conception', on the ground that it violated privacy, which is included within the right of due process guaranteed by the 14th Amendment.[84] Similarly, in 2003 the US Supreme Court held that the statute criminalising intimate sexual conduct between two consenting adults of the same sex violated the Due Process Clause of the 14th Amendment and therefore was unconstitutional.[85]

I believe that it is about time to think more coherently about subjecting criminalisation to constitutional constraints, and to develop human rights discourse within the area of substantive criminal law. Such a discourse would grant the harm principle,[86] for example, constitutional status, and crimes that do not seek to avoid harm would be held to be unconstitutional.[87] Even when the crime seeks to avoid harm, subjecting the issue of criminalisation to constitutional control would require evaluating whether there are alternative means, less intrusive than the criminal law, to prevent individuals from causing such harm.

[83] *Griswold v Connecticut* 381 US 479 (1965). For the doctrine of 'substantive due process', see E Chemerinsky, 'Substantive Due Process' (1999) 15 *Touro Law Review* 1501; DO Conkle, 'Three Theories of Substantive Due Process' (2006) 85 *North Carolina Law Review* 63; RC Williams, 'The One and Only Substantive Due Process Clause' (2010) 120 *Yale Law Journal* 408.

[84] *Griswold*, above n 83.

[85] *Lawrence v Texas* 539 US 558 (2003).

[86] Above n 64.

[87] It should be noted that granting constitutional status to the harm principle does not preclude granting constitutional status to additional principles, such as the 'offence to others' principle (J Feinberg, *Moral Limits of Criminal Law: Offense to Others*, vol 2 (Oxford, Oxford University Press, 1985). Constitutional status may even be granted to alternative principles, such as the Kant-inspired dignity principle, according to which 'the main goal of criminal law is to defend the unique moral worth of every human being' (M Dan-Cohen, 'Defending Dignity', in his *Harmful Thoughts: Essays on Law, Self, and Morality* (Princeton NJ, Princeton University Press, 2002) 150).

13

Beccaria on the Human Rights Committee? An Excursus on the Parameters of Human Rights and Penology

LESLIE SEBBA AND RACHELA ER'EL*

I. INTRODUCTION

CESARE BECCARIA HAS long been familiar to criminologists as the 'father' of the 'classical school' of criminology, with penologists in particular being impressed by his opposition to the death penalty and his scepticism as to the deterrent effect of the severity of punishment, in particular his view that deterrence would better be achieved by increasing the likelihood of punishment (generally referred to as 'certainty') rather than its harshness, a view confirmed in recent times by empirical research.[1] However, while all who have read Beccaria's seminal essay on the criminal justice system (*Dei Delitti e Delle Pene*, hereinafter '*Dei Delitti*') cannot fail to note its emphasis on what later criminal law scholars would refer to as 'due process', Beccaria has not been especially identified by criminologists – or indeed by other scholars – as a pioneer of human rights.

This may have been so in part because until recently criminologists and penologists have generally not shown much interest in the field of human rights (excepting the burgeoning field of international crimes and transitional justice).[2]

* The authors thank Noy Eitan for her research assistance. The two authors contributed equally to this chapter.

[1] A von Hirsch et al, *Criminal Deterrence & Sentence Severity: An Analysis of Recent Research* (Oxford, Hart Publishing, 1999); AN Doob & CM Webster, 'Sentence Severity and Crime: Accepting the Null Hypothesis' (2003) 30 *Crime & Justice* 143.

[2] See, eg, J Savelsberg, *Crime and Human Rights: Criminology of Genocide and Atrocities* (London, Sage Publications, 2010). Sattar makes this point in the reverse direction. Outside transitional justice, he asserts, 'the relationship between human rights and the justificatory foundations of punishment generally, or in the context of domestic penal law, has received much less attention': see A Sattar, *Criminal Punishment and Human Rights: Convenient Morality* (Abingdon, Routledge, 2019) 20.

However, this is beginning to change.[3] Human rights discourses are increasingly central,[4] particularly so in responding to the excesses of punitiveness and mass incarceration in recent decades,[5] and in the continuing struggle to abolish the death penalty.[6] Interest in this field may also have been generated by the increasing institutional and academic activity promoting the application of international human rights law (IHRL) to the field of punishment,[7] as exemplified in a pioneering monograph by Van Zyl Smit and Snacken that links the norms of international law applicable to prison inmates to prevailing penological research.[8]

Indeed, a perusal of their book, and exposure to the discourse of international institutions that monitor states' criminal justice systems, might suggest that penology and human rights are natural bedfellows, with human rights norms acting as a restraint upon states imposing excessive or otherwise unacceptable punishments. This is, however, a simplification to say the least, as indicated in Adnan Sattar's recently published historical analysis of the relationship between human rights doctrines and criminal punishment, which draws attention to the diversity of approaches adopted both by and within these respective fields to the underlying penological justifications for punitive practices.[9]

This chapter addresses the human rights/criminal punishment nexus with a focus on exploring the relationship, if any, between Beccaria's penal policies and contemporary international human rights norms. Our belief in the possibility of establishing such a linkage rests on the following considerations.

First, readings of *Dei Delitti* by non-criminologists make it clear that its framework is considerably wider than the norms and practices of penology. Beccaria enthusiasts over the years (echoing the enthusiasm of some of his contemporaries) have discovered in his writings significant contributions to a wide range of fields, including economics and political science,[10] and some have already connected Beccaria's work to international human rights norms.

[3] See T Murphy & N Whitty, 'Making History: Academic Criminology and Human Rights' (2013) 53 *British Journal of Criminology* 568.

[4] K Sellars, *The Rise and Rise of Human Rights* (Stroud, Sutton Publishing, 2002).

[5] J Simon, 'For a Human Rights Approach to Reforming the American Penal State' (2019) 11 *Journal of Human Rights Practice* 346.

[6] WA Schabas, 'International Law and Abolition of the Death Penalty' (1998) 55 *Washington & Lee Law Review* 797. See also R Hood & C Hoyle, *The Death Penalty: A Worldwide Perspective* 5th edition (Oxford, Oxford University Press, 2015).

[7] See, eg, the publications of Penal Reform International, and in particular the involvement of this organisation in the adoption of the revised Standard Minimum Rules for the Treatment of Prisoners, 8 January 2016, in United Nations General Assembly Resolution 70/175 (the Nelson Mandela Rules). Additional sources are referred to in Sattar, above n 2.

[8] See D Van Zyl Smit & S Snacken, *Principles of European Prison Law and Policy: Penology and Human Rights* (Oxford, Oxford University Press, 2009).

[9] See Sattar, above n 2.

[10] See P Beirne, 'Inventing Criminology: The "Science of Man" in Cesare Beccaria's Dei Delitti e Delle Pene (1764)', (1991) 29 *Criminology* 777.

Thus Gerhard Mueller, an academic criminologist who was for many years Director of the United Nations Crime Prevention and Criminal Justice Branch, in addition to claiming that Beccaria anticipated most of the leading criminological theories prevailing in the late twentieth century, also argued that what he referred to as Beccaria's 'humanistic program' was reflected in various UN-based documents.[11] His list included the prohibition on torture and other cruel, inhuman or degrading treatment or punishment; the movement towards abolition of the death penalty; and the requirements of humane treatment for prisoners, of the independence of the judiciary, of legal education of the public, of the return of prisoners to their own countries, and of open and public trials.[12] While Mueller did not use the term 'international human rights norms' in this context, the overlap is evident.

More recently, John Bessler, in his wide-ranging analysis of Beccaria's life and contributions to penal theory and policies,[13] has drawn attention to the number of UN-based treaties and declarations that 'address the very subjects that Beccaria took up in *On Crimes and Punishments*', and commented that the Convention against Torture and other Cruel, Inhuman or Degrading Treatment or Punishment of 1984 (CAT), like the similar prohibitions that preceded it in the Universal Declaration of Human Rights of 1948 and the International Covenant on Civil and Political Rights of 1966 (ICCPR), 'has roots in Beccaria's advocacy more than two centuries earlier'.[14] He therefore sees 'such declarations, conventions and treaties' as 'part of Beccaria's enduring legacy'.[15]

Second, while explicit linkages between Beccaria and IHRL are comparatively rare, another line of connection between the two can be derived from the perspective of scholars who read *Dei Delitti* less as an essay on penal policy per se than as a work of political philosophy concerned with the rationale

[11] GOW Mueller, 'Whose Prophet is Cesare Beccaria? An Essay on the Origins of Criminological Theory', in WS Laufer & F Adler (eds), *Advances in Criminological Theory* vol 2 (Abingdon, Routledge, 1990) 1. Mueller here provides an illustration of Paul Roberts' observation that academics tend to 'reconstruct … the past from the vantage point of contemporary perspective and framed by the inquirer's current preoccupations'. See Roberts, ch 9 in this volume. In this respect Roberts attributes some of the difficulties in our analysis of Beccaria's opus to the fact that at the time of its writing, disciplinary boundaries were as yet undeveloped.

[12] Mueller, above n 11 at 10–11.

[13] See JD Bessler, *The Celebrated Marquis: An Italian Noble and the Making of the Modern World* (Durham NC, Carolina Academic Press, 2018). This follows in the wake of an earlier volume dealing with Beccaria's impact on the American Revolution, JD Bessler, *The Birth of American Law: An Italian Philosopher and the American Revolution* (Durham NC, Carolina Academic Press, 2014).

[14] Both passages quoted in this sentence are taken from Bessler, *Celebrated Marquis*, above n 13 at 326.

[15] Ibid. Bessler is careful to comment, however, that the legal instruments referred to, although 'part of Beccaria's enduring legacy were, of course, shaped by many individuals and a variety of events and intervening influences' (ibid.).

for a legitimate exercise of the state's power to punish.[16] It was this focus that led Beccaria to consider the optimal form the penal system should assume in practice – including the manner in which criminal prohibitions should be formulated, their breach proved and the penalties to be imposed.[17] Importantly, Beccaria's underlying rationale for the exercise of state power is seen by many interpreters as strikingly similar to John Locke's version of social contract theory, which, in turn, is viewed as one of the intellectual foundations of the international human rights system.

Third, on a more practical level, scholars exposed to – or re-reading – *Dei Delitti* are frequently struck by the enduring validity and relevance of the ideas elaborated therein and the groundwork it laid for the modern penal system, even while acknowledging that a causal chain may be difficult to prove.[18] Our own familiarity with contemporary international human rights norms, in particular those applicable to punishment,[19] has impressed upon us the many instances of comparable principles evident in Beccaria's essay beyond the well-known examples of his aversion to the death penalty and to torture. Examples can be found in his accounts of the cruelties of prison regimes and in his implicit support for a principle that imprisonment – or possibly even punishment in general – should only be invoked as a last resort.

Last but not least, while linguistic analysis of *Dei Delitti* is complicated by its multiple editions and variety of translations, it seems that Beccaria himself employed an expression with a meaning similar to our modern concept of 'human rights'.[20] The reference appears towards the end of a paragraph in which Beccaria reflects on the wisdom of applying the death penalty, torture and corporal punishment, and questions other aspects of penal policy. This paragraph appears in some editions (including Bellamy's) towards the end of chapter 11 on 'Public Peace', but in other editions towards the end of Beccaria's Introduction. In the Bellamy edition, it concludes:

> [I]f, in upholding the rights of men and the invincible truth, I were to contribute to relieving some blighted victim of tyranny or, equally lethal, ignorance, from the spasms and anxieties of death, the blessing and tears of joy of even a single innocent man would console me for the scorn of the multitude.[21]

[16] See Roberts, ch 9 in this volume; and Zucca, ch 1 in this volume.

[17] A modern parallel may be found in A von Hirsch, *Doing Justice: The Choice of Punishments* (New York, Hill & Wang, 1976), the seminal document offering a blueprint for the replacement of the individualisation of sentencing, as promoted by the then-prevailing positivist school, by a 'just deserts' model, and accompanied by an elaboration of its underlying philosophy. *Doing Justice*, however, placed a much greater emphasis on the mechanics (and quantum) of sentencing.

[18] See, eg, Bessler, *Celebrated Marquis*, above n 13.

[19] L Sebba & R Er'el, 'Free-Style Imprisonment': On the Implementation of International Human-Rights Norms in Israel's Prison System' (2017) 10 *Hukim* 123 (in Hebrew).

[20] See also Gur-Arye, ch 12 in this volume.

[21] C Beccaria, *On Crimes and Punishments and Other Writings* edited by R Bellamy and translated by R Davies (Cambridge, Cambridge University Press, 1995) 30.

In other versions the opening phrase is rendered as 'supporting the rights of mankind';[22] 'defending the rights of man'[23] and 'upholding the rights of man'.[24]

These observations have encouraged us to persevere with an exploration of the connections between Beccaria's proposals and the international human rights system through engaging in what one might describe as historical-conceptual discourse analysis. In so doing we do not wish to deny the weighty methodological obstacles such a project faces, especially when the comparison spans three centuries[25] and a variety of cultures.[26] Moreover, given the large number of topics dealt with in Beccaria's essay, on the one hand, and by the expanding network of international institutions and normative regimes focusing on human rights, on the other hand, any comparison of specific norms must necessarily be highly selective.

This chapter does not, however, seek to convince its readers of a congruence between these two sets of norms, let alone of a causal link between them. The comparative approach adopted is instead intended to provide insights into and possibly new perspectives on each of the normative frameworks under consideration.[27] Thus, in addition to specific norms or policies advocated by IHRL and *Dei Delitti* respectively, we will consider their underlying penal objectives and investigate the possibility of integrating Beccaria's proposals and contemporary human rights norms under a broader conceptual framework of 'punishment as a last resort'. In this context, we will address some issues that have so far been treated – in our view mistakenly – as on the margins of human rights discourse, such as the extent to which human rights norms may or should include obligations to criminalise and punish,[28] the aims

[22] C Beccaria, *An Essay on Crimes and Punishments* translated by ED Ingraham (Philadelphia PA, Philip H Nicklin, 1819) 46.

[23] C Beccaria, *On Crimes and Punishments* translated by H Paolucci (New York, Macmillan, 1963) 10.

[24] A Manzoni, *The Column of Infamy Prefaced by Cesare Beccaria's Of Crimes and Punishments* translated by K Foster and J Grigson (London, Oxford University Press, 1964) 13.

[25] David Garland, in his analysis of Foucault, refers to the historians' accusation of 'the mortal sin of anachronism' where the analysis is perceived as an attempt to 'project … contemporary values and meanings into a past that may have been constituted quite differently': D Garland, 'What is a "History of the Present"? On Foucault's Genealogies and their Critical Preconditions' (2014) 16 *Punishment and Society* 365, but see further below n 27. See also Roberts, ch 9 in this volume.

[26] Cf D Nelken, *Comparative Criminal Justice: Making Sense of Difference* (London, Sage Publications, 2010).

[27] Foucault's concept of 'the history of the present' may be relevant here. See Garland, above n 25, at 367, 370. Garland explains that while Foucault's earlier 'archaeological' studies argued that direct comparison between periods (including the Classical and Modern period) were not possible, given the 'different ways of ordering thought and producing discourse', this did not apply to his so-called genealogies, where, like historians, he is using a contemporary interest in part 'as the spur to question the past in new ways' – but primarily to work out a genealogy of the present.

[28] See, eg, K Engle et al (eds), *Anti-impunity and the Human Rights Agenda* (Cambridge, Cambridge University Press, 2016); M Pinto, 'Awakening the Leviathan through Human Rights Law – How Human Rights Bodies Trigger the Application of Criminal Law' (2018) 34 *Utrecht Journal of International and European Law* 161.

of punishment, and the tension between the principle of the universality of human rights and the legitimacy of cultural or national variation. On these topics, some ambivalence may be discerned in the text of *Dei Delitti* as well as in contemporary IHRL.

This ambivalence is at least in part related to uncertainty as to the identity of the field or sub-field[29] (or discipline or sub-discipline[30]) with which the relevant actors and texts are affiliated or identified, that is, whether human rights or penology, or perhaps penal and/or political philosophy. Is the primary concern of Beccaria on the one hand and the human rights community on the other (i) to protect the individual from an excessive exercise of state power (the traditional role of human rights), (ii) to identify the objectives of state punishment (the function of penal philosophy), or (iii) to analyse the processes of the penal system and the institutions of punishment and to identify the optimal policies for achieving alternative options identified in response to (ii) – the function generally attributed to penology?

As noted by Roberts,[31] Beccaria wrote before modern conventions of disciplinary differentiation (and their related terminologies) became crystallised. One might even say that two of these fields – human rights and penology – did not yet exist outside moral and political philosophy, although the discourses stimulated by *Dei Delitti* did much to change this.[32] Moreover, while penology had already developed as an independent field during the nineteenth century,[33] human rights remained a sub-topic of political philosophy until it began to take off as a juridical topic – as well as a social-science topic – in the twentieth century.[34] That said, it is also worth bearing in mind that during recent decades the parameters of these fields have been changing, or at the very least have been characterised by fluidity, to the point where some writers suggest that 'the interaction between

[29] Cf J Page, 'Punishment and the Penal Field', in J Simon & R Sparks (eds), *The SAGE Handbook of Punishment and Society* (London, Sage Publications, 2012) 152.

[30] On alternative meanings of 'discipline' in a criminological context, see D Garland, 'Criminology's Place in the Academic Field', in M Bosworth & C Hoyle (eds), *What is Criminology?* (Oxford, Oxford University Press, 2012) 298. See also A Abbott, *Chaos of Disciplines* (London, University of Chicago Press, 2010).

[31] Roberts, ch 9 in this volume.

[32] The publication of John Howard's *The State of the Prisons* a few years later must also be considered a landmark in the emergence of penology as an autonomous field. See J Howard, *The State of the Prisons in England and Wales: With Preliminary Observations, and an Account of Some Foreign Prisons* [1777] (Cambridge, Cambridge University Press, 2013). This publication, together with the loss of the American colonies and the suspension of transportation, led to the adoption of the Penitentiary Act in 1779, as well as generating wide-ranging debates in the United States on the optimal form of a prison regime during the first decades of the 19th century. See DJ Rothman, *The Discovery of the Asylum: Social Order and Disorder in the New Republic* (Abingdon, Routledge, 1971).

[33] The term 'penology' is attributed to the 19th-century author Francis Lieber: see SM Benson, 'A Political Science of Punishment: Francis Lieber and the Discipline of American Prisons' (2015) 37 *New Political Science* 382. During the first half of the 20th century this concept became increasingly linked to the developing field of criminology, with textbooks incorporating both areas.

[34] See M Freeman, *Human Rights* 2nd edition (Cambridge, Polity Press, 2011).

penology and human rights … is … at the centre of the analysis of the current state of European law and policy'.[35] Thus, the blurring of questions, concerns and arguments associated with these different fields, which we have attributed to Beccaria, may in fact have become present-day policy.

The chapter is structured as follows: section II traces the Lockean roots of Beccaria's application of social contract theory to account for his view of the limitations on the state's exercise of punitive power (section II.A). Given that the development of international human rights norms is linked to 'natural law' and 'natural rights' as reflected in Locke's theory of state (section II.B), the identification of similar links in Beccaria's essay lends support to the view that, like Locke, Beccaria was a pioneer of human rights. Section III delves more deeply into substantive issues covered both by Beccaria and by IHRL, with reference also to the concept of the criminal law/punishment as a 'last resort' as a key to our understanding of the common ground shared by the two normative frameworks. Section IV then turns to an ambivalence that characterises a number of policy issues arising in the context of both *Dei Delitti* and IHRL, and that – as pointed out above – appears related to uncertainty as to the identity of the field or sub-field (or discipline or sub-discipline) with which the relevant texts are identified. In the Conclusion, we draw some further insights from the continuity of conceptualisation in relation to the foundations of human rights, from John Locke via Beccaria and up to modern times.

II. BECCARIA AND INTERNATIONAL HUMAN RIGHTS NORMS: COMMON ROOTS

While, as noted in section I, recent academic tradition would probably designate Beccaria's *Dei Delitti* as first and foremost a pioneering penological document identified with the classical school in criminology and laying the foundations for a modern conceptualisation of the penal system,[36] there are equally strong arguments for perceiving it as primarily a human rights document with roots in political theory. The case for the latter view can point to both the substance of Beccaria's proposals, with their emphasis on the separation of powers and due process and their critique of prevailing penal practices such as the infliction of inhuman and arbitrary punishments, and to their underlying philosophy in relation to the rationale for the criminal justice system and the limits on the exercise of state power.

One obstacle to the identification of Beccaria with the contemporary school of IHRL derives from his perceived affiliation with utilitarian theory

[35] See Van Zyl Smit & Snacken, above n 8 at xvii.

[36] See, eg, E Monachesi, 'Cesare Beccaria', in H Mannheim (ed), *Pioneers in Criminology* (Montclair NJ, Patterson Smith, 1972) 36 at 49. For a more critical analysis of Beccaria's pioneering status, see G Newman & P Marongiu, 'Penological Reform and the Myth of Beccaria' (1990) 28 *Criminology* 325.

as developed by Jeremy Bentham, who – in keeping with the tenets of utilitarianism – was notoriously unsympathetic to the concept of natural rights.[37] Indeed, the core criterion for social action adopted by utilitarianism – to bring about 'the greatest happiness for the greatest number', applied by Bentham and his followers in a variety of fields (economics, morality, criminal punishment) – is frequently attributed to the text of *Dei Delitti*.[38] As a result, Beccaria has been associated with a consequentialist approach to penal philosophy (of which utilitarianism is the main exponent), rather than with its historic rival – the deontological school, which builds its theory of punishment on concepts such as retribution or desert. The human rights tradition, by contrast, is closely associated with a deontological approach to penal philosophy identified most strongly with Immanuel Kant, which prioritises the dignity of the individual[39] over the promotion of social objectives.[40]

The simple dichotomy between these two historic approaches is, however, increasingly and rightly perceived as 'fail[ing] to capture the subtle and sophisticated ways in which punishment theory has developed'.[41] It is moreover clear that Beccaria can in any event not be pigeonholed into this framework.[42] A major reason for this is that this dichotomy tends to be constructed within the narrower confines of moral philosophy, which takes little account of the broader issues of political theory with which Beccaria was primarily concerned.[43] The application of this dichotomy therefore misses the broader context that Beccaria presents to the reader when he elaborates his vision for a principled criminal justice system.[44]

While this vision in many respects reflected the prevailing values of the Enlightenment in general, we would argue that Beccaria's views on the exercise of state power in particular are deeply rooted in a Lockean-based liberal political theory and interpretation of the social contract.[45] Moreover, given

[37] See J Waldron, *Nonsense Upon Stilts: Bentham, Burke and Marx on the Rights of Man* (Abingdon, Routledge, 1987).

[38] In Beccaria's text, however, the formulation of this principle reads 'the greatest happiness shared among the greatest number'. See Bellamy's Introduction to *Dei Delitti* as it appears in Beccaria, above n 21 at 7. According to Bellamy, a careful reading of Beccaria indicates that (unlike Bentham), 'Beccaria was concerned to maximize equally the happiness of each person': Bellamy, 'Introduction' ibid at xix; but see Zucca, ch 1 in this volume, who argues in favour of the similarity between the underlying principles of Beccaria and Bentham.

[39] However, opinions are divided as to whether Kant had a theory of human rights. See Freeman, above n 34 at 29.

[40] L Caranti, 'Kant's Theory of Human Rights', in T Cushman (ed), *The Routledge Handbook of Human Rights* (Abingdon, Routledge, 2012) 59; D O'Byrne, *Human Rights: An Introduction* (Abingdon, Routledge, 2013) 31.

[41] M Matravers (ed), *Punishment and Political Theory* (Oxford, Hart Publishing, 1999) 1.

[42] See, eg, Bellamy, 'Introduction', in Beccaria, above n 21; and Sattar, above n 2.

[43] See Bellamy, 'Introduction', in Beccaria, above n 21; and cf G Binder, 'Punishment Theory: Moral or Political?' (2002) 5 *Buffalo Criminal Law Review* 321.

[44] See, however, section IV as to the difficulties in understanding the precise meaning of Beccaria's formulations.

[45] See, eg, AJ Draper, 'Cesare Beccaria's Influence on English Discussions of Punishment, 1764–1789' (2000) 26 *History of European Ideas* 177; DB Young, 'Cesare Beccaria: Utilitarian or

that it is customary to attribute the development of international human rights norms to 'natural law' and 'natural rights' as reflected in Locke's theory of state,[46] the identification of similar links in Beccaria's essay will lend support to the view that, like Locke, Beccaria was a pioneer of human rights. Moreover, insofar as we will be able to identify a number of Beccaria's insights that have survived the test of time (whether in the fields of criminal law, criminal procedure or punishment) and have been explicitly endorsed as human rights norms under international law, it may seem plausible to attribute to Beccaria a direct impact here.

We will seek to establish such connections between Locke, Beccaria and international human rights norms in a two-stage process. The first stage will seek to locate Locke's conception of the social contract in Beccaria's essay and in IHRL respectively. The second stage will be to identify rules and principles deriving from (or at least associated with) *Dei Delitti* among the international human rights norms.

A. Locke, Beccaria and the Social Contract

Although John Locke (1632–1704) and Cesare Beccaria (1738–1794) were not contemporaries, both may be considered part of the European Enlightenment movement, which sought to apply rational secular analysis to questions of morality, public policy and institutional structures.[47] The hierarchical socio-political structure that had attributed the monarch's authority to Divine will would henceforth defer to the recognition of the sovereignty of the people, accompanied by a belief in the right to equality, human dignity and the protection of individual liberties.

Like Hobbes before him and Rousseau after him, Locke adopted the concept of the social contract in order to explore the proper nature and extent of governmental authority. For while in the state of nature 'natural rights' – such as the right to life, liberty and property – belonged solely to individuals, the latter were assumed to have elected to transfer minimal powers to the state in exchange for an undertaking by the state to guarantee their future safety and security and the protection of their natural rights.

Of particular interest in the present context is Locke's analysis of the government's power to punish. According to Locke, as elaborated in an article by Simmons, in the state of nature the power to punish for any act of immorality

Retributivist?' (1983) 11 *Journal of Criminal Justice* 317; DH Clarke, 'Justifications for Punishment' (1982) 6 *Contemporary Crises* 25 at 29–31.

[46] Freeman, above n 34 ch 2. As to Locke as a source of international human rights norms, see section II.B.

[47] See, however, the claim by Beirne that 'there was not just one Enlightenment, but several': Beirne, above n 10 at 786–787.

belonged to the individual as his 'natural executive right'.[48] Locke also maintains that someone who commits an attack on another's rights forfeits their own rights in doing so.[49] This rights forfeiture carries across to the state setting, providing the state with a wide margin of appreciation in meting out punishment to miscreants whose misdeeds have rendered them rightless.[50]

While this might not seem a promising basis for placing limits on the state's exercise of penal force, Simmons points out that many of Locke's constructions concerning the political power of the state and its limits must be understood as conditioned by inexplicit and explicit consent to membership in civil society.[51] Political power can be set limits by explicit consent, provided that such limits are consistent with natural law and the goal of a stable and peaceful society.[52] This makes it possible to argue that the power transferred to the state is one that enables the state to protect the individual's natural rights, and therefore is a limited power granted under the terms of the contract. Such a conclusion is in line with Locke's position that the duty of the state entails only that it punishes the wrongdoers enough to preserve societal peace.[53] As Lang highlights, this means that the (Lockean) state no longer operates with a strong rights-forfeiture theory of punishment. Forfeiture is only a necessary element of rights-respecting punishment, not a sufficient condition.[54]

Given the numerous versions of social contract theory, it is of relevance to establish the degree of similarity between Beccaria's concept and the Lockean one. Devine observes:

> The development of Beccaria's jurisprudence from premises of Lockean liberalism is not superficially evident. However, not only are the premises of the two thinkers

[48] JA Simmons, 'Locke on the Death Penalty' (1994) 69 *Philosophy* 471. The famous passage from Locke is as follows: 'That is how in a state of nature one man comes to have a legitimate power over another. It isn't an unconditional power, allowing him to use a captured criminal according to the hot frenzy or unbridled extremes of his own will; but only a power to punish him so far as calm reason and conscience say is proportionate to his crime, namely as much punishment as may serve for reparation and restraint – for those two are the only reasons why one man may lawfully harm another, which is what we call "punishment". By breaking the law of nature, the offender declares himself to live by some rule other than that of reason and common fairness (which is the standard that God has set for the actions of men, for their mutual security); and so he becomes dangerous to mankind because he has disregarded and broken the tie that is meant to secure them from injury and violence. This is an offence against the whole human species, and against the peace and safety that the law of nature provides for the species. Now, every man, by the right he has to preserve mankind in general, may restrain and if necessary destroy things that are noxious to mankind; and so he can do to anyone who has transgressed that law as much harm as may make him repent having done it, and thereby deter him – and by his example deter others – from doing the same. So for this reason every man has a right to enforce the law of nature and punish offenders.' J Locke, *Two Treatises of Government* [1689] (London, Printed for Thomas Tegg et al, 1823) ch II, § 8.

[49] Ibid §11; B Calvert, 'Locke on Punishment and the Death Penalty' (1993) 68 *Philosophy* 211 at 219–220.

[50] Calvert, above n 49.

[51] Simmons, above n 48 at 471–472.

[52] Ibid at 472; See also Calvert, above n 49 at 220.

[53] See Simmons, above n 48 at 474.

[54] G Lang, 'Forfeiture and the Right to a Fair Trial' (2020) 14 *Criminal Law & Philosophy* 203.

> essentially identical, they also are presented in much the same way. The jurisprudential premises provided by Locke consist ultimately of two points: the elimination of traditional standards for evaluating law, and the substitution of the concept of free and equal individuals authorizing the formulation and execution of laws through consent and within a limited sphere of human activity.[55]

According to Devine, Beccaria follows Locke in 'postulat[ing] a state of total liberty and agrees [with Locke] that the natural despotism of individuals renders the actual enjoyment of this liberty uncertain'.[56] 'Since uncertain liberty is useless', Devine proceeds to summarise Beccaria's position:

> [I]ndividuals sacrifice a part of it to society in order to secure guaranteed liberties. The portion of individual liberty sacrificed by mutual contract constitutes the power of the sovereign. Thus constituted, the sovereign power is limited to the sphere of activity necessary to secure the rights of individuals.[57]

The state's power to punish is thus restricted to a minimum. As summarised by Devine:

> [I]n forming the social contract, individuals cannot be supposed to have surrendered power to the sovereign to deal with them more severely than is necessary to achieve the purposes of the social contract. Thus, any punishment in excess of that needed to defend individual rights is without authority and thus an abuse of government power.[58]

Many of the ideas presented in *Dei Delitti* appear to follow directly (if not always exclusively) from this concept of the social contract.[59] This applies to Beccaria's many castigations of the cruelty of prevailing practices and punishments, and his arguments in favour of mildness and against the death penalty, where he specifically asks rhetorically 'Who has ever willingly given up to others the authority to kill him? How on earth can the minimum sacrifice of each individual's freedom involve handing over the greatest of all goods, life itself?'[60]

It is also worth noting that although Locke and Beccaria held distinctive views about the death penalty,[61] some scholars read Locke in ways that would

[55] FE Devine, 'Cesare Beccaria and the Theoretical Foundation of Modern Penal Jurisprudence' (1981) 7 *New England Journal on Prison Law* 8 at 9.

[56] Ibid at 12, quoting the Paolucci translation of Beccaria, above n 23 at 3–7.

[57] Devine, above n 55 at 12–13.

[58] Ibid at 15, relying on the Paolucci translation of Beccaria, above n 23 at 10–14, 42–44.

[59] See Draper, above n 45 at 181: 'Beccaria's own justifications for the institution of punishment were drawn from a wide range of philosophical sources, the more prominent of which included: the natural law theories of Montesquieu, the contractarian thinking of Locke and Rousseau, the use of "happiness" as an end in itself as found in Hutcheson's and Maupertuis's early discussions, the materialist sensationalism of Helvetius, and the empirical psychology of Condillac.' See also Beirne, above n 10.

[60] Beccaria, above n 21 at 66 (ch 28).

[61] Note, however, that Beccaria would retain the death penalty in relation to a person who 'endanger[s] the security of the nation'. See ibid.

bring his views much closer to Beccaria's than the initial contrast between Beccaria's refusal to include the right to impose death among the state's punishments and Locke's endorsement of a state's right to impose the death penalty would suggest. Thus, when examining Locke's reasoning for the infliction of the death penalty, Calvert points out that Locke adopts utilitarian grounds relating to deterrence rather than retributive grounds. This entails a restrictive application of the death penalty, limited only to cases where the offender's continued existence poses an intolerable threat to society.[62] As such, although the state is permitted to punish deserving criminals with the death penalty, it could be seen as exceeding that right when imposing this penalty in cases where it is not necessary for the maintenance of society. Beccaria, who insists that 'the death penalty is not a matter of *right* … but an act of war on the part of society against the citizen that comes about when it is deemed necessary … to destroy his existence', concedes the possible necessity of such destruction in two situations: 'when the [entire] nation stands to gain or lose its freedom, or in periods of anarchy, when disorder replaces the laws'.[63] If Lockean necessity is similarly narrowly circumscribed, then it might be said that Locke and Beccaria would in most cases reach a similar conclusion when determining whether the death penalty could be imposed.

B. Human Rights and the Social Contract Theory

The influence of Lockean liberal theory on international human rights norms is well documented in the historical, political and legal literature.[64] Locke's philosophy of 'natural rights' assumes the form of an epistemological-legal analysis of what would eventually become recognised as 'international human rights'.[65] While formulations thought to be indicative of human rights have been identified in earlier periods and in various cultures,[66] it is the Lockean natural rights tradition that is generally regarded as the one most closely linked to the development of human rights in international law.[67]

[62] Calvert, above n 49 at 225–226.

[63] Beccaria, above n 21 at 66 (ch 28). Beccaria's exceptional justifications for the imposition of the death penalty thus rest upon utilitarian grounds – but in this case seemingly on grounds of incapacitation as much as deterrence.

[64] See Freeman, above n 34, chs 1, 2 and 9.

[65] See J Donnelly & DJ Whelan, *International Human Rights* 6th edition (Abingdon, Routledge, 2020).

[66] See M Ishay, *The History of Human Rights: From Ancient Times to the Globalization Era* (Berkeley CA, University of California Press, 2008).

[67] See PG Lauren, *The Evolution of International Human Rights: Visions Seen* (Philadelphia PA, University of Pennsylvania Press, 2011).

Standard definitions of human rights contend:

> Human rights are, literally, the rights that one has simply as a human being. As such they are equal rights, because we are all equally human beings. They are also inalienable rights, because no matter how inhumanely we act or are treated we cannot become other than human beings.[68]

As natural rights they are also described as being universal, inherent to the individual (i.e., not dependent on the state), independent and indivisible. The historian Yehoshua Arieli regards the recognition of human dignity and equality (widely linked to the social contract), and of the citizen's liberty and responsibility for his own future, as encapsulating humanity's progress in the Enlightenment period, along with the establishment of democratic states and IHRL.[69]

Social contract theory continues to serve us today as a conceptual basis in various fields,[70] but its most notable expression is found in the discourse relating to Western democracies.[71] The development from liberal theory to liberal democracy is well recorded in the declarations of independence and of human rights in England, in the United States and in France.[72] The connection of the social contract and its liberal interpretation to international human rights can clearly be seen in the constitutive texts formulated in these countries. From an IHRL perspective, the assertion in Article 21 of the Universal Declaration of Human Rights that 'the will of the people shall be the basis of the authority of government' reflects the social contract in its purest form, while the opening words of its Preamble relate to the concept of natural rights with their explicit reference to 'the inherent dignity and … the equal and inalienable rights of all members of the human family [as] the foundation of freedom, justice and peace in the world'.

These formulations, when read alongside the academic sources cited above, point fairly clearly to the Lockean social contract and concept of natural rights as the historical inspiration for modern international human rights norms. The close connection of Beccaria's *Dei Delitti* to that same theoretical infrastructure suggests the existence of substantial overlap between the underlying conceptualisations of Beccaria's seminal essay and of contemporary international human rights norms. Section III of our chapter will explore the overlap of some of the specific ideas incorporated in these two normative regimes.

[68] J Donnelly, 'Human Rights, Democracy, and Development' (1999) 21 *Human Rights Quarterly* 608 at 612.

[69] See Y Arieli, 'On the Necessary and Sufficient Conditions for the Emergence of the Doctrine of the Dignity of Man and His Rights', in D Kretzmer & E Klein (eds), *The Concept of Human Dignity in Human Rights Discourse* (The Hague, Kluwer Law International, 2002) 1.

[70] See M Keeley, 'Continuing the Social Contract Tradition' (1995) 5 *Business Ethics Quarterly* 241.

[71] See P Riley, *Will and Political Legitimacy: A Critical Exposition of Social Contract Theory in Hobbes, Locke, Rousseau, Kant, and Hegel* (Cambridge MA, Harvard University Press, 1982).

[72] See MF Plattner, 'From Liberalism to Liberal Democracy' (1999) 10 *Journal of Democracy* 121.

III. BECCARIA AND INTERNATIONAL HUMAN RIGHTS NORMS: COMMON ELEMENTS?

In the previous section we sought to demonstrate a continuity in the conceptualisation of the foundations of human rights, from John Locke to Beccaria and up to modern times. Consistent with these claims, we also believe that common elements may be identified between some of Beccaria's proposals in *Dei Delitti* and contemporary international human rights norms.

Before we turn to this analysis, we want to draw attention to the direct link between Beccaria's ideas and those of the American Founding Fathers, whose ideas in turn had a great influence on the emergence of international human rights norms. *Dei Delitti* is considered one of the most influential books in America's revolutionary period, and was turned to for guidance by the Founders and early American jurists, such as John Adams and Thomas Jefferson.[73] The American Declaration of Independence, the United States Constitution and the United States Bill of Rights were all shaped by Beccaria's ideas of protecting individual rights and his ideal of a 'fixed code of laws'.[74] These texts later stimulated the insertion of Beccaria's ideas into international human rights conventions, discussed below.

Making similar comparisons between Beccaria's proposals and contemporary international human rights norms, however, is very challenging, given the enormous changes in the socio-economic conditions and the political and legal cultures that took place in the intervening period of two and a half centuries. Moreover, while relative to this period international human rights have had only a brief history, some aspects of their development during this period have been very dynamic, thereby further complicating any attempt at comparative analysis. What is more, the main human rights treaties are somewhat reticent with regard to the norms of punishment, offering little beyond the blanket prohibition on torture and cruel, inhuman or degrading treatment or punishment incorporated in the ICCPR (Art 7), and subsequently the object of a specific Convention of its own (the CAT), and some specific provisions in the ICCPR relating to the death penalty, forced labour and the orientation of prison regimes. Perhaps owing to a tension at the time of the adoption of the earliest United Nations (UN) Conventions between the Kantian rights tradition, emphasising proportionality and autonomy, and the dominance of the positivist school of criminology and doctrine of social defence, which were committed to the individualisation of punishment,[75] the international human rights community did not concern itself

[73] JD Bessler, 'Revisiting Beccaria's Vision: The Enlightenment, America's Death Penalty, and the Abolition Movement' (2009) 4 *Northwestern Journal of Law & Social Policy* 195 at 206–215.

[74] JD Bessler, 'The Italian Enlightenment and the American Revolution: Cesare Beccaria's Forgotten Influence on American Law' (2016) 37 *Hamline Journal of Law & Public Policy* 1 at 49.

[75] This ideology is reflected in the language of Art 10(3) of the ICCPR, requiring that 'The penitentiary system shall comprise treatment of prisoners the essential aim of which shall be their reformation and social rehabilitation.'

much with the specifics of penal policy, or the manner and extent to which these might give rise to human rights issues.[76]

Since then, however, so-called 'soft law' provisions relating to punitive regimes and their administration have proliferated, and may now be found in a large number of UN declarations, policy documents and other sources.[77] The most prominent of these are the Standard Minimum Rules for the Treatment of Prisoners,[78] now known as the Nelson Mandela Rules, the 'jurisprudence' of the Human Rights Committee and its General Comments (and their equivalent under other UN Conventions), and the Universal Periodic Reviews conducted under the auspices of the Human Rights Council.[79]

Moreover, UN-based normative activity has been replicated under regional systems, most notably within the framework of the Council of Europe, which has its own set of Prison Rules,[80] its own inspection system and its own enforcement system. Comparisons with Beccaria could be drawn from any of these extensive systems.

In view of this plethora of punishment-related human rights norms, which are, however, unstructured and lacking any coherent policy, the methodology to be adopted for entering into a comparative analysis of *Dei Delitti* and IHRL is problematic. Given the limited space available, we will select various provisions of *Dei Delitti* that either are directly comparable with contemporary IHRL or will provide insights into Beccaria's normative scheme that will be helpful for our more general comparisons between the two normative frameworks.

The first point to note is that both projects purport to be responding to unacceptable barbarism perpetrated by states during the foregoing periods. Beccaria, after noting that in other respects the eighteenth century had shown itself to be progressive and enlightened, then commented that 'there are very few who have fought against the savagery and the disorderliness of the procedures of criminal justice', while making reference to manifestations of 'cold-blooded atrocity' and 'barbarous tortures'.[81] Similar rhetoric referring to 'barbarous acts which have outraged the conscience of mankind' reflecting disregard and contempt for human rights appear in the Preamble to the Universal Declaration of Human Rights.[82]

[76] Cf Sattar, above n 2.

[77] See, eg, Basic Principles for the Treatment of Prisoners, 14 December 1990, United Nations General Assembly Resolution 45/111.

[78] Sattar, above n 2 ch 5.

[79] Moreover, these bodies appear to have increased their activism over the past two decades, as reflected in the introduction of prison monitoring under the Optional Protocol to the Convention Against Torture (OPCAT), the expansion of the General Comments on the part of the Human Rights Committee, and the appointments of Special Rapporteurs by the Human Rights Council.

[80] Currently the European Prison Rules of 2006, but these are presently under revision.

[81] See Beccaria, above n 21 at 8 ('Introduction').

[82] See Preamble to the Universal Declaration of Human Rights, 10 December 1948, United Nations General Assembly Resolution 217 A(III).

Beccaria based his critique on various grounds: the conditions of imprisonment, its extensive use prior to trial, the failure to respect the principle of the greatest happiness for the greatest number, and above all the principles emanating from the social contract restricting the exercise of coercive power on the part of the government. Such rationales are not found in the texts of IHRL, but declarations consistent with the notion of a social contract may be found, for example, in Articles 28 and 29(3) of the Universal Declaration of Human Rights.[83]

Punishment, in Beccaria's view, is justifiable only for the protection of society, a principle that gives rise to two 'super-constraints' on society's right to punish. In the first place, the punishment must be necessary. 'Every punishment which is not derived from absolute necessity is tyrannous',[84] that is it must serve to protect security and liberty. These same values are reflected in Article 9 of the ICCPR.[85] The second constraint is that prevention will always be preferable to punishment. Beccaria indicated various ways in which crimes may be prevented, such as education, incentives and rewards, and the clarity of the laws.[86]

In the spirit of these constraints, it is similarly clear that Beccaria was in favour of reducing the ambit of the criminal law as far as possible. Much of his essay focuses on reasons for refraining from invocation of the criminal law, such as its probable inefficacy in many situations, and the importance of a feeling of entitlement to do what is not expressly prohibited. He thus seems implicitly to support the principle of using 'the criminal law as a last resort', a principle advocated by some human rights advocates today.[87] On the other hand, it must be noted that criminalisation and punishment are sometimes explicitly required for serious breaches of human rights under IHRL, such as in respect of torture under the provisions of the CAT.

Of greater relevance to our topic is Beccaria's opposition to corporal punishment, torture and the death penalty. His objections to these phenomena – and in particular his concerns with regard to torture – are primarily (but not exclusively) Kantian, all the more so in light of the then-common practice of torture prior to trial.[88] These standpoints are of course shared by central provisions of IHRL, although it should be noted that some use of the death penalty and enforced prison labour have been permitted under the ICCPR.[89]

[83] Ibid.

[84] See Beccaria, above n 21 at 10 (ch 2). The source of this proposition is attributed by Beccaria to Montesquieu.

[85] International Covenant on Civil and Political Rights, 16 December 1966, 999 UNTS 171, Art 9.

[86] Beccaria, above n 21 chs 41–45.

[87] See D Husak, 'The Criminal Law as Last Resort' (2004) 24 *Oxford Journal of Legal Studies* 207; P Minkkinen, '"If Taken in Earnest": Criminal Law Doctrine and Last Resort' (2006) 45 *The Howard Journal of Crime and Justice* 521.

[88] The extent to which Beccaria's arguments about punishment's limits go beyond utilitarian concerns is also discussed by Du Bois-Pedain, Gur-Arye, and Kremnitzer and Gal, chs 4, 12 and 11 in this volume respectively.

[89] Abolition of the death penalty is the subject of two optional protocols: See generally Hood & Hoyle, above n 6. Enforced labour for prisoners is permitted under Art 8 of the ICCPR – but arguably also affected by ILO Conventions. See also on this topic Sattar, above n 2 especially ch 4, and Rules 96–101 of the Nelson Mandela Rules, above n 7.

As noted earlier, Beccaria is known to criminologists as the 'father' of the classical school of criminology (in effect penology), and *Dei Delitti* indeed appears to incorporate sentencing guidelines (albeit not quite in the contemporary sense). We are informed that the primary aim of the sentence is prevention – to deter the offender and others from further offending. This is to be achieved by imposing minimal but proportional sentences. The minimum level would be just enough to outweigh any gain obtained from the crime,[90] and the certainty of implementation would ensure deterrence.[91] *Dei Delitti* also includes proposals as to the appropriate type of sentence for different offence categories.[92] These proposals appear to focus on what today would be seen as penological policies,[93] and bear little resemblance to IHRL documents or indeed to IHRL discourse: traditionally the concern of human rights bodies was (in addition to its focus on punishments that were unacceptable for reasons such as cruelty or inhumanity) merely to prohibit excessive punishment.[94]

These comparisons not only strengthen the impression that Beccaria was a pioneer of both human rights and penology; they also suggest that prevailing conventions, which did not require separation of these fields, enabled him to derive an interconnected set of restrictions on penal power that is more sophisticated and progressive than international human rights norms. One way of interpreting Beccaria is to see all these restrictions as following from a social contract that authorises the state to exercise only minimal powers and only when absolutely necessary. Thus only the minimum sentence sufficient to implement a policy of prevention can be imposed. This approach would also be consistent with his utilitarian views, whereby the suffering of the offender has to be reduced to the minimum required for deterrence. Another construction would approach Beccaria's exhortations as reflecting a sophisticated structure of interrelated principles and policies characterised by primary rules and secondary considerations. Any principles deriving from the social contract would be placed in the first category to which other considerations would defer. The principles of certainty and immediacy – essentially penological principles designed to render the system more efficacious – would be subject to the requirement that the sentence must be just, necessary and the mildest possible in the circumstances.[95]

[90] See Beccaria, above n 21 at 64 (ch 27).

[91] Ibid at 63 (ch 27).

[92] See Beccaria, above n 21 chs 20 and 22–23.

[93] The idea of relating the type of sanction to the nature of the offence may also be connected to penal philosophy and the concept of desert: see RL Lippke, *Rethinking Imprisonment* (Oxford, Oxford University Press, 2007).

[94] See, eg, the grounds for human rights interventions identified by D Van Zyl Smit, 'Punishment and Human Rights', in Simon & Sparks (eds), above n 29, 397 at 397–415.

[95] Cf Bellamy's analysis of Beccaria's attempt to reconcile contractarianism with utilitarianism in a manner that would prevent the sacrifice of the individual to the common good: Bellamy, 'Introduction', in Beccaria, above n 21 at xx–xxi.

IV. PENOLOGY, PENAL PHILOSOPHY AND HUMAN RIGHTS: CHANGING PARAMETERS

In the preceding sections we have sought to document the substantial common ground that Beccaria's seminal essay *Dei Delitti* appears to share with contemporary international human rights norms, in respect both of their underlying conceptualisations and their specific content. This may seem surprising, not only in view of the passage of time between the emergence of these two sets of norms – two whole centuries between Beccaria's publication (1764) and the adoption of the first human rights convention (1966) – but also given the ostensible difference in orientation between these respective normative regimes. For, as we have mentioned, *Dei Delitti* is perceived (at least by criminologists) as essentially a penological document advocating a set of (reforming) penal policies, whereas the primary role of human rights norms has traditionally been to place limits on the exercise of state powers in the field of individual liberties.

Such a simplistic dichotomisation between penology and human rights norms, however, fails to take into account the complexities of determining Beccaria's views owing (i) to the strong component of political theory incorporated in *Dei Delitti*, (ii) to his apparent inconsistencies and occasional lack of clarity, and (iii) to his need to camouflage his views from the censors.[96] We have also noted Roberts' comment to the effect that modern disciplinary divisions were not yet developed at the time Beccaria was writing.[97] With this in mind we have endeavoured here to take account of developing interactions over time between the fields of penal philosophy, penology and human rights norms.

In this section, we will continue the comparison by addressing a number of policy issues where there are indications of ambivalence both in Beccaria's formulations and within IHRL as it has been developing in recent years. Indeed, there even seems to be a degree of similarity in the nature of the ambivalence in some of these matters! The areas to which we refer are (i) the extent of their concern with – or more precisely their lack of focus on – the aims of punishment; (ii) the question of a positive obligation to punish; and (iii) the question of universality of punishment versus the recognition of cultural variance.

A. Aims of Punishment

Our thesis regarding the comparability of *Dei Delitti* and international human rights norms appears problematic in the context of Beccaria's views on the aims

[96] See Beirne, above n 10; Bellamy, 'Introduction', in Beccaria, above n 21; and Roberts, ch 9 in this volume.

[97] Roberts, ch 9 in this volume.

of punishment. Not only has Beccaria, as we have addressed, been perceived as a consequentialist of the same penal-theoretical camp as Jeremy Bentham, while human rights are associated with a deontological approach.[98] More specifically, Beccaria is closely identified with deterrence as the primary objective of punishment, while rights-oriented jurists and penal philosophers in the Kantian tradition have long put forward principled objections against deterrence as a penal aim. Given that Beccaria and Kant are both considered key Enlightenment influences on the development of human rights, one might have expected their divergence on this question to generate rival discourses within the human rights community

Remarkably, however, the international human rights movement (and institutions) has generally been reticent to take a position on the legitimate aims of punishment.[99] The English and US Bills of Rights focused on outlawing cruel and unusual punishments, and this concern was expanded under the UN conventions to prohibit 'torture or … cruel, inhuman or degrading treatment or punishment'. Attention has thus been focused on the practices of punishment rather than their policy or objectives, and one standard account by a leading scholar of punishment and human rights accordingly starts with 'punishments that can never be imposed'[100] before moving on to 'principles governing imposition', where the criteria considered are the 'legality' and 'proportionality' of the punishment, but not its aims or purposes.[101] It is true that the objectives of imprisonment are considered at some length elsewhere by Van Zyl Smit and Snacken – and are indeed specified under Article 10(3) of the ICCPR[102] – but, as clarified by these authors, in this context prison policy is regarded as relatively autonomous in relation to the aims of punishment.[103]

However, although we have argued here that contemporary international human rights norms are more concerned with institutional policies and practices than with the aims of the sentence, the two are not independent. For example, penal policies heavily oriented towards incapacitation and/or general deterrence, such as the notorious 'Three Strikes laws', could potentially fall foul of norms designed to prevent inhuman or disproportionate punishment. This type of criticism has not, however, been associated with Beccaria – in spite of his advocacy of deterrence – since for him the gateway to deterrence was via proportional penalties, and at the same time he was an advocate of the moderation

[98] Text at nn 37–40 above.

[99] It was this insight that provoked Sattar to research this topic for his PhD dissertation. See Sattar, above n 2.

[100] See Van Zyl Smit, above n 94.

[101] See ibid. A third heading is 'Implementation', which focuses on prison conditions and the nature of community sanctions.

[102] See above n 75.

[103] See Van Zyl Smit & Snacken, above n 8 at 76 ff; The authors cite Johannes Feest for the argument that 'prison law must be seen as a branch of administrative law that is largely independent of the criminal law and its attendant theories of punishment'.

of punishment, while enhancing its certainty.[104] Indeed, in these respects his sentencing scale bore resemblance to the moderate desert-based scale advocated by Andrew von Hirsch's seminal *Doing Justice* of the 1970s, which, in fact, mentions Beccaria as one of its sources of inspiration.[105]

B. Positive Obligation to Punish?

The question as to whether there is an obligation to punish pertains primarily to the realm of penal philosophy. Notoriously, Kant would insist on the implementation of a pending punishment even were society on the verge of dispersal, while abolitionists are in principle against punishment. A distinction has to be made, however, between criminalisation in the abstract of the type of conduct under consideration and law enforcement, that is, prosecution and punishment in particular cases. Beccaria, as noted, favoured a minimal societal power to punish, to be exercised when justified on utilitarian grounds. However, although we have indicated that Beccaria thereby moved to the position of imposing punishment only as a last resort, his prioritisation (when wearing his 'penological hat') of the certainty of punishment to ensure deterrence,[106] and his belief in the equal treatment of offenders,[107] both seem to lead to an obligation to prosecute (where there is evidence of the commission of offence) and to punish – albeit in moderation – if the perpetrator is convicted.

Human rights advocates initially had their sights set on the limitation of punishment and not on any obligation to impose it. This was largely reflected in the early UN human rights conventions, in which positive rights featured mainly in the International Covenant on Economic, Social and Cultural Rights, while the positive obligations towards prisoners under the ICCPR related to dignity and resocialisation, not punishment. Subsequently, however, punishment for breaches of human rights began to emerge as the way to ensure compliance with human rights, notably under the provisions of the CAT, while the meaning of 'breaches of human rights norms' in this context was considerably broadened by the merger (at least partial) of IHRL with international humanitarian law and transitional justice,[108] and the anti-impunity rhetoric

[104] For comprehensive discussion of Beccaria's approach to deterrence, see Kremnitzer and Gal, ch 11 in this volume.

[105] Von Hirsch, above n 17 at 6; cf Beccaria, above n 21 chs 6–11 and 27–28.

[106] See Beccaria, above n 21 at 63 (ch 27).

[107] Ibid at 51 (ch 21).

[108] On the developing relationship between IHRL, international humanitarian law and international criminal law, see P de Hert, S Smits & M Holvoet (eds), *Convergences and Divergencies between International Human Rights, International Humanitarian and International Criminal Law* (Cambridge, Intersentia, 2018). Already in 1966 the ICCPR included a provision (Art 6.3) recognising the obligation to prosecute under the Convention on the Prevention and Punishment of the Crime of Genocide, 9 December 1948, 78 UNTS 277.

accompanying the latter.[109] The state's obligation to protect victims' rights was in some cases read as generating an obligation on the part of states not only to criminalise certain attacks on rights, but also to enforce these criminal prohibitions.[110] Thus, 'while human rights have traditionally been used to limit the excesses of security of the state, they are increasingly presented as positive obligations, contributing to the extension of penal power'.[111] It seems that this trend has been particularly strong among members of the Human Rights Committee – often citing the need for deterrence as their motivation.[112] This indicates a possible convergence in a highly sensitive and still contested policy area, although it is hard to assess how Beccaria would have resolved the tensions between these conflicting arguments.

C. Universalism

Whether the focus of the normative regimes under discussion is the 'classic' human rights function of imposing restraint on state institutions involved in the administration of punishment, or whether it may also extend to a positive obligation to punish, a question arises as to the scope and application of the norms in question. International human rights norms are clearly intended to apply universally (except insofar as regional regimes are consciously formed). The universal approach has given rise to heated debates on cultural relativity.[113] Beccaria, of course, saw jurisdiction as limited to the polity governed by the sovereign.[114] But to the extent that he entered the more philosophical terrain of the aims punishment should serve, or indeed the conduct that should or should not be criminalised, Beccaria may well have envisaged a wider realm of applicability for his arguments. Bessler refers to the view that Beccaria and his colleagues promoted a concept of world citizenship.[115] The spirit of Beccaria's proposals certainly seems to have been directed at the totality of the European 'world' as he knew it, while at the same time envisaging variations, especially in respect to the forms of punishment acceptable among different cultures.[116]

[109] See above n 28.
[110] *X and Y v The Netherlands* (1986) 8 EHRR 235; Pinto, above n 28.
[111] Pinto, above n 28.
[112] Ibid.
[113] See, eg, Freeman, above n 34 ch 6.
[114] See Duff and Marshall, ch 3 in this volume.
[115] Bessler, *Celebrated Marquis*, above n 13 at 63.
[116] The latter impression derives from a generalisation of Paolucci's translation of Beccaria's chapter on the 'Mildness of Punishments' in Beccaria, above n 23 at 44, where Beccaria is translated

V. CONCLUSION

The challenge we set ourselves – to examine the extent of the linkage or overlap between Beccaria's seminal publication *Dei Delitti e Delle Pene* and contemporary international human rights norms – did not prove easy to meet. This was perhaps not surprising, given the asymmetry between the two objects of our comparison: on one side, Beccaria's relatively short but very personal and somewhat idiosyncratic critique of the criminal processes with which he was familiar in eighteenth-century Europe; on the other side, innumerable but diffuse provisions in a rapidly developing (sub-)field of contemporary international law that have been generated over the last few decades via a wide range of sources, both formal and informal. While the precise content of 'international human rights law' may be contested,[117] this field (or sub-field) today has high name recognition, as reflected on the shelves of any law library or legal (or social science) bookshop. This was not the case in Beccaria's day. Not only did the term 'human rights law' not then exist, but it is clear that the topics discussed by Beccaria in *Dei Delitti* were in fact more wide-ranging and included what we now call penology.

We therefore sought a methodology whereby we could contextualise the comparison, namely, by identifying the relevant fields or disciplines that prevailed during the respective periods when these normative frameworks were being developed, as well as by considering the histories of these fields and disciplines[118] between these periods. This, we hope, has enabled us to compare the two normative regimes in a more meaningful manner, while at the same time facilitating a better understanding of each of these regimes. The manner in which the issues are approached (or not) during any given period by given individuals or institutions will be determined, inter alia, by the status of the relevant field or discipline and how it is perceived. Following on from these methodological insights, there comes a bonus in the form of a better understanding of particular norms or proposals following their contextualisation. Specifically, and following today's lexicon, while Beccaria explicitly and consciously addressed an issue

as asserting that 'the scale of punishments should be relative to the state of the nation itself'. In this sense Beccaria seems to have pre-empted Durkheim and his 'two laws of penal evolution': see E Durkheim, 'Two Laws of Penal Evolution' [1900] (1973) 2 *Economy and Society* 285. *Note*: the similarity to Durkheim derives from the fact that Paolucci's 'should be' appears to be descriptive rather than prescriptive.

[117] Particularly contentious is the dichotomisation between 'hard' and soft' law: see Sebba & Er'el, above n 19.

[118] We should note that neither of the accepted academic terms 'field' or 'discipline' is entirely appropriate to describe the two normative systems that occupy our attention in this chapter (or, by analogy, 'sub-field' or 'sub-discipline') – neither the study of human rights nor penology having yet achieved the status of independent university departments. Moreover, the term 'field' as used by Bourdieu is employed to analyse the behaviour of those involved in the area in question essentially to protect their turf: see Page, above n 29. Nor do either of the meanings of 'discipline' elaborated by Garland appear appropriate here: see Garland, above n 30.

of political philosophy, namely, the state's right to exercise punitive authority (and, in particular, the extent of this right), he also dwelt extensively on two uncharted areas – human rights vis-à-vis the criminal justice system, and penology. However, by the twentieth century these fields had come into their own, and we are able to compare Beccaria's (implicit) human rights advocacy with the contemporary norms of IHRL. We also find that in spite of differences in the nature of the discourse, there is a strong resemblance between Beccaria's condemnation of cruel and degrading punishments and this strand of IHRL – and we find support in *Dei Delitti* for developing principles of human rights law in the area of criminal law, such as punishment as a last resort. In both contexts, the motivation for the restrictive normative regime was a response to the cruelty of existing or recent abuses on the part of state agencies, and in both cases the ideological basis for the limitation on the state's power to punish was derived, directly or indirectly, from a Lockean vision of natural rights as a part of the social contract.

Our perusal of contemporary academic literature and our impression of the activities of the relevant professional bodies have tended to confirm Sattar's observation that penal philosophy as such has assumed a low profile in contemporary human rights discourses; but also that, in contrast, human rights law is in open conversation with penology, and on occasion will incorporate its findings or exhortations into a human rights norm.[119] Given that this blurring of fields (if perceived negatively) or their integration (if seen positively) may historically be attributable to Beccaria, would this not render him an ideal candidate for the Human Rights Committee?

[119] Sattar, above n 2.

Part III

Locating Beccaria in Eighteenth-Century Criminal Justice

14

Criminal Justice Reform in the Austro-Hungarian Empire, Habsburgian Lombardy and Tuscany: Beccaria's Policy Memoranda in Context

ANTJE DU BOIS-PEDAIN

It is sometimes said that Beccaria's book 'was a success primarily because it advocated changes deemed desirable and supported by public opinion'; because 'Europe was ready for it in 1764'.[1] Such a view is unsurprising if we consider that the Prussian ruler Frederick II wrote to his friend the philosopher Voltaire, in a letter dated 5 September 1777, that 'Beccaria has left nothing to glean after him; we need only to follow what he has so wisely indicated'.[2] But even if his book was full of ideas whose time had come, for the enlightened rulers of his time, whom Beccaria courted as his readers and cajoled into agreeing with him,[3] 'to follow what he [had] so wisely indicated' was far more easily said than done. Beccaria himself clearly believed that changes could, and would, come from the top, their effectiveness depending on the sovereign's ability to force local power-holders to fall in line. His trust in the potential for effective leadership by enlightened rulers and their administrations was surpassed only by his distrust of the willingness of local patricians to engage in meaningful change.[4]

[1] Both passages quoted from E Monachesi, 'Pioneers in Criminology IX: Cesare Beccaria (1738–1794)' (1955) 46 *Journal of Criminal Law, Criminology and Police Science* 439 at 448.

[2] Quoted in MT Maestro, *Cesare Beccaria and the Origins of Penal Reform* (Philadelphia PA, Temple University Press, 1973) 134.

[3] Beccaria, in his prefatory remarks 'To the Reader', hails them as '[t]he great monarchs, the human benefactors who rule us [and who] love the truths which are expounded by humble philosophers': C Beccaria, *On Crimes and Punishments and Other Writings* edited by R Bellamy and translated by R Davies (Cambridge, Cambridge University Press, 1995) 3.

[4] On the latter, see esp E Tavilla, 'Beccaria, l'anti-juriste. Critiques de la culture juridique et résistances aux réformes dans l'Italie du XVIIIe siècle', in P Audegean et al (eds), *Le Bonheur du plus grand nombre: Beccaria et les lumières* (Paris, ENS editions, 2017) 97.

Hence *On Crimes and Punishments* was a passionate appeal to those at the top of the power hierarchy to overhaul criminal justice practices – an endeavour that (as Beccaria made explicit) would involve a complete break with tradition, based on a fundamental reconceptualisation of the sources of political and legal authority.

But for all his belief in the need for decisive top-down intervention, Beccaria did not write a handbook for law reformers. The implementation of his calls for reform is left to others, including the work of translating his ideas into concrete policies.[5] The two policy memoranda included in this collection and introduced in this chapter (section IV.B and section IV.C), which Beccaria submitted to the Habsburg administration, were, by contrast, written precisely in the context of trying to bring about concrete reforms. As such, they give us two small windows into what could and what could not be made to work in criminal justice reform at the time.

Before turning to these memoranda, the chapter traces the difficult and sometimes downright treacherous path of criminal justice reform in that period, focusing on the Austrian crownlands and on Northern Italy, the geographical region that encompassed both Habsburg-ruled Lombardy and neighbouring Tuscany. In so doing it allows readers to place Beccaria's memoranda into the larger landscape of reformist policy. It first (in section I and section II) outlines the main criminal justice projects pursued by Austria's rulers during the reigns of Maria Theresa[6] and Joseph II,[7] before turning (in section III) to reforms undertaken by Leopold II,[8] first over his many years as grand-duke of Tuscany and then during his brief tenure of the Habsburg throne. In section IV the gaze shifts to Lombardy, Beccaria's homeland, and the steps towards reform taken there. Particular attention is given throughout to the death penalty, and more broadly to the range of available punishments.

[5] DM Klang, 'Cesare Beccaria and the Clash between Jurisprudence and Political Economy in Eighteenth-century Lombardy' (1988) 23 *Canadian Journal of History* 305 at 307.

[6] Maria Theresa (also known as Maria Theresia), born 13 May 1717, died 29 November 1780, ruled the Austro-Hungarian Habsburg empire from 20 October 1740 until her death. From 1765 she made her son, Joseph II, co-ruler of the Austrian dominions but still controlled all relevant decisions.

[7] Joseph II, Maria Theresa's eldest son, born 13 March 1741, died 20 February 1790, took full control of Austrian-Habsburg government from 29 November 1780. The leading modern biography of Joseph II is the comprehensive D Beales, *Joseph II* vol 1: *In the Shadow of Maria Theresa, 1741–1780* (Cambridge, Cambridge University Press, 1987) and *Joseph II* vol 2: *Against the World, 1780–1790* (Cambridge, Cambridge University Press, 2009). Still very useful is P von Mitrofanov, *Joseph II. Seine politische und kulturelle Tätigkeit*, 2 vols (Vienna and Leipzig, CW Stern, 1910).

[8] Leopold II, Maria Theresa's third-eldest son, born 5 May 1747, died 1 March 1792, succeeded Joseph II from March 1790. Previously he had, from 1765, been ruler of Tuscany after the death of his father, under constitutional arrangements designed to preserve Tuscany as an independent political entity separate from the Habsburg dominions. The most comprehensive biography of Leopold II is A Wandruszka, *Leopold II. Erzherzog von Österreich, Grossherzog von Toskana, König von Ungarn und Böhmen, Römischer Kaiser* vol 1: *(1747–1780)*; vol 2: *(1780–1792)* (Vienna/ Munich, Herold, 1963/1965).

I. THE CRIMINAL LAW OF THE HABSBURG CROWNLANDS DURING MARIA THERESA'S RULE

Beccaria's acerbic description of the criminal law of his time and place as comprising '[a] few odd remnants of the laws of an ancient conquering race ... jumbled together with the customs of the Lombards and bundled up in the rambling volumes of obscure academic interpreters ... the residue of the most barbarous centuries'[9] was made with reference to Lombardy, but Austria's laws were no less vulnerable to charges of cruelty, irrationality and adherence to obscure tradition.[10] During Maria Theresa's rule, however, the impetus for reform stemmed, at first, not from any perception of oppressiveness of the content of the law but from a concern with improving and streamlining its administration. It was the sheer diversity and parochialism of applicable laws throughout the Habsburg crownlands that troubled the empress's advisors, as this constituted a major obstacle towards more effective governance.[11]

The empress was therefore persuaded in 1753 to task expert committees with the preparation of rationalising compilations of civil and criminal law with a view to codification, and to include reform of the court structure and procedure as an integral part of these changes. While the codification of civil law almost foundered on deep disagreements between traditionalists and modernisers,[12] the drafting of a penal code proceeded more smoothly. Ironically, this may have been for the reason that the project was a less ambitious one, aiming not for thoroughgoing revision but for a mere unifying compilation of law already in force, with the ironing out of regional differences and peculiarities. As such, the product of the compilation committee's efforts passed expert scrutiny by the President of the Prague Appeals Court with flying colours,[13] but caused the empress's chief minister, Chancellor Kaunitz, sufficient alarm for him to persuade Maria Theresa to reconsider bringing it into force. The consolidated code still featured crimes such as witchcraft, which most educated persons, including the empress herself, no longer believed could exist.[14] It also faithfully

[9] Beccaria, above n 3 at 3.

[10] Such charges were indeed made, particularly by Joseph von Sonnenfels, professor of political economy at the University of Vienna, whose views were initially harshly challenged by influential conservatives but eventually became instrumental in persuading Maria Theresa to abolish torture. See MA Cattaneo, 'Beccaria und Sonnenfels: Die Abschaffung der Folter im theresianischen Zeitalter', in MA Cattaneo, *Aufklärung und Strafrecht: Beiträge zur deutschen Rechtsphilosophie des 18. Jahrhunderts* translated by T Vormbaum (Baden-Baden, Nomos, 1998) 49.

[11] On judicial reform in the Habsburg monarchy, see FAJ Szabo, *Kaunitz and Enlightened Absolutism 1753–1780* (Cambridge, Cambridge University Press, 1994) 180–185.

[12] Szabo, ibid at 183, notes that work on the civil code had virtually ground to a halt by late 1773 and that 'a reformed civil code might have died on the vine had Joseph II not performed an abrupt *volte-face*, and put new energy into the process in the 1780s'.

[13] Ibid at 183–184.

[14] The leading study of the witchcraft provisions in the *Theresiana* is MF von Maasburg, *Zur Entstehungsgeschichte der Theresianischen Halsgerichtsordnung, mit besonderer Rücksicht auf das im Artikel 58 derselben behandelte crimen magiae vel sortilegii* (Vienna, Manz'sche Buchhandlung, 1880). In what is an interesting reflection of the differing political and professional

retained legal grounds for – and even helpfully illustrated – permissible modes of judicial torture, and preserved not only the death penalty as such but also the full array of gruesome judicially-ordered forms that its execution might take. To be sure, the code – just like the legal practice immediately preceding it – did not envisage that such punishments would be widely applied. The expectation was rather that the well-established practice of regular judicial mitigation of prescribed punishments (of imposing a so-called *poena extraordinaria* or *poena arbitraria*) would continue unabated. The legal experts called upon by Maria Theresa to address Kaunitz's concerns thus defended the code on the basis that it merely reflected law already in force. Based on this assurance, the code usually referred to as *Nemesis Theresiana ('Theresianische Halsgerichtsordnung')* was promulgated, but no one – including the empress herself – had any illusions about the penal law's urgent need for comprehensive reform.[15]

That the horrifying punishments prescribed in the medieval legal texts, which had nominally been carried across into the *Theresiana*, were in nearly all cases replaced by milder punishments did, of course, significantly mitigate the harshness of criminal law in practice. But it hardly made the position of an accused more secure, as to escape the appallingly cruel punishments prescribed by law he or she depended on such mitigation's being applied in the case by some decision-maker[16] (the judge, or the emperor by way of clemency). The accused moreover remained at the mercy of whatever alternative punishment was then chosen – and many of these were neither particularly civilised nor designed to be survivable.[17] Maria Theresa's immediate 'fix' was to reserve to herself the review of every capital case, and indeed the vast majority of death sentences were converted.[18] But criminal law reform was, for her, a source of

sensibilities of expert jurists and key political advisors, the witchcraft provisions had caused the compilation committee little trouble as they were consistent across the disparate sources. More worryingly, these provisions were not entirely obsolete, with occasional cases of witchcraft being tried in the provinces well into Maria Theresa's reign (see ibid at 5–11 for details on both points). In a fudge between modernisation and tradition typical for the style of government of the Habsburg monarchy, the empress stepped explicitly only on the most irrational tip of the superstitious iceberg, by prohibiting courts from using the most dubious of the traditional sources of evidence for the crime (marks on the accused's body and similar). For the rest, she contented herself with instructing the lower courts that all convictions had to be reviewed by the empress's legal division (for the instructions given, see ibid at 53–54). Maasburg's study also contains Kaunitz's indignant note of remonstration (ibid at 59–60).

[15] See also G Ammerer, *Das Ende für Schwert und Galgen?: Legislativer Prozess und öffentlicher Diskurs zur Reduzierung der Todesstrafe im Ordentlichen Verfahren unter Joseph II. (1781–1787)* (Vienna, Österreichisches Staatsarchiv, 2010) 38–40.

[16] This point was expressly made by Kaunitz in his memorandum to the empress; see Maasburg, above n 14.

[17] On the kinds of alternative punishments that could be imposed at the discretion of the judge, see Ammerer, above n 15 at 45–48. They included various forms of hard manual labour, which, however, often proved difficult to organise and supervise, so that convicts, bound in chains, were often semi-abandoned and reduced to begging for food in the regions to which they had been brought.

[18] Ammerer, ibid at 80, cites figures reported to Joseph II in the 1780s, that in the 1770s only about 30 executions per year were carried out in the Habsburg crownlands.

personal insecurities; she left this field to her son and co-regent, Joseph II, to whom she deferred in her subsequent decisions.[19] The boldest of these was the abolition of torture in 1776; a change Joseph II had argued for.[20] But reforms to the catalogue of sanctions were impeded by the difficulty of devising effective and affordable alternatives to the death penalty – a problem for which Maria Theresa's expert advisors offered her various reports but no solution,[21] allowing whatever impetus for further reforms there might have been during her reign to peter out quietly.

II. JOSEPH II AS SOLE REGENT: NEW PRACTICES AND NEW LAWS

Joseph, by contrast, lost no time after becoming sole regent in 1780 to pick up the threads of criminal justice reform again, with a particular focus on the abolition of the death penalty. Not even three months' after his mother's death, he tasked the Government's legal division (*Oberste Justizstelle*) with preparing submissions on the questions (i) to what extent, if at all, the death penalty needed to be retained; (ii) which types of hard labour were to be used as punishments for other criminals, proportionate to their crimes and appropriate to their gender; and (iii) how the secure incarceration and upkeep of these criminals could be arranged without extensive financial burdens on the state.[22] A mere two weeks later, he instructed the courts by way of a confidential dossier to continue to pronounce but no longer to carry out the death penalty,[23] and in April 1781 he ordered the preparation of a reformed criminal code and criminal procedure.[24]

[19] See H Conrad, 'Zu den geistigen Grundlagen der Strafrechtsreform Josephs II. (1780–1788)', in H Welzel et al (eds), *Festschrift für Hellmuth von Weber zum 70. Geburtstag* (Bonn, Ludvig Röhrscheid, 1963) 56 at 58.

[20] See Conrad ibid at 59–62 for Joseph's consistent position on torture throughout his reign. The empress's concerns against torture were in part due to the risk of permanent disability for a suspect resulting from the level of injury associated with certain practices of torture. At one point during the preparations of the *Theresiana* it was even considered whether alternative torture methods in use in other jurisdictions ought to be introduced. See WE Wahlberg, 'Zur Geschichte der Aufhebung der Tortur in Oesterreich', in his *Gesammelte kleinere Schriften und Bruchstücke über Strafrecht, Strafprocess, Gefängnisskunde, Literatur und Dogmengeschichte der Rechtslehre in Oesterreich* vol 2 (Vienna, Alfred Hölder, 1877) 265 at 268–270.

[21] Between 1775 and 1778 the empress commissioned numerous reports on the fiscal and administrative feasibility of the expanded use of various forms of hard labour and incarceration. The gist of these reports was (i) that suitable sites of imprisonment did not generally exist and would need to be built; and (ii) that the infrastructure and organisation needed to use prisoners for public works was generally also lacking. See Ammerer, above n 15 at 77–78.

[22] Instruction of 26 February 1781, quoted in G Ammerer, '"qui nocuit publico, Serviat publico"… Diskurse um die Arbeitsstrafe unter Joseph II', in B Holcman & M Steppan (eds), *Festschrift für Gernot Kocher zum 75. Geburtstag* (Maribor, University of Maribor Press, 2017) 13 at 15.

[23] Ammerer, above n 15 at 82. As Conrad mentions (above n 19 at 63), despite this de facto abolition of the death penalty it was again carried out in one case in 1786, in a most brutal traditional variant, after Joseph II had personally confirmed the death sentence.

[24] Ammerer, above n 15 at 82.

But with all the impatience in the world, the jurists could only be made to produce drafts at their own pace; drafts that were then extensively commented upon, redrafted and scrutinised again, with frequent personal intervention by the emperor, who held strong views on the subject and did not lack confidence in his ability to push them through.[25] Joseph's zest for the abolition of the death penalty did not, however, stem from humanitarian motivations as such. Rather, his vision of good government was linked to objectives of modernisation and secularisation; the overcoming of what he viewed as general backwardness in his lands.[26] He shared the utilitarian outlook of many Enlightenment philosophers, and rejected torture and the death penalty as anachronisms from an earlier, more irrational age.

A. Joseph's Introduction of Barge-pulling as a Form of Penal Hard Labour

Joseph's ideal of the criminal law was that of a more effective deterrent system, and he was keen to widen the use of hard labour as punishment for serious crime.[27] Frustrated by the inefficiency of his political-administrative apparatus in devising what he considered suitable punishments, he solved the problem in his own way by making provision for criminals to be used to pull transport barges upstream on the banks of the Danube and other waterways: a task so punishing for the body that those serving their sentences in this manner rarely survived it for longer than a few months.[28] Having personally invented this mode of punishment, Joseph was not inclined to reconsider it, even as increasingly alarming reports started piling up of prisoners dying in high numbers.[29] He blamed those figures not on the effects of the punishment on the prisoners' health but on the terrible climate in these regions, where fevers and similar diseases were rife among the population generally.[30]

For Joseph, preserving the deterrent effect of the punishment was more important than ensuring its efficiency as a means of providing a publicly useful

[25] Joseph's regular and detailed interventions in the drafting of the criminal code are traced by Ammerer, ibid passim and by Beales, above n 7 vol 2 at 548–551, as well as by C Hock & HI Bidermann, *Der österreichische Staatsrath (1760–1848)* (Vienna, Wilhelm Braumüller, 1879) 305–322.

[26] See, eg, WE Wahlberg, 'Neuere Praxis und Geschichte der Todesstrafe in Oesterreich', in Wahlberg, above n 20, 138 at 158.

[27] On Joseph's motivations, see Conrad, above n 19 at 63–65; and Ammerer, above n 15 at 79–81.

[28] On the introduction of this form of hard labour in 1783 by way of a direct written instruction from Joseph II, without any formal legislation, see MF von Maasburg, *Die Strafe des Schiffsziehens in Oesterreich (1783–1790). Nebst einem Rückblick auf das altösterreichische Gefängniswesen* (Vienna, Manz'sche Hofbuchhandlung, 1890) 9–11.

[29] Ibid at 17–18. Maasburg calculates that 721 died, out of an estimated total of 1,100 prisoners selected for this type of hard labour between 1784 (when transports began) and 1790 (when it was abolished).

[30] Ibid at 18.

service that unwilling locals had previously been pressed into performing. He therefore insisted that the prisoners stayed chained up even when their chains interfered with their movements on slippery pathways along the riverbanks, and insisted on small food rations and extremely primitive living quarters. Even though the convicts selected for this type of hard labour often had no more than a few years of imprisonment remaining of their sentence, no heed was paid in their selection to the likelihood that they might not survive this type of regime until their release. This punishment – although initially introduced as hard labour quite separately from the abolition of the death penalty[31] – then also appeared to Joseph a suitable replacement for the latter, in that it answered to his criterion of being a greater deterrent than immediate death.[32]

B. Joseph's Criminal Code

Joseph's revised criminal code[33] was promulgated on 13 January 1787 and made a decisive break with tradition. Apart from the complete abolition of the death penalty for all crimes tried in ordinary criminal trials – a very important change, but one that was not unexpected given Joseph II's rejection of the death penalty, which was well known – the code's instant fame was due to its advanced legislative structure and technique. Along with ridding the substantive criminal law of offences born of the superstitions and obsessions of earlier ages, such as witchcraft and heresy, it reorganised the entire criminal law on the basis of a distinction between two classes of crimes: genuine crimes or '*Criminal-Verbrechen*', and policy offences or '*politische Verbrechen*'.[34] These different categories of crimes are regulated in two separate parts of the code; each part with separately numbered provisions. The first part, which deals with '*Criminal-Verbrechen*', comprises 184 provisions and sets out the available types of sanctions for these crimes in its §§ 21–39. The second part, which addresses policy-based crimes, comprises 82 provisions and defines the sanctions available for these offences in its §§ 10–18. The prosecution of genuine crimes is regulated separately in a revised code of criminal procedure that rigorously does away with ossified ritual, rationalising and simplifying the law of evidence in particular, while containing significant protections for the accused. Policy-based crimes are prosecuted in a summary process before police tribunals. Joseph II's flagship codifications of civil law, criminal law, civil procedure and criminal procedure were 'the first codes conceived in the form which would become universal in

[31] Ibid at 12.

[32] On this point, see esp Hock & Bidermann, above n 25 at 329–334.

[33] *Allgemeines Gesetzbuch über Verbrechen und derselben Bestrafung* (Vienna, Johann Thomas Edler von Trattern, 1787); hereinafter 'Joseph II's code'.

[34] On the concept of a policy offence, and the choice of this term for the German '*politische Verbrechen*', see Appendix 1 to this volume, note *.

Europe in the course of the next two centuries', which explains their lasting significance for the development of modern legal systems.[35]

The new criminal code's equally instantaneous infamy stemmed from its regime of sanctions – both as regards the severity of the punishments it prescribed, and as regards their unmitigable nature.[36] Genuine crimes could attract three different types of imprisonment, of which the harshest type was of a kind no prisoner could possibly survive for long, as it required the prisoner to be chained to the wall with a very limited range of movement, and allowed him neither sufficient food nor adequate clothing or rest.[37] Survivable punishments could be more or less gruelling but were often combined with physically painful practices of public humiliation, such as whippings and lashings, and – at the highest end of offence seriousness – with permanent disfigurements such as branding and the like.[38] The image of the legal subject addressed by such punishments is that of an uncultured, hardened individual whose desires and temptations towards crime can only be kept in check by the prospect, and repeated demonstrations, of brutal consequences. If Beccaria was right that the penal law of a nation should be sensitive to its cultural development,[39] then one had to surmise the worst of the Austrian natives.

Notwithstanding the brutalities prescribed in the sanctions regime for genuine crimes, the most contentious aspects of Joseph II's criminal code – and the ones that were immediately targeted in public commentary – related to the code's provisions for policy-based crimes, particularly its extensive reliance on publicly humiliating sanctions such as floggings and whippings, and the prescribed application of these sanctions to nobles and educated people too. A well-known satirical work depicted various absurdities and cruelties mandated by the criminal code in a series of tragi-comic episodes set in an imaginary Judge Schlendrian's courtroom.[40] While the sanctions regime and its application to all

[35] See A Padoa-Schioppa, *A History of Law in Europe* (Cambridge, Cambridge University Press, 2017) 433.

[36] L Garlati, 'Die "grossartige Besessenheit". Das Strafensystem im Josephinischen Gesetz von 1787: Widersprüche eines "aufgeklärten Systems"', in T Vormbaum (ed), *Beiträge zur Geschichte der habsburgischen Strafgesetzgebung in Italien* (Berlin, Lit Verlag, 2010) 1.

[37] Joseph II's Criminal Code, pt 1, § 27.

[38] Joseph II's Criminal Code, pt 1, § 24 (branding); § 32 (whipping and lashing).

[39] Beccaria, above n 3 at 113 (ch 47): '[P]unishments ought to be relative to the state of the nation itself. Stronger and more easily felt impressions have to be made on a people only just out of the savage state. … But as souls become softened by society, sensitivity grows. And as it does so, the severity of punishments ought to diminish …'

[40] Judge Schlendrian – whose made-up surname is suggestive of laziness and only semi-benign incompetence – waxes lyrical to his family upon the promulgation of the new code, praising it for providing 'punishments proportionate to the crime, which do honour to our sensitive and enlightened century', such as '50 or at most only 100 floggings', which is 'surely a lenient, humane punishment. For even if a convict succumbs to these few floggings, he will not have died at the hands of the hangman … and neither the law nor the punishment is responsible for his death but rather his own weak physical constitution which prevented him from surviving even this very mild punishment.' He then proceeds to instruct his staff to order enormous annual supplies of hazel sticks and whips to ready the court for this new, mild regime of sanctions. FX Huber, *Herr Schlendrian oder der Richter nach den neuen Kriminalgesetzen. Ein komischer Roman* 4th edition (Berlin, 1787) ch 1.

subjects without reference to their social status and background had long been a feature of the drafts, some of the most objectionable details were introduced by the emperor, literally on the eve of the code's promulgation.[41]

The prescribed regimes of imprisonment (extremely serious, serious and milder – except for the last, life-threateningly harsh) initially attracted less public comment, perhaps because most people assumed they would not personally be affected by these, or because the conditions of imprisonment were largely invisible to the ordinary citizen. Among those involved in the administration of prisons, by contrast, the close proximity of these stipulations to present realities[42] was perhaps the reason they raised fewer eyebrows than they should have done. The English prison reformer John Howard certainly spoke truth to power when he chastised the emperor for practices that were 'worse than any other torture. Poor wretches are confined twenty feet below ground ... in dungeons chained so closely to the wall that they can hardly breathe,' and declared that 'I would rather be hanged, if it were possible, ten times over, than undergo such continuance of suffering as the unhappy beings endure who have the misfortune to be confined in your majesty's prisons'[43] – but he did not thereby tell Joseph anything he did not already know perfectly well and saw no pressing need to remedy.

Joseph took great pride in his reforms and let it be known that he followed not any philosopher's counsel but his own.[44] As one of his earliest biographers remarked in 1795, his 'moral and political character' was 'a kind of mystery ... a strange mixture of kind-heartedness and harshness, of greatness and pettiness, of well-considered and ill-considered ideas, of far-sighted and short-sighted plans and projects'.[45] The harsh (and, on occasion, strange) punishments prescribed in his criminal code earned him the consternation of legal scholars and educated citizens alike.[46] But the organs of the state were bound to apply

[41] Hock & Bidermann, above n 25 at 321–322 report that the emperor, inter alia, introduced alterations that deprived judges of the competence to reduce a convict's sentence after some time had been served, increased the maximum number of lashes from 50 to 100, and removed prescription.

[42] In many places of detention prisoners were kept under ground, without light or fresh air, and in extremely unhygienic conditions. For detailed descriptions of the appalling conditions that prevailed in different places, see Maasburg, above n 28 at 1–7, 22–63.

[43] JB Brown, *Memoirs of the Public and Private Life of John Howard, the Philantrophist* 2nd edition (London, Underwood, 1823) 468–469 (giving an account of John Howard's audience with Joseph II on Christmas Day of 1786).

[44] Letter by Kaunitz of 2 September 1784 in respect of Joseph II's abolition of the death penalty, cited in A Cavanna, *La codificazione penale in Italia. Le origini lombarde* (Milan, Giuffrè, 1975) 45 note 62. On Joseph II's style of government, see E Weis, 'Enlightenment and Absolutism in the Holy Roman Empire: Thoughts on Enlightened Absolutism in Germany' (1986) 58 *Journal of Modern History, Supplement S181.*

[45] Johann Pezzl, whose *Charakteristik Josephs des Zweiten* appeared in 1790, quoted in FAJ Szabo, 'Changing Perspectives on the "Revolutionary Emperor": Joseph II Biographies since 1790' (2011) 83 *Journal of Modern History* 111 at 119 note 39.

[46] For details of the strong criticisms in pamphlets, in the press and by political representatives at the time, see Mitrofanov, above n 7 vol 2 at 563–571. E Schmidt, *Einführung in die Geschichte der*

what the law prescribed, and – with judges stripped of their earlier discretion – the punishments stipulated in Joseph's code cost more prisoners their lives than the previous four decades of criminal justice practice (including his mother's enforcement of the death penalty) taken together.[47]

III. LEOPOLD II: TUSCANY AS A MODEL STATE, DAMAGE CONTROL IN AUSTRIA

Joseph died in February 1790. His longer-term succession plan had been for his brother Leopold's eldest son, Francis, to follow him on the throne, but now Leopold himself had to step into the breach. It is unlikely that he welcomed this development. Still only in his early 40s, he had at this point been grand duke of Tuscany for 25 years and, notwithstanding a strong hedonistic streak much remarked upon by his contemporaries, had governed it with the energy of a young man and the good judgement of a much older one. His philosophy of government was enlightened, and his style of government anything but despotic. Of the many rulers of his age who self-identified as enlightened modernisers, he was the only one to grasp the new ideal's full constitutional implications. He took an avid interest in North American constitutionalist movements. Far from being repelled by American efforts to throw off the shackles of the Motherland, he viewed constitutions that gave equal rights to citizens as entirely compatible with monarchical modes of government;[48] indeed, one of his many ambitions was to bestow a constitution on his Tuscan subjects (an ambition thwarted by intervention from Joseph II, who did not care for this idea to spread).[49]

Tuscany's rule had fallen to Leopold at a very young age – he was only 18 and had just married when, in 1765, he was called upon to replace his father as grand duke of Tuscany under the rule of succession according to which Tuscany should fall to the second-born son.[50] Immediately he set out to turn the run-down province into a model state.[51] In his political vision, he was far ahead

deutschen Strafrechtspflege 3rd edition (Göttingen, Vandenhoeck & Ruprecht, 1995) 257, cites a leading 19th-century criminal law author, who remarked that Joseph II was 'almost sickly original' when inventing new penalties.

[47] See Ammerer, above n 15 at 20.

[48] A Wandruszka, 'Joseph II und das Verfassungsprojekt Leopolds II' (1960) 190 *Historische Zeitschrift* 18 at 26–27; Weis, above n 44 at 197.

[49] See Beales, above n 7 vol 2 at 355–362 with reference to Wandruszka, above n 8 vol 1 at 368–390. In connection with forestalling Leopold's constitution-bestowing efforts, Joseph in 1784 pressurised Leopold into giving up this principle in return for assurances concerning Joseph's succession and provision for Leopold's numerous offspring. See Beales ibid at 359–363 for details.

[50] Leopold was in fact the third-born son, but the second-born had died young.

[51] On Leopold's reforms, see esp H Holldack, 'Die Reformpolitik Leopolds von Toskana' (1942) 165 *Historische Zeitschrift* 23.

of his advisors.[52] Criminal justice reform was only one element in the grand scheme of reforms, and was preceded by the reorganisation of the entire administrative structure of the province and by thoroughgoing land and tax reforms.[53] He turned his mind to it seriously in 1782. Early on he decided on a complete overhaul of both procedural and substantive law, as opposed to a more gradual and organic reform of the inherited status quo. He then took to drafting a set of instructions that were notable for their internal organisation, their reformed catalogue of punishments, and an appendix that contained a quantitative overview of crimes charged, trials held and punishments imposed by the courts of Tuscany between 1762 and 1782.[54]

His next step was to seek extensive written comments on his draft from four influential sources – the head of police, the head of the judiciary, a prominent member of the Council of State, and a seasoned former administrator and legal expert. Their assessments can only be described as dampening. The administrative expert cautioned against abandoning what in his view worked perfectly well, including such time-honoured practices as secret investigations and trials under the old inquisitorial procedure, the death penalty and even the offence of heresy. The head of police was concerned that police powers could be weakened; the representative of the judiciary counselled against the principle of open justice. The member of the Council of State, while supporting the grand duke's vision of abolishing the death penalty and a general move towards more moderate punishments, still viewed the retention of the possibility of imposing lesser criminal sanctions on those not cleared of suspicion as desirable (imposing such sanctions was a much-used practice under existing procedural law, which set the bar for full proof extremely high). These responses, given by 'practitioners wedded to tradition who ultimately tried to shape the future by taking the past as their model', certainly 'made it plain which elements of the grand duke's intended reforms based on a new ideal conception of criminal justice were likely to see efficient implementation, and which would be perceived as philanthropical pipe-dreams likely to meet with total rejection and resistance in practice'.[55]

Leopold was able to persevere by giving the task of revising the draft to the member of the Council of State, Tosi, who had at least been sympathetic to its broad outlines. The end product, proclaimed by Leopold on 30 November 1786 as '*Riforma della legislazione criminale*', was perhaps not quite the technically

[52] Beales, above n 7 vol 2 at 358, remarks that even Leopold II's chief minister 'could not enter into the spirit of his master's [constitutional] scheme'.

[53] A comprehensive account of Leopold's reforms can be found in ATW Crome, *Die Staatsverwaltung von Toskana unter der Regierung seiner königlichen Majestät Leopold II* vol 1 (Gotha, Justus Perthes, 1795). Specifically on criminal justice reforms, ibid at 120–151.

[54] The drafting process of the code that came to be known as the Leopoldina is traced in H Schlosser, *Die Leopoldina: Toskanisches Strafgesetzbuch vom 30 November 1786: Originaltext, deutsche Übersetzung und Kommentierung* (Berlin/New York, De Gruyter, 2010) 8–15.

[55] Schlosser ibid at 15 (my translation).

finessed piece of legislation that great codifiers aspire to. But its substantive commitment to penal moderation was ground-breaking. The new law uncompromisingly did away with the crime that had given the greatest leeway to manipulative enforcement against social and political 'undesirables' (the vaguely defined crime of lèse-majesté) while relegating heresy to a mere violation of police law. Offences of abuse of office and official corruption were prominently placed at the start of the code, and law enforcement was put on a short leash. Most importantly, the death penalty was abolished and the sanction replacing it – penal servitude for life – reserved for formerly capital crimes; and while the law excluded the possibility that previously existed to seek one's release after 30 years, it refrained from abhorrent modes of hard labour and there are no historical records of prisoners being systematically worked to death. Notable also for its brevity and for the avoidance of over-regulation, Leopold's Tuscan code constituted a clear break with past practice and a fresh start. It was not, to be sure, everything an enlightened philosopher could desire:[56] certain humiliating public punishments were kept, and judges retained the power to impose lesser punishments on those not cleared of suspicion. But the orientation of all punishment towards reintegration directed those who enforced the system away from penal excess, and the egalitarian principles underpinning the Tuscan code were, unlike in the case of Joseph II's code, not a target of public criticisms.[57] As Costa stresses, Leopold was clearly inspired by Beccaria: his prefatory declaration to the code echoes Beccaria's treatise in every important respect, with, however, the exception of the contractual foundation[58] – possibly because accepting it would have turned the abolition of the death penalty from something a wise ruler chooses to do into something he merely acknowledges as a limitation of his power.

Leopold was well aware of the criticisms and carnage his brother's sanctions regime had provoked. After taking over as Austrian ruler in 1790, he quickly put a stop to its most offensive features: barge-pulling as a mode of penal hard labour, the branding of criminals and the public performance of humiliating corporal punishments.[59] The last of these modifications signified a change in the

[56] The English translator of Leopold's code prefaced his translation with the remark that 'there are passages in this Edict which do not consist with that extensive liberty which is the just pride and boast of Englishmen'. Quoted ibid at 42 note 221.

[57] On the Tuscan code's egalitarian commitments, see esp F Jung, 'Die Gleichheit vor dem Gesetz. Cesare Beccaria, das toskanische Strafgesetzbuch von 1786 und die leopoldinischen Verfassungsentwürfe', in A Baumann, S Wendehorst & S Westphal (eds), *Adel, Recht und Gerichtsbarkeit im frühneuzeitlichen Europa* (Oldenbourg, De Gruyter, 2014) 141 at 153–155. For all that, the Leopoldina did not remain untouched for long. Key provisions were changed or adapted within four years. Even the population was less than grateful, with the clergy in particular whipping up the public against changes they alleged were un-Christian and un-Tuscan. See Jung, ibid.

[58] P Costa, '"Voilà le sophisme qui a séduit tant de publicistes". Lectures contractualistes des Délits et des peines dans l'Italie du second XVIIIe siècle', in Audegean et al (eds), above n 4, 197 at 217–218. Another interesting point on which Leopold does not follow Beccaria is as regards the carrying of arms, which the code restricts for everyone. See Jung, above n 57 at 160.

[59] Ammerer, above n 15 at 404–408.

underlying penal objective pursued by corporal punishments, from the deterrence of others to the reform of the criminal himself. But it did not put a stop to corporal punishments as such. Whippings and lashings remained embedded in the administration of penal sentences, particularly sentences of imprisonment, only now they were used as means of discipline rather than justified as a deterrent component of the sentence that had been imposed.[60]

IV. TOWARDS REFORM IN LOMBARDY: BECCARIA'S MEMORANDA IN CONTEXT

A. The Political Situation of Habsburg-Lombardy

In contrast to Tuscany, Lombardy, in which Milan – Beccaria's home town – is located, belonged to the Habsburg empire, having fallen to the Austrian Habsburg line in the peace of Utrecht and Rastatt in 1713/14.[61] It was ruled by a Habsburg-appointed governor, the 'Ministro Plenipotenziario' of Lombardy. This role was occupied from 1756 to 1782 by Carlo di Firmian,[62] one of Beccaria's ardent supporters, and after Firmian's death in 1782 – including when Beccaria wrote the two memoranda – by Johann Joseph von Wilczek.[63] Throughout this time the plenipotentiaries reported to and took instructions from the throne through Chancellor Kaunitz, the chief advisor to Maria Theresa, Joseph II and Leopold II.[64]

Austria's ambitions to incorporate Lombardy more fully into its economic and administrative governance structures were held back by the laws that governed the province, which for the most part preceded Austrian rule. Memorably condemned by Kaunitz in a letter to Firmian as '[a]n impenetrable labyrinth of statutes and laws in which the wealth of her majesty's subjects is

[60] For details, see U Gass, *Die Sanktion der körperlichen Züchtigung im österreichischen Strafrecht des 18. und 19. Jahrhunderts. Eine Annäherung an Foucaults 'Überwachen und Strafen'* (Diploma thesis, University of Vienna, 2013) 97–125.

[61] For details on the political context, see A Ortolja-Baird, 'Cesare Beccaria: Functionary, Lecturer, Cameralist?: Interpreting Cameralism in Habsburg Lombardy', in E Nokkala & NB Miller (eds), *Cameralism and the Enlightenment: Happiness, Governance, and Reform in Transnational Perspective* (Abingdon, Routledge, 2019) ch 8.

[62] On Firmian's period of governance, see E Garms Cornides, 'La destinazione del conte Firmian a Milano: analisi di una scelta', in A de Maddalena, E Rotelli & G Barbarisi (eds), *Economia, istituzioni, cultura in Lombardia nell'età di Maria Teresa* vol II: *Cultura e società* (Mulino, Società editrice, 1982) 1015.

[63] On Wilczek (sometimes spelled Wilczeck or Wilzeck), see C von Wurzbach, *Biographisches Lexikon des Kaiserthums Oesterreich, 56. Theil* (Vienna, Kaiserlich-königliche Hof- und Staatsdruckerei, 1888) 115 (entry on Wilczek, Johann Joseph). Earlier in his career Wilczek had spent some time as Maria Theresa's emissary at Leopold's court in Tuscany.

[64] On Kaunitz, see Szabo, above n 11. To facilitate the administration of the Italian possessions, Kaunitz had created the Italian Department as a separate branch of the monarchy's administration.

lost',[65] the local patriciate retained a firm grasp on their application through their control of the judiciary and the Milan senate.[66] The modernising overhaul of the province began during Maria Theresa's reign,[67] to the welcoming cheers of educated reform-minded youngsters like Pietro and Alexandro Verri, and the rather less enthusiastic reception of the older generation of establishment figures, with wide-ranging administrative, tax and land reforms.[68] In Ingrao's estimation:

> The cosmopolitan outlook of Milan's urban patriciate emboldened Kaunitz to stack its government with a remarkable group of Italian reformers, including Cesare Beccaria and Pietro Verri. Under their direction Lombardy soon emerged as a testing ground for some of Maria Theresia's bolder domestic activities.[69]

Reform often involved lengthy consultations with stakeholders so as to facilitate acceptance, but it could also be decreed from the top. In particular, substantial institutional and procedural reforms to both criminal and civil procedure were pushed through in top-down fashion.[70] As regards substantive law reform, however, the Habsburg rulers chose to proceed more cautiously, though it is hard to know whether this was so because they found the desirable outcomes less clear-cut, the task itself more complex given the danger of introducing confusion and contradiction into existing legal frameworks, or the risk of local political opposition comparatively greater (or less worth taking) than in the case of procedural reform.[71]

Criminal justice became a focal point of reform after Joseph II's accession to the throne. As in the Habsburg crownlands, it was connected to an administrative reorganisation that would, amongst other changes, separate judicial matters from all other business of government (fiscal and administrative). From 1784 he increased the pressure on the governors of Lombardy to move ahead with reforms, and when things – as usual – happened too slowly for his taste, he sent an emissary – Carl Anton von Martini, a legal scholar and member of

[65] Kaunitz to Firmian, letter of 29 December 1795, quoted by J Black, 'The Politics of Law', in A Gamberini (ed), *A Companion to Late Medieval and Early Modern Milan: The Distinctive Features of an Italian State* (Leiden, Brill, 2014) 432 at 452.

[66] D Young, 'Despotism and the Road to Freedom: Cesare Beccaria and Eighteenth-Century Lombardy' (1984) 13 *Studies in Eighteenth-Century Culture* 271 at 272–273.

[67] These developments are traced by Klang, above n 5 at 306–310; and most comprehensively by S Cuccia, *La Lombardia alle fine dell'ancien Régime. Richerche sulla situazione amministrativa e giudizaria* (Florence, La Nouva Italia, 1971).

[68] Cf C Capra, 'Habsburg Italy in the Age of Reform' (2005) 10 *Journal of Modern Italian Studies* 219.

[69] CW Ingrao, *The Habsburg Monarchy 1618–1815* (Cambridge, Cambridge University Press, 1994) 184–185. See also MG Vitali-Volant, 'Pietro Verri, Cesare Beccaria et les réformes en Lombardie autrichienne (1760–1790)', in F Antoine & B Bernard (eds), *Lombardie et Pays-Bas autrichiens: regards croisés sur les Habsbourg et leurs réformes au XVIIIe siècle* (Brussels, University of Brussels Press, 2008) 45.

[70] See MG di Renzo Villata, 'Droit et justice à l'âge des Lumières dans la Lombardie autrichienne', in Antoine & Bernard (eds), above n 69, 125.

[71] See Cuccia, above n 67 chs 1, 3 and 5.

Joseph's close circle of trusted advisors, who was moreover Italian by origin and thus one of the very few Vienna-based experts capable of assessing Italian legal materials – to push the changes through.[72]

Lombardian law was certainly no stranger to outrageous punishments and the widespread use of the death penalty even for crimes not generally considered capital crimes.[73] A Milan church from 1471 to 1760 kept a register of persons given spiritual assistance before the death penalty was inflicted upon them; this register – a copy of which was found among Beccaria's papers – showed that while the frequency of executions declined over time, on average there were still two executions per month(!) performed from 1700 onwards,[74] often on persons who had been convicted of crimes other than murder. As late as 1776, Gabriele Verri, for the Milan Senate, considered the retention of the death penalty necessary even for crimes such as theft, when committed repeatedly by persons with a criminal lifestyle, given that such persons were not deterrable by other punishments.[75]

Joseph II envisaged a comprehensive reform of Lombardian criminal law that would closely follow the blueprint of his Austrian criminal code, which was then in the final stages of drafting. An important part of Martini's mission was to prepare the legal ground for such an extension through a reformed criminal procedure. Martini completed this part of his mission in 1786 by introducing the 'Norma interinale del processo criminale per la Lombardia austriaca' with effect from 1 January 1787.[76]

In April 1787, Chancellor Kaunitz sent an Italian translation of Joseph's code to Wilczek, instructing him to seek out the views of the political and judicial authorities in Lombardy on possible changes to be made to the text of the code.[77] Wilczek turned, inter alia, to the 'Supremo Tribunale di Giustizia' and the head of police. The reports he received showed little appetite for the introduction of the new law in Lombardy. Lack of enthusiasm for the abolition of the death penalty was one of the reasons;[78] rejection of the prescribed catalogue of punishments as 'untraditional' another.[79] A local judge, Luigi Villa,

[72] See A Szántay, *Regionalpolitik im alten Europa* (Budapest, Akadémiai Kiadó, 2005) 105 ff (on Martini's mission, see ibid at 128–129).

[73] Lombardian law imposed the death penalty for a wide range of offences, including against property, homosexuality, heresy, etc, and the authorities were (until Maria Theresia prohibited the use of torture in 1776) empowered to torture suspects where the investigation concerned a crime punishable by death. See A Rinaldini, *Beccaria. Biographische Skizze nach Cesare Cantù 'Beccaria e il diritto penale'* (Vienna, Braumüller, 1865) 11–12 (quoting the relevant Lombardian Statute).

[74] Ibid at 18. On the use of the death penalty in Lombardy in Beccaria's time, see generally I Mereu, *La pena di morte a Milano nel secolo di Beccaria* (Vicenza, Neri Pozza, 1988).

[75] Rinaldini, above n 73 at 73–74.

[76] For details, see Cavanna, above n 44 at 39–40; and G Provin, *Una riforma per la Lombardia dei Lumi. Tradizione e novità nella 'Norma Interinale del Processo Criminale'* (Milan, Giuffrè, 1990).

[77] Personal communication from Professor Paolo Rondini, Professore Associato di Storia del diritto medievale e moderno, Università degli Studi di Milano-Bicocca.

[78] On this point, see Garlati, above n 36 at 15.

[79] Garlati, ibid at 14 note 32.

was tasked with further editorial work on the code, and produced a version containing numerous modifications and changes, especially to the kinds of sanctions.[80] It quickly became evident that an unmodified introduction of Joseph's code in Lombardy was politically untenable. A commission charged with adapting Joseph II's code to Lombardy's particular needs and conditions – the *Giunta Criminale* – was created in October 1787;[81] this commission held various meetings, but the code was not – even in a modified form – introduced during Joseph II's lifetime.

B. The First Memorandum

Milan was not so far from Vienna that notice would not have been taken almost immediately of Austria's new penal law. And indeed it was – not necessarily, however, in a complimentary fashion. This may well have been one reason why Wilczek also sought out the views of one of the Habsburg administration's most trusted and high-ranking officials: Cesare Beccaria.[82]

While it might seem to the modern reader that the part on genuine crimes would be the more contentious part of the code, from a political perspective the opposite was true.[83] It was in relation to policy crimes that respectable citizens were most likely to find themselves at the receiving end of criminal law enforcement – not least because Joseph had, even prior to the coming into force of his code, in some widely publicised cases insisted on the application of publicly humiliating punishments to nobles irrespective of their rank.[84] Beccaria was thus tasked with reporting on the part of the code likely to meet with the greatest concern and resistance amongst persons of influence. It is difficult to know whether he was approached because he was expected to support the egalitarian application of the law that the code prescribed, or because it was hoped that he would ring the bell of moderation.[85] What we do know is that the request came to Beccaria despite the fact that up to this point he had not been involved in criminal justice issues during his entire time in the Habsburg administration.

[80] On Villa's draft code, see P Rondini, *Il progetto di Codice Penale per la Lombardia Austriaca di Luigi Villa (1787): Pietra scartata o testata d'angolo?* (Padova, CEDAM, 2006).

[81] Garlati, above n 36 at 15 (with further references); Cavanna, above n 44 at 60–67.

[82] Beccaria's elevated position in the administration is evident from the organigram sketched in Wilczek's own hand and reproduced in Szántay, above n 72 at 356–357. Following the comprehensive reorganisation of Lombardy's governmental and administrative structures, which Joseph ordered in 1785, Beccaria had become the head of one of seven departments, that for economic and commercial affairs.

[83] See Garlati, above n 36 at 3 and 14 note 32 on public reactions in Lombardy to Joseph's code.

[84] See Beales, above n 7 at 551 for examples and further references.

[85] Kaunitz had certainly always felt that the code's penchant for publicly humiliating punishments was unfortunate and, when applied to the educated classes, toxic. For Kaunitz's remarks on the State council to that effect, see Hock & Bidermann, above n 25 at 310 and 315.

It is certainly not implausible that his input was sought because the administration wanted to arm itself with arguments justifying the introduction of a modified version of the code in Lombardy and, apart from seeking guidance on what needed to be modified, the very fact that modifications were recommended by someone already on record as sharing the major premises of the code might perhaps give Vienna reason to pause.

In writing this report,[86] Beccaria therefore had to walk a diplomatic tightrope, and one cannot doubt that he knew it. He perceived clearly that the code's combination of punishments based on public humiliation for minor crimes with an insistence on applying these punishments to everyone, without differentiation as to station or rank, would be a breeding ground for opposition and delegitimate the Habsburg Government completely in the public eye. But neither can he have been unaware that these were precisely the aspects of the code that were particularly dear to the regent.

Beccaria's grand strategy for silver-tongued moderation is threefold: he repeatedly emphasises the docile, guidable but also fearful disposition of the Lombardian people[87] (the implication being that, in Lombardy, a wise ruler might want to do things differently); he builds on the nature of policy crimes the argument that the main purpose of punishing such crimes is to bring the errant offender back into the fold (the implication being that one therefore must not use punishments that make such reintegration impossible[88]); and he draws on the impact of publicly humiliating punishments on persons of higher standing to argue against such punishments in respect of policy offences on crime-preventive as well as egalitarian grounds.[89] Beccaria then cautions that the very aim of these sanctions, to make the perpetrator infamous in the eyes of the people, is one the legislator cannot be sure to achieve in respect of policy offences, as the societal perception of what crimes bring shame on their perpetrators is one the legislator cannot control directly (although he may seek to influence public opinion indirectly).[90] This allows Beccaria to point to another reason why shaming sanctions should be avoided, this time the implication being: for everyone.

[86] C Beccaria, 'Brevi riflessioni intorno al Codice generale sopra i delitti e le pene per quanto riguarda i delitti politici' in C Beccaria, *Opere* vol 2 edited by S Romagnoli (Florence, Sansoni, 1958) 705–718, here quoted as translated in Appendix 1 to this volume. On the correct dating (June 1787), see Appendix 1 to this volume, n 2.

[87] Appendix 1 to this volume at [22]–[24].

[88] Ibid at [6], [7], [8], [16], [19].

[89] Ibid at [18] and [21]. As regards genuine crimes, Beccaria also considers such punishment – due to its effects – graver for the nobleman than for a member of the lower classes, but argues that for these crimes, punishing the nobleman more harshly is appropriate because, if a member of the upper classes commits a genuine crime, the crime itself is more grave by reason of the fact that society already gave many more advantages and comforts to this person who now commits an act tending to its destruction. Ibid at [20]. This allows him (and possibly his ruler, were he to be attracted to this modification) to remain outwardly consistent with his earlier argument for strict equality.

[90] Ibid at [10], [24].

We should not allow the measured tone of the report and the interweaving style of exposition to detract us from its bold substance. Beccaria's definitional considerations towards the beginning of the report[91] may seem technical and rather dull, but it is on these definitions that he builds his arguments that correction must be the aim of punishing policy offences (which 'render society imperfect, but without tending towards its destruction directly'[92]) since these offenders, albeit errant, could still be useful members of society, additionally stressing that non-rehabilitative punishments for these offences can only have criminogenic effects. In this manner, Beccaria can claim to stay completely in line with the values and objectives underpinning the code, while in substance proposing a complete overhaul of its intensely problematic regime of sanctions. After narrowing the category of policy offences to 'those simple blameworthy acts and transgressions, which do not involve any type of fraud or violence, substantial and malicious incitement to evil', he suggests that 'the tribunal for policy offences should be an authoritative father rather than a judge, correcting and not avenging human actions' and that its sanctions should be limited to 'greater or lesser periods of prison or detention …, bearing in mind that detention could be at home or in a prison completely separate from the prison for criminal offenders' and 'according to the person's station, to deprivation of or suspension from duties of office; to the closure of a business for a fixed period, with a public notice giving the reason; to prohibition from leaving the town; to exile from a given place; to banishment to the country; and to public admonition'.[93] Floggings and whippings, hard labour and onerous modes of imprisonment have dropped off the list.

It is in this context that his suggestion that some of the policy-based crimes should be reclassified as minor genuine crimes must be read. Such mild punishments would not be appropriate for crimes like theft or fraud.[94] After conceding this, however, Beccaria immediately insists that the sanctions prescribed for genuine crimes in Part I of the code are too severe for such minor genuine crimes.[95] Moreover, for these minor crimes, first-time offenders should only be punished with sanctions contained in his (much moderated) list of sanctions for policy offences.[96] In substance, therefore, the upgrading of some policy offences to minor genuine crimes would make the regulatory scheme more consistent but not lead to a harsher regime of sanctions in practice.[97]

[91] Ibid at [5].

[92] Ibid.

[93] All quotations in this sentence, ibid at [25].

[94] Beccaria also suggests the reclassification of adultery, when committed by a married woman, as a minor genuine crime as, in the case of offspring, it undermines society's reliance on genealogy for inheritance. Ibid at [27].

[95] Ibid at [26].

[96] Ibid.

[97] Incidentally, Beccaria's suggestion to introduce an intermediate category of minor genuine crimes resolves a problem that had bogged down the drafters of the code but eluded satisfactory resolution by them: whether the label 'crimes' was, as such, appropriate for policy offences or not. On this disagreement, see Hock & Bidermann, above n 25 at 318–320.

Beccaria's report skilfully demonstrates how a proper division of crimes, and a clear sense of the main aims punishment should serve in respect of these, can ground a much more moderate penal regime. He also highlights the risks of abuse and overreach that follow from the prescribed summary procedure for policy crimes (a procedure he in principle supports, provided that the sanctions are as minor as he suggested they should be). His proposals, if implemented, would convert the emperor's harsh penal code into a much milder one.

On many of these issues, Beccaria echoed or provided additional grounds for positions taken by others, both in public life and in administrative service.[98] This is precisely what gives this document its significance. What Beccaria said confirmed the importance of these views for his superiors and allowed them to slow down, in the time-honoured way of the imperial Habsburg administration that Joseph II had so often railed against, the introduction of Joseph's code in Lombardy – to the point where the project eventually ground to a halt.[99]

C. The Second Memorandum

Soon after his accession to the Austrian throne, Leopold II set the law-reform process back in motion by issuing fresh instructions for the *Giunta Criminale* (taking into consideration, this time, not only Joseph II's Austrian criminal code but also Leopold's Tuscan code).[100] Beccaria was the only member of the commission whose name was suggested by Leopold II himself.[101] A sub-committee was created in July 1791 to consider in particular the question of abolishing the death penalty; this committee – which elected Beccaria as rapporteur – was unable to reach agreement on this question. At the meeting on 22 January 1792 in which votes were taken, Beccaria and the two committee members who supported him declared that they would set out the reasons for their vote in a separate document to be attached to the protocol of the meeting; this is the document analysed here.[102]

That Beccaria found himself in the minority in supporting abolition may appear strange when one appreciates that the commission was created by, and charged with reporting to, a distinctly abolition-friendly administration and monarchy (with Joseph II and Leopold II both embracing abolition). It appears

[98] Eg, by Villa in his draft code; see Rondini, above n 80.

[99] See also Cavanna, above n 44 at 58–59.

[100] Rinaldini, above n 73 at 76–77; Cavanna, above n 44 ch 3. As a matter of fact, the commission appears to have relied heavily on the draft code already prepared by Villa in 1787: see Rondini, above n 80 at 8–11.

[101] Rinaldini, above n 73 at 77.

[102] C Beccaria et al, 'Voto degli infrascritti individui della giunta delegata per la riforma del sistema criminale nella Lombardia austriaca riguardante la pena di morte', in C Beccaria, *Opere* vol 2 edited by S Romagnoli (Florence, Sansoni, 1958) 735–741, translated in Appendix 2 to this volume. The protocol of the commission's meeting on 22 January 1792 is reproduced in C Cantù, *Beccaria e il diritto penale* (Florence, G Barbèra, 1862) 357–358.

less strange, however, if one bears in mind that the commission was heavily staffed with members of the judiciary, and that the cause of abolition had long failed to attract the judicial elite's support.[103]

The report advances three arguments against the death penalty: that it is unnecessary and therefore unjust; that it is less efficacious than perpetual punishment combined with continuous publicity; and that it is irreversible.[104] Regarding the first two arguments, it closely follows Beccaria's earlier arguments in *On Crimes and Punishments*.[105] The third argument is new, and developed in the lengthiest section of the report.[106] The report also goes beyond Beccaria's book in stating, positively, that

> if we look … to those countries both near and far where the death penalty has been restricted to serious crimes, we will find … [that] where punishments have been more moderate, and for that very reason more strictly applied against delinquents (there being fewer reasons to let them go unpunished), crimes have become less frequent …[107]

– an assertion that Beccaria and his colleagues likely felt justified in making based on the post-abolition experience of neighbouring Tuscany. The argument from proportionality, which Beccaria first presented in chapter 27 of his book, is also developed further in an interesting direction: the report, for the first time, exposes the fallacy in the claim that the death penalty is required for the most serious crimes, 'for it is clear that no matter how barbaric a murderer may be, there is always the possibility that someone else may commit even more barbaric crimes and in greater number', such that the quest to devise a punishment that matches the punished crime quickly becomes quixotic and tempts the criminal justice system to amplify the death penalty 'with more atrocious and sophisticated torments', thus 'adding a legal example of cruelty to the rather illogical idea of punishing a homicide with another homicide'.[108]

The only argument missing from the report is the one Beccaria gave greatest prominence to in his book: the claim that the sovereign has no right to punish by death, since that right cannot have been included in the 'sum of the smallest portions of each man's own freedom' that are 'the foundation of sovereignty and

[103] See text at n 75 above for the position of the Milan Senate, and more generally L Garlati, 'Nemo propheta in patria. La proposta abolizionista di Beccaria nel diritto italiano di fine Settecento tra tiepidi entusiasmi e tenaci opposizioni', in L Garlati & G Chiodi (eds), *Un uomo, un libro. Pena di morte e processo penale nel 'Dei delitti e delle pene' di Cesare Beccaria* (Milan, Giuffrè, 2014) ix. That abolition was a 'hard sell' had been no less true for Austria, where the Compilation Commission had in 1781 – in full knowledge of Joseph II's preference for abolition – come out in support of the death penalty. There, only its president, Count Sinzendorf, and the councillors von Keeß and Martini had voted for abolition (Hock & Bidermann, above n 25 at 308).

[104] Appendix 2 to this volume at [4] (final sentence).

[105] Ibid at [5] and [7], with editorial notes 4, 6 and 7 detailing parallel passages in *On Crimes and Punishments*.

[106] Ibid at [9].

[107] Ibid at [6].

[108] All quotations in this sentence: ibid at [8].

its laws'.[109] To the contrary, the report stresses that its authors 'are not motivated by an ill-conceived passion for the wicked – much less by the idea of curtailing the right of the sovereign legislator to prescribe it if in his Great Wisdom he were to think it necessary in order to repress crimes'[110] – a volte-face that is perhaps unsurprising, given that this was the one argument unlikely to meet with the sovereign's approval.

At first blush, this may not seem much of a loss – the argument, one might say, relies on a philosophical construct (the social contract) rather than on anything capable of being evidenced in any event. But this reply misses its true importance. The case against the death penalty is only watertight if it is based on the notion that the state has no right to employ it because the rights of the citizen stand in opposition to it. If that premise is abandoned – something that Beccaria and the other committee members had to do, of course, whatever their personal beliefs on the matter, as it was not open to them to proceed on the basis that the sovereign's powers were in any way curtailed (even Leopold had not admitted that when he abolished the death penalty in Tuscany) – the whole issue is downgraded from a question of principle, and rights, to a mere policy matter. Beccaria and his co-authors add an important policy argument to the mix – the irrevocability of death – and they also point out the practical unsustainability of a competition with the most brutal criminals for the most abhorrent penalty. But all these policy arguments are vulnerable to counterarguments: all punishments are irrevocable, and it is surely doubtful whether it is really easier for a man to look death defiantly in the eye than to contemplate with equanimity the slow but inexorable accumulation of unhappy moments in a life of penal slavery. If the case for the abolition of the death penalty has to rest on these alone, the case for abolition can hardly be a decisive one. A polity that takes itself to have the right to punish by death is difficult to persuade of the greater wisdom of refraining from using it. At the level of policy, as every contemporary committee found, those in favour of retaining the death penalty tended to win out. It was familiar and relatively easy to implement; the alternatives were complicated and expensive to administer, and their superior efficiency was empirically uncertain. Only when treated as a question of principle and right was the case against the death penalty a conclusive one.

V. CONCLUSION

Beccaria's thinking is infused with the idea that rulers have obligations towards those they rule. That thought is not in tension with their supremacy, since (as good rulers, which they are also credited as being, or as aspiring to be) they

[109] Beccaria, above n 3 at 66 (ch 28). The philosophical soundness of Beccaria's argument, and the challenges made against it, are analysed in Du Bois-Pedain, ch 4 in this volume.
[110] Appendix 2 to this volume at [9].

would want to use their power only in legitimate ways. Beccaria helps them think through what it is permissible for them to do – and here is where the thought comes to prominence that people give up only the minimum amount of freedom necessary to secure the enjoyment of their rights. Read in this spirit, the social contract Beccaria refers to is not a theoretical device from which certain conclusions are drawn but reflects an existing political-constitutional convention, rather similar to the sense in which the United Kingdom is said to have a constitution: a set of practices underpinned by what are imagined to be shared assumptions about good and appropriate government and limits to the exercise of sovereign power.[111] Paragraph by paragraph, chapter by chapter, Beccaria builds the political castle of good, enlightened rulership and then holds its door open for the rulers of his time to enter.

It is with this understanding of what he is talking about that Beccaria addresses the rulers of his age. And, interestingly, this is also how he was understood by them – perhaps better than by some of his philosophical interlocutors. This is why Leopold II, who accepted the picture of limited government as the basis of his authority, was happy for his reforms to be understood as responding to Beccaria's call for change; this was perhaps also why Joseph II (jealous to guard, as against this modern one, the earlier understanding of his authority, where the ruler derives his authority from and is accountable only to God and not to those he rules) insisted that his reforms were not inspired by the writings of any philosopher – even though in substance they implemented a good portion of Beccaria's main reform proposals for criminal practice.

But, as this chapter has amply demonstrated, it was not easy being a truly Beccarian policymaker in Beccarian times. Too deeply inscribed in the political imagination were the criminal justice practices of the day. One only has to contemplate Jefferson's Beccaria-inspired (as he himself took it to be) catalogue of mutilations that constituted, for him, proportionate punishments (and which had the good historical fortune of failing to impress his political allies when they got to see it) to appreciate the moral disaster that lay in the wake of misunderstood notions of criminal deterrence and proportionality.[112]

[111] For this reconstruction of Beccaria's conception of the social contract, see Du Bois-Pedain, ch 4 in this volume.

[112] Jefferson's aim was to devise appropriate punishments for formerly capital crimes but his draft bill included mutilating punishments such as castration. After tracing the extent of Beccaria's influence on Jefferson through the latter's notebooks and letters, JD Bessler, 'The Italian Enlightenment and the American Revolution: Cesare Beccaria's Forgotten Influence on American Law' (2016) 37 *Hamline Journal of Public Law & Policy* 1 at 148 observes that 'Some of Jefferson's thinking and language closely tracked what appeared in *On Crimes and Punishments*, but Jefferson – like many early Americans – had difficulty completely breaking away from antiquated common law punishments.'

None of these problems were present in Beccaria's position as set out in *On Crimes and Punishments*. They were distortions that arose when he was read by those who did not have what we would now call the emotional intelligence not only to rationally analyse but also to sympathetically imagine what implementing their policy proposals would be like. Beccaria was able to imagine himself in the criminal's place and station in the world. This leap in sympathetic imagination, which sustained his decisive turn away from penal cruelty, was not one even his most ardent admirers could easily emulate.[113]

[113] The contemptuous dismissal of those punished as less worthy of protection than other citizens shines through, for instance, in Diderot's oblique placing of a question mark behind the worthiness of a concern with how those found guilty of crimes are to be treated: 'To save the life of a man is always an excellent deed, though there may be a presumption against this man [the convicted criminal on the scaffold] which does not apply to the victim of a bad doctor. From this I only draw the conclusion that there are many disadvantages [to Beccaria's ideas] which are in different ways serious and which have not yet received any attention.' Diderot, 'Observations sur le Nakaz', as quoted by C Emsley, *Crime, Police and Penal Policy, 1750–1940* (Oxford, Oxford University Press, 2007) 34.

Appendix 1: Brief Observations on the General Code on Crimes and Punishments *as Concerned with Policy Offences**

(TRANSLATED FROM THE ITALIAN BY JR SPENCER)**

[1][1] I write these brief remarks in obedience to the command of Your Excellency,[2] with very great frankness as they are intended only for him who has supreme power over me, and because this code, though bearing at its head the august name of the Sovereign, has not yet been brought into force by sacred

* The Italian text of the 'Brevi riflessioni intorno al Codice generale sopra i delitti e le pene per quanto riguarda i delitti politici' is printed in C Beccaria, *Opere*, vol 2 edited by S Romagnoli (Florence, Sansoni, 1958) 705–718. On the resolution of the dating difficulty for this report, see n 2 below. The legislation Beccaria comments on is the 'Allgemeine Gesetzbuch über Verbrechen und derselben Bestrafung', promulgated by Joseph II of Austria on 13 January 1787 (hereinafter: Joseph II's code; the code). For details, see Du Bois-Pedain, ch 14 in this volume, section IV.B. The code is divided into two parts, each part consisting of separately numbered provisions. Part I deals with '*Criminal-Verbrechen*' (referred to in this translation as 'genuine crimes' or 'criminal offences'). Part II deals with '*politische Verbrechen*' (rendered here as 'policy offences').The literal translation of '*politische Verbrechen*' is 'political crimes' ('*delitti politici*'), and this is the term used by Beccaria. That phrase, however, brings to mind a very different concept from the meaning given to it in the code, where the expression refers to behaviour that is not, like genuine crimes, considered evil irrespective of the society in which it is performed, but is criminalised in response to the needs of a particular society.

** I am most grateful to Francois du Bois and Paola Filippucci for their help.

[1] The paragraph numbers are not part of the original report but have been inserted into this translation to facilitate cross-referencing from other chapters in this collection.

[2] 'Your Excellency' is the form of address Beccaria used to address Count Johann Joseph von Wilczek, the *ministro plenipotenziario* (head of the Habsburg administration) in Lombardy. While Beccaria's undated report was for a long time thought to have been written only in 1791, when Beccaria was a member of a commission charged with drafting a new penal code for Lombardy, today it is believed that Beccaria wrote this report at Wilczek's request in June 1787. This would explain the tone of the report, which comments on the provisions of Joseph II's 1787 code and does not mention a draft penal code for Lombardy, which was prepared in 1791. It also appears that another report Wilczek received from the 'Supremo Tribunale di Giustizia' on 6 July 1787 takes Beccaria's thoughts into account. The editors thank Professor Paolo Rondini of the Università degli Studi di Milano-Bicocca for kindly providing this information in a personal communication. Professor Rondini additionally refers to A Cavanna, *La codificazione penale in Italia. Le origini lombarde* (Milan, Giuffrè, 1975) 40–53 and C Beccaria, *Edizione Nazionale delle Opere di Cesare Beccaria*, vol IX: *Atti di Governo* (serie IV: 1787) edited by L Firpo and G Francioni (Milano, Mediobanca, 1998) 477.

royal authority. This I do in the best way possible for me, given my well-known circumstances, the shortage of time and the multitude of [my] official duties: namely by simple commentaries.

[2] Under § 1 of Part II of the code,[3] which deals with policy offences, I see so classed only those set out in the code itself: whence it seems that all the other legal transgressions which are dealt with according to the provisions of the specific regulations cannot or should not be classed as falling within the category of policy offences. As the particular regulations in force are so numerous, varied and cumbersome, and the penalties prescribed for them are almost invariably pecuniary, these provisions do not seem readily to fit with § 10, which for all policy offences forbids[4] fines, except for the single case of illegal gambling.

[3] It is therefore necessary to say that there are three categories of offences: genuine crimes carrying the longest and harshest penalties; policy offences with penalties which are lower, in length at least; and regulatory offences punishable with fines. With that in mind it seems to me that the majority of offences in the third category and punishable only with fines already find themselves categorised and specified in the class of policy offences, which makes the reservation set out at the end of § 1 inappropriate.[5] Secondly, it seems to me that if many offences of that type were to fall outside the classification of policy offences, this would fail to heed the purpose set out in the Royal Proclamation published at the head of the code itself: which is to give to punitive justice a clear direction that precludes all arbitrary administration, to conveniently fix the boundary between criminal offences and policy offences, and to establish the proper measure between offence and punishment, in a way that does not give the impression of something purely transitory.

[4] These sacred maxims, worthy of the Sovereign who has dictated them, encourage me to express the wish that in the code the essential nature of criminal offences and of policy offences should be clearly distinguished.

[5] To me it seems that, as distinctions should be made between different offences, we should understand as a criminal offence one whose nature is such that it directly tends towards the destruction of the social bond unless it is punished and repressed; and consider as policy offences those transgressions or faults which render society imperfect, but without tending towards its destruction directly.

[3] § 1 of Part II provides 'Policy offences are only the offences defined as such by this code. Acts not covered by the definitions of this code are not policy offences. However, such other acts, when contrary to [some other] law, will also be given attention by public authorities and will be sanctioned according to the special provisions governing them.'

[4] The Italian text says '*prescrive*' (requires), but this must be a transcription error for '*proscrive*' (forbids), as is clear from the German text of § 10 of Part II of the code.

[5] What Beccaria points to here is the considerable overlap between acts that amount to a policy offence defined in the code, and the various acts prohibited by other laws. The practical upshot, as he clearly sees, is that this gives the authorities a choice under which law to proceed, with very different punishments resulting, and that this undermines the legislator's objective of clarity and predictability in the application of the law.

[6] Following this distinction, I can at once understand the very different principles according to which the one or other type of repressive legislation – criminal or policy – should be regulated; because the regulation of genuine crimes has as its aim more the making of an example than the correction of the individual; with policy offences on the other hand, one should rather have the aim of correcting than of making an example, even though in case of either type of offence both aims should be borne in mind.

[7] Policy offences being principally faults and transgressions rather than true offences, they should be regarded as actions which prepare a person to become truly delinquent and criminal, deserving of public infamy and destined solely to become an example for others. Hence they should be punished by those means which are the most efficacious to correct and restrain a citizen whom the criminal law would wish to preserve, and not be obliged to lose by the necessity of making an example.

[8] In accordance with this, as punishments for genuine crimes should serve principally as an example which is substantial and permanent and brings about deterrence which is not temporary but lasting, it is right to abolish the death penalty in all its forms, and to substitute for it long and repellent punishments, in proportion to the offence.[6] But as the punishments for policy offences should principally serve to correct, and only secondarily set an example, these should be measured in a way that does not undermine correction, which is their principal purpose; and hence they should be of a kind greatly different from the first: far less severe, less long-lasting and, so far as possible, not causing infamy, since if infamy is caused there vanishes all possibility of correction, which is desired, and which ought to arise from punishments for policy offences.

[9] I feel obliged to point out another quite important difference between policy offences and their punishments, and criminal offences and the punishments for these, arising from the distinction previously mentioned.

[10] Criminal offences, tending to the destruction of society, are such that they do not need positive laws in order to acquire their character, because as such they are defined by the law of nature and of peoples, and possess a gravity equally recognised and detested in all climes, in all periods and under all forms of government, in all nations that are civilised and not barbarous or savage. On the other hand policy offences, tending to harm but not destroy society, derive their character principally from positive legislation, which can and should be different according to the period, the clime, the form of government – to summarise, to all the circumstances of a nation; and if for criminal offences the

[6] Joseph's code (§ 20 of Part I) declared the death penalty inapplicable for all crimes except in proceedings under martial law. In respect of its execution, it prescribed death by hanging without any additional torture or mutilation of the body. De facto this amounted to the abolition of the death penalty in all ordinary criminal trials. Beccaria's concern here, however, is not to comment on this provision but to contrast the aim of criminal punishment, which guided the legislator towards replacing the death penalty with other modes of criminal punishment (lasting deterrence), with the aim of punishment for policy offences (correction).

almost invincible public feeling is of a similar strength, with policy offences it should vary with all the variations of the society, and on this public opinion the sovereign does not have a direct influence, but only an indirect influence, through appropriate legislation.

[11] I thought it was proper to set out these general reflections because they seem to me to fit in with the very great wisdom of the Royal Edict discussed above. It seems to me however permissible to reflect that, although in many provisions, in most of them in fact, and particularly in the general division of the policy offences, and in the provisions of general application,[7] they seem to be followed, this is not so in many of the provisions relating to particular offences and the penalties prescribed for them.

[12] That there is a desire to maintain a different scheme for policy offences and criminal offences seems to me to be clearly shown by §§ 2 of Part I and Part II of the code.[8] To render a person liable for a criminal offence presupposes *deliberate malice and free will*; to render him liable for a policy offence presupposes *harmful action which proceeds from free will*. Malice and harm therefore are, according to the code, two different essential requirements for liability for criminal offences in case of the first, and policy offences in case of the second.

[13] Another notable characteristic differentiating policy and criminal offences is found in § 4 [of Part II], where it is said that a mere attempt does not render a person liable for a policy offence; whereas by contrast with a criminal offence the mere attempt does give rise to criminal liability.[9]

[14] According to my principles, indeed, the frequency of attempts to do those things which tend to destroy society is too dangerous by reason of example for these not to be punished. Not so with policy offences, hence it suffices both for correction and for example-setting to punish the [completed] action. If we were to wish to punish attempts, then by reason of the frequency of such misdeeds the cure would be worse than the evil.

[15] On the basis of the foregoing reflections and following the scheme and spirit of the code itself on the nature of policy offences, chapter II [of Part II] deals with the penalties for policy offences, which in [§ 10][10] are limited to

[7] Each Part of the code starts with provisions applicable to all offences in this category of offences, thus containing what we would today describe as the 'General Part'.

[8] § 2 of Part I provides 'Malice and free will belong to a genuine crime. Malice exists when before or during the prohibited act or omission, the harm which follows from it was envisaged and decided upon, such that the unlawful conduct was performed with the aim of bringing this harm about.' § 2 of Part II provides 'The charge of a policy offence refers to an act committed with free will; hence, if an act that would otherwise constitute a policy offence was done in circumstances set out in § 5 of Part I [which provides that agents who are insane, involuntarily intoxicated, not yet 12 years old or subjected to overwhelming force, lack free will] the agent cannot be charged with a policy offence.'

[9] Liability for attempted genuine crimes is provided for in § 9 of Part I.

[10] Beccaria's report says here 'chapter X', but this must be an error. The code contains no 'chapter X'.

punishment by flogging, exposure in the pillory, arrest, public labour in irons, expulsion from a designated place, excluding all financial penalties, except in the sole case of prohibited gambling.

[16] Now it seems to me that with the exception of imprisonment in chains[11] these punishments are nearly the same as those provided in § 21, Part I, for genuine crimes, the only difference being their greater or lesser duration, and certain details concerning the prison regime.[12] The pillory and flogging are in particular punishments that place an indelible mark of infamy on the sufferer. Even though they serve as an example and to deter the innocent from policy offences, they cannot do any good for the correction and reform of the offender, which is the main aim of the punishment of policy offences: indeed the infliction of these punishments, very far from correcting and restraining the commission of similar offences, does nothing but drive and stimulate these offenders to commit greater and real offences, because someone who suffers a profound public stigma, by that alone gradually losing all sense of shame, acquires ever stronger reasons to give way to the vilest passions, which are then the source of the great and [truly] criminal offences. The force of this argument is all the greater in that I see that the pillory and flogging are prescribed without any distinction of persons, whether they are nobility, civil servants, merchants or artisans, albeit that for these persons the milder form of imprisonment[13] can under §§ 14 and 15 be converted into house arrest.

[17] Now in the policy offences the quality of the person is an essential piece of information which should be very seriously considered when weighing up the proportionality of the punishment.

[18] The number of people who are inclined to commit criminal offences is small compared to the very great number who commit or would commit the policy offences listed in the code, because human weakness, the force of passions and so many other physical and moral reasons drive people to commit these; so that use of the pillory, afflictive[14] imprisonment and flogging, in this multitude of cases, instead of correcting the nation would only make it worse. By destroying the feeling of honour in those of nobility and high civic standing, it takes

[11] Imprisonment in chains (Part I, § 25) is the harshest form of imprisonment provided for in the code. Here, amongst other hardships, an iron ring is placed around the body of the convict and connected to the wall, leaving only minimal mobility.

[12] § 21 of Part I provides 'The other criminal punishments are imprisonment in chains, prison with public labour, prison alone, flogging and whipping, and the pillory. The three first-mentioned punishments can, in light of the criminal's condition, be made more severe, either by lengthening their duration or by adding something to their mode of execution that makes them harsher.'

[13] In respect of policy offences, the code provides for a milder and a harsher form of imprisonment. The milder form allows prisoners to have visits and to occupy themselves as they please, provided they have food brought in at their own expense, whereas the harsher form of imprisonment (specified in Part II, § 13) involves wearing an ankle chain, sleeping on bare boards, having only official visitors and performing prison labour.

[14] In the Italian text, '*afflittiva*'.

away from them the principal reason by which they keep themselves spontaneously within the laws of honesty and of the state; and by bringing them down to the level of persons of the greatest infamy and vile condition, depravity and the same vile behaviour are always driven to increase and spread.

[19] In principle it may be noted that infamy arises from the guilt and not the punishment, and that in consequence such blameworthy acts which by nature are infamous in public opinion deserve punishments conferring infamy; but for the others which do not carry infamy, this is inappropriate. This is the case with the greater part of policy offences, which do not presuppose malice, but merely harm committed of free will, and in consequence cannot be considered as carrying infamous blame; and they should not be permitted to render the delinquent infamous to some lesser degree, if it is true that the aim of punishments for policy offences is to correct and deter the person from committing the more serious offences.

[20] I see no great disadvantage in nobles being exposed to the same penalties as common people for offences that are criminal, which for the most part presuppose great malice and wickedness, and in consequence give rise to great infamy. If a person of the highest rank degrades himself by committing such offences, it follows that an infamous punishment can apply, even though it may be true that the long-lasting and afflictive punishments substituted for the death penalty have a longer and more sensitive effect on the delinquent's family, to whom infamy necessarily attaches as a result. In as much as such a person, in proportion to their rank and status, enjoys greater social advantages, in committing the same sort of offence as a common person, he commits a graver crime. Therefore giving him the same penalty, if in reality it means giving him more, is fair, because in a noble it presupposes greater malice, and hence the punishment is in proportion to the nature of the offence.

[21] But in policy offences, which do not presuppose malice, but harm freely committed, and which do not directly tend to the destruction of society, nor offend against natural law, and which are mere faulty acts and not malicious ones; which to adopt the terminology of Roman Law are not *maleficia*, but *quasi malificia*, regard should most certainly be had to the status of the person, because flogging, which might correct a coarse individual, demoralises and destroys a nobleman, an honest merchant, and any civilised person, and involves their whole family in the most miserable infamy. The punishment is no longer proportionate to the offence, but greater by far, with the risk that the damage caused by the punishment is beyond comparison with the damage resulting from the fault.

[22] Another grave inconvenience which arises from the application to policy offences of punishments that are too afflictive and infamous is the terror and consternation that would spread among the citizens upon the publication of a law that is so punitive. The majority of citizens have no inclination to wish to commit grave and criminal offences, nor do they too readily fear that they might be falsely accused, given that the way to defend yourself is simple enough, as

the rules of procedure in criminal cases furnish every assistance to the innocent. But this is not so with policy offences. Everybody knows how easily they may be committed, all the more so when the situations and circumstances in which a policy offence may be committed are increased, and when to become liable for such an offence a voluntary act is all that is required. The excessive number of such offences, which are inevitably committed in a society which is populous, and thereby corrupt, makes it necessary to have a summary form of procedure and a rapidity of process, for otherwise they would go unpunished and the objective of the criminal law would fail. Therefore, everyone would be fearful for himself, and fearful of the hatred of a false accuser, afraid that anyone may turn out to be an informer, and of easily becoming the victim of a summary process, either because of another's dislike or because of his own recklessness. From this general fear and from this general distrust, which corrode society with a damage which is as hidden as it is real, all who can escape, do so. Hence, if in a nation that is docile and submissive they do not give rise to sedition and tumults, they certainly do give rise to an unnoticed and perhaps immediate emigration, so much the more easily accomplished if this nation, like ours, is densely populated, and exists within narrow borders and surrounded by other states, which, due to continuous interactions would not refrain from welcoming the emigrants: with grave damage to our own agriculture, and the greatest damage to our renascent industry. The Milanese people are docile, obedient, and in no way violent, by comparison with many of our neighbours. But they are lazy and easily demoralised. They need encouragement and better education, and to this our paternalistic and providential rulers are indeed attending. The resulting frequency of afflictive penalties for policy offences would undo the effects of this and produce the exact opposite.

[23] Two further considerations relating to the local circumstances of our country move me to argue against the inclusion of punishments that are too afflictive and stigmatising in the Code of Policy Offences and their punishment. The first is that a great number of noblemen and bourgeois families possess much landed property abroad, many of these forming the greater part of their estate. They nevertheless live among us out of love of this country, through a genuine attachment to the august Ruling House, and because of their relatives and acquired habit. But all of these links could dissolve if such a fear, however ill-founded, of suffering such a punishment too easily should take hold of their minds. This could cause harm without compare, which could be avoided if there could be some softening of the punishments for policy offences and for some of the criminal offences.

[24] The second consideration relates to the stigmatising punishments provided for the policy offences. Relationships with family, spouses and arising from the varied dealings with the many neighbours surrounding us are too important to cause us to overlook the unhappy effect of stigmatising punishments on these relationships. To a certain point a sovereign may be able to influence the opinion of subjects by means of the law, when he commands a great and vast

nation; but in no way can he influence in such a matter those nations which obey other governments or princes. Now our situation is such that, having the honour of obeying a great monarch, we do so; but not everything that is applicable to his vast dominions of Germany, Bohemia and Hungary can be suitable for us – who are surrounded on all sides by foreign nations, which, through the many and close relationships we have with them, determine the workings of public opinion in such a way that the general laws of a great monarchy cannot be applied in a simple way without incurring a grave risk of producing harms much greater than the advantages intended by compilation of a general code.

[25] From everything said above, it would seem advisable to me to restrict policy offences within narrower limits than would be done under the code; with regard to such offences, I would wish to limit them to those simple blameworthy acts and transgressions, which do not involve any type of fraud or violence, substantial and malicious incitement to evil, but stem from mere caprice, overheated imagination, formal disobedience to someone who has authority to command: in brief, to all those actions which are on the way towards crimes, but not truly such, and to all others which disturb the order of society, but do not directly oppose it. In brief, legislation concerning the punishment of policy offences should impede the growth of evil, restrain the imprudent person who is on his way to committing serious offences, and correct small and everyday transgressions with a restrained severity, and the tribunal for policy offences should be an authoritative father rather than a judge, correcting and not avenging human actions. Likewise, it seems advisable to limit the punishments to the greater or lesser periods of prison or detention wisely set out in the code for policy offences, bearing in mind that detention could be at home or in a prison completely separate from the prison for criminal offenders; according to the person's station, to deprivation of or suspension from duties of office; to the closure of a business for a fixed period, with a public notice giving the reason; to prohibition from leaving the town; to exile from a given place; to banishment to the country; and to public admonition.

[26] Thefts and frauds, public defamation, real and open incitement of honest people to corrupt behaviour, I see listed in the Code of Policy Offences; and as they presuppose genuine malice, they should be listed in the Code of Criminal Offences, with a punishment greater than I have suggested, but less than those prescribed in Part I, § 21 [of the code]. As regards this type of lesser but genuine offences, the first misdeed should not be dealt with under the rules for criminal offences but under the less serious rules of the policy offences, because a first action, though malicious, does not presuppose habitual malice, nor does it remove the hope of correction for the individual. But certainly recidivists cannot be considered under this approach; however, according to the provisions of the code repeated acts do not always double the punishment, nor do they ever move [policy offences] into the category of criminal offences, although the repetition of such acts presupposes a malice that is established and manifest, and therefore deserves to be considered as criminal. This observation

refers to §§ 29, 30, 31 and 32 [of Part II], which concern petty thefts of less than 25 florins,[15] since repetition of these acts is not taken into account for increasing the punishment, despite the fact that a thief who every day steals less than 25 florins ought to be considered a genuine criminal, beyond correction by punishments for policy offences, but only punishable with the severity of the law as an example to others.

[27] The other policy offences listed include, in § 44, adultery.[16] In this connection the importance of preserving the chastity of the marriage bond, which is a type of reciprocal property, and is the foundation of everything that concerns peace within the family, the bringing up of offspring, social customs and relationships and rights of succession, could be considered perhaps to merit categorising such misbehaviour among the criminal offences. Even if it should be thought more expedient to retain this among the policy offences, it would seem proper to me to distinguish adultery by a man from adultery by a woman, given that this can render someone a father of children who are not his own, unlike the adultery of a man with a loose woman, which cannot cause the same damage to society, and in consequence does not deserve the same penalty. I leave aside here the public scandal [involved], which requires different measures, and for the avoidance of which I find particularly appropriate the decision in the code to make it punishable only on the complaint of the injured party, for their part innocent, and who consistently objected to the adultery of their spouse.

[28] In covering publicly scandalous expression, § 69[17] seems to expose persons who are alleged to be seducers all too easily to doubtful accusations of seduction, and the nature of these offences is such that it is better to keep them quiet than to draw attention to them in order to avoid producing the [very] consequence which the spirit of the law seeks to prevent.

[29] § 75 completely prohibits prostitution, which seems too strict, given that it is not possible to avoid this evil in a populous town without running the

[15] Beccaria's cross-reference is not entirely accurate here: § 29 concerns thefts of goods worth less than the equivalent of 25 Vienna guilders; § 30 concerns illegal wood collection, hunting, and theft of plants and fruits from unenclosed woodland and fields (even if worth more); § 31 covers theft by servants up to the indicated value, as well as fraudulent requests for reimbursement and fraudulent handing over of goods of lesser value; § 32 specifies the punishments.

[16] § 44 provides 'A person linked in lawful marriage to a spouse, and thereby obliged to marital fidelity, commits adultery by engaging in sexual relations with another party, whether that party is married or unmarried.'

[17] § 69 provides 'Whosoever, upon encountering on the street a decent woman of good repute, approaches her with gestures or words that clearly signal the wish to seduce her into impropriety is, upon the complaint of the woman thereby insulted, to be treated as a policy offender.' This is a straightforward statement of *adtemptata pudicitia*, an established form of *iniuria* or *contumelia* – ie insult – in Roman law, which is present throughout Europe in the Middle Ages and well beyond. Perhaps in Italy this came to be known as '*l'espressione di pubblico scandalo*', the phrase used by Beccaria in his report. The provision was the butt of a comic episode in Judge Schlendrian's imaginary courtroom, where 'Judge Schlendrian proves that it is a crime to pay a woman a compliment'. On this comic novel, which exposed aspects of Joseph II's code to public ridicule, see du Bois-Pedain, ch 14 in this volume, n 40.

risk that lustful youths would go and contaminate marital beds, and would find a way to satisfy themselves by secretly corrupting honest persons. It would seem appropriate to punish prostitution when this is accompanied with scandalous and real seduction made with a view to profit, and put up with the rest as a necessary evil, as appears to be suggested, albeit not clearly, by the following § 76.[18]

[30] If time and circumstances had permitted, I would have been able to go through all the other provisions of the Code of Policy Offences and to make many other observations which would have served to clarify and ameliorate many of them, which, truth to say, more by reason of the way in which they are expressed than by their substance, have caused the greatest fear among all classes of citizens:[19] which is not surprising to those who know that the masses, far from interpreting [them] benevolently, tend to think evil of novelties. When it is a question of new systems and new laws, such clarification and amelioration is very necessary in a code, since mankind, which generally regulates itself more by habit than by reasoning, is more disposed to tolerate an evil that is greater but ancient, than one which is lesser but new.

[31] I have also read the instructions for the political authorities concerning the method of enquiry, conviction and execution of sentence against those guilty of policy offences,[20] with which Your Excellency has entrusted me, and I find them generally appropriate. It seems to me that in this Part the manner of execution tempers the severity of the code itself, and it also seems to me that these instructions, adjusted in certain respects in light of our circumstances, should be published, so that everyone can see the limits within which the authority of the magistrates who judge policy offences is restricted, and the nation may be disabused of the ill-founded fear that the Code of Policy Offences seeks to subject the citizenry to the prejudice and caprice of the persons exercising public authority.

[32] A few small observations have occurred to me, which to me seem to deserve some consideration.

[33] *I*. Some thought could be given to § 10 [of the Instructions],[21] in which there is admitted as a legal proof the deposition of a sworn official

[18] In the relevant parts, § 76 provides for double punishment for each repeated commission of the offence, and for harsher punishment when a minor has been seduced.

[19] Here Beccaria alludes, in the most polite way possible, to the 'bad press' Joseph II's code has attracted both in Austria and in Lombardy.

[20] Beccaria appears to refer here to the *Instruktion für die politischen Behörden, über die Anstrengung einer Inquisition, Aburtheilung, und Strafvollziehung, wider einen eines politischen Verbrechens Beschuldigten* (hereinafter: *Instruktion*), brought into effect in Austria and some provinces in March 1787. The *Instruktion* is printed in J Kropatschek (ed), *Handbuch aller unter der Regierung des Kaisers Joseph des II. für die K.K. Erbländer ergangenen Verordnungen und Gesetze in einer Sistematischen Verbindung*, vol 13 (Vienna, Johann Georg Moesle, 1789) 423–432. The institutions in charge of policing the commission of policy offences, referred to in the *Instruktion* as 'the political authority', were effectively the local administrations.

[21] Ibid.

charged with the maintenance of discipline, good order and public safety, who has caught the offender in the act, and has challenged and arrested him. And this proof is equated with a unanimous sworn deposition of two other witnesses, totally unimpeachable, confronting the accused. Now to give the same weight to the sworn statement of one person, even if an official, as would be given to two sworn statements by unimpeachable persons, seems completely unacceptable, however much credibility the official function may add to that of the person giving evidence, particularly when under § 10 it is not specified what level of person has this power. Those charged with arresting offenders in the act are junior people who have an interest in establishing the offence; and these people, and even those of the level above, could use their power very abusively, for vendettas or other purposes, notwithstanding their oath; and this particularly so in the case of offences based on acts [alone], where the non-existence of a *corpus delicti* means the accused is abandoned to the discretion of one single person.

[34] *II.* §§ 14 and 15 of the instructions forbid the authorities who have imposed the penalties of flogging, the pillory or exile for policy offences to execute these punishments before they have been placed before and confirmed by the district authorities and, if the defendant is a member of the nobility or in royal service, by the provincial governor himself; and as far as public labour is concerned, included in this reservation are merchants and artisans, provided they are otherwise of unimpeachable character and of good reputation. Much could be said about this, but to be as brief as possible: A) As the uncertain judgement as to good reputation and conduct is, according to the wording of the paragraph cited, left to the judge of policy offences, it is therefore left to him to choose whether his own sentence is to be confirmed. B) Flogging, the pillory and public labour are punishments so afflictive that they should be excluded from the Code for Policy Offences; but if they must be included, it does not seem enough to protect the safety of the innocent, or at any rate of the minimally guilty, to make the confirmation of such a severe punishment depend on an official in the district administration, who with us would be the Intendant, or his assistant if unavailable; so that the local political authority, who is the first [instance] judge for policy offences, with the confirmation of an Intendant or an assistant can have a merchant or artisan flogged or put in the pillory; whereas for a crime, a criminal court of first instance composed of several persons cannot impose a similar punishment without the confirmation of the court of appeal. C) Then nobles and officials can be flogged and put in the pillory, and merchants [given] public labour, with the confirmation of the provincial governor. Not to repeat what I have said about the inappropriateness of subjecting the nobility and civilised persons, in the case of policy offences, to these penalties, I beg Your Excellency to reflect that although it appears that in such a case the fate of the citizens would depend on a collegiate body, notwithstanding this fact, Your Excellency, when comparing with his penetrating intellect the manner in which the joint decision of the governor's council is

arrived at, and the influence of the vote of a single person, with the functioning of the court of appeal, will understand immediately that those accused of policy offences are in a worse position than those accused of crimes. Your Excellency has too generous a spirit to accuse me of impertinence in making such an observation, which is certainly not applicable at the present time; but circumstances could arise in future which would make this inconvenience manifest, and Your Excellency understands better than I do that laws and codes must be made for the permanence of time, and not for the persons in whose hands public authority resides for the moment.

[35] I have written these observations solely because to me it is an honour to obey not only every command Your Excellency issues to me as my superior, but also every hint he may make to me as my special master and protector. For the rest I beg him to forgive the errors and omissions this paper contains, attributable to the weakness of my talents, to being for a long time uninvolved in criminal matters (in which I have always lacked practical experience), and to the current situation of my work and of my home, of which Your Excellency is well aware.

*Appendix 2: Opinion of the Undersigned Members of the Committee Charged with the Reform of the Criminal System in Austrian Lombardy for Matters Pertaining to Capital Punishment (1792)**

(TRANSLATED FROM THE ITALIAN BY AARON THOMAS AND JEREMY PARZEN)**

[1][1] The Criminal Committee, while drafting the Prolegomena to the new penal code that will be submitted to the approval of the sovereign, and which is based upon the precepts contained in § III of the Royal Dispatch of 13 August 1790, was obliged to list the number and the ranking of diverse punishments that will be prescribed by this code so as to assign them to diverse crimes with the correct proportion, and in doing so followed the praiseworthy example of the Austrian and Tuscan codes that the above-mentioned dispatch mentioned as a possible model.

[2] From the outset, the extraordinarily important question had to be confronted of whether to include the death penalty among these punishments. The opinions of the committee members were so divided that at first it seemed impossible to make any progress in the writing of the Penal Code without first humbling our differing opinions before the sovereign oracle of Your Majesty in

* The Italian text of the 'Voto degli infrascritti individui della giunta delegata per la riforma del sistema criminale nella Lombardia austriaca riguardante la pena di morte' is printed in C Beccaria, *Opere*, vol 2 edited by S Romagnoli (Florence, Sansoni, 1958) 735–741. The report is further analysed in Du Bois-Pedain, ch 14 in this volume, section IV.C.

** This translation was first published in C Beccaria, *On Crimes and Punishments and Other Writings* edited by A Thomas and translated by A Thomas & J Parzen (Toronto, Toronto University Press, 2008) at 153–159 and is reprinted here by kind permission of Toronto University Press.

[1] The paragraph numbers are not part of the original report/translation but have been inserted into this reprint to facilitate cross-referencing from other chapters in this collection.

order to wait for your decision; otherwise we shall be making as many codes as there were opinions among the members of the committee, which would be a great waste of time and effort. But once everyone agreed that capital punishment ought to be restricted to very few crimes, that its pure and simple execution ought to be regarded as the last resort, and that all those useless and ferocious treatments that accompanied the death penalty ought to be omitted, the committee was then able to proceed swiftly in its work in ascribing the ultimate punishment to the most serious crimes, and explained in the margins the opinions of those in favour of the death penalty and those in favour of the punishment that should replace it, which in our opinion should be forced labour of differing degrees of difficulty and commensurate with the crimes themselves. The three of us were of the same opinion that the death penalty should not be prescribed except in the case of absolute necessity, and in the peaceful circumstances of our society, and with the regular administration of justice, we could not think of any case of absolute necessity other than the situation in which the accused, in plotting the subversion of the state, was capable, either through his external or internal relationships, of disturbing and endangering society even while imprisoned and closely watched.[2] Other members expressed the opinion that another case should be added to this, namely, one in which the accused, above and beyond committing a crime worthy of capital punishment in and of itself, aggravates that crime with a murder, as with a highway robber who commits not only a violent theft of property but at the same time takes the life of his victim; other members, still, believed it necessary to extend the death penalty to a number of other crimes, all of them very serious. Everyone agreed, however, with the opinion that in the case of openly seditious activity, riots and gatherings of large crowds, the seditious that are resisting can be killed on the spot because this is not a legal administration of the death penalty, but rather the response to a general declaration of war.

[3] We owe it to ourselves and to the devotion to the public service that drives us, to expose candidly and succinctly the reasons that have brought us to this determination, support for which we found in the combined example of the Austrian and Tuscan codes that we have received as models. The first code, at [§] 20 of chapter II in Part I,[3] clearly prescribes that the death penalty should

[2] This view aligns with Beccaria's position in C Beccaria, *On Crimes and Punishments and Other Writings* edited by R Bellamy and translated by R Davies (Cambridge, Cambridge University Press, 1995) at 66–67 (ch 28). In this work, Beccaria initially appears to be making a second exception for offenders whose execution is the only means of deterring others from crime, but, as Peter Garnsey has pointed out, this apparent second exception is 'a false trail, a phantom hypothesis, for Beccaria [spends] the rest of the chapter refuting the idea that the death penalty can legitimately be considered the only way of preventing crimes': P Garnsey, *Against the Death Penalty: Writings From the First Abolitionists – Guiseppe Pelli and Cesare Beccaria* (Princeton NJ, Princeton University Press, 2020) 144.

[3] For the content of this provision of Joseph's 1787 Code, see Appendix 1 to this volume, n 6.

have no place except in the cases of so-called summary justice – or rather rough justice – and it is clear from the context and the reasoning that such summary procedure is neither admitted nor admissible, save in the case of an imminent danger to the state, as in the case of sedition and riots. Chapter 51 of the second code abolishes the aforementioned punishment for any and all capital crimes, offering an explanation with the most plausible and sincere reasons; and it should be noted that both codes exclude the death penalty for those crimes that pertain to the offences – no matter how serious they may be – directly aimed at the person of the prince.

[4] Even leaving aside for a moment the authority that the aforementioned codes must inevitably have over our subordinate understanding, an authority for which we must have the greatest respect, following in the glorious footsteps of article 51 of the Tuscan Code which we praised above, and the tracks left by the most valiant men who have held the same opinion, we believe that the death penalty is not suitable except in the case we mentioned above. First, because it is not just, since it is not necessary; second, because it is less efficacious than perpetual punishment equipped with a good deal of continuous publicity; third, because it cannot be undone.

[5] To prove that it is not necessary, it is sufficient to note that for a punishment to be just it only needs to have a level of intensity sufficient to deter men from crimes. There is no one who, upon reflection, would choose the total and perpetual loss of one's freedom, no matter how advantageous a crime can possibly be. Thus, the severity of the punishment of perpetual enslavement that replaces the death penalty has itself what it takes to deter even the most resolute mind. Furthermore it is well known that human nature prefers death to a perpetual and miserable enslavement.[4]

[6] For the death penalty to be deemed necessary to serve as an example capable of discouraging the most serious crimes, it would be necessary to prove with facts, showing that where the death penalty has been most frequently employed, such crimes were far fewer in number than in places where the same death penalty was used less or not at all. Now, if we look with the impartial and peaceful eye of the legislator and at bygone times, as well as to those countries both near and far where the death penalty has been restricted to serious crimes, we will find exactly the contrary: where punishments have been more moderate, and for that very reason more strictly applied against delinquents (there being fewer reasons to let them go unpunished), crimes have become less frequent because the nature of man has slowly and surely been shaped by the moderation of the law.

[7] To prove that the death penalty is less efficacious than perpetual and public punishment, it is enough to note that it is not so much the severity of

[4] These considerations are identical to Beccaria, above n 2 at 68, and were added by Beccaria to the third Italian edition of his work (see ibid at 6, starred note).

the punishment as its inevitability – provided that there is proportion between crimes and punishments – that is the most effective means to restrain crimes, and that the strongest impediment to crimes is not the terrible and fleeting spectacle of the death of a wretch, but the long and repeated example of a man deprived of his liberty, who with his labour is paying back the society he offended. This effective and oft-repeated image that we ourselves might be reduced to a long and miserable condition in the event that we commit similar crimes is by far more powerful than the sight of death, which men always see from some vague distance and under the illusion that they might avoid it, and with a feeling of compassion for those who actually fall prey to it. Furthermore, with the death penalty every example for the nation presupposes a crime; with perpetual slavery, one sole crime provides many and lasting examples; and if we really mean to show concretely how powerful our laws are, the death penalty should be used very frequently, which presupposes a high frequency of crimes; so in order for this punishment to be efficacious, it is necessary that it does not make the impression on men that it should, that is, that it be effective and ineffective at the same time.[5]

[8] The death penalty is also less efficacious for the reason that, if we all agree to reserve it for the greatest and most atrocious crimes, because it occurs instantaneously it cannot easily be made proportionate to the number and atrocity of those very crimes, for it is clear that no matter how barbaric a murderer may be, there is always the possibility that someone else may commit even more barbaric crimes and in greater number. To avoid the inconvenience of meting out the same punishment for more serious and numerous crimes, the death penalty ought to be amplified – in reality and not in appearance only – with more atrocious and sophisticated torments, and this would entail adding a legal example of cruelty to the rather illogical idea of punishing a homicide with another homicide.[6]

[9] In conclusion, since it is irreparable, we believe that the death penalty is not at all suited to the inevitable imperfection of human proofs. And even if it were a just punishment, even if it were the most efficacious of all forms of punishment, in order to be correctly applied to a criminal, it would be necessary to demonstrate that he is indeed guilty in a way that excludes the possibility of the contrary. This arises manifestly from the irreparability of the death penalty; if these infallible proofs were indeed required to sentence a criminal, there would never be any possibility of carrying out the death penalty. Nor can we say that it would be wise to leave it on the books so that it may act as a threat, for if it is not practised, the greater efficacy of setting an example – which lies in the inevitability of punishment – is lost, and the power of the other penal laws

[5] This paragraph closely follows passages that can be found ibid at 67 and 68.

[6] This paragraph develops an argument from proportionality already present in Beccaria, ibid at 64 (ch 27) into a somewhat different point.

is weakened at the same time. But the fact of the matter is that an examination of all the laws shows that we can see that the proofs sufficient to sentence a criminal to death have never been such that they could exclude the possibility of a contrary verdict. For neither the witnesses' testimony, even if there were more than two, nor the wealth of circumstantial evidence, even if buttressed by the confession of the accused, are such that they fulfil the limits of moral certainty, which on closer inspection turns out to be nothing but a matter of probability. In almost all nations, it is not unheard of to find examples in which the apparently guilty were sentenced to death because they were shown to be so according to these supposedly incontrovertible proofs. Nor do we intend to attribute this to the incompetence, negligence, or bad will of the judges, but to the necessary imperfection of the law. Whenever these practically inevitable errors of the magistrates have remained under the scrutiny of the public, and whenever time has shown promptly the innocence of those who were supposed to be guilty, such a turn of events has been considered a public calamity, and the magistrates were the victims of public disdain for no fault of their own. If we are to be guided by the not-always-luminous light of moral certainty when arriving at a guilty verdict, there is no comparison between a punishment that may be rectified while the accused is alive and the death penalty that is irreparable after the accused has been killed, even if we are to assume that the punishment was intrinsically just and truly more efficacious than a punishment that lasts a lifetime – an assumption that we are far from making. One might say that even in the one case in which we admit that the death penalty may be employed, the accused is subjected to the same difficulty where the possibility of a contrary verdict is not excluded. But we must keep in mind that in our single case, we are caught between two contradictory necessities. On the one hand, there is the necessity to protect the state from the imminent danger of overthrow, and on the other, we must face the rather remote danger of killing an innocent. Between the two dangers, it is clear that we must confront the latter as a factual necessity in order to avoid the former, which at best could only serve the function of setting an example, that is, a purely juridical function. So in suggesting that we should suppress the death penalty, we are not motivated by an ill-conceived passion for the wicked – much less by the idea of curtailing the right of the sovereign legislator to prescribe it if in his Great Wisdom he were to think it necessary in order to repress crimes. If we thought for a moment that it might be necessary, we would consider it our precise duty to propose it and plea with him to stop following the sublime example set by our present August Sovereign who has abolished it for every situation in Tuscany, as we already dared to do so in the single case of the criminal who, although imprisoned, could nonetheless be influential in overthrowing the state; but even this ought to be left in the hands of His Sovereign's decision after consulting with the supreme magistrate.[7]

[7] This long paragraph develops an argument not present in Beccaria ibid.

[10] Before we conclude our resigned sentiment, we have to take it upon ourselves to add as a corollary that the punishment we recommend in the place of the death penalty entails sufficient and repeated public punishment, and as such, one sole prison relegated to a remote corner of the province does not seem to be the most suitable to give a repeated and persuasive example to the public, which is what we consider necessary. We would maintain, thus, that it is by far better to set up prisons in several cities so as to make sure that the punishment is clear for all to see.

[11] Dividing and classifying types of life imprisonment would be useful in order to find comparable public works that may serve as punishment. And it would help to obviate the disorder that would result if those guilty of different crimes and condemned to sentences of differing severity were to be mixed together in a single place.

[12] This is not the place to develop these ideas further, and it was sufficient to note them here, for the council will take them under more careful consideration. We feel that it is sufficient to have touched upon them here, just enough to demonstrate that the punishment consisting of public works can be the most efficacious and useful for the purposes of any good criminal legislation – which is, first of all, the correction of the criminal whenever possible, as well as the provision of an example to innocents to deter them from the crime. And while the death penalty may be the most rapid way of getting rid of guilty people, it is not the most useful to deter crimes.[8]

Gallarati Scotti
Beccaria Bonesana
Risi

[8] *Translators' note* (reproduced from Beccaria, above n ** at 178–179): 'Francesco Gallarati Scotti, a councillor in the Ministry of Justice, was one of Beccaria's pupils when he taught economics at the Scuole Palatine in Milan. Paolo Risi, an associate of the Accademia dei Trasformati and friend of Parini, authored *Animadversiones ad criminalem jurisprudentiam pertinentes* (Milan, Galeazzi, 1766), a work that took up themes similar to those found in Beccaria's *On Crimes and Punishments*. Beccaria, Gallarati Scotti and Risi held the minority position in the commission. The majority of the members argued to retain the death penalty for serious crimes, based on what they believed to be its deterrent effect. See Carlo Capra, *La Lombardia austriaca nell'età delle riforme, 1706–1796* (Turin, UTET, 1987) 460–2.'

Index

www.ingramcontent.com/pod-product-compliance
Ingram Content Group UK Ltd.
Pitfield, Milton Keynes, MK11 3LW, UK
UKHW020237290926
15470UKWH00002B/588